*An Introduction to Measurement
in Physical Education*

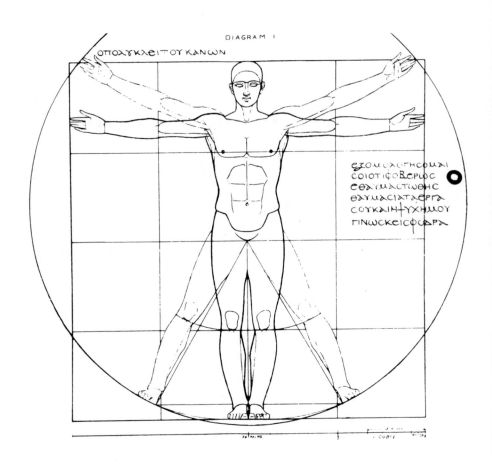

DIAGRAM I

HENRY J. MONTOYE

University of Wisconsin—Madison

An Introduction to Measurement
in Physical Education

Allyn and Bacon, Inc.

Boston   London   Sydney   Toronto

An earlier version of this text was printed in five volumes
in 1970.

Library of Congress Cataloging in Publication Data

Main entry under title:
An Introduction to measurement in physical
   education.
      Includes bibliographies and index.
      1. Physical fitness—Testing.   I.   Montoye,
Henry Joseph.
GV436.I58   1978   613.7   77–20075

ISBN 0–205–05787–X

Contributors

John A. Faulkner
Ray T. Hermiston
W. W. Heusner
Paul Hunsicker
Kathryn Luttgens
William D. McArdle
John F. McCabe
Benjamin H. Massey
James Oestriech
M. Gladys Scott
Peter O. Sigerseth
W. D. Van Huss
Hugh G. Welch

Contents

Foreword

Careful analysis of the program *misnamed* physical education shows that, in the large, it is comprised of three major areas of concern: (1) exercise science—the developmental, hygenic, therapeutic, and other values and uses of big muscle activity; (2) sports culture—the historical, sociological, economic, literary, and other reaches of sport; and (3) dance culture—the historical, sociological, economic, literary, and other reaches of dance. This book relates to the first area, exercise science.

It is to be noted that human beings, viewed in terms of our evolutionary backgrounds, are a product of activity, mainly muscular activity. Evolutionists tell us that our progenitors, developing through a series of stages, wriggled on the ocean floor, swam in the sea, crawled ashore, walked on the land, climbed over obstacles, fended for food, built shelters, fought enemies, and engaged in a host of other self-preserving big-muscle activities.

The point of importance here is that, as a result of this background, human life is geared to this kind of experience. Or, to put the matter more specifically, every aspect of our functioning organism—skeletal system, cardiovascular system, gastrointestinal system, etc.—is tied directly to the neuromuscular system, in other words, big muscle activity. It is quite clear that this type of activity is basic to the health, vigor, and efficiency of all of these systems, or, stated more broadly, to living. This means that big-muscle activity is essential to living a good life.

It is to be noted, however, that until quite recently people got this type of activity automatically, through engaging in the normal affairs of life. During the earler stages of the period called civilization, for example, this consisted of many types of manual labor—clearing and plowing the land; planting, tending, harvesting, and storing crops; raising, tending, and slaughtering animals; hunting; fishing; weaving cloth and making garments; gathering materials and constructing and maintaining shelters; chores such as milking cows, repairing harness, cleaning house, and on, and on, and on.

But, today, for an increasing percentage of the population, particularly in the more advanced nations, these kinds of activities are no longer required. The net effect is that these people face the alternative of accepting a low level of physical ability, health, and vigor, or participating in a program of structured big-muscle activity, or, to use the expression now commonly applied, exercise.

Taking an intensive look at the subject of exercise, however, we find ourselves faced with a host of questions. Examples are:

What are the potential physiological (pulse rate, blood pressure, etc.), performance (endurance, strength, agility, flexibility, etc.), physical (posture, weight, shape, etc.), and other effects of exercise, and what is their relative importance? What constitutes a desirable level of attainment in each area of potential effect for (1) both sexes, (2) all age groups, and (3) the major body types—mesomorphs, endomorphs, and ectomorphs? What contributions may each of the items and sub-items included in the four major categories of activities—sports, dance, designated exercises—and chores, make to each of the potential outcomes?

These are but examples of the benefits of exercise in organic or physical life. There are many others, notably posture, weight control, body appearance. And, too, there are relationships to the mental and social aspects of life.

The point of immediate significance is that most physical education teachers and administrators and, as a matter of fact, many members of the lay public, have some awareness of these relationships and, in consequence, formulate and carry on programs designed to produce certain wanted results. The great difficulty here is that we have so little exact information regarding the various aspects of the subject, that we are forced, *per se,* to formulate programs based solely on generalized observation and experience.

The range of issues faced here may be illustrated as follows: How frequently (daily, three times per week, two times per week), how long (10 minutes, 30 minutes, 60 minutes), and how strenuously should each activity be performed to secure a wanted outcome? What type of daily program (one, two, three, four or more kinds of activities), weekly program (same daily program, different daily programs), seasonal programs (same for all seasons, different progam for each season, two programs for each season) should be used? What types of programs should be carried on by each sex, the different age groups, and the different body types?

This situation can be improved only through conducting a vast array of research studies designed to uncover the particular organic and structural conditions effected by all of the many types of exercise with all of the many kinds of people deciding what conditions are important, constructing tests to measure these conditions, formulating test tables, testing people and recording the results on the test tables, deciding what changes (improvements) are desirable, and then prescribing and/or conducting programs of exercise that can produce the wanted results.

This book constitutes a major contribution to these ends. The data presented, the ideas offered, and the procedures proposed provide solid ways and means for improvement in this most important area of concern.

S. C. Staley, Ph.D., Sc.D.

Formerly, Dean
College of Physical Education
University of Illinois

Preface

The literature on tests and measurements in physical education is copious. Considerable sophistication in statistical terminology and knowledge in a number of areas is required to understand and evaluate much of what is written. In developing this text, it was felt that no one person is capable of selecting the best tests in each area from this extensive literature. For example, in appraising the growth and development of children there have been many techniques proposed, including several growth grids and various indices based on skeletal and other measurements. There obviously is no unanimity of opinion as to which is the best technique for use in the schools. Thus, it does not solve the student's dilemma to include all indices in a text. As a partial solution of the problem of test selection and evaluation, persons who are familiar with a particular area and who have had extensive experience with tests in this area agreed to write on the topic of their competency. Reference lists at the end of each chapter are provided so the interested student may find descriptions or discussions of other tests or measurements in the particular area. An effort is made to acquaint students with likely sources of future studies of tests and measurements applicable to health and physical education.

This series is designed for use in a college undergraduate course in tests and measurements. In the past, such courses have frequently been confined to tests applicable to school-age children. In view of the fact that increasingly more teachers of physical and health education are assuming responsibility for conducting adult fitness and recreational sports programs, graduates in physical education should be familiar with tests and measurements applicable to these programs. Accordingly, discussion and applications in this series are not restricted to school-age children.

It is assumed that the undergraduate student for whom this series is designed has had prerequisite work in the biological or health sciences, general psychology, sociology, growth and development, mathematics, and an introduction to administration of education in the United States. Courses in the health sciences generally include anatomy, general physiology, and physiology of exercise.

Most of the chapters are organized to answer these two questions: (1) why is it important for the physical educator to measure a particular ability or quality, and (2) what are the best tests for measuring this particular ability or characteristic? Each author has selected tests and procedures that he or she would find useful teaching in a college, in an elementary, junior, or senior high school, or conducting a recreation or fitness program. The tests and measurements, therefore, are not necessarily those employed in a university research laboratory.

Standards of performance (achievement scales), or references to standards, are included. Since these are generally in the form of percentile ranks, they represent a deviation from the usual practice in tests and measurements books in physical education. While the authors recognize certain mathematical advantages in other kinds of scores, they are convinced that percentile ranks are preferable for the average teacher. Where available, standards for adults as well as for children and youth are given.

The series differs in other respects from the traditional approach. Tests of sports "potential," physical "capacity," motor ability or "motor educability" are omitted, not because such tests might not ultimately be useful to the teacher, but because insufficient evidence for their validity is available.

Sociometric and personality tests, which have been included in some texts, are omitted in the present series. We believe that physical education, like many other school subjects when properly taught, makes a significant contribution to the mental, emotional, and social adjustment of children and adults. However, we have restricted the series to test areas that are more nearly the responsibility of the physical education teacher.

Batteries of tests, such as physical fitness tests, are not emphasized. We view each item in such test batteries as a measure of a particular characteristic or ability. Being exceptionally fit in flexibility and exceptionally unfit in strength does not add up to an average level of fitness that is acceptable. The individual items are important and should be treated so. Does an individual pass a medical examination by virtue of having exceptionally fine teeth but poor peripheral circulation?

It is hoped that the teacher training instructor will include laboratory experiences as a substantial part of the course to supplement the lectures. A laboratory manual is available for use with this text.

Our final manuscripts were in some measure a compromise as works of this kind must be. Conferences were held in which the co-authors served as sounding boards for each other. This resulted in changes, sometimes drastic ones, in the original drafts of some chapters. However, the final draft of a section was always the responsibility of the particular author or authors preparing it. In combining our efforts in this project, we had as our primary objective the establishment of a more scientific foundation and a practical basis for the teaching of physical and health education.

We are indebted to the many scholars who allowed us to quote from their work so extensively. They and their publishers generously permitted us to reproduce many figures. I am personally happy to acknowledge the help of my wife, Betty, for her encouragement and constructive criticism of many portions of the series.

We wish to express our sincere thanks to Phi Epsilon Kappa Fraternity for publishing the first version of this text and to Dr. R. R. Schreiber and Mr. Nick Kellum for their help in bringing this one to print. Working with them has been a pleasure.

To the students, teachers, and administrators in physical education who use measurement in an effort to improve the quality of education, this series is dedicated.

H. J. M.

I

History
and
Principles

MEASUREMENT IN PERSPECTIVE

1

Benjamin H. Massey

> *"It is the mark of an educated man to look for precision in each class of things just so far as the nature of the subject permits."*
> Aristotle

Some three thousand years ago, centuries before the Golden Age of Greece when Socrates walked the streets of Athens proclaiming the cause of wisdom and justice, a wise man wrote, "Wisdom is the principal thing; therefore get wisdom: and with all thy getting get understanding." (1). Today, many centuries later and in a world entirely different from that known to King Solomon, wisdom still is the principal thing and the getting of Understanding one of our most critical needs. One objective of higher education is the getting of understanding, and measurement and the study of measurement contribute to this end.

Measurement: basic nature and significance

The nature of measurement

Everyone is familiar with measurement in one form or another. It permeates every aspect of our lives. We measure the length of objects. We are measured for the fitting of suits, coats, and shoes. We step on the scale to find out if we are overweight or underweight. We carefully count our change after making a purchase, and we not so carefully count our strokes on the golf course. Despite the all-pervasive nature of measurement and its influence on human affairs, few of us have ever stopped to reflect on its exact nature, the part it plays in shaping our personal and professional lives, and the contribution it makes to physical education. In order for one to understand the role of measurement, one must first have some insight into what measurement is in its most rudimentary form.

Measurements range in form from very simple kinds of measurements such as those mentioned in the preceding paragraph to the very complex measurements of science and research. Measuring the length of a field is relatively simple. Measuring the age of a fossil or the distance of a faint star is considerably more complex, requiring more skill and knowledge on the part of the measurer. Perhaps the most complex of all measurements are those having to do with human beings and their performance, whether physical, mental, emotional, or social.

Physical education has to do with human beings and their performance and consequently, the measurements are at times very complex. In fact, some aspects of human activity are at present too difficult for us to measure; they must await the development of suitable instruments and techniques. Ultimately, these too will be measured, for the overriding premise on which all measurement and advances in measurement rest is the premise that anything that exists must exist in some quantity and therefore can be measured.

The complexity of measurement in physical education is not often appreciated even by experienced teachers, much less by persons who have had little contact with physical education and do not understand its nature. It is not easy to measure an individual's skill in stroking a tennis ball or executing a gymnastic stunt. It is even more difficult to measure attitude, sportsmanship, or the relationships and feelings among teammates and within a group of students in a typical physical education class. There are still only inadequate methods for measuring the stroke output of blood by the heart during running, the energy expended in the course of a football game, the emotions of a coach during the closing minutes of a contest, or a child's will to win.

The measurement process

Measurement in its most elementary form is closely associated with the whole process of thought and learning. From time immemorial, human beings have gained through measurement a clearer understanding of the universe and the world about us. Measurement has satisfied our most basic needs, particularly curiosity. It has been the means whereby we have verified our opinions and objectified our more nebulous and subjective estimates. Measurement and measurement concepts have provided a disciplined and systematic approach to learning.

Measurement always involves four distinct processes: (1) selecting, identifying, and defining that which is to be measured; (2) choosing a familiar object as the basic reference, the scale against which the object being measured is to be compared; (3) comparing the item selected for measurement with the familiar object or scale; and (4) noting and recording the quantitative relationship between the two. If, for example, one wishes to find the length of an object such as a boat, one must first identify precisely what is to be measured. In all probability, this will be the greatest horizontal space intervening from tip to tip. Next, an object, the length of which is already known, is selected as a frame of reference. It may be a stride, the length of a foot, or, if we wish to be more precise, a yardstick. Next, the object to be measured and the familiar object are brought into apposition, one with the other. Last, the quantitative relationship between the two objects is noted in terms of a number of strides, feet, yards or whatever unit was selected for use. The accuracy and usefulness of any measurement will depend on how intelligently and faithfully these steps are followed.

The significance of measurement

Measurement is significant to us for a number of important reasons. For one thing, it is the epitome of disciplined thought and learning. Furthermore, it has been the key to our advancement through the ages. It has been the basis for all technological progress, the backbone of every nation's economy, and the means whereby we have come to understand, predict, and control the world about us. Measurement has served as the basis for the classification and systematization of all knowledge, which makes it important in science. It has enabled us to objectify and quantify our subjective estimates. It has provided the basis for writing formulae, establishing principles, and predicting events. It has made wise and discriminatory decisions possible. In brief, measurement has undergirded all human progress.

It is difficult to imagine a world without measurement. There would be no trading or selling, no exchange of money, no research, no medical science, no diagnosing of illnesses, no ball games, and worst of all, no tests or grade reports at the end of the term. We would have no calendar or clock. The nature of skeletal muscle would still be a mystery. We would not understand the dynamics of the circulatory system, and would be incapable of evaluating the physical performance of individuals. The world as we think of it would not exist.

The implications of this for physical education are obvious. The question is sometimes raised, even by supposedly experienced physical educators, as to whether or not measurement is important. Such a question actually is meaningless, for without measurement in some form, there could be no physical education. The real question to be asked is "How effectively is measurement being used?"

The value of studying measurement

A legitimate question to be asked by anyone undertaking the study of measurement for the first time, especially a student who takes the course as a curriculum requirement, is "What returns can I expect for my efforts?" The answer to this question clearly depends on three principal factors: the quality of instruction, the intelligence of the student, and the extent to which the student concentrates on the subject. The last factor is the most important, for the student can do very little about the first two. Mental effort is extremely important, for measurement is not an easy subject to master. Many undertake the study of measurement poorly prepared academically for the task which confronts them. Fortunately, any sensible person willing to work hard and engage in additional study, particularly in the prerequisite academic subjects, can master measurement theory. Important to success is a reasonably good grounding in the fundamentals of mathematics, familiarity with the anatomy and physiology of the human body, a knowledge of psychology, and a knowledge of basic physics, especially mechanics. A mature philosophy of physical education is also important, for philosophy gives direction and meaning to one's efforts. Last, a willingness on the part of the student to think critically and independently, reflectively considering new concepts and formulating independent principles, is extremely important. Students who unquestioningly memorize whatever is presented may pass an introductory course in measurement but will not be educated. They will not be capable of proceeding to more advanced levels or be able to translate into practical terms what they have learned.

Direct outcomes

The direct outcomes which can be expected from the study of measurement are as follows: First, and perhaps most important from the standpoint of becoming an educated person, is the cultivation of the ability to think in measurement terms. Measurement demands that problems be attacked in a disciplined, orderly fashion. Facts must be marshalled and conclusions drawn on the basis of the best available evidence. In this respect, the study of measurement is similar to the approach used in mathematics. It is important to approach this subject with the intention of establishing basic concepts and principles of thought, rather than memorizing selected tests and procedures as would be expected of a technician with little interest or vision with respect to his work.

A second outcome that may be expected from the study of measurement is a further clarification and crystallization within one's own mind of a personal philosophy of physical education. Measurement, to be meaningful, must be purposeful. Emphasis in measuring should be placed on those aspects of physical education one considers of particular importance. It has been pointed out that the first step in measurement is identification and definition of what is to be measured. The entire measurement process, that is, consideration of what is to be measured, the development of suitable instruments and techniques, and the application of these instruments and techniques, by necessity tends to emphasize the important aspects and brings into proper focus the field in its entirety.

A third and more prosaic benefit to be expected from the study of measurement is the acquiring of skills, tools, and terminology that assist one in other areas of specialization within the field of physical education. What we know about kinesiology, physiology of exercise, methods of teaching, and the psychological aspects of physical performance have been derived through measurement. A knowledge of the units of measurement and measurement terminology assists tremendously in understanding these subjects.

Fourth, an understanding of measurement is essential to understanding and interpreting research. Each year, more and more research pertaining to physical education is published. A professional person has the obligation to keep up with the literature in the field. Research is principally a matter of measurement and interpretation of measurements. The articles appearing in *The Research Quarterly** and other scientific periodicals are highly technical and virtually incomprehensible to persons not trained in measurement.

Last, and quite important, the study of measurement enables one to become a better and more effective teacher. Pupils are interested in their progress and achievement. The teacher is interested in how well the goals set for pupils are being achieved. Measurement is the only method by which this information can be obtained. A physical education program not based on measurement cannot be an effective program.

Basic principles

Up to this point, measurement has been considered in rather general terms. Let us now consider measurement more specifically as it relates to physical education. This will contribute to an overview of the subject and will also serve to lay the ground work for more detailed discussions of various topics which follow in subsequent chapters.

It has been pointed out that the process of measurement always entails four procedures, namely, (1) identification, and definition of that which is to be measured, (2) choosing an appropriate unit or dimension to adequately reflect the nature and quantity of the factor to be measured, (3) selecting a suitable instrument for making the measurement, and (4) analyzing and interpreting the measurements obtained.

Factors measured in physical education

Every subject field, including physical education, considers certain factors particularly worthy of attention. Physicists measure those factors related to the physical universe and its operation, including mechanical force, heat, elec-

*Published by the American Alliance for Health, Physical Education and Recreation.

tricity, and so on. The chemist analyzes and quantifies the elements and compounds found in nature. The psychologist measures mental, emotional, and behavioral phenomena. The biologist is interested in the growth, development, and the physiological processes of living things. The sociologist measures and evaluates the structure and interaction of groups of people.

Physical educators are interested in human beings and their welfare, especially as it is affected by participation in programs of physical activities, sports, and health instruction. The objectives of the program dictate what is to be measured, and these objectives in turn depend on the philosophy of those responsible for the program.

Because a human being is an integrated whole, physical education, presumably, affects all aspects of our nature. We are normally thought of as having four major aspects, namely, the physical, the mental, the social, and the moral (spiritual). Physical education, obviously, most directly affects the physical. Consequently, primary emphasis in measurement is placed on this attribute. The mental and social aspects of our nature also are affected through physical education, but perhaps not so obviously. The spiritual is undoubtedly affected to a marked degree by the experiences encountered through physical education. The gymnasium and play field afford an unusual laboratory for developing ethical codes of behavior and for bringing moral values into focus. Little attention, however, has been given by physical educators to measurement in this area, even on a research basis.

Units of measurements

Of particular importance in measurement are the units selected for use. When the decision has been reached about what is to be measured and it has been clearly defined, the next step is the selection of a unit which provides an appropriate frame of reference. There is generally a great variety of units which can be selected for the task at hand, or, if suitable units are not available, new ones can be devised. When people began to explore outer space, the need arose for some type of standard solar "yardstick." The unit selected as the space yardstick was an astronomical unit, the mean distance between the earth and the sun, 92,960,104 miles. The reporting of distances in space between planets and stars can now be accomplished easily and with an acceptable degree of accuracy.

At times, the unit selected may, for practical reasons, be quite crude. This is the case when we select runners on the basis of the order in which they finish a race, when the height of a tennis net is measured with a racquet, or when points are assigned in judging diving. At other times, a measurement may be quite precise, as when we measure to a thousandth of a second the speed of movement of an arm or the velocity at which a ball is traveling.

The kinds of measurement used by a profession reflect favorably or unfavorably on that profession and the quality of its work. The use of crude or inappropriate units indicates ignorance and ineffectiveness. The more advanced and sophisticated the profession, the more refined and sophisticated are its units of measurement.

Measurement is essentially a process of proceeding from the known to the unknown. The unit selected should serve as the known quantity or frame of reference for discovering the amount or extent of the factor being measured. Hence, any unit selected must (1) be a quantity which is familiar and interpretable, (2) be of appropriate size to reflect the measurement at the desired level of accuracy, and (3) have stability.

The importance of familiarity with a unit of measurement is illustrated by the Biblical account of Goliath, the Philistine. Goliath, we are told, was 6 cubits and a span tall and carried a spear weighing 600 shekels. Most of us, without other information, would infer nothing from these measurements. We have been told, however, that Goliath was a giant. Was he bigger than our present day basketball players? Let us see. A cubit is the distance from the tip of the elbow to the tip of the middle finger, and, as standardized by the English, equaled 18 inches. A span is the width of the hand from tip of thumb to tip of little finger with fingers spread. As standardized by the English, it was 9 inches. A shekel, an ancient coin, supposedly weighed about .036 pounds. Now Goliath's size and strength become more understandable, for we can relate his physical attributes to units with which we are familiar. A little calculation tells us that Goliath was a man well over 9 feet tall and handling a spear weighing around 20 pounds, somewhat heavier than the official collegiate javelin. By modern standards, Goliath was quite an athlete.

It is difficult to visualize a muscle fiber ranging in diameter from 10 to 100 microns and in length from a few millimeters to 40 or more millimeters without the ability to visualize a millimeter and micron. It is just as difficult to think in terms of calories, ergs, joules, candle power, and degrees of temperature for those unfamiliar with these units. Should the time on the 100-meter dash be faster than for the 100-yard dash? Should an American wrestler weighing 120 pounds be matched against a 120-kilogram European wrestler?

Just as important as familiarity with the nature of a unit is the matter of the appropriateness of the size of a unit for the task at hand. Only a very foolish individual would attempt to measure the distance from New York to San Francisco in inches, for not only would this be time consuming, but the level of accuracy in reporting the measurement would be misleading. It would be assumed that, since inches were used, the measurement was accurate to the nearest inch. For a distance this great, such accuracy is a virtual impossibility. Just as inappropriate would be the reporting of a basketball player's height in miles. How excited should a coach get about a prospective player who is .0011 miles tall? The unit selected must be of appropriate magnitude if the measurement is to be meaningful.

The importance of stability in a unit is obvious. If the unit selected is continually fluctuating, it is not a particularly useful unit. The plotting of lots for building a large housing development certainly could not be based on dimensions obtained by stepping off the distances. Much more precise measurements based on stable units are needed. In early days, the units used were not particularly stable. Figure 1–1 illustrates an early unit of measurement. Distances were measured by body parts such as the cubit, span, foot, and hand. They varied from man to man. Weight was measured using pieces of money, such as the shekel. Today, units used on a large scale are quite stable. Both in the business world and in the scientific world, measurement units ·are strictly defined by international agreement and models have been constructed to serve as standards. The standard yard, for instance, established in 1854, is represented by the distance between two parallel lines crossing two gold studs set in a platinum bar housed in London. The distance between the two lines actually is an exact yard only when the temperature is 62 degrees Fahrenheit and the barometric pressure 30 inches. Consider, if you will, the precision of this standard "yard" as compared with the units of the past such as the hand or cubit which varied from man to man, or for that matter, with the badly marked and warped wooden yardsticks we sometimes use today. Other units of linear measure such as feet, inches, rods, and miles are defined using the standard yard as the basic unit.

The traditional units of physical measurement used in the United States are the yard as the unit of linear distance, the pound troy and the pound avoirdupois as the units of weight, and the gallon as the unit of volume. Other units of linear distance, weight, and volume are fractions or multiples of these standard units. Models of these basic units are kept at the Bureau of Standards in Washington, D.C.

Throughout much of the world, the metric system is the most widely used system of measurement. This system is a decimal system, and lends itself to ease of calculation. It is commonly used in the basic sciences, chemistry and physics. It also is the system of units used in the Olympic games.

A principal limitation associated with measurement in physical education is the absence of, or disregard for, standardized, stable, refined units. A sit-up or a pull-up is a less than desirable unit because it fluctuates from day to day and from person to person. And so it is with many of the kinds of units and scales used. One of the great challenges facing the physical educator of the future is to establish standardized units of measurement or to adapt to already established units of measurement. The present confusion with respect to physical fitness and the level expected of pupils arises from the lack of adequate, standardized units for measuring this attribute.

Measuring instruments

Units reflect the quantity of something measured in a form which is understandable. Instruments are devices used for making measurements, that is, converting or relating that which is being measured to the desired units. Using an old-fashioned balance scale, we can determine a baby's weight in pounds or ounces by placing him on one pan of the scale and then placing ounce weights on the opposite pan in the amount just needed to balance the baby's weight. In this way, we quantify the baby's weight in ounce units. The scale

- Inch and Foot -
Three barley corns taken from center
of ear placed end to end equals one inch.
(Edward II 1324)
A foot ranged from 9¾ inch to 19 inches.

FIGURE 1–1.   Courtesy of Dr. L. Earle Arnow of Warner-
Lambert Research Institute, The C V Mosby Company, and
Kaufmann and Fabry Company.

is the measuring instrument. Carrying this line of thought further, we can consider every measuring instrument as operating somewhat like a balance scale in that it serves to equate that which is being measured with that which has been selected as the frame of reference, namely, the unit. Even a written objective test is such an instrument. The items on the test are analogous to the ounce weights, with the items correctly answered presumably equivalent to one's knowledge. Tapes, watches, calipers, rating sheets, questionnaires, and checklists are familiar instruments used by instructors and coaches in their measurement work. Dynamometers, ergometers, audiometers, sphygmomanometers, electrocardiographs, electromyographs, electron microscopes, counters, and oscilloscopes are somewhat less familiar, but also are used by physical educators, especially in research and physical fitness testing.

A very familiar instrument and one that is a particularly favorite tool is the test. The word *test* comes from the Latin word *testum,* which means an earthen vessel. In ancient times, a porous, cuplike vessel was used for assaying and refining precious metals. This process, in which intense heat was frequently used, was designed to discover the value of the material being assayed or tested. Many physical education tests today have the same purpose. The test is generally a method of trying someone out, or of putting one to the test in order to discover the quality and amount of any characteristic possessed. As in those early days, a test today which truly taxes an individual's ability can be a trial by fire. An oral examination, an attempt to vault a high bar, or an endurance run can be both a challenging and an agonizing affair. Often, a test not only measures the quality of the performance, but also serves to refine and mature the one being tested. Growth and maturation cannot take place without adversity and struggle. A team never put to a real test in its own league has little hope of winning outside its league. A runner cannot expect to finish a marathon race, much less win it, if he has never competed in such an event. Those who wish to excel must welcome testing. A test above all else contributes to quality performance. A teacher who does not test is selling the students short. Testing is essential to learning.

Error in measurement

Perfection is impossible to attain. This applies especially to measurement. An ancient proverb states that "he who begins to count begins to err." There is always error in measurement. Some errors are due to ignorance or carelessness, hence are avoidable. Others, however, are unavoidable, the result of human limitations and imperfections. Seldom, if ever, are we able to obtain precisely the same reading on two consecutive measurements, even with something as objective as measuring the length of a board. Not only will slight changes occur in the tape and its position, but all information we acquire must be filtered through and processed by our nervous systems, which have limited capacity. We can never be certain that what we observe is correct. We can only estimate with a reasonable degree of assurance. Hence, in all measurement work we must, of necessity, accept a certain amount of error. The size and amount of this error will depend, in large part, on how much error we are willing to accept in the interest of haste and the care we take in obtaining the measurement. Such error, however, can never be eliminated entirely, no matter how much time and effort is put forth. It can only be minimized and noted. This error, inherent in the process of measurement, results from the interaction of many forces beyond the measurer's control. Repeated measurements taken on the same thing will fluctuate, sometimes in one direction causing an overestimate and sometimes in the other, causing an underestimate. The numbers, or scores, obtained with repeated trials tend to form a distribution with a few extreme plus and minus deviations, but with most of the scores hovering around the average. This type of unavoidable error, inherent in measurement work, is referred to as "measurement" or "chance" error.

Measurements obtained by repeated trials will vary depending on the stability and quality of the instrument being used, environmental factors affecting the instrument, the measurer, and the stability of the thing being measured. Living organisms, in particular, are subject to change, especially where performance is involved. This is a major source of variation.

Because measurement error is always present, and because the human mind has difficulty comprehending and properly interpreting large amounts of data, statistical procedures have been devised which aid the process of analysis and evaluation. The statistical procedures currently used are based on the laws of chance and form a branch of applied mathematics. Statistical methods provide a basis for the selection of tests and other measuring instruments. They are essential in the analysis and interpretation of data, and are useful in comparing the performances of individuals and groups of individuals. These and related applications make statistics an important measurement tool.

REFERENCES

1. Arnow, L. E. and M. C. D'Andrea, *Introduction to Physiological and Pathological Chemistry* (4th ed). St. Louis: Mosby, 1953, p. 508.

2. Clark, H. H., *Application of Measurement to Health and Physical Education*. Englewood Cliffs, N. J.: Prentice-Hall, 1959, p. 528.

3. English Bible, King James Version. Prov. 4:6.

4. Howe, H., *Introduction to Physics*. New York: McGraw-Hill, 1942, p. 557.

5. Larson, L. A., and R. D. Yocom, *Measurement and Evaluation in Physical, Health, and Recreation Education*. St. Louis: Mosby, 1951, p. 507.

6. Lindquist, E. F., ed., *Educational Measurement*. Washington, D.C.: American Council on Education, 1951, p. 819.

7. Meyers, C. R., and E. T. Blesh, *Measurement in Physical Education*. New York: Ronald Press, 1962, p. 473.

8. Peloubet, F. N., and A. D. Adams, *Peloubet's Bible Dictionary*. Philadelphia: Winston, 1925, p. 798.

9. Peterson, H., *Essays in Philosophy*. New York: WSP, 1959.

10. Scott, M. G., ed., *Research Methods in Health, Physical Education, Recreation*. Washington, D.C.: American Association of Health, Physical Education and Research, 1959, p. 536.

11. Smithells, P. A., and P. E. Cameron, *Principles of Evaluation in Physical Education.* New York: Harper, 1962, p. 478.

12. *The New York and Wagnalls Encyclopedia.* New York: Unicorn Press.

13. Van Norman, R. W., *Experimental Biology.* Englewood Cliffs, N.J.: Prentice-Hall, 1963, p. 243.

14. *Webster's New World Dictionary of the American Language,* (College ed.).

STUDY QUESTIONS • *Chapter 1*

1. State the rationale for this textbook. Why was it written when there are other texts on the market? What two objectives were outlined for chapters on various kinds of tests?

2. Why are "motor ability" and "sports potential" tests not included?

3. Describe five values (outcomes) one would expect in the study of measurement.

4. Why are measurements in physical education sometimes quite complex and difficult to make?

5. Explain the four common processes in measurement.

6. Why are careful measurements important in athletics?

7. How and for what purpose are tests and measurements used in research?

8. Describe how tests and measurements can contribute to an effective physical education instructional program.

9. What is the difference between evaluation and measurement?

10. How might an administrator in physical education use tests and measurements?

11. How do tests and measurements in physical education differ from those in other academic areas?

12. What are important considerations in selecting the units of measurement?

13. Is a cubit more or less than 12 inches?

14. About how many microns are there in an inch? In a millimeter?

15. How are the following conversions made:
    inches to centimeters
    miles to kilometers
    yards to meters
    cubic inches to cubic centimeters
    cubic yards to cubic meters
    cubic inches to cubic feet
    pounds to kilograms
    ounces to grams
    square inches to square feet
    square yards to square meters
    square inches to square centimeters
    square centimeters to square meters
    quarts to liters

16. What is the derivation of the word *test?*

17. Explain what is meant by "systematic" errors or a "bias."

18. Explain what is meant by "chance" errors.

19. What is the purpose of statistical analysis?

MEASUREMENT: HISTORICAL REVIEW

2

Benjamin H. Massey

In this chapter is presented a brief history of the development of measurement and testing in physical education in the United States. The intent is to present an overview of the development of measurement, focusing on those incidents, personalities, and instruments which will contribute to better understanding and appreciation of the nature of modern measurement in physical education.

The beginning of measurement

It is a truism to say that measurement began with the human race, for it has already been pointed out that measurement in a very basic way is associated with the process of thought itself. The early Chaldean priests observed and charted the course of the stars, laying the foundation for our present calendar. The Egyptians as far back as 3000 B.C. measured and plotted their land following the flooding of the Nile and constructed pyramids based on mathematical principles and measurement. Without belaboring the point or going into tedious detail, it can be asserted that, throughout the course of history, the rise of each civilization and all technological advances have been directly related to advances in the science of measurement.

Edward Hitchcock, the father of
physical education measurement

Prior to the middle of the nineteenth century, there was little formalized physical education measurement in the United States. The emphasis in education was on classical studies and physical education did not exist in the sense in which we think of it today.

Measurement in physical education had its formal beginning in 1861 when Dr. Edward Hitchcock was appointed Professor of Physical Education at Amherst College, the first professorship in physical education. Medically trained and interested in the physical welfare of the students, Dr. Hitchcock approached his task of caring for the students' health in a scientific manner. In connection with his physical education program, he inaugurated a strong testing program centered around anthropometric measurements and strength tests. Each student, five times during the course of his college career, was measured with respect to height, weight, finger reach, chest girth, lung capacity, and pull-ups. For a period spanning fifty years, Hitchcock and his successor Phillips continued to compile records of this sort. It is interesting that more than one hundred years later many of the measures used by Hitchcock still play an important part in physical fitness evaluation.

Dudley Sargent: strength testing

During the last half of the nineteenth century, interest in strength swept the country and held sway for the next fifty years. This interest was stimulated not only by such persons as Dio Lewis, honorary doctor of homeopathy, who convinced many public school officials of the importance of physical training using his system of exercises, Catherine Beecher, a sister of the famous writer, Harriet Beecher Stowe, who insisted on the importance of systematic exercises for young women, and William Blaikie and William B. Curtis, enthusiastic proponents of strength development, but also by an influx of strong men from Europe who toured the country for over half a century demonstrating feats of strength.

In 1879, Dudley Sargent, like Hitchcock a physician, assumed the directorship of physical training at Harvard University. Interestingly, this was the year that Blaikie, a Harvard graduate, published his well-known book on systematic exercise, a book which in all probability influenced Sargent's thinking. Sargent, like Hitchcock, was interested in anthropometry and formulated a series of some forty body measurements, including such items as height of the sternum, girth of the arm at the elbow, and height of the pubic arch. Sargent was especially interested in determining the ideal proportions for the American male and female, so much so that at the 1893 Chicago Exhibition he exhibited statues depicting the ideally proportioned American male and female based on measurements he had taken from a number of individuals. The interest engendered by Hitchcock and Sargent in anthropometry spread to other colleges, to the Y.M.C.A., and even into secondary schools. The period from 1885 to 1900 has been called the "golden age" of anthropometry.

Sargent, undoubtedly influenced by the popular enthusiasm for strength development, and recognizing that anthropometry alone did not reflect best the effects of physical training on the human organism, turned in the 1880s to strength testing. He devised a test battery to measure the strength of college males that came to be known as the Intercollegiate Strength Test. This battery included measurements of the strength of the legs, back, and grip using a spring dynamometer; strength of the arms as indicated by pull-ups and parallel bar dips; and lung strength (strength of the respiratory muscles) indicated by blowing against a pressure gauge. This test battery was so popular that it was used as the basis for intercollegiate competition, involving practically all students in the participating schools. Through the years, this test has continued to be used, appearing in modified forms under other names. Frederick Rand Rogers in 1925 modified the test, calling it the Physical Fitness Index (PFI), and later C. H. McCloy, a student of Sargent, further refined the test.

Sargent's contribution to the field of measurement was not confined solely to anthropometry and strength. In 1902, he constructed a test designed to measure physical performance in more general terms. This test, called the "Universal Test for Strength, Speed and Endurance," was based on calisthenic exercise movements. There were six exercises in all. Also, in 1920 Sargent proposed the vertical jump test, perhaps one of the most popular and widely used tests in physical education at the present time. This test, a very simple one, involves jumping directly upward. Its popularity is due to the importance of leg power in most forms of athletics and the simplicity of its administration. It is difficult to exaggerate the importance of his contribution to and influence on the field.

1880 to 1900

The period from 1880 to 1900 saw physical education become an accepted part of American education, and measurement an integral part of the physical education program. Major emphasis during these years was on anthropometry and strength testing, but the ground work was laid for the expansion of measurement into other areas, especially athletics.

The first meeting of the Association for the Advancement of Physical Education, today the American Alliance for Health, Physical Education, and Recreation, was held in 1885. This meeting can be identified as the beginning of physical education on an organized basis in the United States. It is interesting to note that discussion at this first meeting involved measurement. Hitchcock presented a plan for measuring the physical health of college students utilizing a medical examination and anthropometric measures. Problems of uniformity in testing and the use of norms were discussed. These still are major problems in measurement work.

By 1885, athletics which had been introduced into American colleges earlier in the century were fairly well established in even the smallest and most isolated colleges with some type of organized competitive program. Physical education at this time continued to be thought of primarily as physical training with emphasis on calisthenics and gymnastics, with athletics considered primarily recreational in nature. Because of the obvious bearing athletics has to physical development and the enthusiasm of students for sports, it was natural that an amalgamation of the two types of programs take place. Physical education and sports began to be synonymous in the minds of many. This new dimension to physical education demanded an expansion in the concept of measurement.

The first athletic testing instrument of any consequence was constructed in 1890 for the Athletic League of the Y.M.C.A. by Luther Gulick. The test was a pentathlon, consisting of a 100-yard dash, running high jump, hop-step-jump, 16-pound shot put, and a hand rope climb. It was administered as part of the Cleveland Turnerbund Festival of 1894. Not until after the turn of the century, however, with the continued expansion of athletics, did significant progress occur in athletic measurement.

The period of transition: 1900–1920

The period from 1900 to 1920 represents a period of transition in the conceptual nature and objectives of physical education. Both the expansion in athletics and a shifting educational philosophy affected physical education and, ultimately, measurement. Both educators and the public were beginning to recognize that there were important things to be accomplished through the school experience other than the training of minds. The philosophies of John Dewey and G. Stanley Hall placed emphasis on the importance of experience and the necessity for learning by doing. Reflecting the trends of the time, Thomas Woods and Clark Hetherington from 1900 to 1910 spearheaded a move to extend the horizons of physical education to incorporate the expanding educational philosophy. Hetherington, an influential personality, outlined four objectives for this "new physical education": organic development, psychomotor education, character education, and intellectual education.

The changing philosophy concerning physical education was reflected in the ever expanding number of tests constructed and utilized during this period. Sargent in 1902 proposed his *Universal Test for Strength, Speed and Endurance of the Human Body.* Luther Halsey Gulick, author of the Pentathlon for the Y.M.C.A., constructed for the Public School Athletic League in New York City the *Athletic Achievement Test.* Ward Crampton, a physician, presented in 1905 his famed *Blood Ptosis Test,* an instrument based on changes in the dynamics of the circulatory system with changes in body position.

George Meylan of Columbia University in 1907 set up a College Achievement Test for marking students. This was an important step, for it represented one of the first attempts to integrate measurement with the process of instruction in physical education. Meylan's test battery consisted of the following measures: (1) a written examination on personal hygiene and sanitation, (2) good carriage and graceful movement, (3) ability to perform three motor skills: the high jump, bar vault, and swinging jump, (4) endurance, and (5) swimming. J. H. McCurdy, a well-known Springfield College professor, in 1910 worked out norms for heart rate and blood pressure, providing a basis for interpreting circulatory fitness. In 1913, Meylan constructed a test of cardiovascular efficiency and in the same year the American Playground Association adopted the *Athletic Badge Test,* establishing minimum standards for performance. Schneider during World War I presented his classic *Schneider Test,* which was based on heart rate and blood pressure response to mild exercise.

Around 1917, interest arose in the formulation of classification indexes useful for the grouping of students for activity. Frederick J. Reilly presented one of the first such indexes. His index, widey used for a number of years, was based on age, weight, height, and grade in school. F. L. Kleeberger in 1918 utilized a rather comprehensive battery of items at the University of California for the assignment of students to activities. The Kleeberger battery included a measurement of *health; agility* as indicated by the ability to perform the hand vault, high jump, broad jump, and the 100-yard dash; *defense,* represented by skill in wrestling, boxing, and fencing; *swimming;* and *sportsmanship.* Failure in any phase resulted in assignment to a program intended to strengthen that area of weakness.

A survey taken in 1920 of the tests used at the secondary level gives some indication of the status of measurement at that time. The tests most frequently used with boys in physical education classes were the running high jump, pull-ups, short dashes, standing and running broad jumps, rope climb, pushups, and the shotput. Basketball throw for distance, short dashes, rope climb, and vaulting were used in testing girls.

Period of rapid growth: 1920–1940

The scope of modern measurement in physical education had been determined by the early 1920s. Physical educators were interested in measuring physique, posture, physical performance, athletic skills, the physiological effects of exercise, knowledge, attitude, and social relationships. Measurement technique, however, was as yet relatively crude and unreliable. The next twenty years were characterized by rapid advances in the technical aspects of measurement.

From 1920 to 1940, the field of educational measurement underwent a complete metamorphosis. Testing and measurement prior to this time had been primarily a matter of good judgment and subjective estimates. Advances made during the twenties and thirties by mathematicians in the area of statistics and by psychologists in test construction provided educators with tools hitherto unknown. These advances laid the basis for scientific and objective measurement of biological phenomena. Tests could be constructed on grounds other than empirical evidence. Measurement instruments of all types could be tried out, their validity and reliability evaluated in terms other than personal prejudices. During this period, measurement in physical education was translated from an art into a science. Textbooks were written on the subject and special training was required of those wanting to become measurement experts. In physical education as well as in the general field of education, a measuring instrument had to demonstrate an acceptable degree of precision and validity to be accepted.

The interest of physical educators in measurement was directed into many channels. David K. Brace, a name familiar in measurement for many years, in 1924 constructed an instrument designed to measure the basketball-playing ability of girls. He is also credited with introducing at about the same time the first formal, objective written test, a true-false test of basketball knowledge. Elizabeth Beall (1925) constructed a test for tennis. Dr. Brace (1927) introduced a battery of stunts for measuring motor ability. This battery later was modified by Charles H. McCloy. It consists of twenty physical performance stunts scored on a pass or fail basis. The stunts are similar to those frequently tried by school boys, for example, kneeling on both knees and attempting to jump to a standing position, jumping over a stick held with both hands, and performing a deep knee bend on one leg, touching the opposite knee to the ground. An attempt was made in 1928 by Van Buskirk to measure those moral qualities and social traits presumably influenced through physical education. Frederick W. Cozens, 1929, constructed a test of the athletic ability of men, and McCloy, 1930, attempted to measure "character."

Interest in measurement received a distinct boost in 1930 when the *Research Quarterly* came into being. Not only was the importance of measurement emphasized through its use in research studies, but research directly bearing on test construction and the validation of tests had a published outlet.

Measurement continued in the thirties along the same lines it had followed during the twenties. Interest was shown in developing instruments for the homogeneous grouping of pupils for instruction; the measurement of health status, physical development, and organic efficiency; the measurement of athletic ability; the ascertainment of knowledge and attitudes; and the appraisal of character, personality, and social attitudes. Interest in these last was undoubtedly heightened by the depression, with its emphasis on human problems and social relations.

World War II

The onset of World War II virtually paralyzed all aspects of education. By popular demand, the emphasis in physical education, particularly for males, swung radically toward physical fitness. Each of the military services set up batteries of tests which presumably measured fitness. These tests consisted of the customary feats of strength and endurance, such as pull-ups, situps, and dashes. Physical education as it had been in peace time no longer existed. It became physical training with emphasis on calisthenics, combatives, and running obstacle courses. The influence of the military reached down into the secondary schools, where the major emphasis for boys was on stamina. It was only in programs for girls that a reasonable semblance of interest in the educational objectives of physical education was maintained.

Post-war measurement

The war profoundly influenced physical education. Measurement at the close of the war was considered synonymous with physical fitness testing. Thousands of men had been exposed to this type of testing during their military service and to them, this was the beginning and end of all measurement. To many, physical education was repulsive. A reaction set in producing an immediate swing back toward the social objectives of the prewar years.

Movement away from physical fitness objectives continued up until the early fifties, when Hans Kraus, a physician, brought to the attention of President Eisenhower, what he, Dr. Kraus, considered the deplorable physical condition of children in the United States as compared with their counterparts in Europe. The Kraus-Weber test on which this report was based consisted of six items scored on a pass-fail basis. These test items measured the strength and flexibility of the body in the region of the hips and trunk. Concerned by this report, the President immediately formed a Council on Physical Fitness. Physical educators, always alert to public opinion, reversed their field and once more returned to emphasis on physical fitness and conditioning. A test of physical fitness, somewhat more extensive in scope than the Kraus-Weber test, was devised under the auspices of the American Association for Health, Physical Education and Recreation. This test battery, consisting of pull-ups, situps, a 40-yard shuttle run, standing broad jump, 50-yard dash, softball throw for distance, and 600-yard run-walk, was administered on a national scale and norms tables constructed. The AAHPER test, coupled with the sustained activity of the President's Council on Physical Fitness, created a peace-time interest in physical fitness hitherto unknown in the United States. This interest continued unabated through the fifties and on into the seventies.

Other facets of life following the war years also influenced the character of measurement. The tremendous expansion in the number of colleges and universities offering a major in physical education, and the continual upgrading in curricula due both to the competition between schools and the new emphasis on science and research, caused an ever-expanding interest in measurement. In 1930, there were less than two hundred schools offering a major in physical education. By 1960, there were more than six hundred schools. Graduate work mushroomed, with nearly one hundred schools offering a doctoral program in 1960. Many of the graduate programs centered around research, impressing on the students recognition of the need for a greater grasp of measurement concepts and skill in the use of measurement tools. Further, much of the research undertaken in one way or another was directed toward improving measuring instruments.

Measurement during this post-war period, 1946 to 1970, steadily expanded as evidenced by a marked increase in the number of young physical educators interested and knowledgeable in the subject, by the utilization of measurement in research, by an ever-increasing number of colleges requiring a course in measurement as part of the basic curriculum for future physical educators, and by the increase in the number of physical education measurement textbooks.

Measurement from an historical perspective

Measurement as viewed from the vantage point of history leaves one with certain well-defined impressions. First, one is impressed by the close association between the growth of measurement and research in physical education. Through the years, those interested in establishing physical education on a sound scientific basis have been the leaders in refining measurement. Consequently, measurement has been more than tinged with the researcher's approach, so much so that it has not always been relevant to the practical problems encountered in instruction. Unfortunately, to many physical educators, measurement remains a tool only for the investigator. Its importance and relevance to instruction escapes them.

Second, one is impressed with the diversity of factors which have interested physical educators through the years and the variety of instruments and approaches employed. This stems both from the broad base on which physical education rests and also from the fact that the scope and philosophical concepts relative to the field have continually expanded and changed. Measurement in physical education has drawn on many disciplines, including mathematics, logic, physics, chemistry, biology, psychology, and sociology.

The challenge

The importance of measurement to any subject field or profession was well expressed by James Maxwell over ninety years ago:

> "The most important step in the process of every science is the measurement of quantities. Those whose curiosity is satisfied with observing what happens have occasionally done service by directing the attention of others to the phenomena they have seen; but it is to who endeavor to find out how much there is of anything that we owe all the great advances in our knowledge. Thus every science has some instrument of precision, which it has advanced, by enabling observers to express their results as measured quantities. In astronomy we have the divided circle, in chemistry the balance, in heat the thermometer, while the whole system of civilized life may be fitly symbolized by a foot rule, a set of weights and a clock."

Today, there are signs of more interest in measurement and recognition of the importance of measurement on the part of physical educators than at any previous time in history. The profession, at last, seems to be awakening to the fact that without measurement there can be no knowledge and without knowledge there can be no profession.

REFERENCES

1. Brace, D. K., "Tests and Measurements in Physical Education," *The Making of American Physical Education,* edited by A. Weston. New York: Appleton-Century-Crofts, 1962, p. 319.

2. Clarke, H. H., *Application of Measurement to Health and Physical Education.* Englewood Cliffs, N.J.: Prentice-Hall, 1959, p. 528.

3. Jokl, E., *Clinical Physiology of Physical Education: A Medical Theory of Gymnastics,* pp. 85–92, 2: a Lingiaden Stockholm, 1949, Kongressen II.

4. Larson, L. A., and R. D. Yocom, *Measurement and Evaluation in Physical Health, and Recreation Education.* St.

Louis: Mosby, 1951, p. 507.

5. Massey, B. H., et al., *The Kinesiology of Weight Lifting.* DuBuque, Iowa: Brown, 1959, p. 175.

6. McCloy, C. H., *Tests and Measurements in Health and Physical Education.* New York: Appleton-Century-Crofts, 1942.

7. Sullivan, J. W. N., *The Limitations of Science* (Mentor ed.). Viking, 1933, p. 189.

8. Van Dalen, D. B.; E. D. Mitchell; and B. L. Bennett, *A World History of Physical Education.* New York: Prentice-Hall, 1953, p. 639.

STUDY QUESTIONS · *Chapter 2*

1. Publication of what journal was important in the development of tests and measurements in physical education? Why?

2. Identify the following persons in the history of measurement in physical education. Describe their contributions:

Luther Gulick	Dio Lewis
Hans Kraus	C. H. McCloy
Dudley Sargent	George Meylan
Edward Hitchcock	J. H. McCurdy
Ward Crampton	Fredrick Rand Rogers
Catherine Beecher	David Brace

3. What effect did the onset of World War II have on physical education tests?

4. What is meant by "Ptosis"?

5. Describe the Intercollegiate Strength Test.

6. Anthropometry refers to what kinds of measurements?

SELECTION AND CONSTRUCTION OF TESTS

3

Henry J. Montoye

> *"The power to test is the power to define the curriculum."*
> Stanford C. Erickson*

Introduction

From the first two chapters, it is apparent that the imaginative teacher will see many applications for tests and measurements in physical education and recreation programs. The specific purpose of testing must be clearly defined if one is to select or construct a test intelligently. Many offices contain reams of data, in many cases carefully collected data, which have never been used because the teacher had no understanding of why the tests were administered in the first place. For example, it will make a difference in selecting a test whether the teacher wants to classify students for elementary sports instruction, or to select members of a varsity team. The first step, therefore, in either

---

*Director, Center for Research on Learning and Teaching, University of Michigan. Reproduced with permission of the author.

selecting or constructing a test is to determine how the results are to be used.

Having determined the "why" of testing, there are several considerations in determining the suitability of a test, including validity, reliability, objectivity, and practicability (administrative feasibility).

Validity

Definition

The traditional definition of validity is the extent to which the test measures what it purports to measure. A highly valid tennis performance test is one in which the score reflects accurately one's performance in the game of tennis. A valid test of knowledge of the rules in soccer is a test in which an individual with an excellent knowledge of the rules scores high in the test whereas a person whose knowledge is limited scores poorly. The definition is simple. Establishing the validity of certain test is frequently not so simple. For example, the measurement of fitness for muscular work is of significance to the physical educator and the exercise physiologist. But despite years of effort, the validity of most of the tests proposed for assessing this capacity is still questionable. Appraising the validity of tests has occupied considerable time and energy of scientists in many disciplines.

Criteria

Some standard is required in order to assess the validity of a test. Every field of science requires standards of measurement. A research laboratory in physical education will frequently have a good set of calibrated weights available so that scales and dynamometers may be checked at regular intervals.

Face validity

Fortunately, good criteria are frequently available for measuring physical performance, particularly sports performance. In some instances, tests almost define the sport itself. The essence of target archery is accuracy in shooting. The best criterion of overall performance in golf is obviously the score in the game. Running time in the 100-yard dash is another example. A rules test in a particular sport is generally developed from the official rules governing the sport. Tests of these kinds are often accepted on the basis of their "face validity."

Tournament scores

In dual sports (tennis, badminton, handball, etc.), a game score is not available in the same sense as in golf or archery. It is common practice to employ the number or percentage of games won in a singles tournament as a criterion in such sports. A valid test of badminton skills will rank the players in about the same way they would finish in a singles round-robin tournament. However, one should not expect perfect validity as measured by pure skills tests, since it is virtually impossible in a testing situation to duplicate game conditions precisely. In other words, non-skill factors enter into tournament play that are not measured in a skills test. The badminton test proposed by Lockhart and McPherson (6) is an example of a test in which tournament results were employed as one of the criteria. In this study, 27 college sophomores took the skills test, which consisted of volleying a badminton shuttle cock against a wall for thirty seconds. These same 27 girls played a round-robin tournament in which each girl played every other girl in the tournament. The percentage of games won by each contestant was compared to the score she made on the skills test. When the subjects were ranked on their tournament performance and then on the basis of the skills test, the rankings were very similar. Those who performed well in the tournament also performed well on the skills test. Hence, the skills test was a reasonably valid measure of badminton ability. The criterion was the tournament results.

Subjective ratings

In a complex team sport, such as basketball, it is impossible to arrive at an individual point score or number of games won. One can intuitively analyze the game as comprising certain skills such as throwing, shooting, dribbling, etc. Tests of these abilities can be devised, but ultimately one must ask if such a battery of test items really measures "basketball ability." Many times, tests are validated by administering the test battery to children and then assembling a group of experienced teachers or coaches to observe and rank or rate the children during actual game play. The criterion scores in this instance are the average ratings of the children by the panel of "experts." To a person used to absolute standards, subjective ratings of this sort appear less scientific. However, under proper conditions, the results can serve a useful purpose. Frequently there is no alternative. Objective posture tests are often validated in this way. For example, Elliott (3) describes an experiment in which posture photographs were taken of a large group of children. Fourteen judges rated the posture of each child on a numerical scale. The criterion was the sum of the judges' ratings for each child. Certain objective measurements on the photographs were made. In order to study the validity of these measurements, they were compared with the sum of the ratings of the fourteen judges. The validity of a basketball skills test was similarly investigated (5).

Established tests

There are some tests or measurements which have been well validated but, because of practical considerations (equipment, space, time, etc.), it is not feasible to make use of them routinely. It is sometimes possible, however, to devise simpler tests which compare quite favorably with the original, more elaborate test. When such a simpler test is compared with a well-established one, the latter is being used as a criterion.

One method of determining the percent of fat (body composition) in an individual is to weigh him in air and then under water. By Archimedes' principle, it is possible to calculate with a fair degree of accuracy the body density of the individual. Then, by making certain reasonable assumptions, the percentage of the person's weight due to fat can be estimated. This is a fairly well accepted procedure. But it is impractical in most situations in which the physical education teacher wishes to assess the fatness in men and women or boys and girls in his classes. In recent years, widespread use is made of the technique of measuring the subcutaneous fat by means of fat calipers. This test will be described later in the text. The most common method of validating such skinfold thickness measurements is to compare the results with the underwater weighing just described. In this case, the most generally accepted test is used as a criterion. An example of such a comparison in young men is described in a paper by Pascale and collaborators (8).

Contrasting groups

It is desirable or necessary at times to use the contrast between two extreme groups as a method of establishing the validity of a test. A valid test of field hockey ability should discriminate between beginners and players of recognized superior ability. Similarly, tests of other sports, physical fitness, dancing, and many other abilites can be validated in this way. The discrimination between the two groups serves as a criterion to determine the validity of the tests. The use of this technique is demonstrated in the report by Kelly and Brown (4). To validate a written knowledge test in field hockey, four groups of subjects were chosen: (a) experts (nationally recognized players, coaches, and umpires), (b) physical education majors who had had considerable training and experience in field hockey, (c) nonmajor students who had completed one or more seasons of field hockey, and (d) nonmajors who had never had any experience in field hockey. When the proposed knowledge test was administered to these students, the mean scores of the four groups were decidedly different.

Concomitant change

An obvious change in ability or condition should produce a corresponding change in the score in a test that purports to measure that ability or condition. The use of such a criterion is illustrated by the heart rate test proposed by Brouha (1, 2). The test rests on the assumption that individuals who have good cardiovascular-respiratory fitness, when subjected to a standard amount of work, will show a lower heart rate at a fixed time after the work is completed than will individuals whose cardiovascular-respiratory fitness is poor. The test was administered to a group of 21 oarsmen before and after a training program.

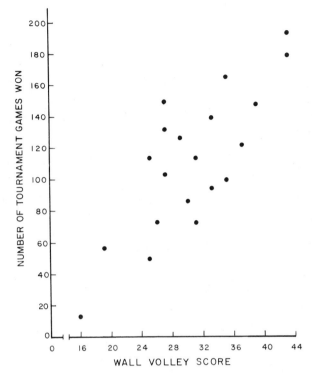

FIGURE 3–1. Scatterdiagram showing the relationship between wall volley test scores and tennis tournament results.

The scores before training, when the men were in poorer condition, were distinctly inferior to those obtained when the men were in better condition.

Measuring validity

Correlation

Most test data in health and physical education consist of numerical scores such as inches, pounds, seconds, games won, correct answers, etc. The criterion also consists of numerical values (a) when an absolute score is available, for instance, the number of strokes required to play 36 holes of golf, (b) when tournament scores are utilized, (c) when scores on an established test are available and, (d) when subjective ratings are used. In all such instances, validity may be expressed in terms of the correlation of the test scores with criterion scores.

Until mathematicians developed methods of measuring and expressing this correlation, one could only plot the relationship in what is sometimes called a scatter diagram or correlation plot. This is illustrated in Figure 3–1. A

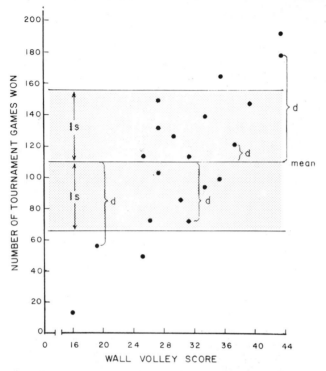

FIGURE 3–2.   The same scatterdiagram of Figure 3–1, but
also showing the mean number of tournament games won
(solid line), standard deviation on each side of the mean (dotted
area marked ls), and deviation of a few of the scores from
the mean (marked d).

wall-volley test has been used as a measure of tennis ability.   In this test, the
subject hits the tennis ball against a wall above a three-foot net line while remaining behind a restraining line.   The score is the number of good hits in one
minute.   In order to determine the validity of the test, the boys who took the
test also played a round-robin tournament in which every boy played six games
with every other boy in the class.   The total number of games won in all matches
constituted the tournament score for each boy.   The results for a sample of the
boys is shown in Table 3–1.   From Table 3–1, it is difficult to assess the relationship between the wall-volley test scores and the criterion (tournament
results).   However, when the data are plotted as in Figure 3–1, the correlation
is clearly evident.   The boys with the higher test scores also, in general, won
the most tournament games.   Thus, the test scores reflected tennis ability as
measured by tournament results.   Although plotting the scores in a scatter
diagram does give us a general impression of whether or not the two sets of
scores are related, it does not give a quantitative measurement of this relationship.   Furthermore, the publication of a scatter diagram to illustrate every
relationship is expensive.   In order to overcome these two limitations, a so-
called "correlation coefficient" is often calculated.

   There are many other statistical techniques that can be employed to quantify relationships but a discussion of them is beyond the scope of this text. However, because the correlation coefficient is used so extensively in validating tests in health and physical education, it will be explained in some detail.

In statistical work, the "arithmetic mean," or simply the "mean," is calculated by summing the scores and dividing by the number of scores. This is called the "average" in simple everyday discourse. The mean number of games won for the 20 boys (Table 3–1) is 110.9, which is illustrated by the horizontal line in Figure 3–2. Some of the scores are above and some are below the mean. In other words, there is some variation or variability of scores. The most common method of expressing the variability of scores is by means of the standard deviation, abbreviated *S.D.* or *s*. When referring to the standard deviation in a total, usually theoretical, population, the Greek letter σ may be used. The standard deviation may be computed by measuring the deviation or difference of each score (d in Figure 3–2) from the mean, squaring each of these deviations, summing them, dividing by the number of scores minus 1, and finally extracting the square root of the result. It is not necessary at this point to understand completely the mathematics involved, but one should appreciate that the larger the numerical value of the standard deviation, the greater the spread or variability of the scores. The calculation of the standard deviation will be illustrated in a later chapter. For the data on number of games won in Table 3–1 and Figure 3–2, the value of s turns out to be 45.3 and is indicated by the shaded area in Figure 3–2.

TABLE 3–1
Wall Volley Tennis Test Scores and Tennis Tournament
Results for 20 Boys

Subject	Wall-Volley Score	Tournament Games Won
BL.	35	165
NO.	27	132
TH.	16	13
AB.	33	139
MO.	30	86
CH.	25	113
FO.	31	72
FA.	43	192
SM.	25	49
AN.	37	121
ER.	26	72
GI.	39	147
RI.	27	102
LA.	35	99
WH.	43	178
SO.	33	94
LY.	31	113
PR.	27	149
JA.	19	56
OL.	29	126

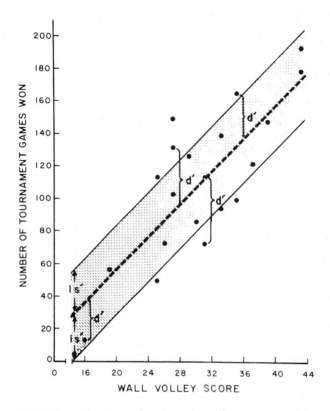

FIGURE 3–3.   The same scatterdiagram of Figure 3–1, but
also showing the best fitting (regression) line for the relationship
between tournament games won and test scores. This is
illustrated by the heavy broken line. The standard deviation
of the points about this line is the shaded area marked ls′.
Deviations (differences between several of the points and the
best-fitting line) are marked d′.

Consider now the plot of Figure 3–1. A straight line is fitted through
the points as shown in Figure 3–3.*   All of the points do not fall on this line;
there is a certain amount of spread or variance of the points around the line.
These deviations from the line are labeled d′, in Figure 3–3.   The standard
deviation of these points about the fitted line can be calculated just as was done
for the deviations about the mean.   For these data, the value turns out to be
27.7 and is illustrated by the shaded area on each side of the diagonal line in
Figure 3–3.   It will be observed that the closer the points cluster about the
line, the smaller are these deviations.   This will result in a smaller ratio of the
standard deviation of the points about the diagonal line to the standard devia-

*In practice, this is done in a precise way to minimize the sum of the squared deviations
from the line. When test and criterion scores in physical education are plotted, a straight
line often fits the data fairly well. This is one of the assumptions justifying the computation of a correlation coefficient.

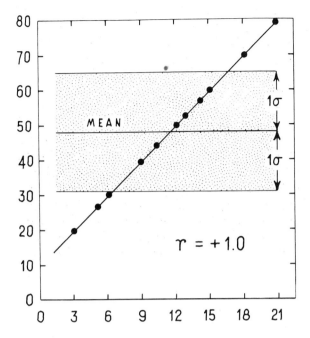

FIGURE 3–4a.   Perfect positive correlation.   Standard
deviation of points about the best fitting (heavy solid) line.
ls′ is not shown since its value is zero.

tion of the points about the mean.   In fact, a ratio of the squares of these two
standard deviations can be formed thus: $\frac{s'^2}{s^2}$.   If this ratio is subtracted from
one and the square root taken, the result is the correlation coefficient (r) which
may be either positive or negative.

$$r = \sqrt{1 - \frac{s'^2}{s^2}} = \sqrt{1 - \frac{(27.7)^2}{(45.3)^2}} = 0.79**$$

By convention, r is positive if the scores on the one axis increase with an increase in the scores on the other.   If, however, the scores of one variable
increase as the others decrease, the correlation coefficient is labeled negative.
The larger r becomes, either positive or negative, the closer is the correlation
of the two scores and, therefore, the higher the validity of the test.   This is
perhaps better understood by looking at extreme examples.   If the correlation
between two sets of scores were perfect, the points would form a straight line
as shown in Figure 3–4A.   Then the ratio $\frac{s'^2 \text{ (diagonal line)}}{s^2 \text{ (mean)}}$ would be zero

**This is not the usual computational formula.   A later chapter will include an example
of how the correlation coefficient is generally computed.

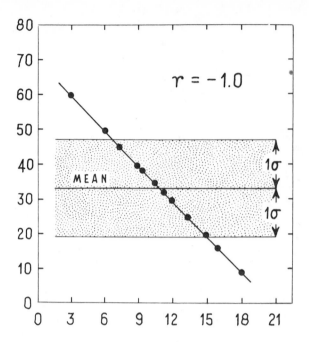

FIGURE 3–4b.   Perfect negative correlation.   Standard
deviation of points about the best-fitting (heavy solid) line.
1s′ is not shown since its value is zero.

because the standard deviation of the points about the line (the numerator of
the ratio) would be zero and the correlation now becomes:

$$r = \sqrt{1 - \frac{s'^2}{s^2}} = \sqrt{1 - \frac{0}{s^2}} = \sqrt{1} = +1$$

The correlation would be -1 if the scores were perfectly but inversely (negatively) correlated as shown in Figure 3–4B.   On the other hand, consider the
situation illustrated in Figure 3–5, in which there is almost no correlation
between the two tests.   In this case, the variance of the scores around the fitted
line is almost as great as the variance of the scores around the mean.   The
numerator in the ratio $\dfrac{s'^2}{s^2}$ approaches the numerical value of the denom-
inator and r approaches zero, thus:

$$r = \sqrt{1 - \frac{s'^2}{s^2}} \qquad \text{but } s'^2 \text{ approaches the value of } s^2$$

$$\text{and } \sqrt{1 - \frac{s'^2}{s^2}} \text{ approaches } \sqrt{1-1} = 0$$

Summarizing then, the correlation coefficient may vary from -1 (perfect
negative correlation) through 0 to $+1$, (perfect positive correlation).   The

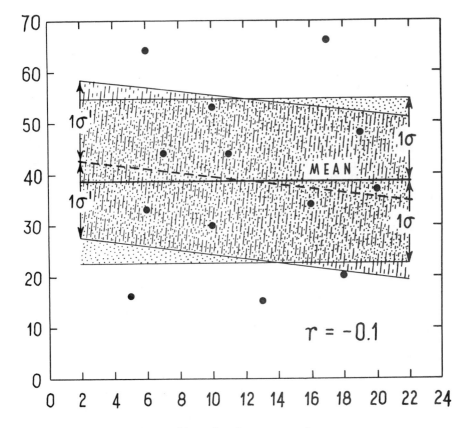

FIGURE 3–5. Scatterdiagram illustrating almost no correlation. The standard deviation of the scores (shaded area marked s′) about the best-fitting line (heavy broken line) is almost as large as the standard deviation of the scores (dotted area marked ls) about the mean (heavy solid line).

closer r approaches either $+ 1$ or $- 1$, the closer the test is correlated with the criterion and hence the higher is the validity of the test.

A better interpretation of r is still needed. The value of r has no units; it is a pure number. An r of 0.30 is not 50% as good as one of 0.60. How, then, can we interpret this number? One way is to recall the formula on p. 38, $r = \sqrt{1 - \dfrac{s'^2}{s^2}}$ where s'^2 is a measure of the variance around (or deviation from) the "best fit" line (See Fig. 3–3) and s^2 is a measure of the variance around (or deviation from) the mean (See Fig. 3–2). By squaring each side of this formula and rearranging the terms, one obtains $\dfrac{s'^2}{s^2} = 1 - r^2$. The quotient on the left is a ratio of the variance or spread of scores around the fitted line divided by the variance of scores around the mean. From the data in Table 3–1, the correlation coefficient representing the relationship between tournament games won and wall-volley test scores is .79 (see p. 33). If this value is substituted in the formula above

$$\frac{s'^2}{s^2} = 1 - r^2 = 1 - (.79)^2 = 1 - 0.62 = 0.38$$

This means that the variance around the "best-fit" line is, on the average, 38% of the variance around the mean. Suppose there were 20 boys in the next room and you were asked to guess the number of tournament games won by Boy "A," knowing only that the mean for all twenty was 110.9. Your best guess would be the mean. However, your guess would likely be in error by some amount since any particular boy is apt to be above or below the mean. However, suppose I now told you his wall-volley test score was 24. What would be your guess for Boy "A" now? A wall-volley test score of 24 is lower than most, as shown in Figure 3–3. You would likely find 24 on the horizontal axis of this figure and then follow this point upward until it intersects the fitted broken line. The estimated number of games won (on the vertical axis) corresponding to this test score is about 78. This would now be your best guess. But how much better is this? Since the correlation coefficient between games won and wall-volley test is 0.79, knowing the test score enabled you to guess or predict the games won with an average error about 38% as great as if you knew only the mean of the group and nothing at all about a person's wall-volley test score.

Since the reduction in error is proportional to the square of r and not r itself, a large r is needed to greatly reduce the error. For example, if we wanted to reduce the error to 10% rather than 38%, the correlation coefficient would have had to be 0.95 instead of 0.79. $(1 - r^2 = 1 - 0.95^2 = 1 - 0.90 = 0.10.)$

Another way of interpreting the correlation coefficient would be to square it and multiply the correlation coefficient by 100. Under most conditions, the resulting value represents the percentage of the total variation in the criterion that is associated with the particular test. In the case above (r = 0.79), approximately 62% of the variation in number of games won is associated with the wall-volley test score: $100 \ r^2 = 100 \cdot (0.79)^2 = 62.41$. As another example, Miller (Chapter 12) gave a similar wall-volley badminton test to 20 college girls and then had them play a round-robin tournament. The correlation coefficient expressing the relationship between the wall-volley test score and performance in the tournament (the criterion of badminton ability) was 0.83. If this coefficient is squared and multiplied by 100, the result is a value of 68.89 which means that 68.89% of the variation in ability to play badminton is related to (or accounted for) by the variability in the volley test. By the same token, 31.11% (100 − 68.89) of badminton ability is not accounted for (not measured by) the volley test. Another example, if the correlation coefficient between height and weight is 0.7, then 49% of the variation in weight is associated with the variation in height. Again, it becomes clear that high correlation coefficients are needed if we are to account for a high percentage of the variance. A coefficient of 0.9 still leaves 19% of the variance unaccounted for. For this reason, the student can understand why one requires a more valid test for selecting members of a varsity team than for grouping children for instruction.

Comparison of groups

As discussed above, tests are sometimes validated by comparing scores of two groups of people who are known to differ. For example, Table 3–2 contains data on resting heart rates and post-exercise heart rates of 10 young college men not in training [Brouha and Savage (2)]. The exercise consisted of 5 minutes of stepping onto a 20-inch bench at the rate of 30 steps per minute. Table 3–2 also contains similar data on 10 well-conditioned basketball players. It may be difficult to determine from the table whether either of these heart rates (resting or post-exercise) differentiates the two groups. From Figure 3–6, however, the relative validity of the two measures can be compared. Not only is the difference between means of the two groups important, but of equal importance is the variability within each group as this determines the overlapping of the distributions. It is obvious that the post-exercise heart rate differentiates between the two groups more effectively than the resting heart rate. The standard deviations are illustrated by the shaded area. In addition to a graphic assessment of the validity of tests as illustrated in Figure 3–6, it is possible to express the validity in quantitative terms by using more advanced statistical techniques that are beyond the scope of this text.

When a change in the subjects is employed as a criterion, a graphic or statistical analysis can be employed to measure validity. As an illustration,

TABLE 3–2

Resting and Post-Exercise Heart Rates of 10
Trained and 10 Untrained Young Men

TRAINED BASKETBALL PLAYERS			**UNTRAINED YOUNG MEN**		
Subject	**Resting Heart Rate**	**Post-Ex. Heart Rate**	**Subject**	**Resting Heart Rate**	**Post-Ex. Heart Rate**
Fe.	53	65	Qle.	72	132
Hal.	55	88	Gow.	70	114
Hi.	54	98	Ro.	62	122
Co.	59	85	To.	64	92
De.	65	94	Ba.	70	118
Ols.	59	80	Haw.	74	122
Pe.	51	68	Gov.	65	131
Ar.	65	74	Jo.	58	115
Ra.	71	100	Va.	62	124
Gor.	61	90	St.	71	138

From Brouha and Savage (2). Reproduced with permission of the publisher.

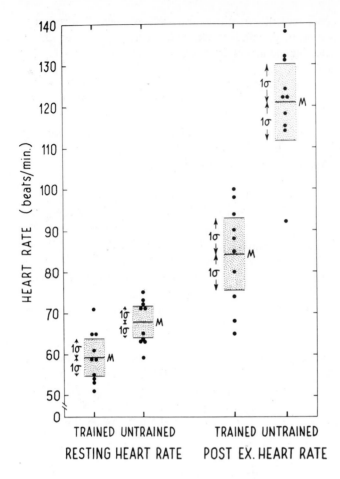

FIGURE 3–6.   Comparison of trained and untrained young
men in resting heart rate and in heart rate after a standard
exercise.

Table 3–3 contains more data on the 21 oarsmen of Brouha and Savage.
Training improves the cardiovascular-respiratory condition of individuals.
From Figure 3–7, based on the oarsmen data in Table 3–3, it is also clear that
maximum heart rate during a standard exercise reflects this change and, hence,
gives evidence of the validity of this test for measuring cardiovascular-
respiratory condition.

Words of caution

Test batteries in physical education are sometimes published in which tests
have been validated against an "internal criterion."   At times, there is some
justification for this procedure.   In most instances, however, the situation is

TABLE 3–3
Maximum Heart Rate During Standard Exercise in 21 Oarsmen
5 Min Treadmill Run, 7 Mph, 8.6% Grade

Subject	Heart Rate (Beats/Min)	
	Before Training	**After Training**
Cu.	172	158
Mar.	173	170
Er.	180	164
Gi.	185	172
No.	185	172
Ri.	190	170
La.	190	180
Cha.	190	178
Wh.	190	172
So.	192	174
Ch.	193	186
Ly.	195	180
Pr.	195	195
O.	195	176
Fi.	195	192
Eu.	196	182
Jr.	196	180
Br.	196	168
Mr.	200	180
Sn.	204	178
An.	205	186

From Brouha and Savage (2). Reproduced with permission of the publisher.

similar to the story of a shopkeeper* who was very proud of a clock that was kept in the shop window. One day he met the man whose duty it was to blow the noon whistle at a factory in the neighborhood. During the course of their conversation, the shopkeeper pointed out that his clock was quite an excellent timepiece since in the past several years it had not gained or lost a minute. He went on to point out that when his friend blew the noon whistle, this clock was always right on the dot. "By the way," said the shopkeeper, "What do you use to time the whistle?" "Oh, I always go past your window about ten minutes before noon and I set my watch to your clock," was the answer. (9) While the circular reasoning in this illustration is obvious, the trap can be so well camouflaged in an actual research study that the experimenter as well as the reader can be easily misled. In physical education, this has frequently occurred in the area of physical fitness testing. "New" batteries of tests purporting to measure physical fitness have been validated by comparing them with published physical fitness tests which themselves are of questionable validity.

*Excerpt from *An Introduction to Scientific Research,* Wilson, E. B., Jr., 1952, McGraw-Hill, New York, p. 83. Reproduced with permission of the author and publisher.

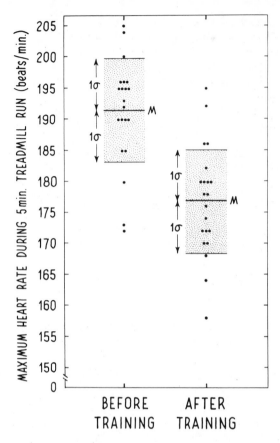

FIGURE 3–7. Maximum heart rate during a standard exercise in 21 university oarsmen before and after a training program. Plotted from data in Brouha and Savage (2).

The physical capacities of individuals have interested various workers in physical education for a long time. C. H. McCloy (7) used the term "General Motor Capacity Score," but various other labels such as "physical potential," "motor educability," and "general motor ability" have been attached to this concept. The implication is that one can measure the ultimate capacity of an individual. Tests in this area are, for the most part, worthless because criteria for studying their validity are not available or were not used.

Too frequently, tests and measurements in physical education have been based on data collected on a very narrow age range. For example, it is not justifiable to assume a test is valid for measuring junior high school girls when the data on which the validity of the tests rests are scores made by male freshmen in college. The data used in validating a test is sometimes referred to as the data population. The term *problem population* defines the population for which the test is developed or is to be applied. Obviously, the data population should be representative of the problem population or at least it should be a reasonable sample of the problem population. In studying reports describing the validity and other characteristics of tests, keep these two populations in mind.

Reliability

Definition

Reliability refers to the reproducibility of scores when the same subjects are tested a second time by the same tester. It also implies that the second administration of the test occurs soon enough after the first that the subjects do not have time to change fundamentally in the characteristic, ability, or knowledge being measured. Some tests and measurements in physical education are reliable, for example, the measurement of body weight, time of an endurance run, and distance a ball can be thrown. If one of these tests were administered to a group of boys and girls and the children were ranked on the basis of their performance, and the next day the test was repeated, and the children ranked again, there would be little difference in the rankings of the children on the two days. On the other hand, target tests (throwing a ball for accuracy, for example), subjective posture appraisal, and many speed tests would frequently give varying results, that is, the subjects' performance would vary from one trial to the next. Reliability is important because it affects validity. Unreliability tends to reduce the validity of the test. Validity demands high reliability in a test. The reverse, however, is not necessarily true. A test can give reproducible results but not necessarily be valid for a particular purpose.

Measuring reliability

Generally, the reliability of a test is determined by correlating the scores of the first administration of a test with those on the second trial. Table 3–4 contains data on leg extension strength. Each boy was tested twice with a few minutes separating the first and second trial. The results are plotted in Figure 3–8. Each point in the diagram represents the score on the first and second trials. The procedure for plotting the data and calculating the correlation coefficient is identical to the procedure described above for the correlation coefficient. In this case, the correlation coefficient was 0.85. However, since reliability is being measured and the two scores for each subject are for a test administered twice rather than a score on two different variables or tests, the result is sometimes called the coefficient of reliability, usually written r_{11}. Mathematically, the coefficient of reliability is the same as the correlation coefficient and the interpretation is likewise the same. The closer the value of r_{11} to 1.00, the higher the reliability of the test. From Figure 3–8, it is clear that this test is very unreliable. For obvious reasons, one would never expect the reliability coefficient to be negative.

    In objective written tests (true-false, for instance) and occasionally in physical tests, the reliability coefficient is calculated by comparing the score

TABLE 3–4
Leg Extension Strength in Pounds Using
Back-Leg Dynamometer Without Belt
(30 College Freshmen)

Subject Number	First Trial	Second Trial	Subject Number	First Trial	Second Trial
1	456	509	16	544	496
2	331	374	17	509	474
3	431	513	18	539	574
4	396	342	19	543	556
5	370	357	20	582	513
6	646	624	21	475	431
7	435	409	22	440	444
8	611	660	23	362	405
9	564	483	24	496	526
10	534	431	25	496	444
11	426	396	26	543	557
12	435	409	27	338	344
13	569	559	28	509	474
14	516	477	29	539	561
15	431	400	30	396	440

on one-half of the test with the score made by the same subject on the other half. In written tests, this is commonly done by calculating a score for each subject on the odd-numbered questions and a second score from the even-numbered questions. The two scores are then handled as if they were scores on a test administered twice and the coefficient of reliability calculated in the usual way. A correction of this coefficient is possible to estimate the reliability of the entire test. The report by Kelly and Brown (4) illustrates the use of this procedure.

Data are sometimes not in the form of a numerical score. There are occasions in physical education when it is desirable to classify individuals into three or four gross categories. If a measure of reliability is desired on the technique used to classify the subjects, the procedure can be repeated twice and the consistency of classifications compared. For example, one can subjectively classify posture of children into good, fair, or poor. The same examiner can then repeat the classification without looking at the original series. The per cent of the subjects who are classified in the same category on both series of examinations is a measure of the reliability of the technique.

Improving reliability

Since this topic will be covered in detail as it pertains to particular tests or measurements, only a general discussion will be included here. Unreliability in tests stems from several sources including (a) change in the subject being tested,

(b) an alteration in the testing environment, (c) lack of precision on the part of the administrator or scorer of the test, and (d) a change in disposition on the part of the administrator or scorer of the test.

Changes in the subjects from one test trial to the next may cause a decrease in reproducibility of scores. A player shooting baskets may be more accurate one day than another day because some internal factor or factors have changed. In one sense, this is not due to lack of reliability, because the test is reflecting a change in the subject. However, in educational testing, we are most often interested in a score that is representative of the subject. Hence, day-to-day variations in a subject are considered chance fluctuations contributing to unreliability. Even a simple measurement such as stature, taken at the same time each day, will vary depending on how straight the subject stands or how he holds his head. This, in turn, may be due to varying degrees of fatigue in the subject.

Effects of changes in the subjects can be minimized by controlling, as much as possible, those factors that might influence the score. For example, in a measurement of resting heart rate or blood pressure, a period of quiet rest preceding the test will eliminate, to some extent, the variations in these measurements due to the physical activity immediately preceding the testing period. Adequate sleep the night before tests are administered is helpful. Also, physical tests should not be administered when an infection (cold, flu, etc.) is present.

If a battery of tests is given, the same sequence of items should be followed

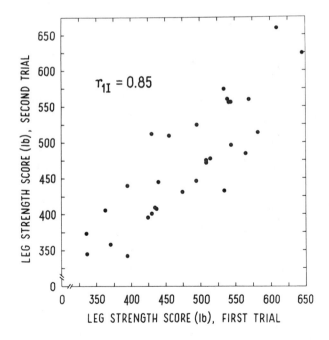

FIGURE 3–8. Scatterdiagram showing the relationship between scores on first and second trials of a leg strength test. The same observer made both sets of measurements. Unpublished data.

each time.   Subjects should be tested at the same time of the day for maximum reliability.   Sometimes the test must be repeated a number of times, as for example in target tests, and a mean taken as the score.   It may even be necessary to test on several different days and average the results before a representative score is obtained.   This amounts to increasing the length of the tests. For example, the percentage of baskets made out of 100 trials (not necessarily on the same day) in a baskeball test is likely to give a better index of ability than when the percentage is calculated on the basis of 25 trials.   Sufficient practice should be given in some tests to avoid the effects of learning.   On the other hand, when an all-out effort is required, it is often necessary to avoid strenuous activities preceding the test.

Variations in the instruments or the testing environment may affect the reliability of tests.   Wind conditions may be a factor in throwing events or running events and will vitiate to some extent the reliability of a test if the effect is not constant for all subjects.   Noise can have a similar effect on written or other tests.   A slippery gym floor will affect dribbling scores or running times. Some instruments are affected by temperature, humidity, or electrical current, and, therefore, it is often wise to calibrate instruments each time tests are given. In short, it is desirable to standardize the testing conditions as much as possible and it is sometimes necessary to have a checklist of important environmental or equipment factors to review before each series of tests.   It should be remembered that a *constant* error in an instrument or an environmental factor does not affect the reliability even though the mean for the group may be changed.   For example, in measuring stature, if the instrument is in error by 1 inch so that each child's true height is 1 inch greater than that recorded, this error will not affect the consistency (reliability) of the test.   If, however, stature is measured with children wearing shoes, the height of the heel may vary greatly from one child to the next, so that the error, although always in one direction, is not a constant one.   If stature is measured on another day and some children are wearing different shoes, this factor will result in a decrease in reliability.

Finally, variations in the tester (administrator) may contribute to unreliability.   He may not consistently read instruments the same.   In scoring written essay examinations, his mood may change sufficiently to result in poor reliability.   Carelessness will contribute random errors and hence, reduce reliability.   In order to minimize errors of this sort, care must be taken in reading and recording scores.   Fatigue and boredom on the part of the administrator of the test should be avoided or reduced if possible.

Objectivity

Definition

Objectivity refers to the reproducibility of scores when two different persons administer the test to the same subjects on two different occasions.   It is similar to reliability but involves two different testers.   The term *objectivity* is opposite in meaning to the term *subjectivity*. The student is no doubt familiar with subjective or essay-type written examinations. When two different individuals grade the examination, there is almost invariably less agreement than when the same person grades the papers twice. This is due entirely to the differences in the persons scoring the examinations. For this reason, most research on written tests is directed towards the development of objective-type examinations (multiple choice, true-false, etc.) where scoring is so objective that the task may be turned over to machines. However, objective tests rarely lend themselves to the assessment of creativity or self-expression.

Measuring objectivity

Objectivity is generally measured in the same way as reliability. When numerical scores are available, the correlation technique described earlier is appropriate. The resulting coefficient of objectivity has no regularly employed abbreviation or symbol. Mathematically, it is the same as the correlation coefficient and is interpreted in the same way. It should be remembered again that a constant error or bias in one direction will not affect the value of the coefficient. In a gymnastic meet, for example, one of the judges may be consistently higher than the others in grading all the contestants. The effect will be to raise the average score of each performer but will not change the rank of the performers.

In Table 3–5, unpublished data on half-mile run times are shown. The subjects were male college freshmen (the most tested population in America) who had been practicing running for two months. These twenty-eight students were timed in the half-mile run by timer "A" (the instructor) and by timer "B"

TABLE 3–5
One-Half Mile Run Scores as Measured by Two Timers

Subject Number	Time of Run (Min:Sec)		Subject Number	Time of Run (Min:Sec)	
	Timer A	Timer B		Timer A	Timer B
1	2:46	2:46	15	2:15	2:15
2	2:59	2:58	16	2:36	2:37
3	2:24	2:24	17	2:19	2:19
4	2:28	2:27	18	2:34	2:36
5	2:21	2:21	19	2:38	2:37
6	2:20	2:21	20	2:31	2:31
7	2:22	2:22	21	2:08	2:08
8	2:35	2:34	22	2:41	2:42
9	2:55	2:56	23	2:29	2:29
10	2:23	2:23	24	2:31	2:32
11	2:33	2:33	25	2:28	2:28
12	2:36	2:35	26	2:43	2:43
13	2:29	2:28	27	2:39	2:38
14	2:36	2:36	28	2:45	2:45

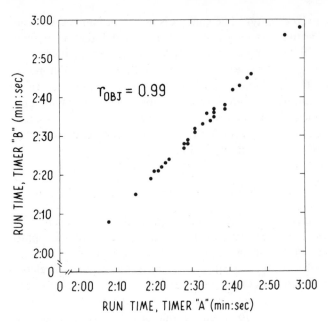

FIGURE 3–9.   Scatterdiagram showing the relationship
between scores made on the half-mile run as recorded by two
timers (observers).   Unpublished data.

(a student in the class).   As can be seen by the results in Figure 3–9, this is a
very objective test.

Improving objectivity

In many physical education tests, there may be little subjectivity; but this is not
true of all tests.   In rating posture or diving performance, for instance, it is
often difficult to reach agreement among several test administrators.   This is
understandable because the rating involves a judgment of aesthetic performance
and will always be partially dependent on individual (subjective) tastes.   But
subjective elements are frequently present when they might easily be eliminated.
Often the unreliability exists because there is a lack of understanding or agreement among the testers on how to measure or test.   Carefully prepared standardized instructions generally eliminate or minimize errors from this source.
High objectivity is important to the average teacher.   This indicates students
or others may be employed to help administer the tests.

Other considerations

Of great importance in selecting or constructing tests are the practical considerations which dictate whether or not it is feasible to use a test or measurement in a specific program.   Despite the fundamental importance of these

considerations, they will be touched upon only briefly in this section for several reasons. In the first place, the ideas are easily understood and hence require little amplification. Secondly, the authors of specific chapters will discuss the feasibility of using particular tests. Finally, practical considerations vary so much in each school or recreation program that teachers ultimately must decide for themselves whether a particular test can be employed in a given situation.

Time requirement

Some tests may be administered quickly while the time necessary to administer others may be prohibitive. The purpose of testing will frequently determine whether the time required is a limiting factor. In some instances, the administration of a test may be done quickly but the analysis of results is very time consuming. In this situation, students or help from other sources can be mobilized outside of class.

Interest

Learning takes place in proportion to the interest or motivation of the learner. This applies to testing just as it does to any other phase of teaching. Furthermore, in many physical tests, motivation is essential for optimum results. Hence, the wise teacher will consider the age and sex of the pupils when selecting tests and measurements to be employed.

Facilities and equipment

It is obvious that no matter how valid, reliable, and objective a particular test is, its usefulness will depend on the availability of necessary equipment and/or facilities. Physical educators have frequently demonstrated resourcefulness in improvising and constructing satisfactory equipment for the testing program. Very often, other departments, such as Industrial Arts, are cooperative in this regard.

Achievement scales

All things being equal, tests for which achievement scales have been published are more useful than those in which no standards are available. This is particularly true when the published scales have been developed from representative populations of the state, country, and even other countries. The Youth Fitness Test (10) is a case in point. The Youth Fitness Achievement Scales make it possible for teachers to compare the fitness of the boys and girls under their direction with standards based on a cross section of the United

States. This factor is at least partially responsible for the widespread popularity of this test battery.

REFERENCES

1. Brouha, L., "The Step Test: A Simple Method of Measuring Physical Fitness for Muscular Work in Young Men." *Res. Quart.,* 14:31–36, 1943.

2. Brouha, L. and B. M. Savage, "Variability of Physiological Measurements in Normal Young Men." *Rev. Canad. Biol.,* 4:131–143, 1945.

3. Elliott, R., ed., "Grading Anterposterior Standing Posture." *Res. Quart.,* Supp., 9:79–88, 1938.

4. Kelly, E. D. and J. E. Brown, "The Construction of a Field Hockey Test for Women Physical Education Majors." *Res. Quart.,* 23:322–329, 1952.

5. Lehsten, N., "A Measure of Basketball Skills in High School Boys." *Physical Educator,* 5:103–109, 1948.

6. Lockhart, A. and F. A. McPherson, "The Development of a Test of Badminton Playing Ability." *Res. Quart.,* 20: 402–405, 1949.

7. McCloy, C. H., "The Measurement of General Motor Capacity and General Motor Ability." *Res. Quart.* supp., 5: 46–61, 1934.

8. Pascale, L. R.; M. I. Grossman; H. S. Sloane; and T. Frankel, "Correlations between Thickness of Skinfolds and Body Density in 88 Soldiers." *Body Measurements and Human Nutrition,* edited by J. Brozek. Detroit: Wayne University Press, 1956, pp. 55–66.

9. Wilson, E. Bright, *An Introduction to Scientific Research.* New York: McGraw-Hill, 1952, p. 83.

10. American Association for Health, Physical Education and Recreation, *Youth Fitness Test Manual.* Washington, D.C.: The Association, 1958, p. 56.

STUDY QUESTIONS • Chapter 3

1. How much of the variance in speed can be accounted for by strength if the correlation coefficient between the two is 0.5?

2. Describe three ways of improving the reliability of a test such as the dribbling test in basketball.

3. List four examples of criteria used in validating tests in physical education.

4. Explain what is meant by "validity of a test."

5. Explain what is meant by "reliability of a test."

6. Explain what is meant by "objectivity of a test."

7. Could you use students in administering a test even though the objectivity of the test is low, as long as the reliability is high? Why?

8. Is a correlation coefficient of 0.6 twice as good as a coefficient of 0.3? Explain.

9. To what does the split-halves method refer? Explain.

10. Does a correlation coefficient of + 0.7 indicate a closer relationship than one of − 0.7? Why?

11. Explain what a percentile score of 18 means.

12. What is another name for a correlation chart? Describe.

13. What are two common kinds of graphs for showing distribution of scores?

14. Besides validity, reliability, and objectivity, list four other criteria you would consider in selecting a test to be used in the schools.

15. What are the numerical limits of the correlation coefficient?

16. Give an example of "face validity" of a test.

17. A new basketball test for women is published. The test was validated using 60 college freshmen by correlating the scores on the test with the average rating during game play for each woman as judged by five experts. The correlation coefficient is 0.60. The reliability coefficient was reported to be 0.99 and the objectivity coefficient 0.70. What can you conclude about this test? How would you interpret these coefficients?

18. Identify the following

    A. r E. r_{11}

    B. $\frac{\leq X}{N}$ F. ━

    C. S.D.   G. s

    D. M

19. Explain the meaning of the correlation coefficient. For what purpose is it used? How can you interpret it? Use diagrams or anything else you need to explain your answer.

20. What can be done to study the reliability of a written objective test, if it is not possible to give the test a second time?

21. What will be the effect on the correlation coefficient (i.e., validity) if the reliability of a test is decreased?

22. What two methods are available for studying the reliability of a written test?

23. Explain what is meant by the word *criteria* as used in tests and measurements.

24. If you wished to validate a test of table tennis for 9th-grade boys, how would you go about it? How about a basketball test, a test of cardiovascular fitness, a measure of golf ability?

25. What is the meaning of a negative correlation coefficient?

26. The correlation coefficient reflects a ratio of two standard deviations. Explain.

27. A basketball test has been validated for high school girls, ages 15–18. Can we assume this test is also valid for junior high school girls? Explain your answer.

28. Explain what is meant by "data population" and "problem population."

29. How does unreliability affect the validity of a test?

30. Can a test be reliable without being valid? Explain.

31. List some of the factors that can affect the reliability of the measurement of height (stature).

32. Does a constant factor such as an error of 2 inches in the measuring tape affect the reliability of a standing long jump test? Why?

33. Do random errors affect reliability? Validity? Objectivity? Why?

34. Why is the objectivity of a test important?

35. List and explain things about a test, other than validity, reliability, and objectivity, which should be considered in selecting or evaluating a test.

II

Physical Fitness
and Physique

STRENGTH, POWER, AND MUSCULAR ENDURANCE

author W. W. Heusner
W. D. Van Huss

4

The terms strength, power, and muscular endurance often have been used in a confusing and inconsistent manner. At times, these terms are even erroneously used interchangeably. As tested, *strength* simply means the maximum effective force which a muscle or group of muscles can exert once; *power* implies the maximum strength which can be exerted once at a maximum rate of movement; and *muscular endurance* denotes the duration of time, or the number of repetitions, that a given contraction can be performed.

The general topic of muscle function has been a subject of major interest to physical educators and allied workers since well before 1900. Readers desiring to review this history are referred to the works of Leonard and Affleck (49) and Rice (58) and to the particularly noteworthy contributions of Kellogg (44), Sargent (61), and Rogers (60). Although muscle function (strength, power, and muscular endurance) has been studied repeatedly over the years, the topic still is not well understood and remains a subject of controversy. More extensive coverages of the research literature than this chapter can afford may be found in the reviews of Clarke (11, 12), Hunsicker and Greey (34), Hellebrandt and Houtz (30), and Hettinger (33).

The topic of muscle function is yet to be mastered due to the extreme complexity of the phenomena involved. Strength, power, and muscular endurance result from close coordinations of complicated mechanical, biochemical, neural, and endocrine functions. Additional perspective on these functions requires intensive study of the underlying physiology. The excellent monograph on muscle edited by Rodahl and Horvath (59), the review by Guth (24), and the basic work of Seyffarth (62) on motor unit activity are particularly helpful. Attempts to oversimplify, lack of standardized terminology, the extreme specificity of adaptation of the muscular system, poor correlations of most of the strength parameters with performance criteria, and inconsistencies in research findings all have contributed to the confusion about muscle function.

The purpose of this chapter is to present briefly a basis for a working knowledge of muscle function through a synthesis of research evidence and to identify tests for use in the schools that are practical, functional, interpretable, and require a minimum of equipment. This task is attempted with full recognition of the fact that there is current controversy regarding the nature of muscle function and the fact that it is highly questionable whether maximal strength, power, or muscular endurance ever can be measured precisely. For example, the strength test is yet to be devised that cannot be altered by motivational procedures.

The student of muscle function must maintain an open mind and be willing to accept the idea that future modifications of the concepts presented here are inevitable. Dramatic new evidence, as yet insufficiently confirmed for practical use, may force revisions. Since we are involved at this time in an accelerating explosion of knowledge, it is imperative that all practitioners, teachers, and researchers recognize the plasticity of our basic body of information and be prepared to remold their operating principles on the basis of new evidence.

Importance of strength, power, and muscular endurance

Muscular contraction provides the force necessary for all static postures and dynamic movements in humans. Individuals having reasonable levels of muscular strength and endurance are capable of achieving and maintaining efficient postural alignments and are not readily subject to fatigue in work and play.

In addition, the individual usually looks better when his or her muscles are well conditioned. (It is not by chance that the bathing suit models selected by manufacturers are active men and women with relatively high levels of strength.) Unfortunately, the relationship between strength and attractiveness often is overlooked by women. In many circles, it is not considered feminine to be strong. This idea is based on a misconception. The female hormones (especially estrogen) tend to prevent the development of excessive musculature by a protein catabolic effect (25). Thus, a layer of fat will be maintained over the muscles (3) causing firm but smooth contours to result from even the most vigorous of activity programs. The extreme muscle definition possible in the male is not found in the female except in a very few individuals having high masculine genetic components.

The role of strength and muscular endurance in the prevention of postural deformities and injuries is an important area of study that cannot be treated here in detail. It is an area in which all physical educators should keep themselves well informed, but it is not one that generally is recognized when the importance of strength and muscular endurance is considered. In the ankle, elbow, and shoulder, the principle of injury prevention is relatively simple. If a force is applied which tends to move the joint into a range of motion where ligament damage could occur, a stretch reflex is elicited that results in contraction of the opposing musculature in an attempt to stop the movement. If the musculature and attachments are sufficiently strong, the movement will be stopped and injury will be prevented. Obviously, the greater the strength of the muscles around these joints, the fewer the injuries (57).* Muscular strength has been shown to be important for the prevention of injuries in other parts of the body. For example, by a combined program of exercise and the teaching of the proper mechanics of lifting, Anderson (2) has achieved dramatic reductions in the incidence of lower back injuries in industry.

The primary competency that all physical educators should have is an expertness in exercise and work. Therefore, understanding of muscle functions and knowledge of assessment techniques for strength, power, and endurance performances are imperative. In the material that follows, where the evidence is clear, it has been documented. Where gaps exist in the current information, an attempt has been made to provide "educated" guesses.

Definitions

Static strength

Static strength is the maximum effective force that can be applied once to a fixed object by an individual from a defined, immobile position. No movement of the object, which usually is attached to a measuring device, or of the body segments is involved.† The force applied in a hand dynamometer test is an example of static strength.

Dynamic strength

Dynamic strength is the maximum muscular force that can be exerted once to move a load through a specified range of motion of a joint with the body in

---

*In selected instances, this principle does not apply, e.g., in lateral stress on the knee where the joint is not structured for such motion and there is no specific controlling musculature.

†It is common for the terms static strength and isometric strength to be used interchangeably. However, the preferred term is static strength since, by definition, "isometric strength" implies no movement of the muscle. Considerable muscle movement is involved in an *in vivo* static muscular contraction.

some defined position.* In measuring dynamic strength, the rate of movement should be sufficiently slow so that supplementary inertial effects are avoided. The military press with maximum load and the I-RM (repetition maximum) contractions advocated by DeLorme (14) are examples of activities involving this type of strength.

Power

Power is the amount of work which can be accomplished per unit of time. It usually is measured in terms of the maximum effective work the subject can perform once at a maximum rate of movement, where *effective work* means work done moving one's body or an object. Strength and speed are both involved in the execution of power activities. Explosive movements such as shot putting and high jumping are examples of power movements. The 60-yard dash in track also can be considered to have a large power component.

Static muscular endurance

Static muscular endurance is the ability to maintain a given amount of force in a fixed position for a prolonged period of time. Holding a heavy suitcase is an example of an activity requiring this type of endurance.

Dynamic muscular endurance

Dynamic muscular endurance (DME) represents a continuum of ability. It ranges from the strength required to perform a minimum of two repetitions of a task involving high-intensity work to that required to repeat a task involving low-intensity work many times. Since DME is a continuum, any schema used to partition it into subdivisions must be arbitrary. Nevertheless, we believe that the nine overlapping levels of DME shown in Table 4–1 are physiologically identifiable. These levels are defined in terms of time intervals for maximum performance. They can be distinguished from one another, at least theoretically, by *absolute* values of the common energy metabolism variables and/or by *relative* contributions of the major energy sources for muscle contraction.

A few of the entries in the body of Table 4–1 represent little more than subjective judgments. The actual data needed to draw firm conclusions are not available in some cases, and much of the indirect evidence is contradictory. In particular, the estimates of the relative contributions of blood glucose to DME-5 through DME-9 are quite tenuous. This limitation does not seriously weaken the classification system, however, since each pair of adjacent levels is differentiated by the changing of at least two physiological criteria.

One might question the validity of functional subdivisions for DME that

---

*The terms *dynamic strength* and *isotonic strength* often are used synonymously. The preferred term is *dynamic strength* since, by definition, *isotonic strength* implies constant muscle tension. Considerable alteration of muscle tension is involved in an *in vivo* dynamic muscular contraction.

TABLE 4-1
Arbitrary Subdivisions of Dynamic Muscular Endurance (DME)

DME Level	Approximate Time of Maximum Performance (min:sec)	Energy Metabolism in Subjects Trained for these Durations			Relative Contributions of the Major Energy Sources for Muscle Contraction				Examples for Trained Athletes	
		O$_2$ Uptake (per min)	Total O$_2$ Debt	Muscle Lactate	Endogenous ATP and PC	Muscle Glycogen	Blood Glucose	Total Lipids	Running Events	Swimming Events
DME-1	to 0:08	Very Low	Low	Very Low	High	Low	Very Low	Very Low	60 yd	
DME-2	0:06 to 0:15	Very Low	Low	Low	High	Moderate	Very Low	Very Low	100 yd	25 yd
DME-3	0:12 to 0:30	Low	Moderate	Moderate	Moderate	High	Very Low	Very Low	220 yd	50 yd
DME-4	0:25 to 1:30	Moderate	High	High	Moderate	High	Low	Very Low	440 yd	100 yd
DME-5	1:20 to 3:30	Mod-High	High	High	Low	High	Moderate	Very Low	880 yd	200 yd
DME-6	3:00 to 7:00	High	High	High	Low	High	Moderate	Low	1 mile	500 yd
DME-7	6:00 to 12:00	High	Moderate	Moderate	Very Low	Mod-High	Moderate	Moderate	2 mile	1000 yd
DME-8	10:00 to 40:00	High	Low	Low	Very Low	Moderate	Moderate	Mod-High	5000 mtr	1650 yd
DME-9	35:00 to 240:00	High	Low	Low	Very Low	Low	Moderate	High	Marathon	4 mile

so neatly encompass the standard running and swimming events. Undoubtedly, our preliminary thinking was influenced by the desire to understand how a skilled performer can dominate one event and yet often be defeated in a longer or shorter race. But Table 4–1 was not constructed to conform to any given program of events. On the contrary, attempts to explain the physiological adaptations that accompany improved muscular endurance led first to the conclusion that there are different identifiable levels of the DME continuum and second to the realization that the events listed in Table 4–1 exemplify those levels. In retrospect, the correspondence between DME levels and the standard running and swimming events is not surprising. It should not be viewed as a coincidence. After all, years of trial and error ought to have produced programs of competitive events that test measurably different capacities. Continuing the line of thinking that there is a biological basis for most common practices, it appears there may be other levels of DME that, as yet, are undefined. For example, at present we would classify the 10,000-meter run, along with the 5,000-meter run, as a DME-8 event. This might not be correct. The 10,000-meter run may reflect a substantially different metabolic requirement.

Viewing DME as a continuum of ability with many possibilities for diverse individual adaptations, we have been reluctant to list numerical values for the energy metabolism variables shown in Table 4–1. The subjective terms used appear to be reasonably self-explanatory when interpreted relative to established norms, by age and sex, for maximum oxygen uptake capacity and maximum oxygen debt and lactate tolerances. We have used the same terminology for the relative contributions of the major energy sources. However, in this case the following rough percentage interpretations are possible: Very Low = 0% to 10%, Low = 5% to 25%, Moderate = 15% to 45%, Mod-High = 30% to 70%, and High = 50% to 100%. Overlapping ranges of percentages are necessary to accommodate individual variability.

It is clear that there is a gradual shift from anaerobic to aerobic processes as the time of maximum performance increases. Accompanying this shift is a corresponding change from dependence on endogenous energy sources to carbohydrate metabolism and finally to lipid utilization. In accord with these observations, we assume that increasing use of lipids for exhaustive work of long duration (DME-7 through DME-9) is an expression of a glycogen-sparing mechanism that prolongs the time a fit subject can perform a given submaximal task. The same mechanism may operate as early as DME-5 through an enhanced uptake of blood glucose—but that possibility must remain in the realm of conjecture at this time.

Although the preceding discussion has been provided as rationale for the DME tests that will be presented later, the information contained in Table 4–1 has many other implications for physical education teachers and coaches who are interested in improving performance. Unfortunately, the problem of designing training regimens to achieve specific performance goals is outside of the scope of this text.

Anatomical-physiological basis

A brief review of the anatomical-physiological basis of muscle function is presented here to provide background for the material which will follow. Although the treatment is relatively superficial, the documentation provided will enable the interested reader to delve profitably beyond this discussion.

Muscles are made up largely of contractile fibers grouped into small bundles of parallel fibers called *fasciculi*. These fasciculi are surrounded by connective tissue which forms a harness so that the pull of the muscle fibers may be applied. Each muscle has at least two attachments to bones or other parts of the body. A contraction serves to bring these attachments, the origin(s) and insertion(s), closer together. The arrangement of the fasciculi within the harness is variable. In longitudinal muscles (e.g., sartorius, the long muscle of the thigh), they are parallel to the direction of pull and provide maximum range of motion with only moderate strength; in penniform muscles (e.g., peroneus longus, connected to the fibula), or multi-penniform muscles (e.g., gastrocnemius, the large muscle of the calf), they are at an angle to the direction of pull and provide greater strength at the expense of range of motion.

Each muscle fiber contains from 5 to 36 myofibrils, each about 1 micron in diameter. The myofibril is the site of the contractile process (39, 40). The myofibrils contain the proteins actin and myosin which combine to form actomyosin during contraction. The exact mechanisms involved in this process are not completely clear (65). However, it is known that length changes in the contractile system take place by a relative sliding motion of two types of protein filaments (F-actin and L-myosin). Muscular tension appears to be developed by an interaction (involving calcium ions) of these two types of filaments (37, 38, 42).

All skeletal muscle fibers are not the same. Some are small, red, slow-contracting fibers with a high capacity for prolonged work. These fibers have a rich capillary supply and numerous mitochondria which contain the enzymes required for efficient aerobic metabolism. They may be called red oxidative (RO) fibers.* Other fibers are large, white, and fast-contracting. These fibers have low aerobic capacity, minimal capillarization, and few mitochondria but are high in contractile proteins. They may be called white glycolytic (WG) fibers. Fibers of the WG type store considerable quantities of glycogen and the enzymes usually associated with anaerobic metabolism. Both of these fiber types are known to be present in man. There is a third fiber type in animals which can be called red oxidative-glycolytic (ROG). These ROG

---

*The fiber type we have called "red oxidative" has been given a variety of names by different investigators (e.g., intermediate, slow-twitch intermediate, red-slow, slow-twitch oxidative, Type I, Type A, etc.). In fact, fiber-type terminology seems to be in a continual state of flux. We prefer the names used here because they are simple, descriptive, and defensible in terms of the common histochemical techniques used to type fibers.

fibers are red in appearance, have good capabilities for both aerobic and anaerobic metabolism, and are fast contracting. Whether or not the ROG fiber type is present in human beings is controversial at this time. Whole muscles differ in the relative numbers of the different fiber types they contain. Some muscles such as the gastrocnemius are mixed in fiber type while others have primarily white fibers (e.g., extensor digitorum longus, muscles of fingers and toes) or red fibers (e.g., soleus, the broad flat muscle of the calf).

The most generally accepted viewpoint concerning the effects of training on the number of muscle fibers present in a muscle is based on the early findings of Morpurgo (53). Each person is thought to have a given number of skeletal muscle fibers at birth, and it is supposed to be impossible to increase that number (hyperplasia) through training. However, it is known that fiber size may be increased (hypertrophy) by training and that fibers may be destroyed by various means.

Morpurgo's concept should not be abandoned, but it should be recognized that conflicting evidence exists and that ultimately it may be necessary to revise this viewpoint. Van Linge (69), Reitsma (56), and Carrow (9) have demonstrated the possibility that hyperplasia may occur in the voluntary muscle of the rat. Histological sections show the budding off of new fibers following strenuous prolonged training. (Mitotic figures which usually are evident in cell division were not shown, and the necessary tests for amitotic division were not conducted.) In order to obtain these dramatic results, both Van Linge and Reitsma transplanted the insertion of a muscle prior to stressing it heavily with exercise. Carrow, on the other hand, has observed fiber splitting followed by increased numbers of fibers in cross sections of skeletal muscles from normal animals subjected only to strenuous exercise programs. It is interesting that the concept that has been held for so long is suspect. Unquestionably, marked changes in the current thinking about exercise and training will be necessary if confirmation of hyperplasia in normal voluntary muscle is obtained.

Principles of motor unit activity

The best working principles of strength, power, and muscular endurance probably can be derived from an understanding of motor unit activity. Within each motor nerve there are many separate motor fibers (alpha fibers). Each alpha fiber branches to a number of motor end plates (myoneural junctions) and thus is capable of stimulating a number of muscle fibers. A motor unit consists of a single alpha fiber, all of its branching, and all of the muscle fibers it innervates. The motor unit is the smallest functional component of muscle action. Alpha fibers that are involved in very sensitive movements, such as those controlling the extrinsic eye muscles, may supply as few as seven muscle fibers. In the larger muscles that produce gross movements, the nerve-fiber to muscle-fiber ratio may be as high as 1 to 1600 (66).

Multiple motor end plates from branches of different alpha fibers are known to exist on individual muscle fibers (17). These have been isolated anatomically. It also has been established that growth of new nerve endings can occur under controlled laboratory conditions when one of several nerves entering a muscle is severed and capped to prevent regeneration (1, 70). It is not clear at this time whether or not the growth of additional nerve endings (resulting in multiple motor end plates) can be stimulated physiologically in normal muscle as a direct result of physical activity.

Whenever a motor nerve is activated, it transmits an impulse to all of the motor end plates of the individual muscle fibers within the unit. However, some of the muscle fibers may not contract because of the synaptic function of the myoneural junction. The greater the rate of neural firing, the greater the number of fibers that contract.

A muscle with its innervating nerve trunk is an assemblage of groups of motor units. When a muscle is contracted in a skilled static contraction, there is a definite sequence in the firing of the activated motor units. Each time the contraction is repeated at a given joint angle with a given load, the same motor units are active in the same order (15, 62). The sequential motor-unit pattern can be determined since each motor unit yields an identifiable electromyographic tracing.

If only the load involved in a static contraction is increased, additional motor units will be recruited. For example, if motor units designated as F, C, E, and A are fired repeatedly in that order during a contraction, with an increased load at the same joint angle, the sequence might be F, C, E, A, H, K, and M. Units H, K, and M thus are recruited to handle the additional load (45). The order of recruitment of motor units for the addition of load in a contraction with the body position held constant is always the same. On the other hand, if the joint angle in a static contraction is changed even slightly, an entirely different repetitive sequence of motor unit activity may result.

As long as a contraction is submaximal, motor unit firing remains sequential and the force application is constant. That is, the units involved will fire in order repeatedly to maintain the force. When a contraction is maximal, however, motor unit firing no longer occurs in an orderly sequence. Motor units fire over and over simultaneously. As a result, the contraction becomes tremulous; and the longer it is held, the greater will be the tremor (15).

Dynamic movements are performed in much the same way as static contractions. The only difference is that many sequences of motor unit activity are involved as the joint angle changes from moment to moment. Each time a submaximal skilled movement is repeated with the same load, the successive sequences of motor unit activity will be identical. If the load is increased, again there is a definite order in which motor units are recruited. However, if either the pattern of the movement (joint angles) or the speed of the movement is changed, the sequence of motor unit firing may be altered. There may even be a change in the motor units that are active. This implies the formation of a neural synthesis specific to both the movement pattern and the rate of the movement.

Recruitment and isolation of effective motor units

In learning a complex new skill, there is likely to be little initial similarity of movement patterns from one repetition to another and thus no standard order of motor unit firing.   Contractions may be present in efficient motor units and even antagonistic motor units.   As the skill is repeated, it is learned by neuromuscular trial and error in conjunction with feedback from various internal and external sources.   Fewer and fewer noneffective motor units are used so that the energy expenditure of performing a given task gradually is reduced during the learning period.   Finally, the basic motor unit sequence is established. Indeed, *the process of learning a specific motor skill may be thought of physiologically as the progressive recruitment and isolation of effective motor units.*

The fact that motor unit activity is specific to rate of movement explains why this process of recruitment and isolation is expedited when a new skill is practiced at approximately the desired speed of performance.   Practice at any other speed will result in the subject learning a different neuromuscular task. Subsequent learning and relearning problems then are encountered.

Consideration of motor unit activity also places limitations on practice duration if motor learning is the primary goal.   Whenever a movement is repeated to the point of localized exhaustion, the movement pattern will have to be altered for the task to be continued.   The effect of muscular fatigue, therefore, is to interrupt the establishment of an effective motor unit sequence. The overall result may be the serious impairment or even total frustration of the intended motor learning.   At least some of the continuing controversy over massed versus distributed practice could be resolved by adherence to the principles of motor unit function.

Muscular fatigue presents a similar problem for the already skilled performer, but the solution is somewhat different.   In this case, a conscious attempt should be made to modify the movement pattern *slightly* so that other *efficient* motor units can be recruited to aid in accomplishing the basic task. If such minor modifications in the movement pattern are not made voluntarily as the work progresses toward exhaustion, other inefficient motor units and finally other assisting muscles may be recruited involuntarily.   When this occurs, the pattern of the movement will be changed grossly, and the total movement may cease to be efficient.   In fact, participants in exhaustive events requiring repetitive movements would be wise to learn two or more slightly different movement patterns which can be used interchangeably.

An interesting observation has been made regarding warm-up prior to the execution of a power event.   If an individual warms-up with an overload and then performs with the standard load for that event, the resulting performance will be better than if the warm-up had not included an overload.   This phenomenon has been demonstrated under controlled conditions with the baseball throw (68).   Theoretically, it appears that efficient, but otherwise unused, motor units are recruited to handle the extra load.   When the additional load is removed, the individual retains the ability to recruit these motor units for subsequent maximal performances.

A routine laboratory experiment, which produces an almost immediate increase in measurable static strength, reflects the previously mentioned fact that motor learning is a process of recruitment and isolation of effective motor units. Improvements of 20 to 30% in knee extension strength often can be obtained during a period of only 30 minutes by repeatedly contracting the extensors submaximally. If the subject then walks on a treadmill at 4 miles per hour for 5 minutes and is measured again right after the walk, further improvements of 10 to 20% may be observed. Increases of this magnitude in such a short period of time can be attributed only to motor learning, certainly not to morphological changes.

It has been determined recently that motor units are homogeneous with regard to fiber type (46). Thus, in a mixed muscle such as the gastrocnemius, one motor unit would have only aerobic RO fibers whereas another would have only anaerobic WG fibers. The applications of this information are of special importance in training. For example, it would appear obvious that motor units with RO fibers should be recruited and conditioned specifically by participation in DME-7 through DME-9 activities, which require economy of movement. Conversely, strength, power, and DME-1 through DME-3 activities should be used to train motor units with WG fibers.

Implications of motor unit activity for testing

The principles of motor unit activity explain why static strength measured at various points in the range of motion of a joint often are not highly correlated. If the strength of an individual is pretested at various angles throughout a range of motion and the subject then is trained at one angle only, the improvement seen will be greatest at the angle of training and will be progressively less at angles further away from that angle.

Static and dynamic strength do not correlate as highly as one might anticipate ($r = 0.70$ approximately) (5). Since a dynamic contraction throughout the range of motion employs many motor unit sequences and a static contraction at a single angle uses only one sequence, this is not surprising. However, since dynamic strength in a slow movement can be regarded as an infinite series of static contractions, a high correlation might be expected between the static strength at the angle at which an individual is weakest and dynamic strength. Bender's results confirm this hypothesis (4). Consequently, if an individual trains statically at the angle(s) at which he or she is weak, dramatic improvements in dynamic strength are possible in short periods of time.

Relatively low correlations ($r = 0.40$ or less) are found between power performance tests and static strength measures (18). This does not mean that strength is not a factor in power performances. It merely means that specifically defined static strength tests usually do not measure those strengths which are critical in the performance of the practical tasks that are involved in sports and daily living.

Neuromuscular control

In voluntary muscles and joints, sensory nerves originate in muscle spindles, Golgi tendon organs, spiral endings, and end bulbs. These proprioceptors provide feedback information of tension and compression so that the amount of contraction may be related accurately to the effort required (27).

The muscle spindle is the most complex of these receptors and appears to be the most important. It responds in proportion to the amount of tension placed on it through the graded radiation of stimuli from intrafusal fibers located within the spindle. These intrafusal fibers receive stimulation from small motor (fusimotor or gamma) nerve fibers which have a low repetitive discharge rate of 0.5 to 1 per second when the muscle is quiescent (6). Several phenomena will increase the gamma fiber discharge rate which in turn increases the activity of the spindle (16, 35).

Muscular contractions and any movements resulting from them are, in fact, sensorimotor experiences. The proprioceptors that are stimulated during the performance of an activity provide a vast amount of coded information that reflects muscle lengths and tensions as well as joint positions. This feedback data goes to various levels of the central nervous system where it is processed, integrated, and used to initiate motor signals that appropriately modify the performance. The degree of muscular contraction and the amount and type of musculature necessary for a task may be determined largely by these proprioceptive feedback mechanisms. It has been shown, for example, that the stretch reflex elicited by a mild force recruits motor units with small red fibers, whereas the stretch reflex elicited by a high-intensity force recruits motor units with large white fibers (31, 32).

Proprioceptive feedback and the initiation of motor stimuli which direct muscular contractions generally are below conscious level. In maximal contractions, however, motor stimuli are initiated centrally under voluntary control and either bring about the necessary contraction or augment the motor impulses which are integrated from proprioceptive feedback. Maximal voluntary strength thus is the result of both central nervous system activity and reflex mechanisms of muscular contraction.

From *in vitro* studies, it is clear that isolated muscles are capable of producing far greater tensions than have been achieved in voluntary strength tests. The reason for this is that the mechanisms of central nervous system control of muscle activity are threefold: (a) as is shown in experiments on decerebrate animals, various centers in the brain stem potentially stimulate muscular activity continuously; (b) the motor cortex acts to inhibit the otherwise continuous stimuli from the brain stem; and (c) the cerebellum integrates the output of the central nervous system to produce coordinated movements.

Conscious muscular contractions then can be thought of as resulting from the selective release of cortical inhibition of brain stem activity. As the release of this cortical inhibition increases, strength will increase. The formation of neural syntheses to release cortical inhibition would result in increased strength. That is, to decrease the inhibitory effect would constitute "learning" to contract the muscle to greater tensions. Conversely, the formation of neural syntheses to increase the inhibition provided by the motor cortex would constitute "learning" to relax or remove muscular contraction.

Central attention (concentration), motivation, and fear all serve to release cortical inhibition and therefore to increase maximal voluntary strength measures. Ikai and Steinhaus (41) found strength to be significantly improved by firing a gun just prior to contraction. Many astounding feats of strength have been reported in situations where individuals were under severe emotional stress.

Effects of training on muscle

The demands placed on muscle tissue are quite different for various types, intensities, durations, and repetitions of contractions. In turn, the adaptation of muscle tissue to various training regimens involves numerous specific changes at the cellular level. For example, a training program which is based upon DME-1 through DME-3 activities will produce an elevation of structural proteins (but not sarcoplasmic proteins) and substantial hypertrophy of muscle fibers (20, 21, 22, 23, 29).

On the other hand, participation in DME-7 through DME-8 activities will result in an elevation of sarcoplasmic proteins (but not structural proteins), a relative increase in the number of functional capillaries in red muscle and an actual decrease in muscle fiber size (8). Training of this type also has been shown to decrease the excess lactate level in prolonged standard exercise (72). The excess lactate level is a rough measure of anaerobic metabolism and reflects the inability of the muscle to function aerobically at a rate sufficient to meet its needs. Thus, a decrease in excess lactate indicates improved biochemical and transport capacities which result in more efficient aerobic metabolism.

It is clear that the type of work performed in a training program is important in dictating the adapted functional capacity of the muscle cell. The mechanisms of the adaptation process are less clear. As has been noted previously, one would expect strength, power, and DME-1 through DME-3 activities to involve primarily those motor units having anaerobic WG muscle fibers. Participation in DME-7 through DME-9 activities should involve the less powerful motor units with aerobic RO fibers. The unanswered question concerns the extent to which muscle fibers can be altered by these and other specific training stimuli. There are four possibilities: (a) The existing fibers of a given type may be trained to perform their designated tasks more effectively. (b) The fibers of one type may acquire, through training, the addi-

FIGURE 4–1. Examples of strength measurement instruments.

tional metabolic capability required to assist overloaded fibers of another type. (c) Fiber type may be mutable so that training can produce actual shifts from one fiber type to another along with necessary changes in the neural innervation of the affected fibers. (d) The number of functional fibers of a given type may be increased by the splitting of existing fibers into several small fibers with each having an adequate blood supply and a neural innervation as well as the capacity to hypertrophy to normal size with further training. The first two of these mechanisms are well established, and there is limited evidence supporting both mutability (24) and fiber splitting (9). It is our current opinion that muscle tissue may adapt very specifically to the type of training stress placed on it by all four of these methods. Further research is needed to either confirm or reject this position.

Techniques of measurement

Static strength

Any instrument that yields a reliable force measure with minimal movement can be used for the measurement of static strength. The most common types of instruments include: (a) dynamometers—modified spring scales, (b) strain gauges—electronic methods for measuring tension or compression, (c) cable tensiometers—modified versions of the spring scale principle which measure tension in a cable, and (d) hydraulic systems—instruments by which force is transmitted, usually through a piston, to a closed fluid reservoir with a pressure gauge attached. Figure 4–1 shows several typical instruments.

Static strength measures are extremely valuable for determining suscep- tibility to injury, for evaluation in rehabilitation, and for research purposes. Specific techniques of measuring static strength at specified angles in the major joint actions of the body have been presented by Clarke (10). These special tests are excellent when used in the situations for which they were designed.

However, for the following reasons static strength measures are *not* recommended by the writers of this chapter for general use: considerable equipment is involved, testing is time consuming, there is danger of injury when tests are administered by inexperienced personnel, and the results are very difficult to interpret. Proponents of static strength testing would reject this viewpoint on the basis that static strength is related to general well-being (19), to maturity (12, 43), and to academic achievement (28). These arguments are not to be denied, but the tests which are recommended later reflect such factors equally well. If it is felt that if a static strength item should be included in a battery of tests, then grip strength is recommended as the best single measure (18), the safest, and the one requiring the least expensive equipment.

Dynamic strength

The I-RM (repetition maximum) test used by DeLorme (14) and the maxi- mum military press are examples of dynamic strength measures. The N-K exercise unit shown in Figure 4–2, which is used to determine maximal knee extension strength and to exercise the knee, is an example of a dynamic strength measurement tool.

To determine a I-RM load, it is important that the subject does not know how much weight is being lifted. The I-RM load must be established by

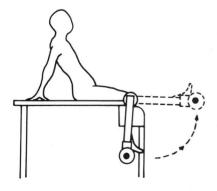

FIGURE 4–2. The N–K exercise unit.

adding or subtracting weight between trials. To obtain reasonably reliable results, a minimum of two minutes should elapse between trials (30).

Dynamic strength measures also are not recommended for general use. Testing is time consuming, excessive equipment is required, and this testing is potentially even more dangerous than static strength testing. For rehabilitation purposes or as research tools, dynamic strength tests are extremely valuable; but for general evaluation purposes, the results obtained are not worth the time, effort, or risks involved.

If neither static nor dynamic tests of strength are recommended, what tests should the practicing physical educator use to evaluate strength, power, static muscular endurance, and dynamic muscular endurance? We believe that the following tests are both necessary and sufficient to provide adequate and meaningful information with a minimum cost, a minimum expenditure of time and effort, and a maximum of safety.

Power

The best single measure of the individual's overall body power is the vertical jump. Its execution is shown in Figure 4–3. All that is needed for the test is a board with numbered marks one-half inch apart which is mounted on a wall. The subject's fingers either are moistened on a wet sponge or are dusted with chalk. The subject is instructed to stand next to the board and to touch the board as high as possible while keeping the heels on the floor. This "stretch height" is recorded. The subject then jumps upward and touches the board as high as possible at the top of the jump with the hand closest to the board. This "jump height" is measured and recorded. The difference between the stretch height and the jump height, to the nearest one-half inch, is the subject's score for that single execution. No forward movement of the feet is permitted prior to the jump.

For reliable results, the subject should take several practice jumps and a minimum of three trials should be averaged for a final test score. If one of the three trial scores is widely divergent from the other two, that value should be disregarded and an additional trial should be allowed. For greater accuracy in reading the jump heights, it is suggested that the test administrator stand on a step ladder or a bench.

The standing broad jump, the softball throw for distance, and similar tests may be used to measure the power performances of selected body parts in more specific movements. However, for overall utility and ease of interpretation, the vertical jump is recommended as the best single test of power.

Static muscular endurance

Only one practical test of static muscular endurance is recommended here. That is the flexed-arm hang for time. This test measures the ability of the subject to support his or her own body weight.

a. FLEXED ARM HANG

b. BENT KNEE SIT UP

c. PUSH-UP

d. PULL-UP

e. VERTICAL JUMP

FIGURE 4–3. Recommended tests.

The flexed-arm hang is administered using a horizonal bar. The subject is helped into the pull-up position with the palms forward (away from the body) and the chin just above the bar (Figure 4–3). The test administrator starts timing with a stop watch as soon as the subject is in the hanging position and stops timing when the subject's chin touches the bar or when the head is tipped back to keep the chin off of the bar. The time is recorded to the nearest second (73).

Dynamic muscular endurance—
DME–1 through DME–3

Although each of the nine levels of dynamic muscular endurance which are presented in Table 4–1 are believed to be physiologically identifiable, practical considerations suggest that the levels should be grouped for routine testing purposes. Tests of DME-1 through DME-3 are highly recommended for use by the practitioner since they are relatively easy and safe to administer and require minimal time and equipment. In general, they test the ability of the individual to handle his or her own body weight in high intensity tasks for short periods of time. The specific tests recommended here are the 100-yard dash for time and the number of repetitions which can be completed in 20 seconds of the pull-up, push-up and bent-knee sit-up tests. (The pull-up and pushup tests are not recommended for girls or women). Note that for the pull-up, pushup, and sit-up tests, the procedure of counting the number of repetitions completed in 20 seconds is preferred to that of counting the maximum number of repetitions which can be completed with no time limit. The reasons for this are: (a) the timed and untimed measures are highly correlated (18); (b) test administration time is saved; (c) the effects of motivation are minimized—especially in the sit-up test; and (d) the extreme muscular soreness often resulting from prolonged testing is avoided.

These recommended tests are administered as follows:

The 100-yard dash is conducted by having the subject run 100 yards on a grass surface as fast as possible while wearing tennis shoes. A regulation track start is used, except that starting blocks are omitted. The time required to run the distance is measured with a stop watch to the nearest, slower 0.1 of a second.

Pull-ups are measured by having the subject jump to a hanging position from a bar with the palms forward (away from the body). After hanging for about one second, the subject is given the starting signal. He pulls himself up until his chin just clears the bar and then lets himself down until his elbows are straight (Figure 4–3). He continues until he can do no more or 20 seconds have elapsed. The test administrator stops any swaying and does not permit any kicking, twisting, or stopping. Each completed pull-up is counted as one. If the last pull-up attempted cannot be completed, it is not scored.

Pushups are measured by having the subject assume the prone position. The hands are placed flat on the floor, beside the chest, just below the shoulders, and with the fingers forward. The feet are together and the body is held straight. No bending at the waist is permitted. The elbows are straightened raising the body and then flexed until the chin and chest barely touch the floor (Fig. 4–3). No stopping is permitted. The test continues until 20 seconds have elapsed or the subject is unable to completely straighten his arms. Each completed pushup is counted as one.

Bent-knee sit ups are measured by having the subject assume the supine position as shown in Fig. 4–3. The hands are clasped behind the head and the knees are bent. A helper should be used to hold the feet down. When ready, the subject sits up by rolling the trunk off of the floor one vertebra at a time in a curling movement until the chin touches the knees. The subject then returns to the lying position by uncurling. No stopping is permitted. The subject continues until 20 seconds have elapsed or it is impossible to perform another complete sit-up.

Dynamic muscular endurance—DME-4 through DME-9 In order to provide a complete picture of dynamic muscular endurance, the entire continuum was discussed earlier in this chapter. However, the DME-4 through DME-9 levels commonly are considered to represent "endurance" abilities requiring specific cardiovascular adaptations. Therefore, functional tests of DME-4 through DME-9 will be reserved for the chapter on endurance testing.

Interpretation of measures

Strength, power, and muscular endurance measures may be interpreted in a number of ways. First, the individual's results in percentile values can be determined from tables based on normative samples of subjects of the same age and sex. This will tell how the person's performance ranks in a grossly defined population.

If, however, each subject's performance is to be interpreted as it should be in an individualized physical education program, a percentile based on a population which is defined only by age and sex yields but one part of the picture. For example, the interaction between body weight and the factor being tested must be considered. Individuals of different body weights should not be expected to perform equally well on all tests. Static strength measures are positively correlated with body weight (e.g., grip strength—$r = 0.49$); thus, heavier subjects have an advantage and tend to score higher on static strength measures than do lighter subjects. On the other hand, static muscular endurance items are negatively correlated with body weight (e.g., flexed-arm hang — $r = -0.48$). Lighter individuals have an advantage and tend to score higher on these measures. Power tests which involve moving the total body weight quickly, such as the vertical jump, are negatively related to body weight ($r = -0.21$), whereas, those power measures which involve moving an object, such as the medicine-ball put, are positively correlated with body weight ($r = 0.39$) (18). These various correlations with body weight are sufficiently high to warrant the development of normative tables based on age, sex, and body weight.

An important dimension still is missing—the hereditary potential of the individual. With the development of reliable methods of determining somatotype, normative tables should be established for strength, power, and muscular endurance tests by body-type groupings. Such tables would facilitate better determinations of the individual's current status in relation to his or her real potential.

Principles for improvement

The physical educator needs a basic knowledge of the physiological phenomena underlying strength, power, and muscular endurance as well as an understanding of the appropriate methods of assessing these factors. In addition, the practitioner must be an expert in the application of various techniques to produce improvements in such abilities. It is clear that dramatic training changes are possible, but the best procedures for eliciting maximal muscular performances have not been identified yet. Solutions are needed for fundamental training problems such as: To what extent is improvement attainable? What are the best methods of achieving improvement? What is the minimum amount of time or work needed to bring about significant improvement? Although these and many other specific questions still are unanswered, there are a number of general principles that can serve as guides in devising training regimens to improve strength, power, and muscular endurance (67). Some of these principles have been covered previously; several others warrant brief mention.

Overload is required for improved performance

This fundamental physiological principle is as applicable and as important in the rehabilitation of the disabled as it is in the training of athletes. To improve in any training program, the overload principle may be utilized by one or a combination of the following techniques: (a) the load may be increased, (b) the work rate may be increased, (c) the duration of work may be increased, and (d) the rest intervals between bouts of exercise may be decreased. The technique(s) to be used would depend on the type of improvement or adaptation desired.

Rate of improvement is directly related to intensity of training

Within the limits of exercise tolerance, the greater the intensity of the overload, the greater will be the rate of improvement. This has been shown clearly in weight-training studies where the data obtained by using few repetitions with heavy loads have been compared with those obtained using many repetitions with light loads. Greater rates of improvement in dynamic strength always are found to result from programs involving few repetitions with heavy loads, even when all subjects perform as many repetitions as they can during each training period (67).

The effects of training are specific to the overload used

The response to training is far more specific than generally is recognized. An example can be shown relative to dynamic strength. If two groups matched on dynamic strength are placed on different weight training programs, quite dissimilar responses may be obtained. That is, if one group lifts maximal loads with few repetitions, a progressive improvement in dynamic strength will result. If the other group is placed on a program in which a designated moderate load is to be lifted a maximal number of times, negligible improvement will be found in dynamic strength, but muscular endurance will be increased (67).

Retrogression often precedes improvement

It is common for performances to deteriorate during the early stages of training. The body requires time to adapt to the overload being applied. During this period, in which the adaptive mechanisms are being mobilized, retrogression is to be expected. It is important that the naive individual not become discouraged when this happens since improvement will occur later.

Repetition is essential for muscular efficiency

Numerous repetitions of a specifically defined movement must be completed, at the desired work intensity, to establish the basic neuromuscular syntheses necessary for efficient movement. That is, repetition is necessary for the recruitment and isolation of effective motor units. Eventually, a plateau is reached where motor learning is complete and no further improvements in muscular efficiency are possible in that given movement. Additional improvement then can be achieved only by altering the basic skill pattern to one which inherently is more efficient.

Response to training is individual and unique

Fitness status, past experience in training, activity background, and hereditary potential all contribute to the rate at which each individual responds to a given training program. Subjects with high mesomorphic components generally improve at fast rates. Also, individuals who start a given training program, having participated in that type of training previously, tend to improve at faster rates than those embarking on such a program for the first time. That is, training appears to establish patterns for future responses to training.

Motivation is essential for effective training

Since the primary objective of training is adaptation to overload, especially in strength, power, and muscular endurance programs, it is clear that the individual must be motivated adequately to attempt progressively greater work intensities.

From these principles, it is obvious that training goals should be defined carefully. Once this has been done, the regimen outlined should be specific to the goals. Every effort then should be made to motivate the individual to attempt progressive overloads if optimal results are to be attained.

Maintenance

The maintenance of strength, power, and muscular endurance throughout life is of primary concern to physical educators. However, at present there is inadequate research available on which to base sound principles of maintenance. Evidence is needed to determine: (a) the extent to which it is possible to maintain these attributes at various stages in life, (b) the particular attributes which must be maintained for optimal health, (c) the levels at which strength, power, and muscular endurance should be maintained for satisfactory and satisfying performances in work and play, (d) the best techniques of maintenance, and (e) the minimum amount of time or work necessary for maintenance. Until such evidence is available, the physical educator must proceed with caution and use good judgment in these matters.

REFERENCES

1. Aitken, J. T., "Growth of Nerve Implants in Voluntary Muscle." *J. Anat.*, 84:38–49, 1950.

2. Anderson, T. McClurg. Personal communication.

3. Bard, P., *Medical Physiology* (11th ed.). St. Louis: Mosby, 1961, p. 862.

4. Bender, J. and H. Kaplan, "Determination of Success or Failure in Dynamic (Isotonic) Movements by Isometric Methods." *Res. Quart.*, 37:3–8, 1966.

5. Berger, R. A. and J. M. Henderson, "Relationship of Power to Static and Dynamic Strength." *Res. Quart.*, 37:9–13, 1966.

6. Buchtal, F. and V. John, "Spontaneous Activity in Isolated Muscle Spindles." *Acta Physiol. Scand.*, (Supp. 145) 42:25–27, 1957.

7. Carpenter, A., "An Analysis of the Relationships of the Factors of Velocity, Strength and Dead Weight to Athletic Performance." *Res. Quart.*, 12:34–39, 1941.

8. Carrow, R. E., R. E. Brown; and W. D. Van Huss, "Fiber Sizes and Capillary to Fiber Ratios in Skeletal Muscle of Exercised Rats." *Anat. Rec.*, 159:33, 1967.

9. Carrow, R. E., W. W. Heusner; and W. D. Van Huss, "Exercise and the Incidence of Muscle Fiber Splitting." *Proc. 18th Int. Cong. Sports Sci.* (Oxford), 1970.

10. Clarke, H. H., *Cable Tension Strength Tests.* Chicopee, Mass.: Brown-Murphy, 1953.

11. Clarke, H. H., "Development of Volitional Muscle Strength as Related to Fitness." In *Exercise and Fitness.* Chicago: Athletic Institute, 1960, pp. 200–213.

12. Clarke, H. H., *Muscular Strength and Endurance in Man.* Englewood Cliffs, N. J.: Prentice-Hall, 1966, p. 159.

13. Coleman, J. W., "Pure Speed as a Positive Factor in Some Track and Field Events." *Res. Quart.*, 11:47–53, 1940.

14. DeLorme, T. L. and A. L. Watkins, *Progressive Resistance Exercise: Technique and Application.* New York: Appleton-Century-Crofts, 1951.

15. Denny-Brown, D., "Interpretation of the Electromyogram." *Arch. Neurol. and Psychiat.*, 61:99–128, 1949.

16. Eyzaguirre, C., "The Motor Regulation of Mammalian Spindle Discharges." *J. Physiol.*, 150:186–200, 1960.

17. Feindel, W.; J. R. Hinshaw; and G. Weddell, "The Pattern of Motor Innervation in Mammalian Striated Muscle." *J. Anat.*, 86:35–48, 1952.

18. Fleishmann, E. A., *The Structure and Measurement of Physical Fitness.* Englewood Cliffs, N. J.: Prentice-Hall, 1964.

19. Gallagher, J. R., "Rest and Restriction." *Am. J. Pub. H.*, 46:1424–1428, 1956.

20. Gordon, E. E.; K. Kawolski; and M. Fritts, "Changes in Rat Muscle Fiber with Forceful Exercise." *Arch. Phys. Med. and Rehab.*, 48:577–582, 1967.

21. Gordon, E. E.; K. Kawolski; and M. Fritts, "Adaptations of Muscle to Various Exercise." *J.A.M.A.*, 199:103–108, 1967.

22. Gordon, E. E.; K. Kawolski; and M. Fritts, "Protein Changes in Quadriceps Muscle of Rat with Repetitive Exercises." *Arch. Phys. Med. and Rehab.*, 48:296–303, 1967.

23. Gordon, E. E., "Adaptation of Muscle to Different Exercise." *J.A.M.A.*, 201:755–758, 1967.

24. Guth, L., "Trophic Influence of Nerve on Muscle." *Physiol. Rev.*, 48:645, 1969.

25. Guyton, A. C., *Textbook of Medical Physiology*, (2d ed.). Philadelphia: Saunders, 1961, p. 1068.

26. Harris, J. E., "The Differential Measurement of Force and Velocity for Junior High School Girls." *Res. Quart.*, 8:114–121, 1937.

27. Hammond, P. H.; P. A. Merton; and G. G. Sutton, "Nervous Gradation of Muscular Contraction." *Brit. Med. Bull.*, 12:214–218, 1956.

28. Hart, M. E. and C. T. Shay, "Relationship between Physical Fitness and Academic Success." *Res. Quart. Supp.*, 35:443–445, 1964.

29. Helander, E. A. S., "Influence of Exercise and Restricted Activity on the Protein Composition of Skeletal Muscle." *Biochem. J.*, 78:478–482, 1961.

30. Hellebrandt, F. A. and S. J. Houtz, "Mechanisms of Muscle Training in Man." *Phys. Ther. Rev.*, 36:371–383, 1956.

31. Henneman, E. and C. B. Olson, "Relations between Structure and Function in the Design of Skeletal Muscles." *J. Neurophysiol.*, 28:581, 1965.

32. Henneman, E.; G. Somjen; and D. O. Carpenter, "Functional Significance of Cell Size in Spinal Motoneurons." *J. Neurophysiol.*, 28:560, 1965.

33. Hettinger, T., *Physiology of Strength.* Springfield, Ill.: Thomas, 1961.

34. Hunsicker, P. and G. Greey, "Studies in Human Strength." *Res. Quart.*, 28:109–122, 1957.

35. Hunt, C. C. and A. S. Parntal, "Spinal Reflex Regulation of Fusimotor Neurones." *J. Physiol.*, 143:195–212, 1958.

36. Hutto, L. "Measurement of the Velocity Factor and of Athletic Power in High School Boys." *Res. Quart.*, 9:109–128, 1938.

37. Huxley, A. F., "Interpretation of Muscle Striation: Evidence from Visible Light Microscopy." *Brit. Med. Bull.*, 12:167–170, 1956.

38. Huxley, A. F. and L. D. Peachey, "The Maximum Length for Contraction in Vertebrate Striated Muscle." *J. Physiol.*, 156:150–165, 1961.

39. Huxley, H. E., "The Ultra-Structure of Striated Muscle." *Brit. Med. Bull.*, 12:171–173, 1956.

40. Huxley, H. E., "The Contraction of Muscle." *Sci. Am.*, 199:67–82, 1958.

41. Ikai, M. and A. H. Steinhaus. "Some Factors Modifying the Expression of Human Strength." In *Health and Fitness in the Modern World.* Chicago, Ill.: Athletic Institute, 1961, pp. 148–161.

42. Ingels, N. B. and N. P. Thompson,

"An Electrokinematic Theory of Muscle Contraction." *Proc. 18th Comp. Eng. in Med. and Biol.*, 7:127, 1965.

43. Jones, H. E., "The Sexual Maturing of Girls as Related to Growth in Strength." *Res. Quart.*, 18:135–143, 1947.

44. Kellogg, J. H., "A New Dynamometer for Use in Anthropometry." *Modern Med. and Bact. World*, 2:269–275, 1893.

45. Knowlton, S. C.; R. L. Bennett; and R. McClure, "Electromyography of Fatigue." *Arch. Phys. Med.*, 32:648–652, 1951.

46. Kugelberg, E. and L. Edstrom, "Differential Histochemical Effects of Muscle Contractions on Phosphorylase and Glycogen in Various Types of Fibers: Relation to Fatigue." *J. Neurol. Neurosurg. Psychiat.*, 31:415, 1968.

47. Larson, L. A., "A Factor and Validity Analysis of Strength Variables and Tests with a Test Combination of Chinning, Dipping and Vertical Jump." *Res. Quart.*, 11:82–96, 1940.

48. Larson, L. A., "A Factor Analysis of Motor Ability Variables and Tests, with Tests for College Men." *Res. Quart.*, 12:499–517, 1941.

49. Leonard, F. E. and G. B. Affleck, *A Guide to the History of Physical Education.* Philadelphia: Lea and Febiger, 1947.

50. McCloy, E., "Factor Analysis Methods in the Measurement of Motor Abilities." *Res. Quart.*, 6:114–121, 1935.

51. McCloy, C. H., "The Measurement of Speed in Motor Performance." *Psychometrika*, 5:173–182, 1940.

52. McCloy, C. H., "The Measurement of General Motor Capacity and General Motor Ability." *Res. Quart.* Supp., 46–61, March 1934.

53. Morpurgo, B., "Ueber Activitäts–Hypertrophie der willkurlichen Muskeln." *Virchows Archiv. fur Path. Anat.*, 150:522–554, 1897.

54. Phillips, M., "Study of a Series of Physical Education Tests by Factor Analysis." *Res. Quart.*, 20:60–71, 1949.

55. Rarick, L., "An Analysis of the Speed Factor in Simple Athletic Events." *Res. Quart.*, 8:89–105, 1937.

56. Reitsma, W., *Regeneratie, Volometrische en Numeriere Hypertrofie Van Skeletspieren bij Kikker en Rat.*, Amsterdam: Drukkerij, J. Ruysendaal, 1965.

57. Rhodes, E.; W. Van Huss; and R. Nelson, "The Effects of a Pre-Season Ankle Exercise Program on the Prevention of Ankle Injuries in High School Basketball Players." *J. Phys. and Ment. Rehab.*, 14:78–79, 1960.

58. Rice, E. A., *A Brief History of Physical Education.* New York: Barnes, 1926.

59. Rodahl, K. and S. Horvath, ed., *Muscle as a Tissue.* New York: McGraw-Hill, 1962.

60. Rogers, F. R., *Physical Capacity Tests in the Administration of Physical Education.* New York: Bureau of Publications, Teachers College, Columbia University, 1925.

61. Sargent, D. A., "Intercollegiate Strength Tests." *Am. Phys. Ed. Rev.*, 2:216–220, 1897.

62. Seyffarth, H., "The Behavior of Motor Units in Voluntary Contraction." *SKR. Norke Vidensk AKAD.*, 1 Mat.–Mat. Kl. No. 4, 1940.

63. Sills, F. D., "A Factor Analysis of Somatotypes and Their Relationships to Achievement in Motor Skills." *Res. Quart.*, 21:424–437, 1950.

64. Szent-Gyorgi, A., *Bioenergetics.* New York: Academic Press, 1957.

65. Szent-Gyorgi, A., "Muscle Research." *Science*, 128:699–702, 1958.

66. Torre, M., "Nombre et Dimensions des Unites Motrices dans les Muscles Extrinse ques de L'Oel et, en General, Dans les Muscles Squellettique delies a Des Organes des sens." *Schweizer Archiv. Suisse Neur. und Psychiat.*, 72:362–376, 1953.

67. Van Huss, W. D.; J. Friedrich; R. Mayberry; R. Neimeyer; and H. Olson, *Physical Activity in Modern Living* (2nd ed.). Englewood Cliffs, N.J.: Prentice-Hall, 1969.

68. Van Huss, W. D.; L. Albrecht; R. Nelson; and R. Hagerman, "Effect of Overload Warm-Up on the Velocity and Accuracy of Throwing." *Res. Quart.*, 33:472–475, 1962.

69. Van Linge, B., "The Response of Muscle to Strenuous Exercise." *J. Bone and Joint Surg.,* 44–B:711–721, 1962.

70. Weiss, P. and M. V. Edds, "Spontaneous Recovery of Partially Denervated Muscle." *Am. J. Physiol.,* 145:587–607, 1945.

71. Wendler, A. J., "A Critical Analysis of Test Elements Used in Physical Education." *Res. Quart.,* 9:64–76, 1938.

72. Williams, C. G.; C. H. Wyndham; R. Kok; and M. J. E. von Rahden, "Effect of Training on Maximum Oxygen Intake on Anaerobic Metabolism in Man." *Int. z. Angew. Physiol.,* 24:18–23, 1967.

73. American Association of Health, Physical Education and Recreation, *Youth Fitness Test Manual.* Washington, D.C.: The Association, 1965.

STUDY QUESTIONS • Chapter 4

1. Define static muscular endurance.

2. Are static and dynamic muscular endurance tests highly correlated? Give evidence to support your answer.

3. How does motor unit activity relate to static muscular endurance?

4. What factors limit performance in static muscular endurance?

5. How does body composition affect DME-1 through DME-3?

6. List sports in which DME-4 through DME-6 is the primary fitness required.

7. Is the 440-yard run for college men a good measure of DME-7 through DME-9? Why?

8. Respond to the following statements. Give reasons or evidence to support your answers:

   In hypertrophy, the number of muscle fibers increases.

   As the joint angle in the arm changes, the sequence of motor unit firing is changed.

   As a skill is perfected, the same number of motor units continue to be used as before the skill was developed.

   The correlation between tests of power and tests of static strength are high ($r = 0.80$).

   Removing cortical inhibition makes possible a greater strength effort.

   Rate of improvement in strength development is not related to intensity of training.

9. Define static muscular strength.

10. Define hyperplasia.

11. Explain the difference in white and red fibers as it relates to strength and endurance testing.

12. Is it necessary to correct for body weight in comparing children in grip strength? Why?

13. Why is it important for the average young man or woman to be strong?

14. Explain the differences between static strength and power as related to tests and measurements.

15. Is the rate of improvement in dynamic muscular strength related to intensity of training? Give evidence or justification for your answer.

16. Describe the difference between static and dynamic strength tests. Give an example of each.

17. Which of the three tests of power (vertical jump, standing long jump, softball throw) appears to be most practical from the standpoint of administration? Which has been most adequately validated?

18. Can you improve power with training? Give evidence to support your answer.

19. What effect would you expect strength exercises, as weight lifting, to have on power? Why?

20. List several sports in which power is a characteristic of the successful performer.

21. How would you determine if success in a particular sport is related to power?

22. Name three sports and three occasions in civilian or military life when absolute static strength is more important than static strength per body size.

23. Is strength in boys of elementary and high school age correlated with health? What evidence can you give to support your answer?

24. Which type of test, dynamic or static strength, imposes a greater load on the circulatory system? Why?

25. Why will strength training generally not produce the muscle definition in females that it does in males?

26. Is maximum oxygen debt capacity more closely related to DME-4 or DME-9? Explain your answer.

27. In what kind of dynamic muscular endurance (DME) would maximal oxygen uptake capacity be most closely related? Why?

28. If the load on a muscle is increased, how does this affect the recruitment of motor units?

29. How does learning a skill affect the sequence and number of motor units involved?

30. How does training in static strength at a particular joint angle affect the static strength as measured when the joint is flexed at other angles?

31. How does "overload" warm-up affect one's performance in a power test? Give an explanation of your answer.

32. Explain neuromuscular feedback.

33. Why is the isolated muscle capable of greater force (tension) than the same muscle in the intact human being?

34. What does 1-RM mean in the measurement of dynamic strength?

35. Give an example of an activity in everyday life in which each of the following are important.
    a. static muscular strength
    b. static muscular endurance
    c. DME-1 through DME-3
    d. DME-7 through DME-9

36. What is, in your opinion, the best test of a, b, c, and d in the previous question for high school girls?

ENDURANCE

5

Hugh G. Welch

Introduction

Endurance and fatigue

Endurance is a term more easily defined than understood. The dictionary definition of endurance is the ability to withstand pain, distress, or fatigue. This definition is probably satisfactory to most physical educators, especially when pain, distress, and fatigue are thought of in relation to prolonged physical activity.

Understanding endurance is more complicated, perhaps because of our inability to adequately define fatigue. The conceptual difficulty with this term may be appreciated when an eminent authority on the subject, Dr. D. B. Dill, former director of the famous Harvard Fatigue Laboratory, purposely avoids attempting to define the term, but instead chooses to describe some of the manifestations of fatigue under various conditions (10). A recent text on the subject of fatigue identified over 8500 references published since 1940, in addition to an older literature dating back over 100 years (23).

Regardless of the difficulties involved, most workers in the field would accept the idea that fatigue implies an impairment in the capacity to do work, and that this impairment is a result of prior exertion. This will serve as an operational definition for the purposes of this chapter.

Stamina

The term stamina frequently appears in the literature as an approximate synonym for endurance. The relationship between the two terms has never been made clear and some confusion exists in the current literature. Fleishman, for example, has described stamina as a sort of whole body endurance or cardiovascular endurance (a term to which we shall return) as opposed to endurance of specific muscle groups. He also suggests that stamina is presumably related to heart muscle capacity (13).

There seems to be little rationale for this distinction. Dictionaries and works on English usage present the terms *endurance* and *stamina* as synonymous. The etymology of the terms is interesting and perhaps offers some basis for differentiating between them. Endurance is derived from the Latin verb *indurare,* meaning to harden, hold out, or make lasting. The term *stamina* had its origin in the Latin noun *stamen,* or *thread,* a botanical term. In usage, however, it came to indicate the "life-threads spun by the Fates," thus, the present implication of perseverance in the face of adversity, illness, or fatigue. Interestingly enough, in this context, stamina does imply a resistance on the part of the whole organism. Basically, however, there seems to be little reason to justify the use of two different terms for the concept implied; the remainder of this discussion will use the term *endurance.*

Capacity and performance

What is the difference between the so-called tests of cardiovascular condition (chapter 6) and those of endurance? Primarily, the "cardiovascular tests" seek to determine the present physiological capacity of the individual in the same way that intelligence tests attempt to determine mental capabilities. These tests are not concerned with motivational problems; they are valid if and only if they are able to assess the capacity of the individual.

On the other hand, endurance tests are primarily performance tests and are presumably greatly affected by the motivation of the subject. The two objectives are thus quite different and the investigator should be certain before selecting a given test whether the concern is with capacity or performance. It should be noted that physiological capacities are not necessarily fixed qualities, incapable of change. The capacity of the body for physical work can certainly be increased with training, and will decrease with deconditioning. Therefore, tests of physiological capacity are only valid for the point in time at which they are administered.

It might be supposed that cardiovascular tests are more desirable than endurance tests on the basis of their "neatness," that is, they are more precise, less affected by day-to-day subject variability, and are easier to understand physiologically. This may be true in the clinic and the research laboratory, but it is not necessarily so in the realm of physical education testing. Indeed, it could be argued with some conviction that endurance is the essence of physical fitness and perhaps the single most important factor to be determined in a fitness profile. Obviously both types of test are important and serve useful functions.

One last point should be made in this discussion. Under conditions of extreme motivation (or stress), endurance tests may represent reasonable approximations of the individual's capacity. World record running times are examples; the normal testing environment is, however, not likely to produce these conditions.

The nature of endurance

Why is this characteristic called "endurance" of such importance that it is included in almost every battery of fitness tests? What basis is there for the statement in a preceding paragraph that endurance may be the single most important factor in fitness testing?

There is no definite evidence to support this statement; there are, however, some suggestive data available. McCloy (17) argued that many of the characteristics of a fitness test are essential for good performance on an endurance item. For example, a reasonable level of strength is necessary. In other words, one might argue that a high performance on an endurance test would be indicative of a high degree of "fitness" in other important areas. This hypothesis draws support from Cureton's study of twenty-eight different fitness tests in which the mile run showed the highest correlation with the overall test score (9, as cited in reference 15). A correlation coefficient of 0.708 was obtained with the composite test results.

On a practical level, participation in many sports activities would seem to depend on an acceptable level of endurance. Tennis, skiing, and skating are three examples of many that could be mentioned. It would also seem that an increase in endurance, particularly for middle-age adults, would make available a greater variety of leisure activities and thus add another dimension to life. It has been suggested for some time (but as yet not proven) that a greater level of endurance should allow one to feel less fatigued at the end of the day, making more energy available for leisure hours.

Along this line, Balke has presented data indicating that an individual with a greater work capacity can sustain effort at submaximal levels of work longer than those with lower capacities (3). Does this suggest that with some endurance training, a housewife might be less fatigued at the end of a regular working day? Åstrand and Rodahl have presented the idea, based on only a few observations, that an individual can work for an eight-hour day at a rate not exceeding about 50% of his maximal working capacity (2, p. 292). Unfit individuals are probably not even capable of that figure, despite the fact that their maximal work rates are also lower. In other words, unfit individuals have lower work capacities to begin with, and are able to sustain smaller percentages of their maximal values.

The importance of this endurance characteristic may also be defended on physiological grounds. The reader is not asked to accept uncritically the following argument but to consider it as an interesting possibility. There are a number of workers in the field who feel that the health of the heart and the vascular system is the single most important consideration in fitness programs. Since the function of the cardiovascular system is to transport oxygen and other nutrients to tissues and to transport carbon dioxide and other waste products away, then the healthier heart ought to perform this function more effectively than the less healthy one. The ability to "endure" a severe work load for some period of time depends, at least in part, on a healthy circulatory apparatus. Or, to turn the statement around, a high degree of performance on an endurance test should indicate a sound heart and vascular system. Though this argument is by no means proven, it does seem reasonable and offers a basis for concern with endurance training and testing.

Physiological bases of endurance

Physiologically, the quality that differentiates endurance from other fitness characteristics is the continued demand for energy over a period of time. Since energy cannot be stored in great amounts in readily utilizable forms, it is necessary to synthesize it from stored potential energy (primarily carbohydrate and fat). The ability to synthesize energy in a useful form over a long period of time demands a steady supply of oxygen and a removal of waste products. If the rate of energy expenditure is lower than the individual's maximal rate, then the activity may be sustained as long as there is a supply of carbohydrate and fat. If, on the other hand, the demand for energy is greater than the rate at which it can be supplied, the available sources of stored energy are quickly consumed and fatigue ensues.

The rate at which work can be done in the former condition is presumably dependent on the rate at which oxygen can be supplied to the tissues (hence the term *aerobic work*). This includes the DME-7 through DME-9 levels of muscular endurance referred to in Chapter 4. In the latter condition, analogous to DME-4 through DME-6, oxygen cannot be supplied rapidly enough and the rate of work is dependent on the amount of energy available from nonoxidative sources. This is usually referred to as "anaerobic" work. The exhausting of the available energy (which must be replenished during recovery) has led to the concept of an oxygen debt. Endurance in shorter events like the 440- and 880-yard runs is usually considered primarily a function of one's oxygen debt, while endurance in longer events is considered a function of one's maximum oxygen uptake.

Let it suffice to say at this point that the evidence implicating oxygen as the limiting factor in performance is not overly impressive. The above explanation is satisfactory for the present, but future research may require some modification.

This discussion might prompt one to conclude that fatigue in aerobic work is due to the depletion of carbohydrate and fat stores and that fatigue in anaerobic work is due to the depletion of nonoxidative energy sources. In the intact human (as opposed to an isolated muscle), this is probably not the case. There is reason to believe that the site of fatigue in humans is in the central nervous system rather than in the muscle (5). The fatigue that we see in athletes is probably never due to total exhaustion of energy stores but to some response of the nervous system. Thus, motivation may be more important in endurance tests than maximum oxygen uptake.

Endurance tests

Endurance tests are legion; in fact, almost every conceivable exercise has at one time or another been utilized as an endurance test. Norms are available for many of these activities (18), and they may be adequate for certain conditions. However, the validity of many of these tests is suspect. There ought to be a reasonable compromise between the precise laboratory tests and the questionable field tests that are often proposed.

The maximum oxygen uptake test

There has been an increasing interest in recent years in the use of the maximum oxygen uptake test as a test of physical fitness. Although some workers are hesitant to accept this one test as a criterion by itself, there appears to be general agreement that it is an effective index of the circulatory capacity of the individual (6, 20, 24; see especially references 20 and 24 for a more thorough discussion of this concept). The maximum oxygen uptake test, however, is basically a laboratory test and is not generally practical for normal testing situations.

Recently, Balke developed a simple field test to predict maximum oxygen uptake with an acceptable degree of accuracy (4). The test employs a 15-minute run around a track or other known distance at the individual's best effort. That is, the subject covers as much distance as possible in the time allotted. Tables are available by which the subject's performance may be evaluated.

Cooper modified the Balke test by shortening the time of the run to 12 minutes and by establishing a slightly different analysis of the performance levels (7). According to the classification of Cooper, an individual must cover 1.5 miles in the 12-minute period to be considered in "good" condition (Table 5–1). Performance tables are presently being prepared which will make adjustments for age and sex differences. Where these are not available, it should not be difficult for teachers to establish norms for the population with which they are concerned.

TABLE 5–1
Levels of Fitness based on Performance in the 12-Minute Run Test

Fitness Level	Distance Run in 12 Minutes (Miles)
Very poor	1.0
Poor	1.0–1.24
Fair	1.25–1.49
Good	1.50–1.74
Excellent	1.75 or more

Data from Cooper (7)

The advantage of the field test proposed by Balke and Cooper is that it requires very little equipment, namely an accurately measured track, a stop watch, and a whistle or horn for indicating the end of the 12-minute period.

Indications at present are that the test can adequately predict the maximum oxygen uptake. Cooper reported a correlation of 0.867 with the field test and the laboratory oxygen uptake tests with adults (7). Other studies have generally supported these results. Ribisl and Kachadorian reported an r of 0.85 between a running test and the laboratory test using middle-aged men as subjects (22). Studies with younger boys (19) and with women (14) have indicated slightly lower correlations.

In comparison, much lower correlation coefficients are usually obtained when shorter runs are utilized. Reported values have typically been around 0.60 when comparing the 600-yard run (as in the AAHPER Test) and the maximal oxygen uptake (8, 11, 12). Some of these studies leave much to be desired, and further verification would be helpful, but the fairly consistent results from various sources suggest that, at present, the shorter runs are of more limited usefulness for endurance testing.

Thus Balke's original contention that longer runs (10–15 minutes duration) are necessary to predict maximal oxygen uptake seems a sound principle with good experimental support (8, 21, 22). The study of Ribisl and Kachadorian (22) is especially interesting in this regard in that they compared maximal oxygen uptake with running performance from 60 yards to 2 miles, finding that the predictive ability of the run improved as the distance increased.

The individual must decide if the apparent gain in predictive ability is worth the extra effort required of the subject. There is evidence that a run of 1 kilometer (about 1100 yards) works very well with preadolescent boys (ages 8–13). An r of 0.93 has been reported for this group when comparing the maximal oxygen uptake test and the results of the run test (16). It is also important to keep in mind that the discussion of the previous paragraphs is based on a small number of experimental studies and that further investigation is very much needed.

Other considerations

Anyone considering using a field test should still keep several factors in mind. The performance levels in Table 5–1 are still, to a large extent, arbitrary. There is still no proof that the ability to run 1.5 miles in 12 minutes indicates a measure of safety from cardiovascular disease, for example. Also, caution must be taken to ensure that deconditioned older subjects do not undertake the test without proper medical supervision. In fact, in these cases, a medical examination should precede a testing and training program.

Almost all the information to date has been obtained from male subjects. There is little comparable information for females at any age level. One of the serious problems that may be encountered here is the possibility that school-age girls may lack the motivation to make the test results useful. This remains to be established.

Another consideration that should be considered by any concerned teacher is the evidence that maximal oxygen uptake capacity (or endurance) is largely determined by genetic factors and can be influenced only to a relatively small degree by training (16). If this is true, the question of using 12-minute run test scores as a basis for grades, as has been suggested by Cooper, is a debatable practice. The purpose of this chapter is not to discuss the philosophy of grading, but it is hoped that any physical educator who considers using endurance scores in this fashion does so only after carefully thinking through the justification.

Recommendations

As far as school testing programs are concerned, perhaps the single most important recommendation is that no test of this type be given without the thoughtful consideration of the instructor. No one test is available over the wide range of ages and ability levels to be found among school-age young people; a teacher insensitive to these problems can do more harm than good.

Tests of anaerobic capacity, or DME-4 through DME-6, as it is termed elsewhere in this text, are not recommended for school testing programs. They may be useful for athletic training programs but they have no particular importance in physical education classes or adult fitness programs. These tests will not be discussed further except to point out that if one especially desires to investigate this quality, probably the 440- or 880-yard run events are most appropriate.

More important to the physical educator are the tests of "cardiovascular endurance" or aerobic work capacity. The longer run-walk tests of the type described by Balke and Cooper are probably the most scientifically sound tests of this category. Because of the small apparent differences in their predictive abilities, the shorter test (the 12-minute run) may be more desirable. Also at this writing, Cooper's work is more accessible than Balke's. One drawback is that both those studies were conducted on adult samples and extrapolation of the results to school-age populations should be made with caution. Cooper's lower age limit is about that of the typical high school junior or senior.

Table 5–2 shows data collected from a Canadian high school physical education program on the Balke field test and allows a rough comparison to be made with adult groups. Some modification of the data was required (see explanation, Table 5–2). With these limitations in mind, it may be seen from the table that about 50% of the 16-and 17-year-old subjects scored in the good or excellent category as defined by Cooper. This drops to about 30% scoring in these two categories at the 14- and 15-year levels. It does not seem reasonable to assume large differences in the relative fitness levels between 14–15-year-olds and 16–17-year-olds; it more likely suggests that the established norms are not useful for the younger group, and that the criteria defined by Cooper should be used with caution if at all with subjects under 17 years of age. There are reports of the adult criteria being applied effectively with junior high students (ages 13–16), but only a small number of subjects was utilized and the results must be used cautiously.

The discussion to this point may be taken to suggest that the 12-minute run is an appropriate measure for certain groups. It is probably useful in adult programs (with proper supervision) and with mature high school students. It may also be useful with subjects of junior high school age if consideration is given to the question of establishing a different set of norms for the age group.

TABLE 5–2
Results of High School Age Boys on the
Balke Field Test of Physical Fitness*

Percentile	14-yr-olds	15-yr-olds	16-yr-olds	17-yr-olds
99	1.75	1.71	1.99	1.92
90	1.59	1.60	1.73	1.71
80	1.53	1.53	1.63	1.63
70	1.48	1.47	1.58	1.58
60	1.44	1.45	1.55	1.54
50	1.41	1.43	1.49	1.48
40	1.38	1.41	1.43	1.45
30	1.29	1.37	1.39	1.41
20	1.22	1.29	1.32	1.35
10	1.13	1.20	1.24	1.28
1	0.91	1.01	1.14	1.23
N=	25	45	43	55

*Data were made available courtesy of Dr. J. K. Barclay. The original data were from the 15-minute run, and performance was expressed as average running velocity in yards per second. I have taken the liberty to convert the data to the distance covered in 12 minutes at the given rate so that the performances could be compared to a 12-minute equivalent run. With apologies to Dr. Barclay and to the reader, this should introduce no serious error and allows for comparisons to be made with Dr. Cooper's data. If there is any error, it is toward making the values above slightly lower than they should be.

With this younger group, however, there is reason to think that a shorter test might be more desirable, a run, for example, of 8 minutes or of 1 mile. Instructors should be able to develop their own norms for these shorter tests. Present evidence (which is admittedly sketchy) suggests that the 600-yard run is not an effective test of aerobic capacity in subjects of junior high or high school age.

For subjects of elementary school age, the 600-yard run-walk as described in the AAHPER Test (1) is probably as appropriate as any. It is debatable whether any endurance test is especially useful with this age group because of the motivational problems. The reader will have to make a decision as to the desirability of these tests at that level. The results of Klissouras (16) suggest that a run of 1 kilometer may be used successfully with boys aged 8–13. Below that age, he found that motivation probably was a limiting factor. Again, norms would have to be established for that test.

The occasional concern one hears from parents regarding endurance runs is worthy of some consideration. There is no evidence that healthy children can be harmed by efforts as strenuous as those required in the tests described and, in fact, their normal play frequently involves as much work as that done in the tests.

Summary

To effectively test "cardiovascular endurance" or aerobic work capacity, a test must be sufficiently long to minimize the contribution of anaerobic work (oxygen debt). It appears that, in adult populations, this means an effort of greater than 10 minutes' duration. The 12-minute run test proposed by Cooper and the 15-minute test described by Balke seem most appropriate. The need for proper supervision with older, deconditioned subjects cannot be overemphasized.

For younger subjects, it is unlikely that the test need be as long as for more physically mature individuals. Accordingly, the length (or time) of the run may be adjusted for age down to something like the 600-yard run-walk for elementary children. Intermediate tests can be established for junior high subjects. The lack of available norms for these tests at certain age levels should not be seen as a serious disadvantage. Enterprising teachers can, and probably should, establish their own norms for the given test and population.

REFERENCES

1. American Association for Health, Physical Education, and Recreation, *Youth Fitness Manual.* Washington, D.C.: The Association, 1961.

2. Åstrand, P. O. and K. Rodahl, *Text-*

book of Work Physiology, McGraw-Hill, New York, 1970.

3. Balke, B., "The Effect of Physical Exercise on the Metabolic Potential: A Crucial Measure of Physical Fitness."

In *Exercise and Fitness*. Chicago: Athletic Institute, 1960, pp. 73–81.

4. Balke, B., *A Simple Field Test for the Assessment of Physical Fitness*. CARI Report 63–6. Oklahoma City: Civil Aeronautical Research Institute, Federal Aviation Agency, April 1963.

5. Basmajian, J. V., *Muscles Alive* (2d ed.). Baltimore: Williams and Wilkins, 1967, pp. 76–84.

6. Chapman, C. B. and J. H. Mitchell, "The Physiology of Exercise." *Sci. Amer.*, 212:88–96, 1965.

7. Cooper, K. H., "A Means of Assessing Maximal Oxygen Intake," *J. Amer. Med. Assn.*, 203:201–204, 1968.

8. Costill, D. L., "The Relationship Between Selected Physiological Variables and Distance Running Performance." *J. Sports Med.*, 7:61–66, 1967.

9. Cureton, T. K., *Endurance of Young Men*. Washington, D.C.: National Research Council, Society for Research in Child Development, 1945, p. 160.

10. Dill, D. B., "Fatigue and Physical Fitness." In *Science and Medicine of Exercise and Sports*, edited by W. R. Johnson. New York: Harper, 1960, pp. 384–402.

11. Doolittle, T. L. and R. Bigbee, "The Twelve-Minute Run-Walk: A Test of Cardiovascular Fitness of Adolescent Boys." *Res. Quart.*, 39:491–495, 1968.

12. Falls, H. B.; A. H. Ismail; and D. F. MacLeod, "Estimation of Maximum Oxygen Uptake in Adults from AAHPER Youth Fitness Test Items." *Res. Quart.*, 37:192–201, 1966.

13. Fleishman, E. A., *The Structure and Measurement of Physical Fitness*. Englewood Cliffs, N.J.: Prentice-Hall, 1964.

14. Katch, F. I.; W. D. McArdle; R. Czula; and G. S. Pechar, "Maximal Oxygen Intake, Endurance Running Performance, and Body Composition in College Women." *Res. Quart.*, 44:301–312, 1973.

15. Kenney, H. E. and S. C. Staley, *A Program in Sports-Dance-Exercise*. Champaign, Ill.: Stipes, 1961.

16. Klissouras, V., "Prediction of Potential Performance with Special Reference to Heredity." *J. Sports Med.*, 13:100–107, 1973.

17. McCloy, C. H., "A Factor Analysis of Tests of Endurance." *Res. Quart.*, 27:213–216, 1956.

18. McCloy, C. H. and N. D. Young, *Tests and Measurements in Health and Physical Education* (3rd ed.). New York: Appleton-Century-Crofts, 1954, pp. 165–192.

19. Maksud, M. G. and K. D. Coutts, "Application of the Cooper Twelve-Minute Run-Walk Test to Young Males." *Res. Quart.*, 42:54–59, 1971.

20. Mitchell, J. H.; B. J. Sproule; and C. B. Chapman, "The Physiological Meaning of the Maximal Oxygen Uptake Test." *J. Clin. Invest.*, 37:538–547, 1958.

21. Olree, H.; C. Stevens; T. Nelson; G. Agnevik; and R. T. Clark, "Evaluation of the AAHPER Youth Fitness Test." *J. Sports Med.*, 5:67–71, 1965.

22. Ribisl, P. M. and W. A. Kachadorian, "Maximal Oxygen Intake Prediction in Young and Middle-aged Males." *J. Sports Med.*, 9:17–22, 1969.

23. Simonson, E., ed., *Physiology of Work Capacity and Fatigue*. Springfield, Ill.: Thomas, 1971.

24. Taylor, H. L.; E. Buskirk; and A. Henschel, "Maximal Oxygen Intake as an Objective Measure of Cardio-respiratory Performance." *J. Appl. Physiol.*, 8:73–80, 1955.

STUDY QUESTIONS • Chapter 5

1. Explain the difference between "cardiovascular tests" and "endurance tests." Which of the two is what physical educators would call primarily a "performance" test?

2. What evidence can you cite that "endurance" is important in our society?

3. Is endurance important in sports performance? Give examples if you believe the answer is yes.

4. What connection, if any, do you see between endurance and health?

5. Can a great deal of immediately useable forms of energy be stored in large quantities in the body? Explain.

6. Can fat be utilized to synthesize energy? How about carbohydrates? Protein?

7. Explain "aerobic" work. Give an example.

8. Explain "anaerobic" work. Give an example.

9. How are aerobic and anaerobic work related to DME 1–3, DME 4–6, and DME 7–9?

10. What is meant by "oxygen debt"?

11. Why do you think an individual stops working when exhausted? In other words, where is the site of fatigue? Give reasons for your answer.

12. If maximal oxygen uptake determines one type of work capacity, why don't we measure this ability in school children?

13. Describe the 12-minute run for distance. How was the test validated? Is it a valid test of endurance? Is it a reliable test?

14. Describe the 600-yard run test. Is a score in this test as closely correlated to maximum oxygen intake as a score on the 12-minute run? Explain your answer.

15. Are tests of anaerobic capacity recommended for school testing? Why?

16. What test of endurance would you use in the elementary school? In the high school? Would they be the same? Why?

17. Do you know of any national standards for any endurance test? Which one?

CIRCULATORY-RESPIRATORY FITNESS

6

Henry J. Montoye

Introduction

Health and disease

The term *circulatory-respiratory fitness,* when used by a physician, may imply freedom from cardiovascular or pulmonary disease. It is not surprising, therefore, that the inclusion of heart rate or blood pressure tests in a physical education program is sometimes not understood. Evidence accumulated in recent years strongly suggests that regular physical activity is a factor in preventing or delaying heart disease. Yet when physical educators or coaches measure the circulatory-respiratory fitness of a boy or girl by means of a simple test, they are not attempting to diagnose heart disease or any other pathological condition. They are generally trying to estimate or judge the capacity of the circulatory-respiratory system to function during sports or other physical activities which require sustained effort. It is in this sense that the term *circulatory-respiratory fitness* (sometimes called *cardiovascular fitness*) is used in this chapter.

Work capacity

The use of complicated physiological tests may appear inappropriate when it would be much easier and more accurate to determine an individual's endurance with a stop watch on the running track. Endurance, such as one's ability to run a mile, certainly can best be determined with a stop watch. However, in the previous chapter on endurance, it was pointed out that work capacity or endurance depends on a number of factors besides the capability of the circulatory-respiratory system to adapt to increased metabolic demands (exercise). An endurance performance is determined in part by motivation and skill. But the physical educator frequently wishes to assess the fitness of the circulatory-respiratory system without involving "non-physiological" factors. Furthermore, in appraising the fitness of middle-aged or older subjects it is often inappropriate, even unsafe, to require subjects to perform a maximum exertion test.

Anaerobic and aerobic work

The anaerobic and aerobic mechanisms which play important roles in work performance, were discussed in the previous chapter. The ability to develop a large oxygen debt depends primarily on the willingness of the individual to subject him or herself to the pain associated with a relatively high concentration of metabolic products in the tissues. It is possible to measure "aerobic capacity" directly but an all-out endurance performance on the part of the subject is required. Therefore, a method of estimating aerobic capacity by means of submaximal work tests has practical significance.

The search for a valid and practical test

Early approaches

Resting measures

Blood pressure. Among healthy children and young adults, there is little evidence that resting blood pressure has validity for measuring circulatory-respiratory condition. Also, there are practical problems associated with blood pressure determination in connection with physical education or recreation programs. Rarely is there a quiet place or the available time to obtain accurate resting measurements on large groups of children.

Heart rate. The characteristic lower heart rates among endurance athletes as compared to sedentary or untrained men and women have been recognized for a long time. That the resting heart rate decreases with training has also been demonstrated many times in both human beings and animals. Among a highly select group of runners competing in the N.C.A.A. 4-mile cross country championships (90), there was a correlation between resting heart rate and performance in the run; the lower the heart rate the better the performance, but the relationship is not strong ($r = 0.52$). Recently Costill (32) reported similar results in cross-country runners. The relative low correlation is not surprising because the resting heart rate is sensitive to many factors besides training including emotional state, age, environmental conditions, etc. Hence, the resting rate is of very little value in classifying individuals in terms of circulatory-respiratory fitness. Besides, as in the case of blood pressures it is difficult for a physical educator, under the usual working conditions, to obtain true resting heart rates.

Lung function. Vital capacity (maximum expiratory volume) is related to body size, principally height, but it also decreases markedly with age. However, there is insufficient evidence at the present time to indicate that resting respiratory rate, vital capacity, timed vital capacity, maximum expiratory flow, or maximum breathing capacity reflects an individual's aerobic capacity. Hence the expense in time and equipment for measuring vital capacity and associated pulmonary measurements in the school or recreation program appears unjustified at the present time.

There is also insufficient evidence to recommend breath-holding ability as a measure of cardiovascular-respiratory condition. This capacity is to a large extent dependent on motivation and practice (84, 85). It is possible for some individuals to be sufficiently motivated to hold their breath until they become unconscious (84). Hence, it may be unwise to subject children to this test.

Physiologic response to a change in posture

Since the beginning of the twentieth century, a sudden change in posture (for example, from a reclining to a standing position) has been used as a physiologic stress. The rapidity with which the neurocirculatory system can adapt to such a change in position has been interpreted as a measure of circulatory-respiratory fitness. It is well known that when there is poor tone of the abdominal muscles and blood vessels, assuming an erect position causes a pooling of blood in the large vessels (i.e., the formation of "blood lakes"). There is consequently a marked increase in heart rate, a relatively large change in blood pressure, and perhaps dizziness. These extreme symptoms, as most people know, may be seen in individuals who stand erect or attempt to walk after several weeks of bed confinement. Individuals who have good tone of the nervous, muscular, and cardiovascular systems will react to the effects of gravity with little change in blood pressure or heart rate and thus maintain what Dr. Cannon called "homeostasis." Crampton was one of the first to utilize this phenomenon in his "blood ptosis" test (34, 35).

The Crampton test and several of the other earlier tests embodied the measurement of circulatory reactions to a change in posture (34, 35, 77, 81, 108, 127). While such a test differentiates sick people who have been confined to a bed from healthy subjects, they have not proved to be useful to the physical educator.

Physiologic response to a standard exercise

When an automobile or airplane motor is evaluated it is usually tested under dynamic conditions. Although defects may not be detected when the motor is idling, when revved-up, it is often possible to detect malfunction or roughness in tuning. For a long time this same principle has been applied to the testing of human beings, the hypothesis being that a mild or moderate exercise stress will distinguish finer gradations in circulatory-respiratory fitness than is possible under resting conditions. In some of the earlier tests by Meylan (81), Foster (47), Barringer (15–17), Schneider (108, 109), and McCurdy (177), heart rate and/or blood pressure changes were studied following exercise. However, in these early tests the exercise was not well standardized and was so mild as to differentiate only those subjects who were at opposite ends of the distribution. The tests have not stood up well under critical investigation using modern statistical methods.

Estimation of maximal oxygen uptake

As noted earlier in this chapter, maximal oxygen uptake (i.e., the maximal rate at which oxygen can be taken in from the air and delivered and utilized in the tissues) is perhaps the most fundamental criterion against which other tests are compared. However, this is not the only criterion for judging the validity of a circulatory-respiratory fitness test.

Maximal oxygen uptake is being studied in children and adults in many laboratories throughout the world. It is often expressed in liters of oxygen per minute. However, since a large person will generally have a large maximal oxygen uptake, the value is usually divided by body weight so that people of various sizes may be compared. This value is then expressed in milliliters per minute per kilogram body weight (ml/min/kg). The measurement of maximal oxygen uptake requires the subject to work to exhaustion, usually on a motor-driven treadmill, a stationary bicycle (i.e., bicycle ergometer) or by bench-stepping. Expensive equipment and considerable time and training of the technician is required. Since the measurement of maximal oxygen uptake is not practical in school and recreation programs, the search for a simple, valid method of estimating this capacity in individuals of various ages and capacities has been under way for a long time. In order for the student to appreciate some of the approaches and problems of developing a simple test, some basic physiological relationships will be discussed.

The circulatory and respiratory responses (heart rate, ventilation, blood pressure, etc.) to exercise of various intensities and durations have been studied by many investigators. The strenuousness or intensity of an exercise (in other words, the oxygen requirement or oxygen uptake) is closely correlated with the heart rate in any one individual. This is illustrated in the middle panel of Figure 6–1 which contains unpublished data on one subject while he walked at 3 miles per hour on a motor-driven treadmill. The angle of the

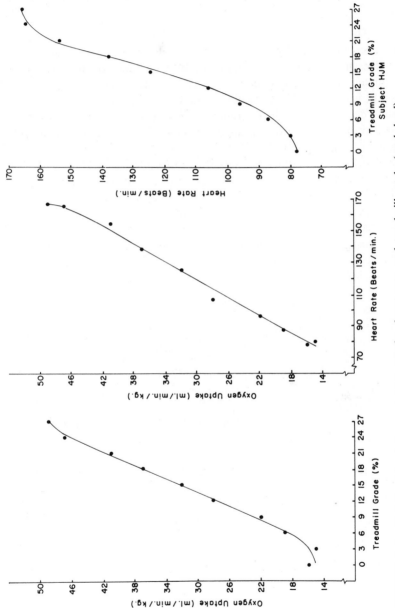

FIGURE 6–1. Relationships between oxygen uptake, heart rate, and treadmill grade (work load) in one subject.

treadmill was increased 3% every 3 minutes, thereby increasing the strenuousness of the exercise (87). It is clear from the figure that oxygen uptake and heart rate are closely related.* Since this is generally true for any one individual on a given day, there have been a number of schemes for extrapolating to an estimated maximal heart rate from the *submaximal* heart rate-oxygen uptake points.

The procedure just described is an alternative to the possibly hazardous practice of exercising middle-aged and old men and women to exhaustion. It does not satisfy the needs of the physical educator, however, because the equipment and skill to measure oxygen uptake, even at submaximal work loads, is rarely available to him. Many investigators have recognized this and have devised methods of estimating maximal oxygen uptake from heart rate and exercise load, two parameters which are fairly easy to measure. Let us examine this approach.

Figure 6–2 shows the oxygen uptakes for 8 men, age 35, walking at various treadmill grades. † Let us suppose that it was possible to exercise these men to exhaustion at gradually increasing work loads but it was not possible to measure oxygen uptake. Since we actually measured the oxygen uptake and heart rates of these men at various work loads, Figure 6–2 could be constructed. This information would not usually be available but data of this kind are in the literature, and if we make the assumption that the best-fitting line (as in Figure 6–2) represents the average for all men, age 35, we could use Figure 6–2 or other published data. In the second column of Table 6–1 is shown the maximal treadmill grade reached by each of the 8 men. Using Figure 6–2, the maximal grade is found on the abscissa (horizontal axis) and the corresponding *estimated* maximal oxygen uptake is read on the ordinate (vertical axis) from the fitted line. These estimated values are given in Table 6–1 with the measured maximal oxygen uptake. The average error in estimating maximal oxygen uptake from work load alone was 3.0 ml/min/kg. (Table 6–1.)

Now suppose it were considered unwise to exercise these men to exhaustion. If the director of the fitness program is not able to measure oxygen uptake but can exercise the men at a gradually increasing load while recording heart rate, up to a reasonable rate (for example, 150 beats per minute), it is still possible to obtain an estimate of each person's $\dot{V}o_2$ max. This is done by plotting the heart rate against work load up to a heart rate of 150 and then extending the fitted line (that is, extrapolating), to a heart rate of 185, the average maximum heart rate reached by men of this age working to exhaustion. Figure 6–3 contains an illustration for one subject. The work load corresponding to a heart rate of 185 from Figure 6–3 for this subject

---

*In Figure 6–1, when the subject is close to maximal work, the oxygen can be seen to increase slightly with little or no increase in heart rate, resulting in a departure from linearity. This is not uncommon when exhaustion is approached.

†These were the first 8 men, age 35, tested on the treadmill in the Tecumseh Community Health Study under Research Grant No. CD00246, National Institutes of Health, U.S. Public Health Service, H. J. Montoye, Principal Investigator.

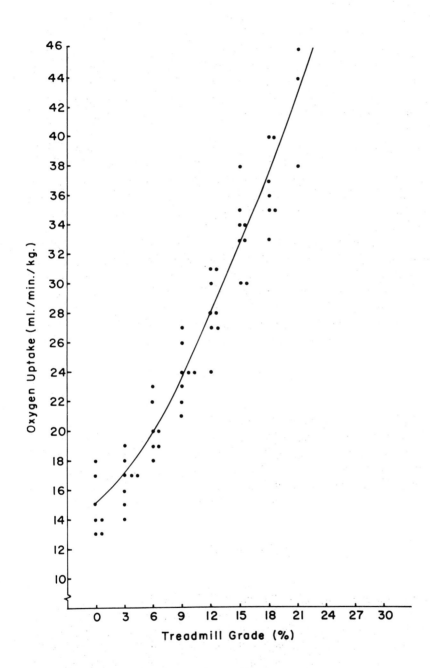

FIGURE 6–2.   Relationship of oxygen uptake and treadmill
grade (work load) in 8 35-year-old men.   Unpublished
data collected under grant HE-12755, National Institutes of
Health, USPHS, H. J. Montoye, principal investigator.

TABLE 6–1

Maximal Oxygen Uptake in Ml/Min/Kg in 8 Men,
Age 35, Measured Directly and Estimated
from Measured Maximal Work Load

Subject Number	Maximal Treadmill Grade %	Estimated Max. O_2	Measured Max. O_2	Difference
2560	18	37.4	34.9	2.5
4507	21	43.0	38.1	4.9
6103	15	32.8	29.8	3.0
3136	18	37.4	32.5	4.9
109	18	37.4	36.2	1.2
6294	21	43.0	43.8	−0.8
3294	15	32.8	36.8	−4.0
4560	21	43.0	45.8	−2.8
Mean|Difference|				3.0

TABLE 6–2

Maximal Oxygen Uptake in Ml/Min/Kg in 8 Men,
Age 35, Measured Directly and Estimated from
Submaximal Heart Rates and Work Loads

Subject Number	Measured Max. O_2	Estimated Max. O_2	Difference
2560	34.9	31.2	−3.7
4507	38.1	46.5	8.4
6103	29.8	33.3	3.5
3136	32.5	46.5	14.0
109	36.2	41.9	5.7
6294	43.8	40.0	−3.8
3294	36.8	41.0	4.2
4560	45.8	42.5	−3.3
Mean|Difference|			5.8

(21%), is used to enter Figure 6–2 and, as before, the maximal oxygen uptake is estimated (in this subject, 43.3 ml/min/kg). This was done for the 8 subjects and the resulting estimates are compared to the measured maximal oxygen uptake in Table 6–2. The average error is now 5.8 ml/min/kg.

These results are presented here for illustration only. Obviously if one repeated the test a number of times on each subject and averaged the results, somewhat better estimates would be obtained. If Figure 6–2 were based on more subjects and if finer graduations in work load were used, further improvement would result. However, it is clear that, in order to simplify the testing, more assumptions are involved, and poorer estimates of $\dot{V}o_2$ max. results. In fact, from Table 6–2 it is obvious that only crude estimates of

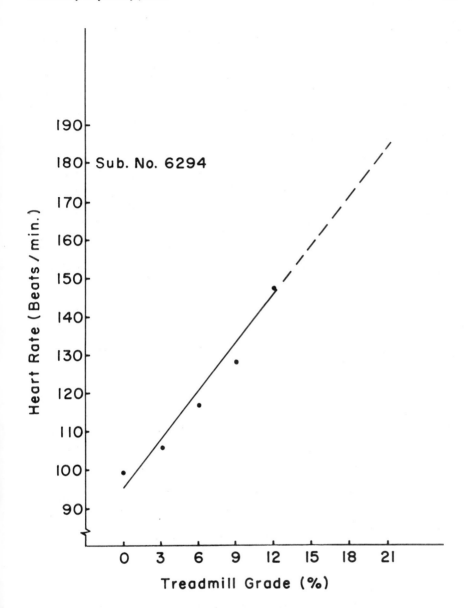

FIGURE 6–3. Relationship of heart rate and treadmill grade (work load) up to a heart rate of 150 and extrapolated to a heart rate of 185. One 35-year-old man. Unpublished data collected under grant HE-12755, National Institutes of Health, USPHS, H. J. Montoye, principal investigator.

maximal oxygen uptake can be made from submaximal heart rate and work load alone. This is not surprising considering (a) the many factors which can affect the heart rate without affecting oxygen uptake, (b) the assumption that efficiency is the same for everyone (Figure 6–2), (c) the assumption that all men this age reach the same maximal heart rate, and (d) the relationship between work load and heart rate is assumed to be linear. Some of the problems can be seen in Figure 6–4 which contains data from four identical treadmill tests on the same subject. From the left side of this figure, it is clear that the oxygen uptake at any particular work load is fairly reproducible (i.e., reliable). Heart rate (right side of Figure 6–4) varies considerably; some days the heart rate is consistently higher or lower for any particular work load or oxygen uptake.

The measurement of heart rate *during* exercise under field conditions is not as convenient or as accurate as measuring the heart rate after the exercise is terminated. It is well known that the heart rate taken soon after exercise is closely correlated with the heart rate during the last moments of exercise. The Harvard Step Test, the most popular test in which post-exercise heart rate is employed, will be discussed in detail below. In this test, as in others of a similar nature, the exercise for almost all subjects is standardized and submaximal; hence, the more fit person is expected to have lower exercise and post-exercise heart rates.

The Harvard step test

Early development

The so-called Harvard Step Test evolved as a result of the basic work by Dr. David B. Dill and his colleagues at the Harvard Fatigue Laboratory.

Some of the Fatigue Laboratory workers developed an index based on running on the treadmill at 7 miles per hour, up an 8.6% grade for 5 minutes (or less if the subject was not able to finish). The index was calculated as follows:

$$\text{Index} = \frac{(\text{Duration of exercise up to 5 minutes, in seconds}) \times 100}{2 \times \text{sum of pulse counts from } 1\text{–}1\ \frac{1}{2},\ 2\text{–}2\ \frac{1}{2},\ \text{and } 4\text{–}4\ \frac{1}{2} \text{ minutes after exercise}}$$

Several other types of exercises were used instead of the treadmill run including: pulling a "stoneboat" loaded by one-third of subject's body weight, rowing against heavy resistance, and riding a bicycle ergometer against a load proportional to body weight. Data were presented to show that athletes and others trained for hard work had a high index. Also it was shown that the index increases when relatively sedentary subjects embark on a conditioning program or even do manual work (52–56).

Because treadmills and even bicycle ergometers are not practical in many instances, Brouha and his colleagues from the Fatigue Laboratory utilized the same principles and almost the same scoring system but substituted stepping up onto a bench. This test has come to be known as the Harvard Step

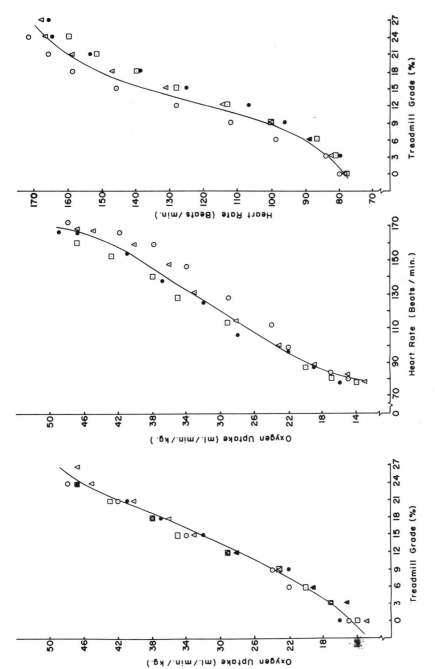

FIGURE 6–4. Relationships between oxygen uptake, heart rate, and treadmill grade (work load) in one subject repeated four times with at least a week between tests. ● first test, □ second test, △ third test, ● fourth test. Unpublished data collected under grant HE-12755, National Institutes of Health, USPHS, H. J. Montoye, principal investigator.

101

Test (23, 25). The Five-Minute Test is equivalent to walking up and down about thirty flights of stairs.

In the administration of the test to males, the subject

1. Steps up onto the 20-inch bench with the left foot.
2. Steps up onto the bench with the right foot. He should now be standing on the bench with legs straight.
3. Steps down to the floor with the left foot.
4. Steps down to the floor with the right foot.

The exercise is repeated at the rate of 30 four-count routines per minute for 5 minutes. At the end of the 5 minutes the subject sits down. If the subject cannot continue for the full 5 minutes he is free to stop at any time. His pulse is counted for 30 seconds for three periods of time after the termination of exercise, namely 1–1 ½, 2–2 ½, and 3–3 ½ minutes. This information is recorded along with the duration, in seconds, that the subject exercised. In most instances, the duration will be 300 seconds, as the majority of young men will be able to finish the 5 minutes of prescribed stepping. The pulse counts are substituted in the formula above except that the 3–3 ½ minute pulse count replaces the 4–4 ½ pulse count.

After further work on the treadmill and bicycle ergometer, the height of the bench was changed to 18 inches and duration to a maximum of 4 minutes for young women (29, 58) and young boys (whose surface area is less than 1.85 square meters) (49, 50). For girls, ages 12–18, the bench height recommended was 16 inches and the duration 4 minutes (51). Later the test was further modified for boys and girls 8–11 years, by reducing the bench height to 14 inches and exercise duration to 3 minutes. For children under 8 years, the bench was also 14 inches high but the duration was changed to 2 minutes (24). Recently, it was demonstrated that scores for women using a 17-inch bench are comparable to a 20-inch bench for men (118). Standards for the original test with young men and for most of the various modified versions were presented in the form of score ranges for categories designated as very poor, poor, average, good, or superior.

In summary, the early validation of the test rests on (a) the intercorrelation of performance, lactic acid accumulation, and heart rate on a submaximal work test, (b) a comparison of individuals in obviously different states of fitness or training; the athletes scoring high and the relatively inactive, poorly conditioned subjects scoring low, and (c) the increase in the index which follows a training program.

Further studies of the step test

Reproducibility. The reproducibility of heart rates taken after the step test will be affected by errors in counting heart beats, by a change in physical condition of the subject from one trial to the next and by differences in the environment or other aspects of the test conditions. Apparently when time is taken to train individuals to measure the pulse rate, accurate and reproducible results may be obtained. Thus, when the recorded heart rate (from an electrocardiogram) is compared with pulse rate recorded by palpation of the carotid artery in the neck, an r of 0.974 was obtained (117). The assistants in this study were, for the most part, physical education majors. In another study, very high correlation coefficients (0.992 to 0.995) were obtained when post-exercise pulse rates, as recorded by fairly inexperienced assistants, were compared (102).

When the entire step test is repeated a second time within a week or two with the same subjects, the reproducibility is not quite as good but is still acceptable. Coefficients of reliability ranging from 0.73 to 0.94 with all but one above 0.82 have been reported (40, 64, 70, 80, 98, 100, 117).

Effect of body build. Although earlier reports suggested a slightly different bench height for extremes in body surface area among children and young adults (49–51), this appears to be an unnecessary refinement, at least for young subjects. In various populations of children and young adults there is almost no correlation of the step test score with height, weight, surface area, or lower extremity length (21, 22, 27, 36, 61, 63, 67, 68, 80–82, 86, 104, 111, 119). The obese subject generally does poorly (67, 119) but in most instances this is due to poor fitness in this group and the additional work imposed by the extra fat tissue. Even among older adults where the range in fatness is greater, no clear-cut evidence has been presented indicating a need to correct for body weight.

Correlation with work capacity. In general, maximum work capacity or endurance performance is not highly correlated with the heart rate response in the step test (18, 21, 32, 38, 39, 40, 62, 64, 73, 86, 100, 110, 122). From the step test heart rate, it is obviously not possible to predict with much accuracy on an individual basis who will perform well or poorly on a maximum work test.

Step test and maximal oxygen uptake. Several reports have appeared during the last few years on the relation of maximal oxygen uptake to the step test. These results are summarized in Table 6–3. Even allowing for laboratory error in determining maximal oxygen uptake and heart rate, it is clear that the step test score does not give a very precise measurement of maximal oxygen uptake in young men. After the discussion in the section "Estimation of Maximal Oxygen Uptake" above, this should come as no surprise.

Effects of training. Although one cannot predict work capacity with much precision from the heart rate response to the step test, evidence is quite clear that physical training lowers the post-exercise heart rate (i.e., raises the Harvard Step Test Score). This was demonstrated in young men some years ago by Dr. Brouha and colleagues (25, 132). These results have been confirmed a number of times in young men (5, 22, 29, 57, 80, 81, 86, 99, 101,

TABLE 6–3
Relationship of Maximal Oxygen Uptake
to Step Test Heart Rate Response

Subjects	Correlation Coefficient	Reference
96 men, age 23–62	.41	58, 103
96 men, age 23–62 (corr. for body size)	−.43*	58, 103
100 young men	−.35**	40
24 young men (mean age = 23.4)	.63–.65	54
16 young men (age 20–26)	.77	42
24 young men, before training	.64	57
23 young men, after training	.44	57
73 young men	.39	44
41 college women	−.75*	73, 74

*Modified test procedure. Score also modified to result in negative correlation coefficient.
**Pulse count was used rather than original score, hence the negative correlation coefficient.

109, 118, 126), in middle-aged men (39, 97, 114) and in old men (19). In fact, the evidence indicates that heart rate following a standard exercise is more sensitive to a training program than maximal oxygen uptake.

Comparison of groups. When young male athletes are compared to non-athletic groups, the post-exercise heart rate is lower and hence the Harvard Step Test Score is higher in the athletes (25, 28, 63, 87, 120, 122, 123). The same results are true in girls and young women (28, 117). Male physical educators score higher than other students (78, 111) as do women majors (68, 78). Boys who are physically active have significantly higher scores than do boys who lead a more sedentary life (107). Men whose occupations require more physical effort score higher (5, 126) as do older men who have a special interest in sports (48).

Modifications of the Harvard step test. Because the sum of the three heart rates during recovery following the Harvard Step Test is almost perfectly correlated with the heart rate taken 1–1½ minutes after the test (28, 31, 57, 65, 66, 86, 123), it is quite wasteful to take the last two counts. Because of the high correlation between the three post-exercise pulse counts, the classic Harvard Step Test formula

$$\frac{\text{Duration of Exercise in Sec} \times 100}{5.5 \times \text{sum of three recovery pulse counts}}$$

has been modified using only the 1–1½ post-exercise count, thus:

$$\text{Score} = \frac{\text{Duration of Exercise in Sec} \times 100}{5.5 \times 1\text{–}1\frac{1}{2} \text{ min pulse count}}$$

This version apparently is as valid as the original formula and shortens the time required for the test (26). The height of the bench, rate of stepping, and duration of exercise may be varied in most populations to alter the intensity of the exercise and hence, the heart rate response. McArdle and others (75) proposed a bench height of 16¼ inches, 22 steps per minute for 3 minutes for college women. This is less strenuous than the original test proposed for college-age women. Standards based on 300 college women have been reported (76).

A panel of members of the Czechoslovakian Society of Sports Medicine (27) recommended a bench height of 51 centimeters (20 inches) for men, 45 centimeters (18 inches) for women, and 30 centimeters (12 inches) for children; not much different from the recommendations of the original Harvard Fatigue Laboratory group.

One of the problems with the Harvard Step Test and later revisions results from the fact that some subjects are unable to complete the stepping. Reducing the step height, rate of stepping, or duration of stepping so that all may complete the test reduces the validity of the test. In the original Harvard Step Test, duration of stepping in seconds appeared in the numerator of the formula so that if the subject was not able to finish the stepping his score was reduced accordingly. However, the score in this case reflects almost entirely the duration of stepping whereas in those who complete the test, the score is dependent on the heart rate response to the exercise (100). Motivation can thus influence the results of the test. Carver and Winsmann (26) have proposed a modified rapid form of the Harvard Step Test for men which appears to adjust for duration of stepping and still reflects heart rate response to exercise in all subjects. It appears to be as valid or more valid than the original Harvard Step Test. The suggested formula is as follows:

$$\text{Score} = \frac{\text{Duration of Exercise in Sec} \times 100}{5.5 \times 1\text{–}1\tfrac{1}{2} \text{ min pulse ct.}}$$
$$+ .22 \ (300 \ \text{Duration of Ex. in Sec})$$

Other factors affecting heart rate. It is common knowledge that the emotions have a very marked effect on resting heart rate. It is also known that the heart rate will increase sometimes by as much as 100% in anticipation of exercise. This will likely affect the heart rate during and after the step test. However, it is believed that the more strenuous the exercise, the less will be the effect of emotions on heart rate, but more work needs to be done on this point. In administering the step test, effort should be made to reduce the influence of emotional factors by familiarizing the subject with the test (repeated testing) and by testing when the influence of emotional factors can be expected to be minimal.

Increased circulation is one method the body has for dissipating heat. Therefore, it is not surprising that the heart rate is higher for the same amount of work done in high ambient temperatures and/or high humidity. In order to better standardize conditions, the step test should not be given when the ambient temperature is more than about 75–80 degrees F, particularly if the humidity is also high.

Eating a large meal raises the heart rate during work (71, 125), but how much influence this factor has on the step test has not been determined. Dehydration is reported to raise the exercise heart rate (8) but probably the variations usually encountered in normal subjects do not affect the step test score to a significant degree.   There is evidence that fatigue raises the heart rate for the same amount of work (71).

Certain diseases affect the resting heart rate (20) and, presumably, the exercise heart rate as well.   Within the normal range among individuals of the same sex, blood hemoglobin concentration apparently is not related to exercise heart rate (106) or the step test score (36) but, as one might expect, persons with anemia have poor circulatory capacity for strenuous work (121) and poor scores on the Harvard Step Test (29).   According to one report (111), women scored as well during menstruation as did women who were in other phases of the menstrual cycle.

The heart rate response to a standard work load on a bicycle ergometer, similar in principle to the Harvard Step Test, has also been studied.   The results (32) indicate that the heart rates were not closely related to running endurance ($r = 0.54$).   In one study the submaximal exercise heart rates were, for the most part, unrelated to maximal oxygen uptake in young girls (7–13 years) and in adults the correlations were significant but not very high; $r = -0.52$ for 23 males and -0.70 for 20 females (33).   Similarly, the heart rate response to a standard walk on the treadmill was not closely correlated ($r = -0.56$) to the time of an all-out run on the treadmill (177) or to maximal oxygen uptake ($r = -0.59$).   These results on the bicycle ergometer or treadmill are not much different than Harvard Step Test results.

Multi-staged work tests

Tests in which the work load is gradually increased and the subject's physiologic response (heart rate, ventilation, blood pressure, etc.) is monitored are frequently referred to as multistaged work tests.   Data obtained in a treadmill test of this kind were discussed in the first part of this chapter.   As also pointed out earlier, graduated work loads may be obtained by means of a treadmill in which the belt speed and/or grade is increased or by means of a stationary bicycle in which the peddling rate and/or resistance is increased.   Treadmills are generally too expensive for use in school programs but a relatively inexpensive light-weight bicycle such as that devised by W. von Dobeln (129) and modified slightly by Åstrand (9) is available.   In the case of a bicycle ergometer, pedal and handlebar adjustments may be necessary for some subjects.

Another technique is to have the subject step for a period of time on a low step and move to higher steps at regular intervals.   Nagle and colleagues (93) have described a step which may be raised as the subject is being tested. Rodahl and coworkers also described an inexpensive adjustable bench (105). However, two disadvantages are apparent when a variable step test is employed: (1) as the step becomes fairly high there is a danger of tripping and consequent injury, and (2) localized fatigue and soreness in the legs frequently occurs, especially among unconditioned people.

Several methods of utilizing pulse rates during multistaged work tests have been proposed but it remains to be seen whether any of them are more valid for studying young healthy adults than the traditional Harvard Step Test. In older adults, however, from the standpoint of safety, a multistaged test in which heart rate and, if possible, other physiological parameters are monitored is essential. A fixed task, such as the Harvard Step Test, even when the bench is low, will be too strenuous for some subjects but will understress others.

The most popular multistaged tests in which heart rate is recorded will be described briefly even though their value and feasibility for mass testing remains to be demonstrated.

Amplitude-Puls-Frequenz (APF)

The APF reported by Lehmann and Michaelis in 1941 was probably the first of the multistaged tests (69). It is a complicated test in that the load increments are small and frequent. The original validation of the test rests primarily on a comparison with subjective fitness ranking of children by their teacher. It has since been shown to be of little value in estimating maximal oxygen uptake (61, 105).

PWC$_{170}$

The bicycle ergometer has been a more popular testing instrument in Europe than in the United States. A few years after the APF test was reported, a series of papers by Wahlund (130, 131) Lundgren (71) and Sjostrand (114) appeared describing another bicycle ergometer test with modifications. In these tests (a) the work is continuous, (b) 4–10 minutes are allowed at each load for a steady state to be reached, and (c) heart rate and/or a change in heart rate and in some cases respiratory rate were observed during the test. The work load one can maintain up to a heart rate of 170 was considered to reflect the work capacity of the subject. As Sjostrand has said, ". . . on other grounds one might as well choose pulse 160 or 150 or extrapolate to an hypothetical maximal pulse rate. Nothing more is gained with this even if the value is expressed as maximal oxygen uptake instead of work at pulse rate 185 or 190, the preferred pulse rate." (115)

Since a bicycle ergometer is used, and the subject's weight is partially supported during the test, PWC$_{170}$ is correlated with body size (133). Therefore, a correction of some kind is necessary, particularly among children. Dr. Forest Adams and his colleagues at the University of California, Los Angeles, have found the bicycle ergometer test useful in measuring the work capacity of normal children and those with disabilities (1, 2, 3, 45). The reliability of the test has not been studied in subjects of both sexes and various ages. In young men, the test gives similar results when the subjects are retested on a separate day within a week. The mean difference in work achieved at a heart rate of 170 was 4.9%.

PWC$_{170}$ has been compared to maximal work in exhaustive exercise. The relationship of PWC$_{170}$ with maximum endurance performance appears to be a little better than the relationship between the Harvard Step Test score and endurance (Table 3–3).

Results on the PWC$_{170}$ have also been used to estimate maximal oxygen uptake. Correlation coefficients between PWC$_{170}$ and maximal oxygen uptake in 16 young men ranged from 0.57 to 0.88 depending on how the PWC$_{170}$ was corrected for body size (44). In the same study, the Harvard Step Test correlated 0.77.

The coefficients of correlation in a small sample of 10- and 11-year-old girls and boys between PWC$_{170}$ and $\dot{V}o_2$ max. were 0.87* and 0.84* respectively, with both measures corrected for body size. Obviously the relationship between PWC$_{170}$ and maximal oxygen uptake needs to be studied further but these preliminary relationships are not much different from the correlation of maximal oxygen uptake with the Harvard Step Test.

Balke test

In 1952 (11) and in subsequent articles (12, 13, 94, 96, 97, 132), a multi-staged treadmill test is described by Dr. Bruno Balke and colleagues. This test is very similar to the PWC$_{170}$ test except that a treadmill is used. The test begins with the subject walking on the horizontal treadmill at approximately 3.5 miles per hour.† At the end of one minute the slope of the treadmill is increased to 1% of the belt travel. The slope is thereafter increased 1% each minute. The test is terminated among normal subjects at a heart rate of 180 or, in a few cases when the subject appeared to approach exhaustion, before reaching a heart rate of 180. The criteria of physical performance were the duration of the test in minutes and the work done (kg/min, disregarding the energy cost of horizontal walking). Usually blood pressure as well as heart rate are recorded continually or measured manually every minute. In laboratory applications, more elaborate physiological parameters may be monitored, such as oxygen uptake, electrocardiogram, etc. The test has the obvious advantage of safety when compared with a single work load test, particularly with older subjects, in that the heart rate (and perhaps other parameters) are monitored as the load is increased. This avoids, in most cases, the overstressing of some individuals and understressing others. We have changed the test slightly and tested about 1400 males and females, age

---

*Calculations by the present author from data in the original article (37).

†This is the way the test is usually administered to normal subjects but slightly different belt speeds and variations in increases in angle during the first few minutes have been reported by the authors.

10–69, with very satisfactory results (89). The test also has been modified for particular kinds of subjects (4, 12, 13, 14, 95, 97).

Nagle, Balke, and Naughton have also described a multistaged step test in which the procedures are roughly the same as in the treadmill test but a step is gradually raised to increase the work load (4, 93). One such test proposed by this group (93), requires the subject to rest quietly in a chair for a period of 10 to 20 minutes. This is followed by brief exposure to the test in which the subject steps for 3 minutes at 33 mounts per minute on a bench 4.5 centimeters in height. These four-count mounts are executed in the same way as the Harvard Step Test. It is useful to use a metronome set at 132 beats per minute or a tape recording in which instructions to the subject and the metronome cadence have been pre-recorded. After a 2-minute rest period, the test itself begins. The subject steps on and off of a box or platform 4.5 centimeters high at a rate of 33 mounts per minute. After each 2-minute period the stepping height is increased 4.5 centimeters without any interruption of the stepping rate. In this way the work may be increased gradually from a very light load to a very rigorous one.

Heart rates may be taken manually during the last 30 seconds at each bench height. This is not as easy to do as when the subject is riding a bicycle but with a little practice, accurate results can be obtained. The test can be terminated at a heart rate of 160 and the heart rate at each bench height plotted against bench height and the line extrapolated to some estimated maximal heart rate. However, it is just as logical to score the subject on the bench height reached at a heart rate of 160. The more fit subject would achieve a higher bench height by the time his heart rate reaches 160. The test, scored in this way, is almost identical to the PWC_{170}. However, there are two distinct advantages to this progressive step test, (a) the equipment needed may be constructed very easily and cheaply and (b) more importantly, no correction is needed for body size.

The author described abbreviated step tests and also modifications for subjects with disabilities (4).

Åstrand test

The test proposed by Dr. Per-Olaf Åstrand and Irma Astrand of the Kunglia Gymnastika, Central Institute, Stockholm, Sweden, is not necessarily a multistaged test. However, like the other tests discussed in this section, it is based on the assumption that work intensity within certain limits determines the rate of oxygen uptake and the corresponding heart rate at which the subject performs the task. Furthermore, it is assumed that not only are these three factors (work intensity, oxygen uptake, and heart rate) linearly related in young healthy subjects, but the rates of increase in heart rate and oxygen uptake for a given increase in work intensity is considered to be about the same for various people. Further, variation in mechanical efficiency within a given age group is assumed to be insignificant. In administering the test, reasonably standard conditions should prevail; that is, temperature and humidity within a comfortable range; no unusual emotional stimulation, no large meal just preceding the test, no undue fatigue, no smoking for at least 30 minutes before the test, and no strenuous activity preceding the test. The intensity of the work in this test should be such as to elicit a heart rate in a steady state of between 125 and 170. To obtain this, a subject is to work from 5 to 6 minutes at a specific load during which time he should have reached a steady state. Work may be done on a bicycle ergometer, treadmill, or by stepping up and down on a bench. Nomograms and tables (7, 9, 11) are available to extrapolate from either the submaximal heart rate and corresponding oxygen uptake or the submaximal heart rate and work load to estimate the maximal oxygen uptake. Since maximal heart rate decreases with age, correction factors are provided for subjects 30 years of age and older. Also, if the step test is used as the work task, a correction factor for body weight is provided. The test has been modified for subjects who are not able to use their legs (6).

If the proper load (that is, intensity) is selected to start the test, it is not necessary to continue the test beyond the one work level. However, if the work is not sufficiently strenuous, the load on the bicycle or treadmill may be increased until the required pulse rate (125 to 170) is reached. In these instances, the task becomes a multistaged test but only because the load is insufficient at the start. The results using this procedure compared to measured maximal oxygen uptake are shown in Table 6–4. The coefficients in Table 6–4 are about of the same order as those for the Harvard Step Test (Table 6–3).

Margaria nomogram

Dr. Margaria and his colleagues (74) at the Institute of Physiology, University of Milan, have proposed a test similar to Åstrands'. The subject steps up

TABLE 6–4

*Maximal Oxygen Uptake Measured Directly Compared to
That Estimated by the Åstrand Nomogram
Using Heart Rate and Work Load*

Subjects	Correlation Coefficient	Reference
76 women, mean age 33.6	.65	7
129 men, mean age 44.3	.72	7
28 policemen, age 20–30	.47	105
24 young men, mean age 23.4	.63–.77	56
25 high school boys	.43–.65	72
23 high school girls	.33–.51	72
16 men, age 20–26	.522	44
10 sedentary subjects	.872	112

and down on a bench 40 centimeters high at the rate of 15 and 25 times per minute. The heart rates are measured at the 4th and 5th minute at each exercise. These heart rates are entered in a nomogram (which has a correction for age) and the maximal oxygen uptake in ml/min/kg. body weight is estimated. Since the test was proposed so recently there have been few reports in which the validity was investigated. Davies (43) concluded that neither the Åstrand nor Margaria nomograms estimate maximal oxygen uptake very precisely. In 24 young men, Shephard and others (113) reported slightly better predictions using the Margaria nomogram compared to that of the Åstrands if the subject exercised on a bicycle or step test but poorer if the subject walked on a treadmill. Obviously, more research needs to be done but the Margaria test is among the simplest multistaged tests to administer.

Recommendations

School children and college students

The Harvard Step Test or a modification is recommended for use in the general classes of normal children (approximately age 8–22). This is the simplest of the proposed tests since heart rate is taken after, not during, the exercise and the only equipment needed is a stop watch and a bench of the prescribed height. None of the tests discussed in this chapter in which only heart rate and work load are measured give precise estimates of maximal oxygen uptake—not as good, for example, as a 12-minute run (Chapter 5). However, the relationship between maximal oxygen uptake and the Harvard Step Test is about as good as between that and any of the other practical tests. There is also ample evidence that the Harvard Step Test is sensitive to a training program, at least in young men and women.

It is recommended that (a) the test be given on several different occasions so the subjects become accustomed to the test and emotional effects are minimized, (b) the test not be given when the ambient temperature is above about 75–80 degrees F, (c) the test be administered at approximately the same time of day for any one subject, and (d) the test not be given following strenuous or moderately strenuous activity, following recent illness, following a meal, or when the subject is known to be fatigued or under emotional stress.

Instead of calculating the Harvard Step Test Score it is only necessary to count the pulse beats from 30 seconds to 1 minute *after* the exercise. Performance standards based on this 30-second pulse count can be developed, the higher counts reflecting poorer fitness. If a subject cannot complete the stepping, he or she obviously ranks in the lowest percentiles, unless some unusual event such as a severe leg cramp occurs. In the subjects who are not able to complete the test, a pulse rate need not be recorded. It is also not necessary to correct for body size. The table below is a suggested plan for modifying the

TABLE 6–5
Suggested Specifications for the Step Test

Age and Sex Group	Height of Bench (in.)	Rate of Stepping (4-ct. cycles/min)	Maximum Duration (min)
Age 8–10, Boys and Girls	8	24	3
Age 10–12, Boys and Girls	12	24	3
Age 12–14, Boys and Girls	18	24	3
Age 15–22, Girls	18	24	3
Age 15–22, Boys	20	30	5

test for particular age groups. Using this plan only a small percentage of the subjects will not be able to complete the stepping. The average heart rate during the test will exceed 150 in most cases.

Adults, age 22–34

If classes are fairly large, or if the subjects are to test themselves, there is no objection to using a modification of the Harvard Step Test among healthy subjects in this age group. The specifications for girls 15–22 may be used for women and those for boys age 15–22 may be used for men (see Table 6–5).

Whenever time and conditions permit, it is preferable to use a multistaged test. If a treadmill is available, the Balke Test is preferred by this writer with heart rate recorded at each load (i.e., each minute) and score (treadmill grade or time) recorded at a heart rate of 180. If the test is terminated before this heart rate is reached, a line fitted to the heart rate-treadmill grade points and extrapolated to a heart rate of 180 may be used.

If a treadmill is not available, as would generally be the case, a bicycle ergometer may be employed with a pedalling speed of 50 revolutions per minute and the ride starting at zero load. Each minute during a continuous ride the load can be increased by 0.5 kiloponds* until a heart rate of 180 is reached. As with the treadmill test, if the exercise is terminated before the 180 heart rate, one can extrapolate to this heart rate. Heart rates should be taken during the last 30 seconds of each minute (i.e., work load). The score is the load in kp. at a heart rate of 180. This is the PWC_{180}. If this score is to be compared with other subjects of the same age and sex, the score should be divided by body weight.

If a treadmill is not available, the multistage step test described on page 109 may be used. The score is the bench height reached at a heart rate

*One kilopond (abbreviation, kp.) is equal to one kilogram at sea level. On the Monarch bicycle, the load may be increased in a few seconds while the subject continues to ride.

of 160. Stepping at the prescribed rate (33 mounts per minute) when the bench is fairly high is difficult and sometimes results in local leg fatigue; hence, stepping beyond a heart rate of 160 is not recommended.

Adults: age 35 and older

There is a medical risk in testing subjects in this age group. Physical educators should not administer tests of fitness to men or women 35 years of age and older unless they are planned in cooperation with a physician. When tests of fitness are given to people in this age group, a physician should be present.

Final statement

Simple circulatory-respiratory exercise tests discussed in this chapter do not give precise estimates of maximal oxygen uptake and have limited usefulness in comparing one individual with another. They should generally be used only for rough screening when various people are to be compared. However, the test scores are sensitive to changes in condition in a single individual. Therefore, the tests are most useful when the same individual is to be studied at different times, for example, before and after a conditioning (training) program.

REFERENCES

1. Adams, F. H. and E. R. Duffie, "The Physical Working Capacity of Children with Heart Disease." *J. Lancet,* 81:493–496, 1961.

2. Adams, F. H.; L. M. Linde; and H. Miyake, "The Physical Working Capacity of Normal School Children: I. California." *Pediat.,* 28:55–64, 1961.

3. Adams, F. H.; L. M. Linde; and H. Miyake, "The Physical Working Capacity of Normal School Children: II. Swedish City and Country." *Pediat.,* 28:243–257, 1961.

4. "Advanced Exercise Procedures for Evaluation of the Cardiovascular System." Milton, Wis.: The Burdick Corp., p. 17.

5. Anderson, K. L., "Performance and Recovery Pulse Rate Studies in the Norwegian Army." Paper presented at the National Convention, American Association for Health, Physical Education and Recreation, 1954.

6. Asmussen, E. and I. Hemmingsen, "Determination of Maximum Working Capacity at Different Ages in Work with the Legs or with the Arms." *Scand. J. Clin. and Lab. Invest.,* 10:67–71, 1958.

7. Åstrand, I., "Aerobic Work Capacity in Men and Women with Special Reference to Age." *Acta Physiol. Scand.,* 49: 1–92, 1960.

8. Åstrand, P.-O., "Human Physical Fitness with Special Reference to Sex and Age." *Physiol. Rev.* 36:307–335, 1956.

9. Åstrand, P.-O., "Work Tests with a Bicycle Ergometer." Pamphlet published by A. B. Cykelfabriken Monark, Varberg, Sweden.

10. Astrand, P.-O., and I. Rhyming, "A Monogram for Calculation of Aerobic Capacity (Physical Fitness) from Pulse Rate During Submaximal Work." *J. Appl. Physiol.*, 7:218–221, 1954.

11. Balke, B., "Correlation of Static and Physical Endurance. I. A Test of Physical Performance Based on the Cardiovascular and Respiratory Response to Gradually Increased Work." *Air University, USAF School of Aviation Medicine*, Project No. 21-32-004, Report No. 1, April 1952.

12. Balke, B., "Optimale Körperliche Leistungsfähigkeit, Ihre Messung and Veränderung in Folge Arbeitsermüdung." *Internat. Zschr. Angew. Physiol.*, 15: 311–323, 1954.

13. Balke, B.; G. P. Grillo; E. G. Konnecci; and U. C. Luft, "Gas Exchange and Cardiovascular Functions at Rest and in Exercise Under the Effects of Extrinsic and Intrinsic Fatigue Factors. A. Work Capacity After Blood Donation and After Exposure to Prolonged Mild Hypoxia." *Air University, USAF School of Aviation Medicine*, Project No. 21-1201-0014, Report No. 1.

14. Balke, B.; G. P. Grillo; E. G. Konnecci; and U. C. Luft, "Work Capacity After Blood Donation." *J. Appl. Physiol.*, 7:231–238, Nov. 1954.

15. Barringer, T. B., Jr., "Studies of the Heart's Functional Capacity." *Arch. Internal. Med.*, 20:829–839, 1917.

16. Barringer, T. B., Jr., "Studies in the Heart's Functional Capacity as Estimated by the Circulatory Reaction to Graduated Work." *Arch. Internal. Med.*, 17:670–676, 1916.

17. Barringer, T. B., Jr., "The Circulatory Reaction to Graduated Work as a Test of the Heart's Functional Capacity." *Arch. Internal. Med.*, 17:363–381, 1916.

18. Baumgartner, T. A. and M. A. Zuidema, "Factor Analysis of Physical Fitness Tests." *Res. Quart.*, 43:443–450, 1972.

19. Benestad, A. M., "Trainability of Old Men." *Acta Med. Scand.* 178:321–327, 1965.

20. Boas., E. P. and E. F. Goldschmidt, *The Heart Rate.* Springfield, Ill.: Thomas, 1932, pp. 166.

21. Bookwalter, K. W., "A Study of the Brouha Step Test." *Phys. Educator,* 5:55, 1948.

22. Bosco, J. S., J. E. Greenleaf; R. L. Kaye; and E. G. Averkin, "Reduction of Serum Uric Acid in Young Men during Physical Training." *Amer. J. Cardiol.*, 25:46–52, 1970.

23. Brouha, L., "The Step Test: A Simple Method of Measuring Physical Fitness for Muscular Work in Young Men." *Res. Quart.*, 14:31–36, 1943.

24. Brouha, L., and M. V. Ball, *Canadian Red Cross Society's School Meal Study.* Toronto: Univ. of Toronto Press, 1952, pp. 55.

25. Brouha, L.; N. W. Fradd, and B. M. Savage, "Studies in Physical Efficiency of College Students." *Res. Quart.*, 15:221–224, 1944.

26. Carver, R. P. and F. R. Winsmann, "Study of Measurement and Experimental Design Problems Associated with the Step Test." *J. Sports Med. and Phys. Fit.*, 10:104–113, 1970.

27. Chrastek, J., "A Lecture Evening on Step Test in Prague." *J. Sports Med. and Phys. Fitness,* 4:190–191, 1964.

28. Chrastek, J.; I. Stolz; and L. Samek, "On Determination of Physical Fitness by the Step-Up Test." *J. of Sports Med. and Phys. Fitness,* 5:61–66, 1965.

29. Cifuentes, E. and F. E. Viteri, "Physical Fitness, Iron Deficiency and Anemia in Agricultural Laborers of Central America." *Fed. Proc.*, 31:719, 1972.

30. Clarke, L., "A Functional Physical Fitness Test for College Women." *J. of Health and Phys. Educ.*, 14:358–359+, 1943.

31. Cogswell R. C.; C. R. Henderson; and G. H. Berryman, "Effects of Training on Pulse Rate, Blood Pressure and Endurance in Humans, Using Step Test (Harvard), Treadmill and Electrodynamic Brake Bicycle Ergometer." *Am. J. Physiol.*, 146:422–430, 1946.

32. Costill, D. L., "The Relationship Between Selected Physiological Variables and Distance Running Performance." *J. Sports Med. and Phys. Fitness,* 7:61–66, 1967.

33. Cites, J. E.; C. T. M. Davies; D. G. Edholm; and J. M. Tanner, "Factors Re-

lating to the Aerobic Capacity of 46 Healthy British Males and Females, Ages 18 to 28 years." *Proc Royal Soc. Lond.,* 174:91–114, 1969.

34. Crampton, C. Ward, "A Test of Condition: Preliminary Report." *Med. News,* 87:529–535, 1905.

35. Crampton, C. Ward, "Blood Ptosis." *New York Med. J.,* 49:916–918, 1963.

36. Cullumbine, H., "Survey of Physical Fitness in Ceylon." *Lancet,* 2:1067–1070, 1949.

37. Cumming, G. R. and R. Danzinger, "Bicycle Ergometer Studies in Children. II. Correlation of Pulse Rate with Oxygen Consumption." *Pediat.,* 32:202–208, 1963.

38. Cureton, T. K., *Physical Fitness of Champion Athletes.* Urbana: University of Illinois Press, 1951.

39. Cureton, T. K., *Physical Fitness Workbook.* St. Louis: Mosby, 1947.

40. Cureton, et al., "Endurance of Young Men." *Monographs of the Society for Research in Child Development,* Vol. 10, No. 1, Serial No. 40, 1945.

41. Cureton, T. K., and E. E. Phillips, "Physical Fitness Changes in Middle-Aged Men Attributable to Equal Eight-Week Periods of Training, Non-Training and Retraining." *J. Sports Med. and Phys. Fitness,* 4:87–93, 1964.

42. Cureton, T. K., and L. F. Sterling, "Interpretation of the Cardiovascular Components Resulting from the Factor Analysis of 104 Test Variables Measured in 100 Normal Young Men." *J. Sports Med. and Phys. Fitness,* 4:1–24, 1964.

43. Davies, C. T. M., "Maximum Oxygen Uptake: Prediction from Cardiac Frequency During Submaximal Exercise." *J. Physiol.,* 189:77–78P, 1967.

44. De Vries, H. A., and C. E. Klafs, "Prediction of Maximal Oxygen Intake from Sub-Maximal Tests." *J. Sports Med. and Phys. Fitness,* 5:207–214, 1965.

45. Duffie, E. R., and F. H. Adams, "The Use of the Working Capacity Test in Evaluation of Children with Congenital Heart Disease." *Pediat.* Supp. Part II, 32: 757–768, 1963.

46. Flandrous, R. and J.-R. Lacour, "L'Aptitude physique chez le Jeune universitaire Francais. Comparison de differents tests avec la consommation maximale d'ozygene." *Schweizerische Zschr. f Sportmedicine,* 14:49–55, 1966.

47. Foster, W. L., "A Test of Physical Efficiency." *Amer. Phys. Educ. Rev.,* 19:632–636, 1914.

48. Frolkis, V. V.; S. F. Golovchenko; S. M. Dukhovichnyi; and S. A. Tamn, "Functional Changes of Circulation and Respiration with Age." *Klinicheskaya Meditsina,* 40:87, 1962. Translation in *Fed. Proc.,* pp. T-1169-T1172, Nov.-Dec. 1962.

49. Gallagher, J. R. and L. Brouha, "Simple Method of Evaluating Fitness in Boys: The Step Test." *Yale J. Biol. and Med.,* 15:769–779, 1943.

50. Gallagher, J. R. and L. Brouha, "A Simple Method of Testing the Physical Fitness of Boys." *Res. Quart.,* 14:23–30, 1943.

51. Gallagher, J. R. and L. Brouha, "A Method of Testing the Physical Fitness of High School Girls." *Revue Canadienne de Biologie,* 2:395–406, 1943.

52. Gallagher, J. R.; C. D. Gallagher; and L. Brouha, "A Practical Bicycle Ergometer Test of Fitness for Adolescents." *Yale J. Biol. and Med.,* 15:679–688, 1943.

53. Gallagher, J. R. and L. Brouha, "Dynamic Physical Fitness in Adolescence." *Yale J. Biol. and Med.,* 15:657–670, 1943.

54. Gallagher, J. R. and L. Brouha, "The Evaluation of Athletic Programs by Means of Fitness Tests." *Yale J. Biol. and Med.,* 15:671–677, 1943.

55. Gallagher, J. R.; C. D. Gallagher; and L. Brouha, "The Evaluation of a 'Body-Building' Program Utilizing a Bicycle Ergometer Test." *Yale J. Biol. and Med.,* 15:689–692, 1943.

56. Glassford, R. G.; G. H. Y. Baycroft; S. W. Sedgwick; and R. B. J. Macnab, "Comparison of Maximal Oxygen Uptake Values Determined by Predicted and Actual Methods." *J. Applied Physiol.,* 20:509–513, 1965.

57. Graybiel, G., and H. West, "The Relationship between Physical Fitness and Success in Training of U.S. Naval Flight Students." *J. of Aviation Med.,* 16:242–249, 1945.

58. Hardy, L.; H. L. Clarke; and L. Brouha, "Testing Physical Fitness in Young Women." *Revue Canadienne de Biologie,* 2:407–415, 1943.

59. Harper, D. D.; C. E. Billings; and D. K. Mathews, "Comparative Effects of Two Physical Conditioning Programs on Cardiovascular Fitness in Man." *Res. Quart.,* 40:293–298, 1969.

60. Hettinger, T.; N. C. Birkhead; S. M. Horvath; B. Issekutz; and K. Rodahl, "Assessment of Physical Work Capacity." *J. Appl. Physiol.,* 16:153–156, 1961.

61. Hodgkins, J. and V. Skubic, "Cardiovascular Efficiency Test Scores for College Women in the United States." *Res. Quart.,* 34:454–461, 1963.

62. Hodgson, P., "A Study of Some Relationships between Performance Tests and Certain Physiological Measures Associated with Maximal and Submaximal Work." *Res. Quart.,* 17:208–224, 1946.

63. Ishika, T., "Aerobic Capacity and External Criteria of Performance." *Canad. Med. Assoc. J.,* 96:746–749, 1967.

64. Karpovich, P. V., "A Comparative Study of the Behnke and the Harvard Step-Up Tests for Physical Fitness." Report 1, Project No. 148, Army Air Forces, School of Aviation Medicine, August 1943.

65. Karpovich, P. V. et al., "Physical Reconditioning After Rheumatic Fever." *J. Amer. Med. Assoc.,* 130:1198–1203, 1946.

66. Karpovich, P. V., M. P. Starr, and R. A. Weiss, "Physical Fitness Tests for Convalescents." *J. Amer. Med. Assoc.,* 126:873–877, 1944.

67. Laubach, L. L., B. L. Hollering, and D. V. Goulding, "Relationships between Two Measures of Cardiovascular Fitness and Selected Body Measurements of College Men." *J. Sports Med. and Phys. Fit.,* 11:222–226, 1971.

68. Leedy, H. E., A. H. Ishmail, W. V. Kessler, and J. E. Christian, "Relationships between Physical Performance Items and Body Composition." *Res. Quart.,* 36:158–163, 1965.

69. Lehman, G. and H. Michaelis, "Die Messung der Körperlichen Leistung-

sffähigkeit." *Arbeitsphysiologie,* 11:376–392, 1941.

70. Liverman, P. D., "Daily Variability of a Three-Minute Work Test." In *Exercise and Fitness,* edited by B. D. Franks. Chicago: The Athletic Institute, 1969.

71. Lundgren, N. P. V., "The Physiological Effects of Time Schedule Work on Lumber Workers." *Acta Medica Scand.,* supp. 13:41, 1–137, 1946.

72. Macnab, R. B.; M. L. Howell; R. W. Norman; R. C. Hyde; and H. J. Green, "The Åstrand Maximal and Submaximal Bicycle Ergometer Test: Validity, Reliability, Intra- and Inter-Individual Differences." Paper presented at 16th Biennial Convention, Canadian Association for Health, Physical Education and Recreation, University of New Brunswick, June 21, 1965.

73. Manahan, J. E., and B. Gutin, "The One-Minute Step Test as a Measure of 600 Yard Run Performance." *Res. Quart.,* 42:173–177, 1971.

74. Margaria, R., "Assessment of Physical Activity in Oxidative and Anaerobic Maximal Exercise." *Fed. Proc.,* 25:1409–1412, 1966.

75. McArdle, W. D.; F. I. Katch; G. S. Pechar; L. Jacobson; and S. Ruck, "Reliability and Interrelationships between Maximal Oxygen Intake, Physical Work Capacity and Step-Test Scores in College Women." *Med. and Sci. in Sports,* 4:182–186, 1972.

76. McArdle, W. D.; G. S. Pechar; F. I. Katch; and J. R. Magel, "Percentile Norms for a Valid Step Test in College Women. *"Res. Quart.,* 44:498–500, 1973.

77. McCurdy, J. H., "Adolescent Changes in Heart Rate and Blood Pressure." *Amer. Phys. Educ. Rev.,* 15:421–432, 1910.

78. McGuinness, W. B. and A. W. Sloan, "Dynamic Fitness for Young Adults and Its Relation to Physical Training and Body Fat." *J. Sports Med. and Phys. Fit.,* 11:179–184, 1971.

79. Metz, K., and J. Alexander, "An Investigation of the Relationship between Maximum Aerobic Work Capacity and Physical Fitness in Twelve- to

Fifteen-Year-Old Boys." *Res. Quart.,* 41:75–81, 1970.

80. Meyers, C. R., "A Study of the Reliability of the Harvard Step Test." *Res. Quart.,* 40:423, 1969.

81. Meylan, G. L., "Twenty-Years Progress in Tests of Efficiency." *Amer. Phys. Educ. Rev.,* 18:442–446, 1913.

82. Michael E. D., "Cardiovascular Responses to Training for Underwater Swimming." *J. Sports Med. and Phys. Fitness,* 3:218–220, 1963.

83. Michael, E. D., Jr., and A. J. Gallon, "Pulse Wave and Blood Pressure Changes Occurring During a Physical Training Program." *Res. Quart.,* 31:43–59, 1960.

84. Montoye, H. J., "An Analysis of Breath-Holding Tests." *Res. Quart.,* 21:322–330, 1950.

85. Montoye, H. J., "Breath-Holding as a Measure of Physical Fitness." *Res. Quart.,* 22:356–376, 1951.

86. Montoye, H. J., "The 'Harvard Step Test' and Work Capacity." *Revue canad. de biol.,* 11:491–499, 1953.

87. Montoye, H. J., "The Prediction of Daily Endurance Performance." *Bulletin, Federatione Internationale Education Physique,* 2:96–100, 1955.

88. Montoye, H. J.; W. D. Collings; and G. C. Stauffer, "Effects of Conditioning on the Ballistocardiogram of College Basketball Players." *J. Appl. Physiol.,* 15:449–543, 1960.

89. Montoye, H. J.; D. A. Cunningham; H. G. Welch; and F. H. Epstein, "Laboratory Methods of Assessing Metabolic Capacity in a Large Epidemiologic Study." *Amer. J. Epidemiology,* 91:38–47, 1970.

90. Montoye, H. J.; W. Mack; and J. Cook, "The Brachial Pulse Wave as a Measure of Cross-Country Running Performance." *Res. Quart.,* 31:174–180, 1960.

91. Montoye, H. J.; P. W. Willis; and D. A. Cunningham, "Heart Rate Response to Submaximal Exercise: Relation to Age and Sex." *J. Gerontology,* 23:127–133, 1968.

92. Montoye, H. J.; P. W. Willis; D. A.

Cunningham; and J. B. Keller, "Heart Rate Response to a Modified Harvard Step Test: Males and Females, Age 10–69." *Res. Quart.,* 40:153–162, 1969.

93. Nagle, F. J.; B. Balke; and J. P. Naughton, "Gradual Step Tests for Assessing Work Capacity." *J. Appl. Physiol.,* 20:745–748, 1965.

94. Naughton, J.; B. Balke; and F. Nagle, "Refinements in Method of Evaluation and Physical Conditioning Before and After Myocardial Infarction." *Amer. J. Cardiol.,* 14:837–843, 1964.

95. Naughton, J.; B. Balke; and A. Poarch, "Modified Work Capacity Studies in Individuals with and without Coronary Artery Disease." *J. Sports Med. and Phys. Fitness,* 4:208–212, 1964.

96. Naughton, J. and F. Nagle, "Peak Oxygen Intake During Physical Fitness Program for Middle-Aged Men." *J. Amer. Med. Assoc.,* 191:899–901, 1965.

97. Naughton, J.; G. Sevelius; and B. Balke, "Physiological Responses of Normal and Pathological Subjects to a Modified Work Capacity Test." *J. Sports Med. and Phys. Fitness,* 3:201–207, 1963.

98. O'Connor, M. E. and T. K. Cureton, "Motor Fitness Tests for High School Girls." *Res. Quart.,* 16:302–314, 1945.

99. O'Donnell, T. V.; E. R. Nye; J. H. Heslop; and J. D. Hunter, "Middle-Aged Men on a Twenty-Week Jogging Programme." *New Zealand Med. J.,* 67:284–287, 1968.

100. Patterson, J. L.; A. Graybiel; H. F. Lenhardt; and M. J. Madsen, "Evaluation and Prediction of Physical Fitness, Utilizing Modified Apparatus of the Harvard Step Test." *Amer. J. Cardiol.,* 14:811–827, 1964.

101. Petroskey, H. M., "A Study of Improvement in Fitness of College Freshmen Women." *Res. Quart.,* 16:257–265, 1945.

102. Phillips, M.; E. Ridder; and H. Yeakel, "Further Data on the Pulse Ratio Test." *Res. Quart.,* 14:425–429, 1943.

103. Rasch, P. J. and W. R. Pierson, "The Effects of Bicycle Riding on Some Physical Fitness Scores and on Flexibility." *J. Assoc. for Physical and Mental Rehab.,* 13:16–17, 1959.

104. Reedy, J. D.; G. L. Saiger; and R. H. Hosler, "Evaluation of the Harvard Step Test with Respect to Factors of Height and Weight." *Internat. Z. Angew. Physiol.*, 17:115–119, 1958.

105. Rodahl, K. and B. Issekutz, Jr., "Physical Performance Capacity of the Older Individual." In *Muscle as a Tissue,* edited by K. Rodahl and S. M. Horvath. New York: McGraw-Hill, 1962, Ch. 15, pp. 272–301.

106. Rowell, L. B.; H. L. Taylor; and Y. Wang, "Limitations to Predictions of Maximal Oxygen Intake." *J. Appl. Physiol.*, 19:919–927, 1964.

107. Ruffer, W. A., "A Study of Extreme Physical Activity Groups of Young Men." *Res. Quart.*, 36:183–196, 1965.

108. Schneider, E. C., "A Cardiovascular Rating as a Measure of Physical Fatigue and Efficiency." *J. Amer. Med. Assos.*, 74:1507–1510, 1920.

109. Schneider, E. C., *The Physiology of Muscular Activity.* Philadelphia: Saunders, 1933.

110. Scott, M. G.; M. Mordy; and M. Wilson, "Validation of Mass-Type Physical Tests with Tests of Work Capacity." *Res. Quart.*, 16:128–138, 1945.

111. Seltzer, Carl C., "Anthropometric Characteristics and Physical Fitness." *Res. Quart.*, 17:10–20, 1946.

112. Shephard, R. J., "Commentary." *Canad. Med. Assoc. J.*, 96:744–745, 1967.

113. Shephard, R. J.; C. Allen; A. J. S. Benade; C. T. M. Davies; P. E. di Prampero; R. Hedman; J. E. Merriman; K. Myhre; and R. Simmons, "Standardization of Submaximal Exercise Test." *Bull. World Health Org.*, 38:765–775, 1968.

114. Sjostrand, T., "Changes in the Respiratory Organs of Workmen at an Ore Smelting Works." *Acta Med. Scand.* Supp. 196:687–699, 1947.

115. Sjostrand, T., "Testing of the Physical Working Capacity: Definition, History and Application." *Forsvarsmedicin,* 3:141–144, 1967.

116. Skinner, J. S.; J. O. Holloszy; and T. K. Cureton, "Effects of a Program of Endurance Exercises on Physical Work." *Amer. J. Cardiol.*, 14:747–752, 1964.

117. Skubic, V. and J. Hodgins, "Cardiovascular Efficiency Test for Girls and Women." *Res. Quart.*, 34:191–198, 1963.

118. Sloan, A. W., "A Modified Harvard Step Test for Women." *J. of Applied Physiology,* 14:985–986, 1959.

119. Sloan, A. W., "Physical Fitness and Body Build of Young Men and Women." *Ergonomics,* 12:25–32, 1969.

120. Sloan, A. W. and E. N. Keen, "Physical Fitness of Oarsmen and Rugby Players Before and After Training." *J. Appl. Physiol.*, 14:635–636, 1959.

121. Sproule, B. J.; J. H. Mitchell; and W. F. Miller, "Cardiopulmonary Physiological Responses to Heavy Exercise in Patients with Anemia." *J. Clin. Invest.*, 39:378–388, 1960.

122. Taddonio, D. A. and P. Karpovich, "The Harvard Step Test as a Measure of Endurance in Running." *Res. Quart.*, 22:381–384, 1951.

123. Taylor, C., "A Maximal Pack Test of Exercise Tolerance." *Res. Quart.*, 15: 291–302, 1944.

124. Taylor, C., "Some Properties of Maximal and Submaximal Exercise with Reference to Physiological Variation and the Measurement of Exercise Tolerance." *Am. J. Physiol.*, 142:200–212, 1944.

125. Taylor, H. L.; Y. Wang; L. Rowell; and E. Blomquist, "The Standardization and Interpretation of Submaximal and Maximal Tests of Working Capacity." *Pediatrics,* Supp., 32:703–722, 1963.

126. Torun, B., and F. Viteri, "Response of Guatemalan Rural Men and Soldiers to Heavy Exercise of Short Duration." *Fed. Proc.*, 30:656, 1971.

127. Turner, A., "The Adjustment of Heart Rate and Arterial Pressure in Healthy Young Women during Prolonged Standing." *Amer. J. Physiol.*, 81:192, 1927.

128. Vladimir, H., "Our Experiences with the Harvard Step Test." *Sportnomedicinske Objave,* 3:29–34, 1955.

129. Von Dobeln, W., "A Simple Bicycle Ergometer." *J. Appl. Physiol.*, 7: 222–224, 1954.

130. Wahlund, H., "Determination of the Physical Working Capacity." *Acta Med. Scand.*, Vol. 132: Supp. 215, pp. 1–78, 1948.

131. Wahlund, H., "Heart-Lung-Funktionsprovning Av Militarfall Med Hjartbesvar." *Nordisk Medicine,* 25:219, 1945.

132. Wells, J.; B. Balke; and D. D. Van Fossan, "Lactic Acid Accumulation During Work. A Suggested Standardization of Work Classification." *J. Appl. Physiol.,* 10:51–55, 1957.

133. Wendelin, H.; P. Heikkinen; and L. Hirvonen, "The Physical Fitness of University Students." *J. Sports Med. and Physical Fitness,* 5:224–232, 1965.

134. Woods, W. L.; L. Brouha; and C. C. Seltzer, *Selection of Officer Candidates.* Cambridge, Mass.: Harvard University Press, 1943.

STUDY QUESTIONS • *Chapter 6*

1. When a physical educator talks about tests of circulatory-respiratory fitness, is he or she referring to whether or not someone has heart disease? Explain.

2. How do "endurance" and circulatory-respiratory tests differ?

3. Explain the following terms:
   a. maximal oxygen uptake
   b. vital capacity
   c. metabolic capacity
   d. ventilation
   e. multistaged tests
   f. dehydration
   g. ergometer
   h. anemia

4. If an all-out endurance run predicts (measures) maximal oxygen uptake better than heart rate response to a submaximal exercise, why is the submaximal test useful?

5. Do trained endurance athletes have different blood pressures than untrained persons of the same age? Explain.

6. The resting heart rate decreases with exercise conditioning. Why, then, is simply resting heart rate not a good test of circulatory-respiratory fitness?

7. Why is vital capacity not recommended as a test of circulatory-respiratory fitness?

8. Why is breath-holding not recommended as a test of circulatory-respiratory fitness?

9. Explain the principle of using a change in posture as a circulatory-respiratory test.

10. What were limitations (criticisms) of the early submaximal exercise tests in which changes in heart rate and blood pressure were measured?

11. How does a high room temperature affect heart rate response to a submaximal work task (load)?

12. Explain how one can estimate maximal oxygen uptake by measuring the maximum work (or grade) a person can reach on the treadmill.

13. If we wish to predict (i.e., estimate) the maximal oxygen uptake of which a man or woman is capable from a series of submaximal work loads and heart rates, how do we go about it? Why are the predictions or estimates of maximal oxygen uptake not more accurate?

14. Why do we often measure heart rate after the submaximal exercise rather than during the exercise? Are the two heart rates closely correlated?

15. Why did the Harvard exercise test use a step rather than a treadmill in the later modifications?

16. Describe the Harvard Step Test.

17. The original Harvard Step Test was devised for college men. How was the test modified for children?

18. Can you give an estimate of the reproducibility of the Harvard Step Test from one day to the next?

19. Can physical education students measure the post-exercise heart rate accurately?

20. Is it necessary to correct for body size in the Harvard Step Test? Why?

21. Is work performance (time on a mile run, work on a bicycle ergometer, etc.) closely related to the score on the Harvard Step Test? Why?

22. Is the correlation coefficient between the Harvard Step Test and maximal oxygen uptake about 0.2, 0.5, or 0.9? Thus, about how much of the variation in maximal oxygen uptake among people is accounted for by variation in the Harvard Step Test score?

23. Summarize the evidence that one is justified in using the Harvard Step Test as a measure of circulatory-respiratory fitness.

24. What factors, other than circulatory-respiratory fitness, affect the Harvard Step Test score?

25. How does dehydration affect the post-exercise heart rate?

26. How would anemia affect the heart rate response to a standard submaximal exercise?

27. What are the relative advantages and disadvantages of the treadmill, variable step, and bicycle ergometer for measuring circulatory-respiratory fitness?

28. Describe the following multistaged tests:
    PWC_{170}
    Balke test
    Åstrand test
    Margaria Nomogram
    How do these tests compare in estimating:
    a. maximal oxygen uptake
    b. work capacity (endurance)

29. What circulatory-respiratory test would you recommend for elementary children? Why? For adults age 22–34? Why?

30. Is the Harvard Step Test a good test to use with middle-aged men in a fitness class? Why?

31. Is vital capacity correlated with height? Is vital capacity a good predictor of the state of circulatory-respiratory fitness?

32. How do heart rates of females during a standard exercise compare with heart rates of males?

33. Is it possible for some persons to hold their breath until they lose consciousness?

34. In the original Harvard Step Test, pulse rate after exercise was counted three times. Your text recommends only one count. Why?

35. How was the Harvard Step Test originally validated?

36. Why is an adjustment for weight necessary for work capacity tests on the bicycle ergometer but not on the treadmill?

FLEXIBILITY

7

Peter O. Sigerseth

Introduction

Definition

The term flexibility is derived from adding the adjectival suffix -bilis, meaning in Latin *capacity* or *capability,* to the term *flectere,* which means *to bend.* The term *flexibilis,* thus derived, has been changed to the present English form (26). The term *flex* is presently only in scientific use and refers to the bending of a joint or bony segment by action of muscles. Although the term *flexibility* may be applied to the ability to bend both animate and inanimate objects, the meaning in scientific use pertains to the moving of articulating segments of the body about a joint and can therefore be used to describe movement from a position of extension to that of flexion or the opposite movement.

Although there is general agreement regarding the definition of flexibility as it applies to the functioning of the human body, the research literature, until recently, has been of little help in clearing the existing ambiguities concerning its characteristics. Flexibility, for example, has been commonly treated as a general ability or factor in physical performance rather than what it really is, a number of specific abilities, each of which will vary from one segment of the body to another. The failure to recognize the specificity of flexibility is especially apparent in the construction of so-called batteries of physical fitness tests. Typically, the batteries are composed of a number of tests, each of which purports to measure some factor of physical fitness. Flexibility, being recognized as one of these factors, is then represented by one test that measures, often very accurately, the range of movement about a joint or about paired joints. In selecting the one measure as representative of a person's flexibility, the test designers have evidently been unaware that there is practically no similarity between the degrees of flexibility in the various joints in the body and that, for both sexes, flexibility is not a general quality or factor but one that is specific to each joint or paired joint (3, 7). This means that a person may be highly flexible, for example, in the hip joints and at the same time highly inflexible in the ankle joints. Likewise, in the testing of groups of boys and girls of various ages, very few will be found who are highly flexible or highly inflexible in many joints (7).* Outstanding performers in different sports or specialized physical activities appear to be characterized by above-average flexibility in certain joints and perhaps, to a lesser extent, below-average flexibility in others. In football, for example, differences in flexibility characteristics are even found between linemen and backfield players (24).

Importance

Historically, physical educators, except those who were medically oriented, have not been as concerned with flexibility as have members of the medical profession. The medical literature reveals that the latter have long been involved with restoring injured limbs to normal function and in the process have developed a variety of methods for measuring, not only the limitation of movement of the injured member, but also the range of movement of the uninjured paired limb. Aside from the testing done by rehabilitation and corrective workers, very little has been done regarding the normal range of movement by those engaged in teaching physical education activities. In contrast, coaches in sports, dance teachers, and teachers of highly specialized activities have long recognized the need for more than normal flexibility in certain joints or groups of joints by performers under their direction. To achieve this flexibility they have used special stretching exercise and drills but have provided little in the form of objective evidence regarding the effectiveness of these procedures. Studies have revealed, however, that subjects register significant increases in flexibility measurements following participation in programs designed to increase flexibility (2, 14). Medical records are replete with evidence supporting the effectiveness of prescribed exercise in increasing the flexibility of joints which have been injured.

*It should be noted that generally subjects were grouped by chronological age. Perhaps if physiological age had been used to group subjects, the correlation of flexibility in the various joints might have been greater.

What determines flexibility?

The range of movement about a joint may apparently be governed, within the limitations of its bony structure, by the functions it performs. When the need or demand is for continuously greater flexion and extension in such movements, the range of movement might finally be limited only by the contact of the muscles, fat, and remaining tissues compressed between the articulating segments of the bone. Under normal conditions, however, the range of movement is restricted by the length of the ligaments, muscles, tendons, and other connective tissues which cross the joints. Factors which may influence flexibility are heredity, disease, trauma, sex, specialized activities, heavy work, and even clothing.

Although flexibility seems to vary more as a consequence of the continued activity pattern which boys and girls follow than as a consequence of age, it should be recognized that one of the most pronounced changes associated with advanced age is the gradual impairment of movement. It does not seem possible from the information available to disentangle and separate the interrelated influences of inherited characteristics and physical, environmental, and social factors and definitely designate the role of each in determining the influence of sex, age, and physical exercise on the specific flexibilities of segments of the body.

In the comparison of the sexes, it should be recognized, however, that boys and girls do not vary greatly in the flexibility of principal joints. Forbes (5) found that girls were more flexible in more joints than boys at the age of 12 and that boys in turn were more flexible in more joints than girls at the age of 18. Hupprich and Sigerseth (4) had previously reported that in general, the flexibility of girls increased during the period from age 6 to age 12 and then declined, although even at the age of 18, girls were more flexible in certain joints than girls 6 years of age. In a more recent study of 10-, 11-, 12-, 13-, and 14-year-old girls, Downie (4) also found that flexibility in girls reached a peak at the age of 12 years and then tended to decrease as they became older. These comparisons took into consideration only the number of joints around which the range of movement was the greater and did not consider the total flexibility of the subjects in sums of degrees.

The unanswered question is whether the lessening of the physical skills exhibited by teen-age girls is a change in potential motor ability with a corresponding change in the flexibilities or is a reflection of the conventions which regulate their social life and whose demands are that girls become less active and more ladylike as they reach maturity. There appear to be some reasons why it would be well to refrain from concluding that the lack of participation in vigorous exercise is the chief factor in the lowering of specific flexibilities in girls. It should be remembered that boys also decrease in flexibility in many of the same joints and at the same ages as girls but still continue to improve in physical skills as they progress through junior and senior high school. It is also evident that the universal public approval accompanying increased success in physical activities does not prevent the trend of decreasing flexibility in boys of these ages.

Highly specialized performers in an activity have been found to not only differ significantly from nonspecialized individuals in the flexibility of certain joints but also from specialists in other activities (18, 23, 25, 27). No studies, however, have been continued on the flexibility of such outstanding performers from the time they started as neophytes in an activity until they became very skilled performers. It cannot therefore be stated with certainty whether they initially revealed promise in the activity because of certain above or below normal flexibility characteristics, or whether the changes in these characteristics paralleled the training involved in acquiring the outstanding skills. The evidence, however, supports Leighton's hypothesis (17) that, in the process of developing specialized skills, the continued participation in an activity tends to cause the range of movement about certain joints to become fixed within specific limits which are conducive to the best performance in that activity. For example, when 28 boys of junior high school age participated in a tumbling class for 20 weeks, significant increases in eighteen of thirty flexibility measures were revealed (10). Even more changes were found following an 8-week program, designed for increasing flexibility, in which significant increases were registered in twenty-seven of thirty flexibility measurements (14).

Methods of measuring flexibility

The early literature provided little information about measurement of flexibility that is adequate for application to present day use. A part of the difficulty was an ambiguity in the earlier studies regarding a common form of expressing the measurements, norms, and limits of flexibility. Their chief contributions were descriptions of a variety of methods for measuring movements about joints. The interest in this aspect of flexibility arose chiefly from the need for instruments which would aid in evaluating disabilities of extremities, many of which had been incurred during World War I. The instruments were chiefly devised by or for physicians and usually only the physician who used the instrument could interpret the measurements that were recorded. Although in some instances the physician developed a system of measurement and recording that, when once explained, was understandable, little data concerning joint function was reported in useable form. A common characteristic of the instruments, however, was that they measured angular movement in terms of degrees of a circle.

Physical educators were interested in aspects of flexibility about which the medical people were not especially concerned. They were more concerned, for example, with the development and maintenance of what they termed general body flexibility as it related to posture and trunk movements. Their interests were therefore involved with the movements about articulations in the vertebral column and the pelvic region to a greater extent than such movements in the extremities. Since they dealt with large groups of subjects, they were interested not only in developing tests which would measure these trunk movements, but in tests which would also require a minimum of equipment and could be administered quickly. They therefore tended to measure flexibilities in linear units or on a pass-fail basis rather than in degrees of a circle. The tests were developed in many forms but usually were scored on the basis of whether or not a performer, without bending his knees, could touch the floor with his finger tips, or how far down on an attached scale he could reach while standing on a bench. In other tests, flexibility was determined by how near the floor the person could bring the upper torso while standing.

The validity of such measurements was subject to question. For example, the measurements, thus derived, were governed or influenced by variation in the lengths of body segments, and they could only be applied to the measurement of the movement of a few joints. Other deficiencies were that they often required subjective judgment in scoring, did not provide scoring ranges, and did not restrict measurement of a movement to individual joints. Their use was further limited because it was not possible to develop norms from these types of measurements which could be compared with each other or with those established by the medical profession. Their validity as testing devices was also subject to question by the fact that a person could easily pass many of the tests following relatively short periods of practice.

Of the instruments developed for the measurement of flexibility, a device called the flexometer, first developed and later improved by Leighton (12), has had most general acceptance in physical education medicine and related sciences. In devising the instrument, certain criteria were met which were lacking in other flexibility measuring devices. These were that measurements should use units that were universal to all movements; the instrument and method should not be affected by variation in length of segments, and that the proper functioning of the instrument should not depend on conformity to the structure of the bony segments but must be applicable to the flexibility measurement of all segments in such movements as those of the ankle, neck, and so forth (12). It was later found that the flexometer also more nearly met the criteria set up by the Research Council of the Association for Health, Physical Education and Recreation for the selection and evaluation tests than any other instrument for measuring flexibility (22). Reliabilities, determined by the test-retest method, were found by Forbes (5) to range from 0.901 to 0.983 when the flexometer was used to determine thirty different flexibility measures.

The flexometer, shown in Figure 7–1, was developed to measure movements of body segments in degrees. It functions because gravity pulls the weighted ends of its dial and needle downward. The device is first attached by means of a strap to a segment of the body and the segment is then placed in the starting position for the movement to be measured. The measuring part of the instrument is a metal disk along whose margin is a double row of numbers representing degrees. The zero on the outer row is directly above the zero on the inner row. The outer row continues to the right and the inner row continues to the left to 360°. Both the dial and the needle rotate freely

FIGURE 7–1. The Leighton Flexometer.

around a ball-bearing supported axle. The needle has a point at one end and a weighted balance at the other. At the starting position, when the zero marks on the dial are vertical, the dial is locked in position. The body segment is then moved to its extreme limit and during this movement, the freely swinging needle turns on its axis and remains in the vertical position while the dial moves with the segment. When the body segment cannot move further, the needle is locked and a direct reading is taken on the dial which represents the arc through which the movement takes place.

To facilitate the accurate use of the instrument and to measure correctly, standard directions for thirty flexibility measurements as described by Leighton (15) are provided in the last part of this chapter. Percentile ranks using the Leighton Flexometer are given in tables in the appendix. However, there is considerable variation in scores reported by workers in different parts of the United States; hence teachers are encouraged to develop their own percentiles.

In instances where budget does not permit the purchase of such an instrument, a little ingenuity and access to a few tools will make it possible to improvise an instrument that, although less accurate and convenient to use than the flexometer, will serve the immediate needs in a testing program. Such instruments have been described and illustrated by Leighton (13, 16), McKenzie (21) and McCue (20).

The inexpensive flexometer developed and described by Leighton (13)

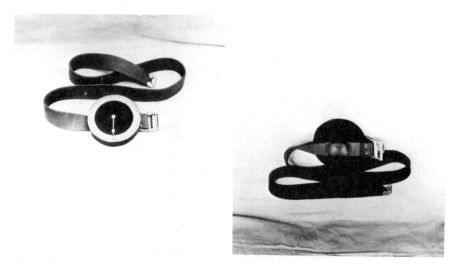

FIGURE 7–2.   An inexpensive flexometer.

is shown in Fig. 7–2.   It is a flat dial made from a circular piece of wood four and one-half inches in diameter.   Its margin is marked off into 360 degrees.   The needle, which rotates freely around the axle, is weighted at its point so that it always points downward when the face of the dial is held perpendicular to the floor.

More recently, electrogoniometers, referred to as elgons, have been developed that are used in increasing numbers in studies involving the measurement of movement about joints (1, 6, 8, 9, 11).   An elgon is a goniometer in which the protractor has been replaced by a potentiometer.   The elgon can record continuously, in degrees, the changes in the angles of joints during movement while a manual goniometer can measure the angles of joints only when they are in stationary positions (8).

Measurement technic: flexometer

Neck

Flexion and Extension.   (Figure 7–3)   *Starting position.*   The subject lies supine on table, head and neck projecting over the edge of the table, shoulders touching the edge, arms and forearms at sides.   The instrument is fastened to either side of head over the ear.

Movement.   Count (1) head is raised and moved to a position as near the chest as possible, the dial is locked; (2) head is lowered and moved to a position as near the end of the bench as possible, pointer is locked; (3) subject relaxes, the reading is taken.

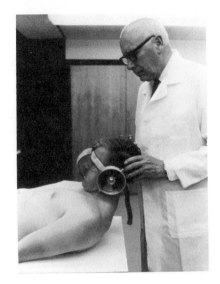 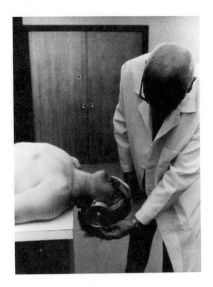

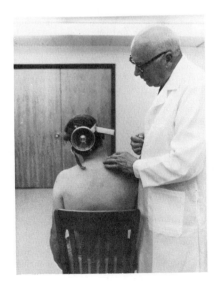 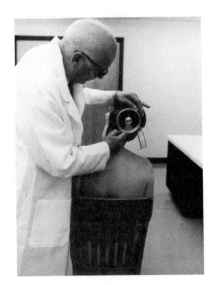

FIGURE 7–3. Neck flexion and extension (upper photographs) and neck lateral flexion (lower photographs).

Caution: Shoulders must not be raised from table during flexion, nor may back be unduly arched during extension. Buttocks and shoulders must remain on table during movement.

Lateral flexion. (Figure 7–3) *Starting position.* Subject assumes a sitting position in a low-backed armchair, back straight, hands grasping sides of the seat of the chair. The instrument is fastened to back of head.

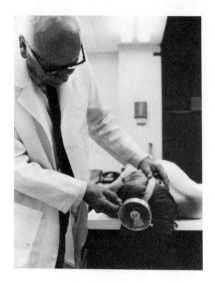
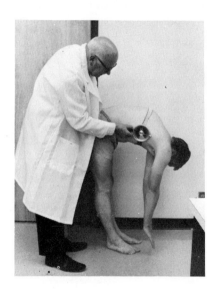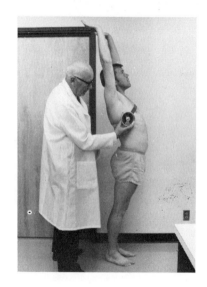

FIGURE 7–4.   Neck rotation (upper photographs) and trunk
flexion and extension (lower photographs).

Movement.   Count (1) head is moved in an arc sideways to the left as far as
possible, dial is locked; (2) head is moved in an arc to the right as far as
possible, pointer is locked; (3) subject relaxes, the reading is taken.

Caution: Position in the chair may not be changed during movement.
Shoulders may not be raised or lowered.

Rotation.   (Figure 7–4)   *Starting position.*   Subject lies supine on the table, head and neck projecting beyond it, shoulders touching edge and arms at sides of table. The instrument is fastened to the top of the head.

Movement. Count (1) head is turned left as far as possible, dial is locked; (2) head is turned right as far as possible, pointer is locked; (3) subject relaxes, the reading is taken.

Caution: Shoulders may not be raised from bench.

Trunk

Extension and flexion. (Figure 7–4) *Starting position.* Subject stands, feet together, knees straight (extended), arms directed above head and palms of hands directed upward. Instrument is fastened to either side of chest just below armpit at nipple height.

Movement. Count (1) the subject bends backward as far as possible, dial is locked; (2) the subject bends forward as far as possible, pointer is locked; (3) subject relaxes, the reading is taken.

Caution: Knees must be kept straight (extended) throughout movement. Feet may not be shifted. Toes and heels may not be raised from floor.

Note: This movement involves trunk and hip extension and flexion. To obtain the measurement of trunk extension and flexion alone, the measure for hip extension and flexion must be subtracted from the score obtained above.

Lateral flexion. (Figure 7–5) *Starting position.* The subject stands, feet together, knees straight (extended), arms at sides. The instrument is fastened to the middle of the back at nipple height.

Movement. Count (1) Subject bends sideways to the left as far as possible, dial is locked; (2) subject bends sideways to the right as far as possible, pointer is locked; (3) subject relaxes, reading is taken.

Caution: Both feet must remain flat on the floor, heels may not be raised during measurement. Knees must be kept straight (extended) throughout movement. Subject may bend sidewards and backwards but must not bend forward.

Rotation. (Figure 7–7) *Starting position.* Subject lies supine on table, legs together, knees raised above hips, lower legs parallel to bench and body. Subject's hands grasp sides of table. The instrument is fastened to the middle rear of either the right or left thigh.

Movement. Count (1) knees are lowered to the left as far as possible, dial is locked; (2) knees are brought back to the starting position and lowered to the right as far as possible, pointer is locked; (3) subject relaxes, reading is taken.

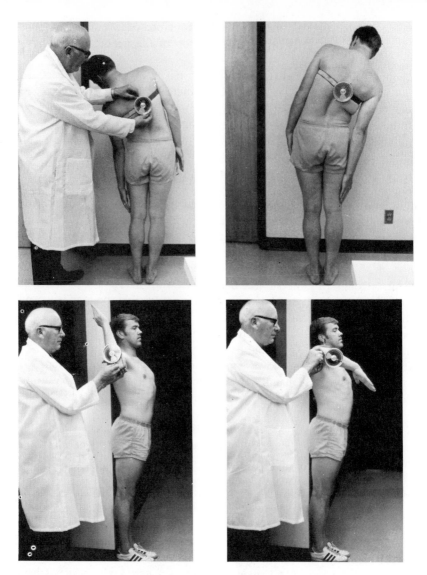

FIGURE 7–5. Trunk lateral flexion (upper photographs) and
arm rotation (lower photographs).

Caution: Subject's shoulders must not rise from the bench during movement. Knees must be moved directly sidewards.

Shoulder joint

Arm flexion and extension. (Figure 7–6) *Starting position.* Subject stands
at the projecting corner of wall, the arm to be measured extending downward
and just beyond projecting corner, arms and forearms at sides, back to wall,

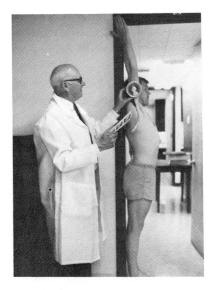 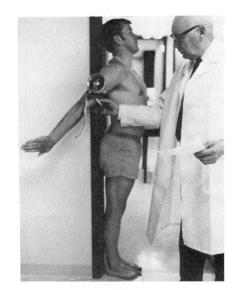

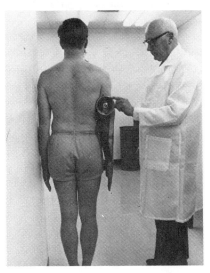 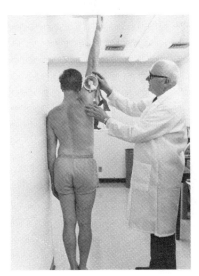

FIGURE 7–6.   Arm flexion and extension (upper photographs) and arm adduction and abduction (lower photographs).

shoulder blades, buttocks, and heels touching wall.   The instrument is fastened
to the side of the upper arm.

Movement.   Count (1) the arm is moved forward and upward and then
backwards in an arc as far as possible, palm of hand held against the wall,
dial is locked; (2) the arm is moved downward and backward in an arc as
far as possible, palm of hand sliding against wall, pointer is locked; (3) subject relaxes, reading is taken.

Caution: Heels, buttocks, and shoulders must touch wall at all times during movement. The elbow of the arm being measured must be kept straight (extended). The palm must be against the wall when dial and pointer are locked.

Arm adduction and abduction. (Figure 7–6) *Starting position.* Subject stands with arms at sides, left (right) side of body towards wall, shoulder touching wall, palms of both hands touching the thighs, feet together, knees and elbows straight (extended). Instrument is fastened to the back of the right (left) upper arm.

Movement. Count (1) the palm of the right (left) hand is pressed against the side of the leg, dial is locked; (2) arm moves sideways, outward and upward in an arc as far as possible, pointer is locked; (3) subject relaxes, the reading is taken.

Caution: The left (right) hand must be kept in contact with the body and wall at all times. Knees and elbows must be kept straight (extended) and body erect throughout movement. The arm and forearm must be raised directly sideways, not forward or backward. Heels of feet must not be raised from the floor.

Arm rotation. (Figure 7–5) *Starting position.* Subject stands at the projecting corner of the wall, arm to be measured abducted sideward and forearm flexed to a right angle at the elbow, right shoulder placed just beyond projecting corner, opposite arm and forearm kept at the side of the body, back to wall, shoulder blades, buttocks and heels touching wall. The instrument is fastened to the side of the forearm.

Movement. Count (1) the forearm is moved downward and backward in a sagittal plane and as far as possible, dial is locked; (2) forearm is moved upward and backward in the same plane as far as possible, pointer is locked; (3) subject relaxes, the reading is taken.

Caution: Upper arm must be directed horizontally sideward and parallel with the floor during movement. Heels, buttocks, and shoulders must touch the wall at all times.

Elbow joint

Forearm flexion and extension. (Figure 7–7) *Starting position.* Subject squats or sits in a chair while facing the table or bench with the upper portion of the arm resting on the table and the armpit resting against its edge. The instrument is fastened to the back of the wrist.

Movement. Count (1) wrist and hand move upward and backward in flexion to a position as near the shoulder as possible, dial is locked; (2) the

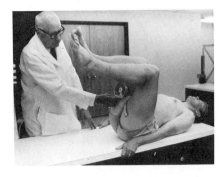 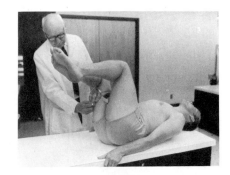

 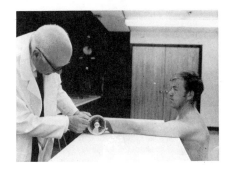

FIGURE 7–7. Trunk rotation (upper photographs) and forearm flexion and extension (lower photographs).

wrist moves forward and downward until forearm is forcibly extended, pointer is locked; (3) subject relaxes, the reading is taken.

Caution: The upper arm may not be tilted or moved during measurement.

Radial-ulnar

Hand supination and pronation. (Figure 7–8) *Starting position.* Subject sits in a chair, back straight, forearm resting on the table, fist doubled and extended beyond the end of the table, the wrist of arm to be measured held straight (extended). The strap is grasped in the hand, the instrument is fastened to the front of the fist. An armchair may be substituted for the chair and table.

Movement. Count (1) thumb side of fist is turned outward and downward as far as possible, dial is locked; (2) thumb side of fist is turned upward, downward and inward as far as possible, pointer is locked; (3) subject relaxes, the reading is taken.

Caution: Body and forearm must remain stationary, except for specified movement, throughout measurement. No leaning of the body is permitted.

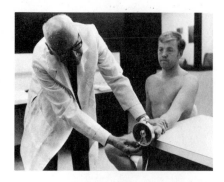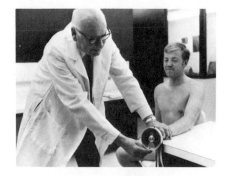

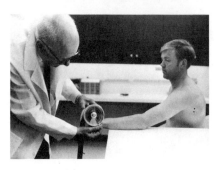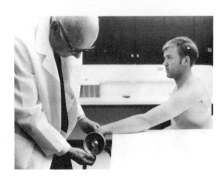

FIGURE 7–8.   Hand supination and pronation (upper
photographs) and hand flexion and extension (lower photographs).

Wrist joint

Hand flexion and extension.   (Figure 7–8)   *Starting position.*   Subject sits
in a chair, back straight, forearms resting on the corner of a table, hands
clenched and extended beyond the ends of the table, the palm of hand to be
measured turned upwards.   The instrument is fastened to the thumb side of
the fist.   A standard armchair may be substituted for chair and table.

Movement.   Count (1) the fist is moved upward and backward in an arc as far
as possible, the dial is locked; (2) the fist is moved forward, downward and
backward in an arc as far as possible, the pointer is locked; (3) subject relaxes, the reading is taken.

   Caution: The forearm may not be raised from the table during movement.

Hand abduction and adduction.   (Figure 7–9)   *Starting position.*   Subject
sits in a chair, back straight, forearms resting on the corner of the table, hands
clenched and extended beyond edge of the table, thumb side of hand to
be measured turned up.   The instrument is fastened to the back of the hand.
A standard armchair may be substituted for the chair and table.

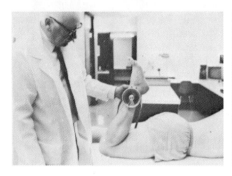 

FIGURE 7–9. Hand abduction and adduction (upper photographs) and leg flexion and extension (lower photographs).

Movement. Count (1) the fist is moved upward and backward in an arc as far as possible, the dial is locked; (2) the fist is moved downward and backward as far as possible, the pointer is locked; (3) subject relaxes, the reading is taken.

Caution: The forearm may not be raised from the chair arm during movement. The fist may not be turned inward or outward during measurement.

Hip joint

Thigh extension and flexion. (Figure 7–10) *Starting position.* Subject stands, feet together, knees straight (extended), arms and forearms directed above the head, palms of hands directed upwards. The instrument is fastened to either side of the hip at the height of the umbilicus.

Movement. Count (1) subject bends backward as far as possible, the dial is locked; (2) subject bends forward as far as possible, the pointer is locked; (3) subject relaxes, the reading is taken.

Caution: Knees must remain straight (extended) throughout the movement. Feet may not be shifted. Toes and heels may not be raised.

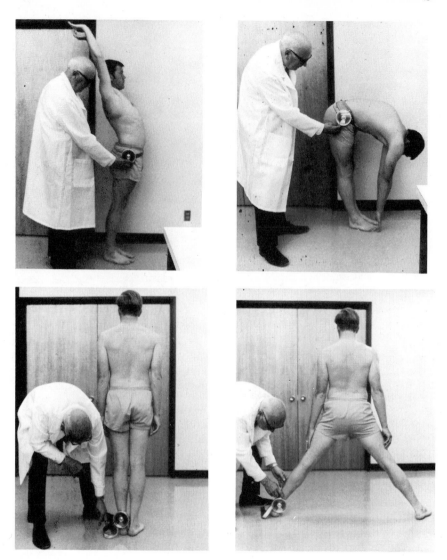

FIGURE 7–10.   Thigh extension and flexion (upper photographs) and thigh adduction and abduction (lower photographs).

Thigh adduction and abduction.   (Figure 7–10)   *Starting position.*   Subject stands, feet together, knees straight (extended), arms at sides.   The instrument is fastened to the back of either leg above the ankle.

Movement.   Count (1) subject assumes starting position, the dial is locked; (2) the leg to which the instrument is not attached is moved sideward as far as possible, the pointer is locked; (3) subject relaxes, the reading is taken.

Caution: The body must remain in an upright position throughout the movement. Knees must be kept straight (extended) with the feet assuming parallel positions.

Thigh rotations. (Figure 7–11) *Starting position.* Subject lies supine on the table with the left (right) leg resting on the table and foot projecting beyond its end, knee straight, right (left) leg flexed at the knee and the foot resting on the table. The instrument is fastened to the bottom of the left (right) foot.

Movement. Count (1) the left (right) foot is turned outward as far as possible, the dial is locked; (2) the left (right) foot is turned inward as far as possible, the pointer is locked; (3) subject relaxes, the reading is taken.

Caution: Knee and ankle joints must remain locked throughout movement. Position of hips may not be changed during measurement.

Knee

Leg flexion and extension. (Figure 7–9) *Starting position.* Subject lies prone on box or bench with knees at end of and lower legs extending beyond the end of bench, arms at sides of body and hands grasping edges of the bench. The instrument is fastened to the outside of either ankle.

Movement. Count (1) foot and lower leg are moved upward and backward in flexion to a position as near buttocks as possible, dial is locked; (2) foot moved forward and downward until leg is forcibly extended, pointer is locked; (3) subject relaxes, the reading is taken.

Caution: Position of upper leg (thigh) may not be changed during movement.

Ankle joint

Foot inversion and eversion. (Figure 7–11) *Starting position.* Subject sits on end of table, knees projecting over its edge and lower legs directed downward. A shoe (low cut) should be worn on the foot to be tested. The instrument is fastened to front of foot.

Movement. Count (1) foot is turned inward as far as possible, dial is locked; (2) foot is turned outward as far as possible, pointer is locked; (3) subject relaxes, the reading is taken.

Caution: Position of lower leg may not be changed during measurement.

Foot flexion and extension. (Figure 7–12) *Starting position.* Subject sits or lies on table with left (right) leg resting on and foot projecting over end of bench, knee straight (extended), other leg flexed and directed downward, foot

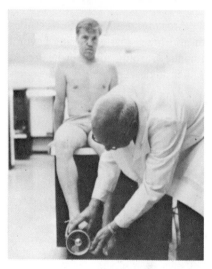
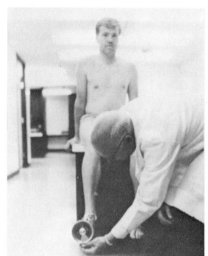

FIGURE 7–11. Thigh lateral and medial rotation (upper photographs) and foot inversion and eversion (lower photographs).

resting on table top. The instrument is fastened to the inside of the left (right) foot.

Movement. Count (1) left (right) foot is turned downward as far as possible, dial is locked; (2) left (right) foot is dorsi-flexed upward and toward the knee as far as possible, pointer is locked; (3) subject relaxes, the reading is taken.

Caution: Knee of leg being measured must be kept straight (extended) throughout movement. No sideways turning of the foot may be allowed.

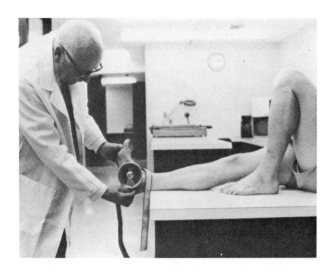

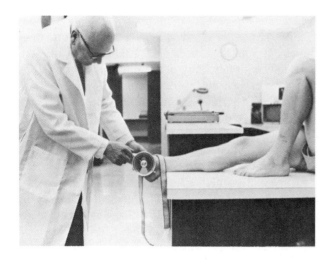

FIGURE 7–12. Foot flexion (upper photograph) and extension (lower photograph).

Improving flexibility

It would appear that the body automatically makes certain adjustments during repeated performances of movement toward optimum flexibility for performance of specific skills. Despite this, it is evident that, through proper direction, such as provided in coaching, some skills may be increased more speedily by purposefully increasing or decreasing the range of motion around certain joints until what would appear to be the optimum flexibility is reached. In providing such direction, it should be realized that too much flexibility, either inherited or acquired, may hinder skillful performance and that the limiting of flexibility in other joints may aid such performance. Thus good teachers, whether they be coaches of sports or instructors in dance, on the basis of their experience and knowledge help their charges in the selection of optimum ranges of motion for the activity in which they engage. The experienced track coach, for example, first teaches high hurdlers special stretching exercises on the grass, and then has them run over one or two hurdles which may be lower and closer together than the 10-yard distance required in official track meets so that the distance between the hurdles can be cleared in three strides. As the hurdlers increase the range or length of their strides, the coach gradually raises the hurdles to regulation height and moves them until they are the official distance apart. Swimming coaches are also aware of the importance of increasing their swimmers' range of movement and teach them special stretching exercises on the deck of the pool before training in the pool. We should also not have to be reminded that dance training far predates sports in terms of emphasizing flexibility through systematic stretching routines.

The physical education teachers who have the chief responsibility for directing the nonspecialized activity programs of normally growing and developing boys and girls have, however, received only limited information applicable to their programs from published research. This is so because the studies involved have dealt chiefly with flexibility of the physically endowed or the physically handicapped. One basic problem is determining what is normal flexibility for normal individuals. Of particular importance to these teachers is knowing whether above- or below-normal flexibility in the different parts of the body will improve a person's health, increase ability to perform everyday functions efficiently, postpone fatigue, or improve motor performance and prevent injury. In some instances, also, a pupil may logically ask the teacher after being tested for flexibility whether he or she made a good score. This is a difficult question to answer since there is little that the teacher can refer to as a criterion. Although the teacher may know that there is evidence of an optimum range of motion in each joint or pair of joints for each specialized activity, there is little evidence to aid in determining what is optimum for the best performance of normal activities. The knowledge that too much flexibility may be as great a handicap to good performance as too little flexibility, for example, is not of much help.

Until more information is available, it is reasonable to assume that the most useful method of determining the flexibility status of nonspecialized students is to compare their flexibility measurements with those in tables of norms derived from measurements of normal boys and girls. The norms provided in the appendix may to some extent aid in interpreting test scores of such nonspecialized subjects.

Exercises for improvement in flexibility, whether they be used to increase or reduce the range of movement in a joint, may be selected and used by the teacher to meet the needs of students who are free of structural and functional changes caused by injury or disease. In instances of deficiencies in flexibility, as revealed in a medical examination or following an injury, exercises should be prescribed by a physician. In either case, special exercises are needed rather than the general warm-up types. It should be realized that in some instances certain warm-up or general stretching exercises may be used before those used in the special cases.

The discussion that follows will deal with exercises that may be used for above or below normal flexibility of nonpathological cases. In administering the exercises, it is necessary to keep in mind the importance of meeting the specific needs and capacities of the individual. It may also be important that other principles be reviewed which apply to such exercises. Daily exercises, for example, are preferable to fewer sessions each week, and periods of intensive exercise should be interspersed with periods of relaxation. Exercises must be continued faithfully for extended periods of time and great changes in flexibility should not be expected overnight. For joints where the flexibility is normal, exercises should be selected which do not strain or require abnormal action. More than normal flexibility should not be sought except in preparation for specialized activities in which the additional flexibility in specifiic joints is desirable. In joints where excessive flexibility has been found, the range of movement should be reduced and the amount of resistance may be increased. Massey and Chaudet (19) concluded that systematic, heavy resistance did not cause the range of movement of joints to be reduced but that if decreases or increases in range of movement did occur, they were due to the training routine and the manner in which the exercises were performed. As a rule, the number of exercises should be relatively small but they may often be varied slightly and thus adapted to different situations. It should be realized that some of the exercises which have been used for decades are still among the best. No set system of exercising has been found that is satisfactory for all flexibility problems. It is still necessary to have well-trained teachers to not only select the proper exercises, but to teach and motivate those who need help. A well-trained teacher in this field will recognize abnormalities involved with joint function. It is most important that this person recognize professional limitations beyond which he must not go, but at the same time assume the responsibility for bringing the abnormal condition to the attention of the parents with the suggestion that a physician be consulted.

The exercises that are briefly described on the following pages are only a few of the many that have been in common use for increasing flexibility of segments of the body. Standard text books in the area of corrective or adaptive physical education will contain many additional exercises or variations of those described.

Circumduction of the head (to increase flexibility of the neck)

While in a standing position with hands resting on hips, begin a rotary movement of the neck by first bending the neck to the left, then backwards, next to the right, and finally forward in a continuous circular movement. The movement should be made both to the left and to the right. The bending movement should be exaggerated.

Towel behind the neck (to increase flexibility in the shoulder joints, wrists, and elbows)

This exercise can be performed by grasping the ends of a face towel and placing it behind the neck. The towel may be alternately moved from left to right, thus varying the ranges of movement in the region of the shoulder girdle and upper extremities. It can also be used on the back of the trunk where it may be moved in different planes. The distance separating the hands can be adjusted at the discretion of the person exercising.

Forward bends (to increase the range of movement in the lower back and hip joints)

From an erect starting position, with feet a foot or more apart, bend the trunk forward and downward at the waist without bending the knees, and stretch the arms and forearms toward the floor. Bob the trunk up and down while the fingers and the palms of the hands gradually come closer to and finally touch the floor.

In a variation of this exercise, grasp both ankles and pull the trunk downward and against the thighs while attempting to touch the knees with the forehead. The knees must not bend during either exercise.

Hamstring stretcher (to increase the range of movement of the lower back and hip joints by stretching the hamstrings and the lumbar fascia)

Assume an erect position, with hands clasped in front of the body and the elbows flexed to an angle of 90 degrees. Bob the trunk up and down at the waist, while trying to touch the floor with the elbows without bending the knees. The distance between the feet should be gradually widened.

Bottoms up (to increase the range of movement in the lower back and hip joints by stretching the fascia of the hamstrings and the lumbar region)

From an erect starting position, with the feet parallel and a foot apart, assume a full-knee-bend position and place the fingers and the palms of the hands on the floor in front of the feet. From this position, raise the hips as high as possible by fully extending the thighs and the legs while keeping the fingers and palms of the hands pressed against the floor.

Psoas stretching (to increase the range of the anterior-posterior movement in the hips by stretching the psoas muscles and the hamstrings)

Assume a position in which the body is supported by the hands and feet in an exaggerated sprinter's starting position. The arms and forearms are perpendicular to the floor and the elbows are therefore fully extended. The most forward knee is placed below the chest and directly above the foot. The hindmost thigh and leg are stretched (extended) back as far as possible. While in this position the hips are "bobbed" up and down as the back, thigh and leg remain extended. Repeat the exercise reversing the legs.

Knee tuck (to increase the range of movement in the areas of the knee, hip, lower back and scapula)

While lying in a supine position on the floor, bring both thighs toward the chest and then clasp the hands around the legs below the knees and pull them as close to the chest as possible.

Situp and roll back (to increase the range of movement in the back, hip, and shoulder girdle regions)

Assume a supine position on the floor with the feet about a foot apart and the arms and forearms stretched beyond the head and the palms turned upwards. Then sit up by forcefully bringing the arms and forearms forward and downward until the fingers touch the toes. Do not bend the knees. Return to the lying position and then raise the thighs and legs overhead and backward, with the knees extended, until the toes touch the floor beyond the head. Then slowly return to the original lying position keeping the knees straight.

Back twist (to increase the range of rotating movement of the vertebral column and pelvic regions)

Assume a supine position with the arms and forearms at right angles to the body. The palms are placed on the floor and the thighs and legs are raised vertically. The thighs and legs are first lowered to the left by twisting the trunk until the left foot touches the floor near the left hand. The legs and thighs are then returned to the vertical position and the exercise is repeated to the right side. The movements are continued alternately to the left and right.

**Supine bicycling (to increase range of movement
in the hips, knees, ankles, and feet in an
anterior-posterior direction)**

Lie supine on the floor with the thighs raised and the legs flexed at the knees
as though they were about to pedal an inverted bicycle. Simulate the leg and
thigh movements involved in pedaling a bicycle and move the feet as though
their paths are in the form of a circle. The range of movement may be increased by bringing the knees closer to the chest during flexion and further
away from the chest during extension, thus increasing the size of the circle the
feet follow in the imaginary pedaling.

**Rocker (to increase range of the extensor
movement in the neck, trunk, and ankles)**

While lying in a pronated position, with the head raised, the hands at the sides
of the thighs, the knees bent and the feet elevated, grasp the ankles and perform a forward and backward rocking movement. Attempt to make the
anterior aspect of the body conform somewhat to the shape of a rocker while
continuing the exercise.

**Creeping exercise (to increase lateral and
anterior-posterior movement in the region of
neck, trunk, and pelvis)**

Perform this exercise on "all fours" (hands and knees) with the trunk kept in
a horizontal position. Move forward by alternately bringing or swinging one
hand and the opposite knee forward simultaneously. At the same time, turn
the head, neck, and trunk to the side of the most forward knee. If for example,
the right hand is moved forward first, bring the left knee forward and turn
or twist the head, neck, and trunk toward the left. The movements are exaggerated and the hands and knees are kept close to the floor, thus resulting
in a creeping movement. Gloves and knee pads should be worn if the exercise is performed regularly.

**Hurdle stretch (to increase range of movement
in the hip joint and in outward rotation of
the thighs)**

Stand back of the right side of a hurdle and place the left heel on top of the
cross bar to simulate a hurdling position. Touch the toes of the right foot
(which is on the ground) with both hands. Return to an erect position while
grasping the top of the hurdle with the left hand. Repeat the exercise in back
of the left side of the hurdle with the right heel resting on the cross bar.

Hurdle stretch on the ground (to increase range of anterior-posterior movement in the hip joint and lower back, and in outward rotation of the thighs)

Sit on the floor in imitation of a hurdler clearing a hurdle. Grasp the leading leg and lean forward until the forehead touches the knee. The other thigh and leg are rotated laterally, the thigh is abducted and the leg is flexed at the knee. Next, lean backward to a sitting position and then repeat the forward and backward movements in a "rocking" manner without changing the position of the legs. Repeat the exercise reversing the legs.

REFERENCES

1. Call, C. B., *An Electromyographic Study of Bioarticular Muscles Involved in Movements of the Tibiofemoral and Iliofemoral Joints.* Unpublished Ph.D. dissertation, University of Oregon, 1967.

2. De Vries, H. A., "Evaluation of Static Stretching Procedures for Improvement of Flexibility." *Res. Quart.,* 33:222–229, 1962.

3. Dickinson, R. V., "The Specificity of Flexibility." *Res. Quart.,* 39:792–797, 1968.

4. Downie, Patricia D., *A Study of the Flexibility Characteristics of Ten, Eleven, Twelve, Thirteen and Fourteen-year-old Girls.* Unpublished D.Ed. dissertation, University of Oregon, 1970.

5. Forbes, J. M., *Characteristics of Flexibility in Boys.* Unpublished D.Ed. dissertation. University of Oregon, 1950.

6. Gollnick, P. D. and P. V. Karpovich, "Electrogoniometric Study of Locomotion and of some Athletic Movements." *Res. Quart.,* 35:357–369, 1964.

7. Hupperich, F. L., and P. O. Sigerseth, "The Specificity of Flexibility in Girls." *Res. Quart.,* 21:25–33, 1950.

8. Karpovich, P. V.; E. L. Herden; and M. M. Asa, "Electrogoniometric Study of Joints." *U.S. Armed Forces Medical Journal,* 11:424–450, 1960.

9. Karpovich, P. V. and G. P. Karpovich, "Electrogoniometer, A New Device for Study of Joints in Action." *Fed. Proc.,* 19:300, 1960.

10. Kingsley, D. B., *Flexibility Changes Resulting from Participation in Tumbling.* Unpublished Masters Thesis. University of Oregon, 1952.

11. Korb, Robert J., "A Simple Electrogoniometer: A Technical Note." *Res. Quart.,* 41:203–205, 1970.

12. Leighton, J. R., "A Simple Objective and Reliable Measure of Flexibility." *Res. Quart.,* 13:205–216, 1942.

13. Leighton, J. R., *A Simple Objective and Reliable Measure of Flexibility.* Unpublished Master's Thesis. University of Oregon, 1942, pp. 10–13.

14. Leighton, J. R., "A Study of the Effect of Progressive Weight Training on Flexibility." *J. for Phys. and Mental Rehab.,* 18:101–105, 1964.

15. Leighton, J. R., "An Instrument and Technic for the Measurement of Range of Joint Motion." *Archives of Physical Medicine and Rehabilitation,* 36:571–578, 1955.

16. Leighton, J. R., *An Investigation of the Flexibility Characteristics of Three Age Groups of Two Specialized Skill Groups Among Males Twelve to Sixteen Years of Age and College Athletes.* Unpublished Ph.D. dissertation, University of Oregon, 1954.

17. Leighton, J. R., "On the Significance of Flexibility for Physical Educators." *J. of Health, P. E. and Rec.,* 31:27–29, 1960.

18. Lemiere, O., *Flexibility of Shot*

Putters and Discus Throwers. Unpublished Master's Thesis. University of Oregon, 1952.

19. Massey, B. H., and N. L. Chaudet, "Effects of Systematic Heavy Resistive Exercise on Range of Joint Movement in Young Male Adults." *Res. Quart.,* 27: 41–51, 1956.

20. McCue, B. F., "Flexibility Measurements of College Women." *Res. Quart.,* 24: 316–324, 1953.

21. McKenzie, R., *Exercise in Education and Medicine.* Philadelphia: Saunders, 1924, pp. 370–371.

22. National Research Council of the Research Section, *Measurement and Evaluation, Materials in Health, Physical Education and Recreation.* Washington, D.C.: American Association for Health,

Physical Education and Recreation, 1950.

23. Pickens, W. L., *A Study of Flexibility in Swimmers.* Unpublished Master's Thesis. University of Oregon, 1950.

24. Sigerseth, P. O. and C. Haliski, "The Flexibility of Football Players." *Res. Quart.,* 21:394–398, 1950.

25. Syverson, M., *A Study of Flexibility in Baseball Players.* Unpublished Master's Thesis. University of Oregon, 1950.

26. The Philogical Society, *The Oxford Dictionary.* Oxford: Oxford University Press, 1961, pp. 319–320.

27. Williams, E. T., *A Study of Flexibility in Basketball Players.* Unpublished Master's Thesis. University of Oregon, 1950.

STUDY QUESTIONS • *Chapter 7*

1. Explain the derivation of the term *flexibility.*

2. Define the following terms:
   articulation
   tendons
   ligaments
   protractor
   goniometer

3. Is flexibility in the various joints closely related? Explain your answer.

4. If an outstanding athlete is flexible in one joint is he or she likely to be flexible in all the other joints? Give evidence to support your answer.

5. Can you increase flexibility through an exercise program or is flexibility inherited? Give evidence to support your answer.

6. Explain what is meant when someone is "muscle bound."

7. Is flexibility related to age? Explain.

8. Is there much difference in flexibility between boys and girls?

9. Of what importance is flexibility in our lives?

10. Describe one of the earlier tests of measuring trunk flexibility. What are some of the reasons this test is not recommended?

11. Describe the "flexometer." Who developed it? Are the flexibility tests using this instrument reliable? To what extent?

12. Describe an electrogoniometer. How does it operate?

13. Give two examples in which flexibility of a particular joint is important in a particular sport.

14. Does weight training (lifting weights) automatically reduce flexibility? Explain.

15. Describe an exercise which will improve flexibility in each of the areas listed.
    a. neck
    b. shoulder joints
    c. lower back and hips
    d. rotation of vertebral column and pelvic region
    e. lateral and anterior-posterior movements of neck, trunk, and pelvis

16. Describe each of the movements listed:

Neck:
    a. flexion and extension
    b. lateral flexion
    c. rotation

Trunk:
    a. extension and flexion
    b. lateral flexion
    c. rotation

Shoulder joint:
    a. arm flexion and extension
    b. arm adduction
    c. arm abduction
    d. arm rotation

Elbow joint:
    a. forearm flexion and extension
    b. hand supination
    c. hand pronation

Wrist joint:
    a. hand flexion and extension
    b. hand abduction
    c. hand adduction

Hip joint:
    a. thigh extension and flexion
    b. thigh adduction
    c. thigh abduction
    d. thigh rotation

Knee:
    a. leg flexion and extension

Ankle joint:
    a. foot eversion
    b. foot inversion
    c. foot flexion
    d. foot extension

MEASUREMENT OF BODY FATNESS

8

Henry J. Montoye

The physical educator should understand the health implications of obesity. Although excessive leanness is a matter of concern to some children and adults, a much more important problem in the United States is excessive fatness. This chapter discusses the relation of body fatness to health, the role of exercise in weight control, and methods of measuring fatness.

Importance of weight control

Mortality and morbidity

During the Renaissance period, Flemish artists often depicted plump, even corpulent, women and children as ideally beautiful. Rubens was a master of this style. Even today in some parts of the world it is considered a mark of beauty and health to be somewhat fat. In some countries of the world, where starvation and diseases such as tuberculosis are serious concerns for a large part of the population, plumpness is, to some degree, an indicator of health.

It is true, of course, that if a baby or young child is not growing or gaining weight, this is frequently a sign of impaired health. Nevertheless, there is no evidence that plumpness in children is healthful. As a matter of fact, laboratory experiments with protozoa, flies, silk worms, rats, and cattle (8) have shown that underfeeding is more healthful and actually increases longevity.

Adipose* or fat tissue, of course, has a useful function. It is an efficient method of storing fuel for metabolism. For example, in zebu (Brahman) cattle and the camel, the hump serves as a store of reserve fat and shows seasonal changes depending on the food supply (8). Salmon, when returning to spawn, are able to swim great distances while utilizing stored fat for energy. Some birds, before migration, store fat in a special organ from which they draw energy during the long flight (63). Subcutaneous fat also serves as insulation and has a certain aesthetic function when deposited in optimum amounts and when distributed properly.

Among adults, the association of obesity† and more moderate degrees of excessive fatness with disease has been the subject of many investigations. Dr. Hundley of the National Institutes of Health (33) has summarized studies of the percentage of adults who are considerably overweight‡ and he concluded that roughly one-fifth of persons past the age of 30 are sufficiently overweight for their health to be affected. Furthermore, in males, the percentage of overweight adults has increased in recent years (50).

It is also clear that obese people, as a group, have a shorter life expectancy than the general population. There is truth in the statement "the longer the belt line, the shorter the life line." A number of research papers have summarized studies which bear on this point (1, 33, 36, 40–43). The decreased longevity associated with obesity appears to be accounted for mainly in the high death rates from cardiovascular-renal and digestive diseases, diabetes, and disorders of the liver (33, 50). However, there is a strong suspicion that excess fatness may be a factor in hypertension, gallbladder disease, degenerative joint disease, certain types of cancer, pulmonary emphysema, appendicitis, venous thrombosis and embolism, and toxemias of pregnancy (33, 58, p. 6). Metabolic and chronic diseases are becoming more important as causes of death; hence, overweight looms as a more important health problem. Excessive body fatness has been implicated as a risk factor in a number of instances. To all this must be added such factors as increased surgical risk in the obese, poor agility and hence greater proneness to injury, and feet and leg complications due to excess weight.

Generally, excess fatness contributes to poorer performance in most sports activities. Often if an overfat child were to lose some of the surplus adipose tissue, his strength per pound of body weight would be increased, even without altering his absolute strength. It is not difficult to see that performance in gymnastics would be improved as a result. There are some activities, of course, in which fatness is not as great a handicap. In synchro-

---

*The terms *adipose* and *adiposity* are derived from the Latin word *adeps*, which means fat (29).

†The word *obesity* is derived from the Latin *obesus*, which means "eaten up or lean." Gradually the term came to have the opposite meaning (62).

‡In most cases, these people are also likely overfat.

nized swimming, the higher percentage of fat in girls and consequently their greater buoyancy likely contributes to a smoother performance in some maneuvers. For this reason, swimming is a relatively safe activity for older adults who wish to become physically active again after a long period of sedentary living.

Is weight control a problem only for adults?

It is well known that a significant number of children are excessively fat (31). One may question whether these children are likely to be obese when they become adults. Dr. Felix Heald (31) has reviewed the research in which obese subjects were studied as children and as adults. All of the studies indicate that the majority of obese children (approximately 80%) will later be obese adults. Also of significance is the observation that adults with a history of childhood obesity tend to be more severely obese and harder to treat effectively than those cases of obesity that began in adulthood. In one study (34) in which longitudinal records were available, about 50% of obese children in high school had been obese during most of their earlier school years. Another third of the children became obese while in the 6th to 8th grade.

In recent years evidence has been accumulating that the total number of fat cells we have is fixed by the time we have reached full growth. After that time, our relative state of obesity is a matter of the size of the fat cell, that is, how much fat each cell contains. During the growing years, however, it appears possible to affect the total number of fat cells the individual will ultimately have. Exercise *in the early years* has been shown to decrease the number and size of fat cells (51, 52). Overnutrition in the young, on the other hand, results in the formation of additional fat cells which "will cry for fat" (48).

Exercise and weight control

Why should weight control be of concern to the physical educator? As teachers and health educators of course, they have an obligation to acquaint children and adults with the health implications of obesity. They must attempt to motivate those with weight problems to do something about them and to influence others to avoid becoming excessively fat. Moreover, because exercise is a potent factor in the prevention of obesity, the physical educator has a very direct role to play.

In most cases, the amount of fat accumulated is the result of a simple equation that includes food intake (calories) on the one hand and energy expenditure (calories) on the other. If a person who is in caloric balance increases food intake without changing the energy expenditure, fat will accumulate. But fat will also accumulate if the food intake is held constant and

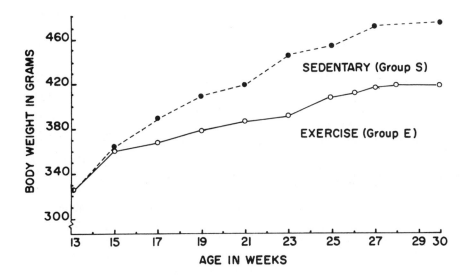

FIGURE 8–1. Mean weight gain for two groups of animals. There were 22 animals in the sedentary group and 20 in the exercise group. From Jones et al. (35).

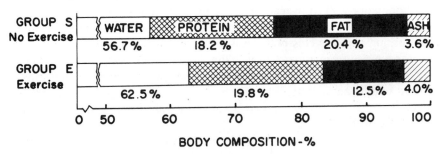

FIGURE 8–2. Mean proximate carcass analysis. It is clear that the exercising animals of Figure 8–1 (Group E) are leaner than the sedentary animals (Group S). From Jones et al. (35).

the energy expenditure is decreased. Conversely, body fat will be lost if energy expenditure is maintained but food intake is decreased *or* if food intake is maintained and physical exercise is increased. This is well known to the farmer who "pens up" animals to fatten them. Figure 8–1 illustrates the same effect in laboratory rats. In this study, the animals in Group E swam about two hours a day; the animals in Group S were confined to small cages which provided little opportunity for exercise (35). Figure 8–2 shows that it is primarily the ratio of fat to muscle that was affected. Similarly, men whose occupation requires little physical activity are fatter, on the average, than men whose occupations require considerable energy expenditure (8, 43, 45).

It is abundantly clear that obese children are less active than children of normal weight, the former having a history of infrequent participation in sports. This observation has been repeated a number of times, both here and abroad. The studies are reviewed elsewhere (43, 45, 46, 49). It is obvious that a vicious cycle develops in which reduced activity results in increased fatness which in turn results in further reduction in activity. However, there is evidence that a decrease in physical activity precedes and is responsible for triggering this cycle in many adolescents (45).

Dr. Mayer, who has done much research on the interrelation of exercise and weight control, has attempted to dispel two erroneous concepts concerning this relationship (43, 46). The first of these is the notion that exercise requires little caloric expenditure and hence is ineffective in controlling body weight. The second is the idea that exercise invariably increases the appetite and therefore any energy expenditure is balanced by increased food intake. Concerning the first of these, it is estimated that a pound of fat is equivalent to about 3500 calories. Walking at 4 miles per hour requires about 490 calories per hour whereas driving an automobile for the same length of time requires about 170 calories (61). The difference of 320 calories per hour indicates that one would have to walk about 11 hours in preference to driving a car for the same time in order to burn up a pound of body fat. However, the walking need not be done at one stretch. If a man living a quarter of a mile from work walked instead of drove to work and walked home for lunch as well, he would expend about 20,000 extra calories in a year (assuming 250 working days). This is the equivalent of roughly 6 pounds of body fat per year for his fifteen minutes of walking, five days per week, and would more than offset the average gain in weight experienced by males from young adulthood to middle age. After all, one should not expect exercise to effectively reduce body fat in a week or two when it has taken ten or fifteen years to accumulate the excess fat.

Furthermore, there is ample evidence that the resting metabolic rate may be elevated for an appreciable length of time after exercise. If this additional expenditure of calories is included, it means that the usual energy cost tables of various exercises may underestimate considerably the importance of exercise.

Evidence also comes from Dr. Mayer's work (43), to refute the second misconception. The food intake and body weight of men in very sedentary occupations were found to be greater than among men doing light work. This supports a study with rats. The food intake and body weight of rats doing one hour of exercise a day was less than animals who were totally inactive. This indicates that appetite (or at least food intake) goes down rather than up when a small amount of activity is added to an otherwise sedentary life (43). It is true, of course, in both studies, that the appetite increases as additional work is done, but only to keep pace with the additional energy expended so that the body weight remains essentially constant. Why sedentary animals and humans consume more food than those moderately active is probably a complicated question. Dr. Cohen and Dr. Serrano (15) suggest the interesting hypothesis that the sedentary animal maintains a lower body and brain temperature, thus serving as a stimulus to the hypothalamic feeding center.

Recent data (45) have shown that obese girls overestimated the amount of exercise they experienced and seemed totally unaware of the role of physical activity in maintenance of normal body weight. It has been demonstrated a number of times that an exercise and nutrition program is effective in reducing body fatness in obese children (17, 45). Whether or not the attitude of these children towards obesity and exercise has been profoundly affected by the exercise program remains to be seen. It is obvious that obesity is an individual matter and involves psychological and sociological forces and needs as well as physiological ones.* However, if the individual can be motivated to maintain even a moderate exercise program throughout life, this can be effective in preventing or reducing the accumulation of excess fat.

Techniques for measuring body fatness

Theoretical considerations

There have been several excellent symposia on the measurement of body composition in recent years; however, the article by Keys and Brožek (37), even though the focus is on adults, remains one of the best discussions of body composition and the measurement of body fatness. The human or animal body may be thought of as being composed of four major substances, namely bone, water, fat, and muscles and internal organs. With regard to measuring body fatness, variation in bone density is of minor significance. Even the change in bone density associated with aging does not introduce a serious error. Hence, variations in bone density between individuals will be ignored in this introductory treatment of the subject.

Alteration in body fluids deserves more consideration but even the influence of this factor does not present serious difficulties in the vast majority of instances. About three-fourths of the body fluid is located within the cells, the rest being in the tissue spaces, blood, etc. The amount of this body water can be markedly altered in certain diseases, unusual salt concentration in the body, or extreme environmental conditions. One should not, for example, attempt to assess the fatness of a boy after a strenuous work-out in the heat when he may have lost considerable body water. In a small percentage of adults and a still smaller percentage of children, edema will seriously affect estimates of body fatness. For the majority of adults and children, however, normal body hydration and bone density can be assumed and for these individuals the assessment of body composition becomes a problem of determining the relative percentage of fat and muscle.

*An accurate and readable discussion of obesity and the many factors involved is contained in the recent book by Mayer (44).

Laboratory techniques

General comments

The physical educator conducting school or adult fitness programs is not generally concerned with the more accurate laboratory methods of measuring body composition and estimating body fatness. However, some of these techniques are used to validate the field methods used. Therefore, it is important for the physical educator to understand how such measurements are made. Excellent discussions of these techniques may be found in one of the references (7). In recent years, a number of new laboratory techniques have been proposed. These include estimating fat under the skin by ultrasonics; estimating body volume by air displacement, helium dilution, or photogrammetry; creatinine excretion; potassium content; or total body water. The more generally employed method of hydrostatic weighing will be discussed in some detail.

Hydrostatic weighing

The density of an object is equal to its mass (or weight) divided by its volume. For inanimate objects, volume often can be determined quite easily by lowering the object into water and measuring the volume of the overflow. Density may in turn be used to calculate specific gravity (S.G.) by dividing the density of the object by the density of the accepted reference, namely water at a specified temperature.

The specific gravity may also be determined by weighing the object in air and in water.
Thus:

$$\text{S.G.} \ = \ \frac{\text{weight in air}}{\text{weight in air} - \text{weight in water}}$$

If the object floats in water (specific gravity less than one) it is necessary to attach a sinker and the formula becomes:

$$\text{S.G.*} = \frac{\text{weight of object in air}}{\begin{array}{c}(\text{weight of an object in air} + \text{weight of sinker in water}) - \\ (\text{weight of object in water} + \text{weight of sinker in water})\end{array}}$$

This technique embodies the ancient principle of Archimedes.

In human beings, it is more accurate to estimate specific gravity by weighing in water rather than by measuring the volume of the water displaced. Attempts to estimate the specific gravity of humans in this way have been carried out for over two hundred years. The underwater weighing can be done in the swimming pool (28), but specially built tanks are more convenient to use. The principal problem with estimating percent body fat from specific

---

*However, it is necessary to correct for water temperature. See reference 37 for a complete discussion of this point.

gravity determined by hydrostatic weighing is the error introduced by the residual air in the lungs.

After the specific gravity has been measured, it can be used to estimate the percent fat in the body by the following formula of Rathbun and Pace (37):

$$\% \text{ Fat} = 100 \left(\frac{5.548}{\text{S.G.}} - 5.044 \right)$$

This is a modification of the formula these authors calculated from chemical analysis of the carcasses of 50 guinea pigs. In the human being, as in animals, the density of fat is less than the density of water, bone, or other tissues. Hence, the higher the percentage of body fat, the lower will be the specific gravity.

Practical methods

Weight change

In many instances, a change in body weight is a simple increase or decrease in body fatness. However, this is a valid procedure only when the change is measured over a short period of time and then only if there have not been unusual changes in hydration (percent body water) or significant changes in muscle mass as a result of a conditioning or deconditioning program. Also, when fat is lost or gained, some supporting tissue and water are also lost or gained. Thus, in overeating experiments by Keys (37), when a man gained 7.1 kilograms of body fat he had an increase of 11.5 kilograms in body weight.

If individuals undergo a strenuous conditioning program, including such muscle-building activities as weight lifting, it is a common observation that body weight increases despite a decrease in body fat. It is also possible for certain body dimensions to decrease on such a regimen even though the body weight stays the same or increases slightly.

Frequently, in middle-aged men or women, weight gain since some arbitrary age (for example, age 25) is used as a measure of body fatness. But the fatness of people at age 25 varies greatly; hence the base line is different for different people. For example, two men may gain 10 pounds from age 25 to age 40. However, the one may have already been bordering on obesity at age 25, and the other might have been a lean athlete at that age. Despite the fact that each gained 10 pounds in the fifteen-year period, they are hardly equally fat at age 40. There are other problems with considering weight gain since some arbitrary age as a measure of fatness. Aside from changes in bone density that may occur with advancing age, and which probably are not of much consequence in interpreting weight changes, there are other sources of error. As people get older, they frequently are less active and muscle mass may decrease. Hence, over a period of years there may be no change in body weight but a decrease in muscle mass balanced by an increase in body fat.

In other cases, an increase in body weight with loss in muscle mass reflects only part of the gain in body fat.

Another measure of a change in fatness over a period of time is in the way clothes fit. A change in clothes size is a meaningful and simple indication of a change in fatness. Even though the body weight has not changed, a person participating in a fitness program might show a decrease in body fatness and a change in size. Of course, the measure is subject to error if there are abnormal changes in hydration. Even normal variations coincident with phases of the menstrual cycle in women are reflected in this measurement and allowances must be made for this in body fatness.

Relative weight

Most, if not all, readers are familiar with the age-height-weight tables for males and females which were developed by insurance company statisticians. Each value in these tables is an "average" weight for a given age, sex, and height. This value is not necessarily an ideal weight but rather the average weight for people of a particular sex, age, and height who are examined for insurance. There have also been extensive tables compiled as a result of measurements of armed forces personnel and in other state and national surveys. More recently tables of "ideal" or desirable weights have been compiled (37) based on the weight for a given height associated with the lowest mortality.

It is well known that people who are muscular and stocky are overweight by these "average" or "ideal" standards even though they may be lean. Dr. W. C. Welhan and Dr. Albert Behnke demonstrated that the usual height-age-sex tables are inadequate when they showed that professional football players were rated very much overweight by the tables and yet these men were quite lean as determined by body specific gravity measurements (65). Keys and Brožek (38) raised the question whether such exceptions are common enough to warrant concern. These workers classified people by the age-height-sex tables and also by more refined methods of measuring body fatness. It was clear that if one wishes to categorize people by body fatness, a large percentage of subjects are misclassified by such insurance company tables.

An early attempt to include body breadth measurements resulted in the tables developed by Dr. Helen Pryor (56). More recently, insurance company tables have included mean values based on three body builds: small, medium, and large frame (37). However, since no objective criteria are provided for classifying body builds, this refinement is of little help. Weight is likely more closely related to volume than to a linear measurement such as height. This has produced a number of studies in which the validity of insurance tables and ratios of height and weight as measures of total body fatness were investigated. This was done by comparing estimates of fatness utilizing a laboratory method with the degree a subject is overweight or underweight according to a height-weight table. Correlation coefficients for these

TABLE 8–1

Relationship of Relative Weight to Other Measures of Total Body Fatness

Measure of Rel. Wt.	Method of Estimating Body Fatness	Correlation Coefficient	Subjects	Reference
	hydrostatic weighing	.63	88 young men	Pascale, et al. (54)
	hydrostatic weighing	.58	94 young women	Young, et al. (69)
Age, ht, sex standards (Insurance Company)	hydrostatic weighing	.48	88 middle-aged women	Young, et al. (69)
	hydrostatic weighing	.78	116 young men	Brožek and Keys (11)
	hydrostatic weighing	.63	214 middle-aged men	Brožek and Keys (11)
	total body water	.75	31 patients	Edwards and Whyte (21)
	total body water	.78*	31 patients	Edwards and Whyte (21)
Wt./ht.	hydrostatic weighing	.70	26 women	Billewicz, et al. (5)
Wt./ht.	hydrostatic weighing	.74	55 men	Billewicz, et al. (5)
Wt./ht.	hydrostatic weighing	.57	97 men	Billewicz, et al. (5)
Wt./ht.	Potassium—40	.56	50 men and women	Forbes, et al. (23)
Wt./ht.^{2}	hydrostatic weighing	.72	26 women	Billewicz, et al. (5)
Wt./ht.^{2}	hydrostatic weighing	.80	55 men	Billewicz, et al. (5)
Wt./ht.^{2}	hydrostatic weighing	.60	97 men	Billewicz, et al. (5)
Wt./ht.^{2}	total body water	.79	31 patients	Edwards and Whyte (21)
Wt./ht.^{3}	total body water	.76	31 patients	Edwards and Whyte (21)
Ht./wt.$^{1/3}$	hydrostatic weighing	.68	26 women	Billewicz, et al. (5)
Ht./wt.$^{1/3}$	hydrostatic weighing	.77	55 men	Billewicz, et al. (5)
Ht./wt.$^{1/3}$	hydrostatic weighing	.57	97 men	Billewicz, et al. (5)
Ht./abd. girth	Creatinine Coefficient	.55	78 young men	Best, et al. (4)
Wt. & abd. girth	hydrostatic weighing	.79**	133 young men	Wilmore and Behnke (66)
Wt. & 4 anthro. meas.	hydrostatic weighing	.85**	133 young men	Wilmore and Behnke (66)
Ht. & wt.	hydrostatic weighing	.52**	176 young men	Cowgill (16)
Ht., knee & wrist diam.	hydrostatic weighing	.71**	133 young men	Wilmore and Behnke (66)
Ht., knee & wrist diam.	hydrostatic weighing	.71**	16 young men, 16 young women	Von Dobeln (64)
Ht., chest & wrist diam.	hydrostatic weighing	.82**	133 young men	Wilmore and Behnke (66)
Ht., chest & wrist diam.	He. Dil. & Tot. Body Water	.84**	31 men	Hechter (32)
Various diameters	hydrostatic weighing	.88–.90**	54 young men	Wilmore and Behnke (67)
Various diameters	hydrostatic weighing	.74–.82**	133 young men	Wilmore and Behnke (66)

*Age, ht, sex standards at age 25 **multiple r

analyses are given in Table 8–1. As can be seen, various height-weight ratios are not much better than insurance tables based on height alone. However, a technique recently suggested by Dr. Behnke, one of the pioneers in this field, is of interest. This approach involves estimating body density or lean body weight from anthropometric measurements, weight and height (3, 66, 67). Percent body fat can then be calculated. (See Table 8–1.)

Skinfolds

It is possible to grasp, between the thumb and index finger, the loose tissue over the abdomen, at the waistline or at other places on the body. This "pinch" of tissue is known as a "skinfold" and includes a double layer of skin plus subcutaneous fat. The thickness of the fold reflects the amount of fat under the skin and is measured in millimeters with a "skinfold caliper."

The early calipers employed were scissor-type, requiring manual or spring pressure on the jaws of the calipers. The pressure exerted was not standardized, which produced variable results, making comparisons of data difficult. This led to the development of a c-shaped caliper at the Laboratory of Physiological Hygiene at the University of Minnesota in which the pressure exerted by the jaws could be maintained at 10 grams per square millimeter (37). Further modifications led to the production of two types of calipers, the Lange and the Harpenden.

The Lange calipers are less expensive, lighter, and easier to handle. The Harpenden calipers provide a more accurate scale for making readings. Both are designed to provide a jaw pressure of 10 grams per square millimeter but, like most instruments, should be calibrated before being used and at frequent intervals thereafter. The two calipers are illustrated in Figure 8–3.*

Technique: The measurement of skinfold thickness is not a difficult procedure. However, several precautions are necessary. The procedure must be standardized with regard to (a) the site on the body where the skinfold is to be taken and (b) the distance from the point at which the skinfold is lifted and the site at which the calipers are applied. This is important because the skinfold should be compressed by the calipers, not by the experimenter's fingers. When pressure is applied with the calipers, the thickness of the skinfold will gradually decrease because tissue is squeezed out from under the jaws of the calipers. This was thought to be a crucial source of error until Dr. H. E. Lewis and colleagues (39) demonstrated that after 2 seconds essentially all compression has taken place and the measurement is stabilized, except in cases of edema. Therefore, if the reading is made between about 2 and 5 seconds, little error from this source will arise.

A number of sites have been proposed for taking skinfolds. A brief

---

*The Lange calipers are sold by Cambridge Scientific Industries, 527 Poplar Street, Cambridge, Maryland. The Harpenden calipers are manufactured by British Indicators, Ltd., but are available in the United States from H. E. Morse Co., 455 Douglas Avenue, Holland, Michigan.

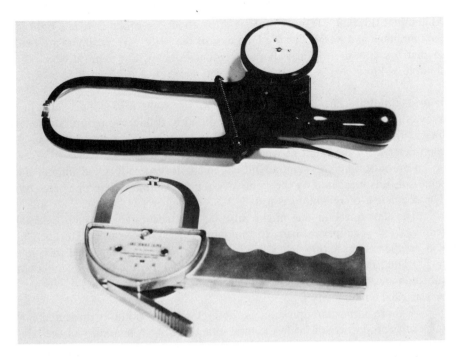

FIGURE 8–3. Skinfold calipers. The Harpenden calipers
are shown above; the Lange calipers, below.

description of the technique for measurement at five of the most common
sites is given below. The measurement in millimeters is the width of a double
skinfold, which is the way values are generally reported.

Biceps skinfold. This measurement is taken approximately over the center of
the biceps muscle of the upper arm. The arm should be relaxed and hanging
freely. The skinfold is lifted about a centimeter below this point along the
long axis of the muscle. The caliper, in a horizontal position, is allowed to
compress the skinfold about a centimeter above the point where the thumb
and finger grasp the skinfolds.

Triceps skinfold. This measurement is taken at a site halfway between the
tip of the acromial process and tip of the elbow. The arm should be hanging
freely. The skinfold is lifted on the back of the right arm parallel to long axis
of the arm about 1 centimeter above the site. Calipers are allowed to compress skinfold about 1 centimeter below the point where the skinfold is lifted.

Subscapular skinfold. The skinfold is lifted at the tip of the right scapula on
a diagonal plane about 45 degrees from the horizontal (laterally downward).
The calipers are used about 1 centimeter laterally downward from this point.

Abdominal skinfold.   The skinfold is lifted about 1 centimeter to the right of the umbilicus and parallel to the long axis of the body.   The calipers are held so that the jaws are vertical about 1 centimeter below the point at which the skinfold is lifted.

Waist skinfold.   The skinfold is lifted on the right mid-axillary line just above the crest of the ilium.   The fold is lifted to follow the natural diagonal line at this point (dorsally upward).   The calipers are again used about 1 centimeter from the point at which the skinfold is lifted.

Reproducibility of skinfold measurement is generally good among the same subjects measured by the same investigators on more than one occasion. The coefficient of reliability is usually 0.90 or higher (2).

The first question one might raise is, how accurately do such external readings with a caliper measure the amount of fat at these sites?   The correlation coefficients resulting from these comparisons are summarized in Table 8–2.   The pinch caliper measurements agree quite well with the thickness of subcutaneous fat as measured after incision or by means of x-ray, ultrasonics, or electrical conductivity.

A more important question is, how closely do skinfold measurements reflect the proportion of fat in the total intact body?   A summary of the relationship between total body fat as measured by skinfolds and as measured by hydrostatic weighing (specific gravity) is shown in Table 8–3.   Using body weight or height in the regression equations does not improve the estimates of fatness from skinfolds (Table 8–3 and reference 18).   Other evidence of validity of skinfolds as a measure of fatness has also appeared in the literature in the form of longitudinal data on weight change (26, 37).   These studies show that when weight is lost or gained, skinfolds decrease or increase respectively.

TABLE 8–2
Relationship between Pinch Caliper Skinfolds and Other
Measures of Subcutaneous Fat

Method of Measuring Subcutaneous Fat	Correlation Coefficient	Subjects	Reference
Incision	.82	19 middle-aged men and women	Fry (25)
Roentgenograms	.61	20 men and women	Fletcher (22)
Roentgenograms	.88	65 young men	Garn and Gorman (27)
Roentgenograms	.85	83 young men	Baker (2)
Roentgenograms	.79	30 young men	Clarke et al. (14)
Roentgenograms	.82	52 middle-aged men	Brožek and Mori (12)
Roentgenograms	.82–.89	Boys	Hammond (30)
Roentgenograms	.84–.90	Girls	Hammond (30)
Ultrasonic	.81	35 men and women	Booth et al. (6)
Electrical Conductivity	.81	14 men and women	Booth et al. (6)

It has been observed (37) that the skinfold measurements of various sites on the same subjects are highly correlated (r = 0.742 to 0.938). We've observed much the same results in the Tecumseh Community Health Study (47) in which the correlation coefficients between triceps and subscapular skinfolds range between 0.6 and 0.8 for age groups spanning 10 years among males and females. When the sum of four skinfolds was correlated with the sum of two, the coefficients were generally near 0.9. This means that the law of diminishing returns applies very soon and a few skinfolds is about as good as taking measurements at many sites. Therefore, to measure skinfolds at more than three or four sites is not worth the additional time.

The use of skinfolds in weight analysis

Skinfold measurements have generally been used in one of two ways, either to classify individuals on the basis of the thickness of one or more skinfolds or to estimate a person's "ideal" weight by means of prediction equations. Classification by skinfolds will be discussed first.

The simplest approach is to add several skinfolds together for each individual and then compare subjects of the same age and sex on the sum of skinfolds. This was the method used in the Tecumseh Community Health Study cited above (47). Skinfolds were measured at four sites; namely, triceps, subscapular, abdomen, and waist, as described in the previous section. These four values were added together. Percentile scores were developed for males and females of various ages. These are shown in Tables 8–4 and 8–5. It was then possible to convert the sum of four skinfolds for a particular individual into a percentile score by using these tables. For example, a 14-year-old boy whose triceps, subscapular, abdominal, and waist skinfolds added up to 98 millimeters had a percentile score of 90. This means that on the average he is fatter than about 90% of boys his age in Tecumseh, Michigan, and leaner than 10% (Table 8–4). On the other hand, a 57-year-old woman with a sum of 98 millimeters for these four skinfolds would have a percentile score of only 25 (Table 8–5). She would thus be leaner than average.

The percentiles in Tables 8–4 and 8–5 may be useful to the physical educator because they include a wide age range and both sexes. However, it is best to develop one's own percentile scores because there is sometimes considerable variation in technique between individuals taking the skinfold measurements. This method was sufficient for purposes of the research in Tecumseh, Michigan, since only a measure of relative fatness for each individual was wanted. However, if a person is overfat, a skinfold measurement or the sum of several skinfolds does not reveal how much weight should be lost. Yet this is what the child or adult would like to know. Hence, equations or techniques have been developed to estimate from the skinfolds what one ought to weigh. This will be discussed next.

Probably the most comprehensive data reported recently using this approach was the study by Durnin and Womersley (20). They measured skinfolds in 209 males and 272 females, age 16–72. They also determined the

TABLE 8–3

Relationship between Pinch Caliper Skinfolds and Total Body Density as Measured by Hydrostatic Weighing

Correlation Coefficient*	Number of Skinfold Sites	Subjects	Reference
.87	3	116 young men	Brožek and Keys (10)
.88	6 plus rel. wt.	116 young men	Brožek and Keys (10)
.74	6 plus rel. wt.	214 middle-aged men	Brožek and Keys (11)
.85	3	88 young men	Pascale, et al. (54)
.86	5 plus rel. wt.	88 young men	Pascale, et al. (54)
.69	12	94 young women	Young, et al. (69)
.69	12	88 middle-aged women	Young, et al. (69)
.74	8	100 young men	Royce (57)
.91	13	50 Chinese men	Chen, et al. (13)
.70	13 (wt. partialled out)	29 Chinese women	Chen, et al. (13)
.90	10	66 boys, age 9–12	Pařízková (53)
.81	10	56 girls, age 9–12	Pařízková (53)
.92	10	57 boys, age 13–17	Pařízková (53)
.83	10	62 girls, age 13–17	Pařízková (53)
.80	2	133 young men	Wilmore and Behnke (66)

r	Measurements	Sample	Reference
.78	7	133 young men	Wilmore and Behnke (66)
.81	4 plus ht.	133 young men	Wilmore and Behnke (66)
.86	7	50 young men	Sloan (58)
.74	2–4	50 young women	Sloan, et al. (59)
.81–.88	2	28 young men	Sloan and Shapiro (60)
.74–.84	2–3	23 girls, age 14–18	Wilmore, et al. (68)
.76–.85	2–3	55 males, age 17–59	Wilmore, et al. (68)
.84**	4	60 males, age 18–34	Durnin and Rahaman (19)
.78**	4	45 women, age 22–29	Durnin and Rahaman (19)
.76**	4	48 boys, age 13–16	Durnin and Rahaman (19)
.78**	4	38 girls, age 13–16	Durnin and Rahaman (19)
.92	1 plus 1 girth and 1 diameter	30 males, age 25–50	Zuti and Golding (70)
.78–.83	2 plus 2 girths	23 girls, age 14–18	Wilmore, et al. (68)
.83	2 plus 1 girth, and 1 diameter	83 women, age 18–22	Pollock, et al. (55)
.89	2 plus 1 girth and cup size	60 women, age 33–55	Pollock, et al. (55)
.7–.9	2–4	481 men and women, age 16–72	Durnin and Womersley (20)

*Minus signs have been omitted. Higher density (i.e., less fat) is inversely correlated with skinfold thickness.
**The inclusion of girths and other anthropometric measurements didn't improve the relationships.

TABLE 8-4
Sum of Four Skinfolds in Millimeters: Males
(Tecumseh Community Health Study)*

Columns 5 through 65-69 are Age (years).

Per-centile	5	6	7	8	9	10	11	12	13	14	15	16	17	18	19	20-24	25-29	30-34	35-39	40-44	45-49	50-54	55-59	60-64	65-69	Per-centile
95	40	59	61	85	77	114	119	144	136	128	160	160	174	138	148	153	170	150	165	143	134	153	154	126	147	95
90	36	42	43	63	52	90	91	124	102	98	112	132	142	113	121	135	150	136	139	126	123	134	149	116	129	90
85	33	36	35	44	48	74	76	104	84	83	91	112	120	94	109	121	138	126	129	116	117	122	130	111	117	85
80	31	34	34	40	42	62	65	88	73	72	79	96	103	81	94	109	126	118	121	110	117	115	122	106	107	80
75	30	32	32	36	38	54	57	74	64	64	70	84	91	71	88	99	117	111	114	104	106	108	115	101	99	75
70	29	30	30	34	36	48	51	64	58	58	64	75	82	65	78	90	110	105	108	99	102	103	109	97	92	70
65	27	29	28	33	31	44	46	55	54	52	60	67	75	60	74	82	103	99	102	94	98	98	105	93	86	65
60	26	27	27	31	29	40	42	48	49	48	56	61	70	57	70	76	96	94	97	90	94	94	100	90	81	60
55	25	26	26	29	28	37	39	43	46	46	52	56	65	56	66	69	90	89	91	86	91	89	96	86	77	55
50	25	25	25	28	27	35	37	40	42	42	50	52	62	55	62	64	83	84	87	82	87	85	91	82	74	50
45	24	25	24	27	26	34	35	37	40	40	48	49	59	54	58	59	77	79	82	78	84	82	87	79	71	45
40	23	24	23	26	25	33	33	36	37	38	45	46	57	53	55	55	71	74	78	74	80	78	83	75	69	40
35	22	23	23	25	24	32	32	34	35	36	43	44	56	52	52	50	65	69	73	70	76	74	79	71	66	35
30	21	22	22	23	23	30	30	32	33	35	40	42	54	49	48	46	59	64	68	65	71	69	75	67	63	30
25	20	21	21	22	22	28	28	30	31	33	38	41	51	46	46	43	53	59	63	60	66	63	70	63	58	25
20	19	20	20	21	21	26	26	28	29	31	34	40	47	43	43	39	48	54	56	54	59	57	66	57	53	20
15	19	19	20	20	20	24	24	27	27	29	32	38	44	38	42	36	41	48	49	47	51	50	62	51	46	15
10	18	19	19	19	18	22	22	23	25	26	28	35	39	34	38	32	35	43	42	41	42	44	56	45	39	10
5	17	16	16	17	17	18	19	20	23	23	25	31	34	28	36	29	28	36	34	33	32	36	44	38	30	5
No. of Cases	127	127	138	110	132	118	127	128	107	103	98	110	90	60	55	239	238	293	325	291	232	174	136	104	71	No. of Cases
Mean	26.1	29.6	30.6	35.1	34.4	45.5	48.7	58.2	54.5	54.7	60.2	67.2	68.0	63.9	77.7	74.3	88.7	85.7	88.6	84.8	87.7	87.1	93.4	84.2	79.0	Mean
S.D.	8.9	16.6	20.8	24.2	24.8	29.1	33.2	39.5	36.2	34.3	34.1	31.9	42.0	32.0	37.4	39.9	41.8	33.8	36.2	33.9	34.5	34.0	32.1	31.0	33.5	S.D.

*The work was supported in part by Research Grant CD-00246 and Program Project Grant HE09814, both of the National Institutes of Health, U.S. Public Health Service.

TABLE 8-5
Sum of Four Skinfolds in Millimeters: Females
(Tecumseh Community Health Study)*

Per-centile	Age																									Per-centile
	5	6	7	8	9	10	11	12	13	14	15	16	17	18	19	20-24	25-29	30-34	35-39	40-44	45-49	50-54	55-59	60-64	65-69	
95	54	57	69	92	116	110	131	141	130	146	170	144	140	175	129	166	209	179	166	200	186	219	195	200	181	95
90	45	47	60	75	75	90	106	114	103	119	143	118	118	136	120	141	165	152	149	171	173	195	174	182	167	90
85	43	43	53	65	65	86	85	96	90	102	126	104	104	117	113	125	139	137	136	154	162	178	165	170	158	85
80	39	40	48	58	54	77	78	84	83	91	114	96	94	107	106	114	124	126	126	138	151	168	158	162	150	80
75	37	37	42	52	50	69	70	76	77	82	104	90	87	99	99	105	112	115	117	126	140	158	152	156	144	75
70	35	35	40	48	46	62	64	69	72	76	96	85	82	92	93	97	106	107	110	117	131	148	147	150	138	70
65	34	34	38	45	43	56	58	64	68	71	87	80	78	87	88	90	96	100	103	109	122	139	141	145	133	65
60	33	33	36	41	40	52	54	60	64	67	82	76	73	82	83	83	89	94	97	103	114	131	139	139	128	60
55	32	32	35	39	39	48	51	56	60	63	77	72	70	77	79	77	83	88	91	97	106	124	131	134	123	55
50	31	31	33	37	37	45	48	52	57	61	73	69	66	72	75	72	78	83	86	91	101	118	126	128	118	50
45	30	30	30	33	36	42	45	48	54	58	70	65	63	68	71	67	73	78	81	86	96	112	120	122	114	45
40	29	29	29	30	34	40	42	46	51	56	66	62	60	64	67	64	68	73	76	81	91	106	115	115	109	40
35	28	29	28	28	32	38	39	43	48	53	63	59	57	61	64	60	64	68	71	77	85	100	109	108	104	35
30	27	28	27	27	32	36	38	41	46	50	60	56	54	57	60	56	60	64	66	72	80	94	104	100	100	30
25	26	27	26	26	29	34	36	39	43	48	55	53	50	53	56	52	55	59	61	67	74	87	98	90	95	25
20	25	26	25	25	27	32	32	37	40	44	52	51	47	50	52	48	51	54	56	61	67	81	92	80	90	20
15	24	24	22	24	25	29	30	35	36	41	48	48	44	47	49	44	46	52	52	57	60	74	84	69	84	15
10	21	23	21	23	25	26	28	34	33	37	42	46	41	43	46	39	41	45	46	52	53	63	75	58	76	10
5	19	20	19	21	23	22	25	28	28	32	34	41	37	40	42	34	35	39	38	44	44	47	61	46	65	5
No. of Cases	118	148	130	118	117	93	122	129	92	101	100	101	70	57	56	268	290	303	351	298	210	154	140	89	71	No. of Cases
Mean	33.7	33.7	37.5	43.1	45.2	55.2	57.9	64.7	65.9	77.0	84.7	77.2	74.6	86.1	80.3	81.2	88.7	94.0	93.2	105.4	111.6	120.9	123.2	123.2	121.4	Mean
S.D.	14.2	12.3	19.0	23.6	26.5	31.7	31.3	35.5	33.0	35.4	43.0	34.0	33.4	46.8	27.2	40.1	47.1	45.4	45.4	48.4	47.2	45.9	38.3	43.5	35.2	S.D.

*The work was supported in part by Research Grant CD-00246 and Program Project Grant HE09814, both of the National Institutes of Health, U.S. Public Health Service.

total body density of each subject by weighing him or her underwater (hydrostatic weighing) as described earlier in this chapter. Equations were then developed to estimate from the four skinfolds the percentage of any particular individual's weight that is due to fat. A table (Table 8–6) was then constructed to facilitate the calculation. In their work, four skinfolds were used; namely, biceps, triceps, subscapula, and suprailiac (waist). An example will illustrate how the table is to be used.

Suppose a male, age 34, had the following skinfolds: biceps, 7 mm; triceps, 10 mm; subscapula, 14 mm; and suprailiac, 17 mm. The total of these is 48 mm. We look for this value in the first column of Table 8–6. This figure does not appear but 45 and 50 are tabulated. Hence we must interpolate between 45 and 50. We may observe that 48 mm falls at three-fifths of the distance between 45 and 50. If we now look under males, age 30–39 (Third column, Table 8–6), we note that 45 mm corresponds to 20.4% fat and 50 mm corresponds to 21.5% fat. Interpolating three-fifths of the distance between the two gives 21.1% fat for 48 mm. This means for a man age 34, 21.1% of his body weight on the average is due to the weight of fat tissue. Frequently an estimate of 15% fat is considered a reasonable figure for an "ideal" body weight for an adult male. This particular subject weighed 162 lb. If we accept the ideal percentage of 15, then we can calculate this man's ideal weight as follows:

Estimated % body fat (from table)   21.1
Estimated ideal weight (15% body fat)   150 lb.

162 lb $\times$ 21.1% = 34.2 lb fat
162 lb — 34.2 lb = 127.8 lb lean body mass

$$\frac{127.8}{85\%} = \frac{X}{100\%}$$

X = 150.35 lb ideal body weight (15% fat)
Overweight = 162 lb — 150 lb = 12 lb

The same calculations can be made for women but in this case 20% is a more reasonable estimate of the "ideal." The last four columns of Table 8–6 are used for women and 80% is substituted for the 85% in the calculations above.

The use of equations developed by someone else implies that the technique of measuring the skinfolds is the same as ours. We can only hope that this assumption is reasonable. In most cases, if the physical educator is careful and uses a good caliper, errors in making the assumption probably are not large.

Unfortunately, Durnin and Womersley in their study did not measure children under age 16. There have been a few similar studies reported in which data on younger children are given. Probably the best of these is the report by Pařízková (53). She also measured skinfolds and underwater weight in her subjects (boys and girls age 9–16). Using just two skinfolds

TABLE 8–6

The equivalent fat content, as a percentage of body weight, for a range of values for the sum of four skinfolds (biceps, triceps, subscapular, and suprailiac) of men and women of different ages.

Skinfolds (mm)	Males (age in years)				Females (age in years)			
	17–29	30–39	40–49	50+	16–29	30–39	40–49	50+
15	4.8	—	—	—	10.5	—	—	—
20	8.1	12.2	12.2	12.6	14.1	17.0	19.8	21.4
25	10.5	14.2	15.0	15.6	16.8	19.4	22.2	24.0
30	12.9	16.2	17.7	18.6	19.5	21.8	24.5	26.6
35	14.7	17.7	19.6	20.8	21.5	23.7	26.4	28.5
40	16.4	19.2	21.4	22.9	23.4	25.5	28.2	30.3
45	17.7	20.4	23.0	24.7	25.0	26.9	29.6	31.9
50	19.0	21.5	24.6	26.5	26.5	28.2	31.0	33.4
55	20.1	22.5	25.9	27.9	27.8	29.4	32.1	34.6
60	21.2	23.5	27.1	29.2	29.1	30.6	33.2	35.7
65	22.2	24.3	28.2	30.4	30.2	31.6	34.1	36.7
70	23.1	25.1	29.3	31.6	31.2	32.5	35.0	37.7
75	24.0	25.9	30.3	32.7	32.2	33.4	35.9	38.7
80	24.8	26.6	31.2	33.8	33.1	34.3	36.7	39.6
85	25.5	27.2	32.1	34.8	34.0	35.1	37.5	40.4
90	26.2	27.8	33.0	35.8	34.8	35.8	38.3	41.2
95	26.9	28.4	33.7	36.6	35.6	36.5	39.0	41.9
100	27.6	29.0	34.4	37.4	36.4	37.2	39.7	42.6
105	28.2	29.6	35.1	38.2	37.1	37.9	40.4	43.3
110	28.8	30.1	35.8	39.0	37.8	38.6	41.0	43.9
115	29.4	30.6	36.4	39.7	38.4	39.1	41.5	44.5
120	30.0	31.1	37.0	40.4	39.0	39.6	42.0	45.1
125	30.5	31.5	37.6	41.1	39.6	40.1	42.5	45.7
130	31.0	31.9	38.2	41.8	40.2	40.6	43.0	46.2
135	31.5	32.3	38.7	42.4	40.8	41.1	43.5	46.7
140	32.0	32.7	39.2	43.0	41.3	41.6	44.0	47.2
145	32.5	33.1	39.7	43.6	41.8	42.1	44.5	47.7
150	32.9	33.5	40.2	44.1	42.3	42.6	45.0	48.2
155	33.3	33.9	40.7	44.6	42.8	43.1	45.4	48.7
160	33.7	34.3	41.2	45.1	43.3	43.6	45.8	49.2
165	34.1	34.6	41.6	45.6	43.7	44.0	46.2	49.6
170	34.5	34.8	42.0	46.1	44.1	44.4	46.6	50.0
175	34.9	—	—	—	—	44.8	47.0	50.4
180	35.3	—	—	—	—	45.2	47.4	50.8
185	35.6	—	—	—	—	45.6	47.8	51.2
190	35.9	—	—	—	—	45.9	48.2	51.6
195	—	—	—	—	—	46.2	48.5	52.0
200	—	—	—	—	—	46.5	48.8	52.4
205	—	—	—	—	—	—	49.1	52.7
210	—	—	—	—	—	—	49.4	53.0

In two-thirds of the instances, the error was within ± 3.5% of the body weight as fat for the women and ± 5% for the men.

From Durnin and Womersley (20). Reproduced with permission of the authors and publisher.

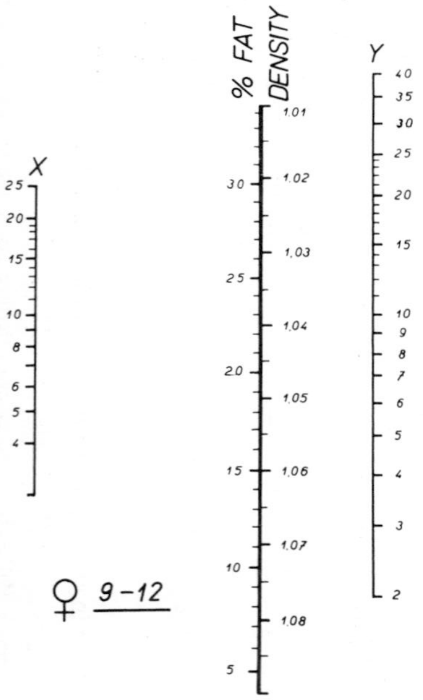

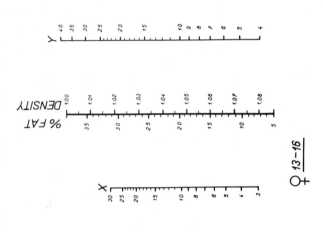

FIGURE 8–5. Nomogram for estimating body density or percent body fat from triceps skinfold (X-scale) and subscapular skinfold (Y-scale) in girls thirteen to sixteen years old. From Pařízková (53). Reproduced with permission of the author and publisher.

FIGURE 8–4. Nomogram for estimating body density or percent body fat from triceps skinfold (X-scale) and subscapular skinfold (Y-scale) in girls nine to twelve years old. From Pařízková (53). Reproduced with permission of the author and publisher.

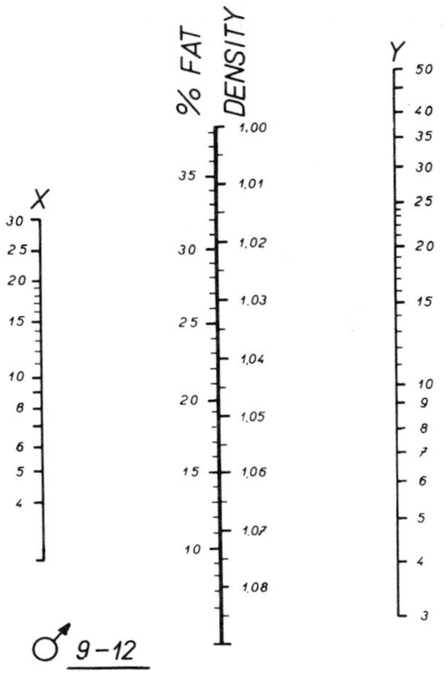

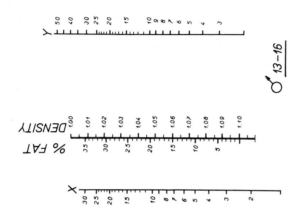

FIGURE 8–7. Nomogram for estimating body density or percent body fat from triceps skinfold (X-scale) and subscapular skinfold (Y-scale) in boys thirteen to sixteen years old. From Pařízková (53). Reproduced with permission of the author and publisher.

FIGURE 8–6. Nomogram for estimating body density or percent body fat from triceps skinfold (X-scale) and subscapular skinfold (Y-scale) in boys nine to twelve years old. From Pařízková (53). Reproduced with permission of the author and publisher.

(triceps and subscapular), she reported the correlation coefficients between hydrostatic weighing and the log of the skinfolds to be from 0.81 to 0.95. She developed nomograms to use in place of her prediction equations. These are reproduced as Figures 8–4 through 8–7. "X" on these nomograms represents the triceps skinfold and "Y" the subscapular skinfold. In order to estimate the percent fat (or density) for a particular individual, it is only necessary to lay a ruler connecting the value of the triceps skinfold on the X-scale with the values of the subscapular skinfold on the Y-scale. The per cent body weight which is due to fat tissue is then read off the middle scale. For example, a girl, age 11, has a triceps skinfold of 15 mm and a subscapular skinfold of 10 mm. Using Figure 8–4, we locate 15 on the X (triceps) scale and 10 on the Y (subscapular) scale. Connecting these two points with a ruler we can now read off 24% on the middle scale. In order to estimate "ideal" weight we follow the same procedure outlined above. This girl weighed 95 lb. Therefore, her fat weight is 95 × .24 = 22.8 lb. Her fat-free weight is estimated at 95 − 22.8 = 72.2 lb. Her "ideal" weight, assuming 20% fat is ideal, is estimated to be 72.8 lb. ÷ 0.80 = 90.3 lb.

REFERENCES

1. Armstrong, D. B.; L. I. Dublin; G. M. Wheatley; and H. H. Marks, "Obesity and Its Relation to Health and Disease." *J. Am. Med. Assoc.*, 147:1007, 1951.

2. Baker, P. T. *Relationship of Desert Heat Stress to Gross Morphology.* Headquarters U.S. Quartermaster Research and Development Command. Environmental Protection Div., Technical Report EP-7, March, 1955. Quartermaster Research and Development Center, U.S. Army, Natick, Massachusetts.

3. Booth, R. A. D.; B. A. Goddard; and A. Paton, "Measurement of Fat Thickness in Man: A Comparison of Ultrasound, Harpenden Calipers and Electrical Conductivity." *Brit. J. Nut.*, 20:719–725, 1966.

4. Best, W. R.; W. J. Kuhl; and C. F. Consolazio, "Relation of Creatinine Coefficient to Leanness-Fatness in Man." *J. Lab. Clin. Med.*, 42:784, 1953.

5. Billewicz, W. Z.; W. F. F. Kemsley; and A. M. Thomson, "Indices of Adiposity." *Brit. J. Prevent. and Social Med.*, 16:183, 1962.

6. *Body Composition in Animals and Man.* Washington, D.C.: National Acad. of Sciences, 1968. Publication Number 1598, pp. 521.

7. Brožek, J., (ed.), "Body Composition." Parts I and II, *Annals of the New York Acad. of Sciences*, 110:1–1018, 1963.

8. Brožek, J., "Body Composition." *Science*, 134:920, 1961.

9. Brožek, J., (ed.), *Body Measurements and Human Nutrition.* Detroit: Wayne State University Press, 1956, pp. 167.

10. Brožek, J. and A. Keys, "Body Build and Body Composition." *Science*, 116:140, 1952.

11. Brožek, J., and A. Keys, "The Evaluation of Leanness-Fatness in Man; Norms and Interrelationships." *Brit. J. Nutrition*, 5:194, 1951.

12. Brožek, J., and H. Mori, "Some Intercorrelation between Somatic, Roentgenographic and Densiometric Criteria of Fatness." *Human Biol.*, 30:322, 1958.

13. Chen, K. P.; A. Damon; and O. Elliott, "Body Form, Composition, and Some Physiological Functions of Chinese on Taiwan." In *Body Composition. Ann. N.Y. Acad. Sci.*, 110:760, 1963.

14. Clarke, H. H.; L. R. Geser; and S. B. Hunsdon, "Comparison of Upper Arm Measurements by Use of Roentgenogram and Anthropometric Techniques." *Res. Quart.*, 27:379, 1956.

15. Cohen, B. J. and L. J. Serrano, "Effects of Exercise and Confinement on Rats." *Laboratory Animal Care*, 13:5, 1963.

16. Cowgill, G. R., "A Formula for Estimating the Specific Gravity of the Human Body with a Consideration of Its Possible Uses." *Am. J. Clin. Nutrition*, 5:601, 1957.

17. Cristakis, G.; S. Sajecki; R. W. Hillman; E. Miller; S. Blumenthal; and M. Archer, "Effect of a Combined Nutrition Education and Physical Fitness Program on the Weight Status of Obese High School Boys." *Fed. Proc.*, 25: Part I, pp. 15, 1966.

18. Damon, A. and G. F. Goldman, "Predicting Fat from Body Measurements: Densiometric Validation of Ten Anthropometric Equations." *Human Biol.*, 36:32, 1964.

19. Durnin, J. V. G. A., and M. M. Rahaman, "The Assessment of the Amount of Fat in the Human Body from Measurements in Skinfold Thickness." *Brit. J. Nut.*, 21:681–689, 1967.

20. Durnin, J. V. G. A., and J. Womersley, "Body Fat Assessed from Total Body Density and Its Estimation from Skinfold Thickness: Measurements on 481 Men and Women Aged 16 to 72 Years." *Brit. J. Nut.*, 32:77, 1974.

21. Edwards, K. D. G. and H. M. Whyte, "The Simple Measurement of Obesity." *Clin. Sci.*, 22:347, 1962.

22. Fletcher, R. F., "The Measurement of Total Body Fat with Skinfold Calipers." *Clin. Sci.*, 22:347, 1962.

23. Forbes, G. B.; J. Gallup; and J. B. Hursh, "Estimation of Total Body Fat from Potassium–40 Count." *Science*, 133:101, 1961.

24. Forsyth, H. L. and W. E. Sinning, "The Anthropometric Estimation of Body Density and Lean Body Weight of Male Athletes." *Med. and Sci. in Sports*, 5: 174–180, 1973.

25. Fry, E. I., "The Measurement of Subcutaneous Tissue by the Harpenden Caliper and by Surgical Incision." *Am. J. Phys. Anthropol.*, 19:98, 1961.

26. Garn, S. M. and J. Brožek, "Fat Changes During Weight Loss." *Science*, 124:682, 1956.

27. Garn, S. M. and E. L. Gorman, "Comparison of Pinch-Caliper and Teleroentgenogrammetric Measurements of Subcutaneous Fat." *Human Biol.*, 28: 407, 1956.

28. Gnaedinger, R. H.; E. P. Reineke; A. M. Pearson; W. D. Van Huss; J. A. Wessel; and H. J. Montoye, "Determination of Body Density by Air Displacement, Helium Dilution, and Underwater Weighing," in *Body Composition, Ann. N.Y. Acad. Sci.*, 110:96, 1963.

29. Greene, R., "Adiposity." *Post Grad. Med. J.*, 22:169, 1946.

30. Hammond, W. H., "Measurement and Interpretation of Subcutaneous Fat with Norms for Children and Young Adult Males." *Brit. J. Prevent. and Social Med.*, 9:201, 1955.

31. Heald, F., "Natural History and Physiological Basis of Adolescent Obesity." *Fed. Proc.*, 25: Part I, pp. 1–3, 1966.

32. Hechter, H., "The Relationship between Weight and Some Anthropometric Measurements in Adult Males." *Human Biol.*, 31:235, 1959.

33. Hundley, J. M., "Need for Weight Control Programs." Ch. 1 in *Weight Control*. Ames, Iowa: Iowa State College Press, 1955.

34. Johnson, M. L.; B. S. Burke; and J. Mayer, "The Prevalence and Incidence of Obesity in a Cross-Section of Elementary and Secondary School Children." *Am. J. Clin. Nutrition*, 4:231, 1956.

35. Jones, E. M.; H. J. Montoye; P. B. Johnson; M. J. M. Martin; W. D. Van Huss; and D. Cederquist, "Effects of Exercise and Food Restriction on Serum Cholesterol and Liver Lipids." *Am. J. Physiol.*, 207:460–466, 1964.

36. Keys, A., "Weight Changes and Health of Men." Ch. 8 in *Weight Control*. Ames, Iowa: Iowa State College Press, 1955.

37. Keys, A., and J. Brožek, "Body Fat

in Adult Man." *Physiol. Rev.,* 33:245, 1953.

38. Keys, A., and J. Brožek, "Overweight versus Obesity and the Evaluation of Calorie Needs." *Metabolism,* 6:425, 1957.

39. Lewis, H. E.; J. Mayer; and A. A. Pandiscio, "Recording Skinfold Calipers for the Determination of Subcutaneous Edema." *J. Lab. and Clin. Med.,* 66:154, 1965.

40. Marks, H. H., "Body Weight: Facts from the Life Insurance Records." In *Body Measurements and Human Nutrition,* edited by J. Brožek. Detroit: Wayne State University Press, 1956, pp. 107–121.

41. Marks, H. H., "Influence of Obesity on Morbidity and Mortality." *Bull. N.Y. Acad. Med.,* 36:296, 1960.

42. Marks, H. H., "Relationship of Body Weight to Mortality and Morbidity." *Metabolism,* 6:417, 1957.

43. Mayer, J., "Exercise and Weight Control." Ch. 12 in *Exercise and Fitness,* edited by S. C. Staley. Chicago: Athletic Institute, 1960.

44. Mayer, J., *Overweight: Causes, Cost and Control.* Englewood Cliffs, N.J.: Prentice-Hall, 1968.

45. Mayer, J., "Physical Activity and Anthropometric Measurements of Obese Adolescents." *Fed. Proc.,* 25: Part I, 11–14, 1966.

46. Mayer, J., "The Role of Exercise and Activity in Weight Control." Ch. 17 in *Weight Control.* Ames, Iowa: Iowa State College Press, 1955.

47. Montoye, H. J.; F. H. Epstein; and M. O. Kjelsberg, "The Measurement of Body Fatness: A Study in a Total Community." *Am. J. Clin. Nutrition,* 16:417, 1965.

48. Munro, H. N., "Impact of Nutritional Research on Human Health and Survival." *Fed. Proc.,* 30:1403–1407, 1971.

49. Novak, L. P., "Physical Activity and Body Composition of Adolescent Boys." *J. Am. Med. Assoc.,* 197:891, 1966.

50. *Obesity and Health.* U.S. Department of Health, Education and Welfare, Public Health Service Publication No.

1485. Washington, D.C.: U.S. Government Printing Office.

51. Oscai, L. B., "The Role of Exercise in Weight Control." In *Exercise and Sport Sciences Reviews,* edited by J. H. Wilmore. 1:103–123, 1973.

52. Oscai, L. B.; S. P. Babirak; F. B. Dubach; J. A. McGarr; and C. N. Spirakis, "Effects of Exercise and of Food Restriction in Early Life on Adipose Tissue Cellularity in Adult Rats." *Med. and Sci. in Sports,* 6:79, 1974.

53. Pařízková, J., "Total Body Fat and Skinfold Thickness in Children." *Metabolism,* 10:794–802, 1961.

54. Pascale, L. R.; M. I. Grossman; H. S. Sloane; and T. Frankel, "Correlations between Thickness of Skinfolds and Body Density in 88 Soldiers." In *Body Measurements and Human Nutrition,* edited by J. Brožek. Detroit, Michigan: Wayne State University Press, 1956.

55. Pollock, M. L.; E. Laughridge; E. Coleman; A. Linnerud; and A. Jackson, "Prediction of Body Density in Young and Middle-Aged Women." *Med. and Sci. in Sports,* 6:74, 1974.

56. Pryor, H.; C. E. Shepard; and R. O. Moody, "Determining Appropriate Body Weight in Relation to Body Build." *J. Lancet,* 56:613, 1936.

57. Royce, J., "Use of Body Components as Reference Standards for Basal Metabolic Rate." *Res. Quart.,* 29:60, 1958.

58. Sloan, A. W., "Estimation of Body Fat in Young Men." *J. Appl. Physiol.,* 23:311, 1967.

59. Sloan, A. W.; J. J. Burt; and C. S. Blyth, "Estimation of Body Fat in Young Women." *J. Appl. Physiol.,* 17:967–970, 1962.

60. Sloan, A. W., and M. Shapiro, "A Comparison of Skinfold Measurements with Three Standard Calipers." *Human Biol.,* 44:29–36, 1972.

61. Spector, W. S., *Handbook of Biological Data.* Philadelphia: Saunders, 1956, p. 347.

62. Spriggs, E., "Discussion on the Causes and Treatment of Obesity." *Proceedings, Royal Soc. Med.,* 29:411, 1935.

63. Tepperman, J., "Adipose: Yang and

Yin." In *Fat as a Tissue,* edited by K. Rodahl and B. Issekutz. New York: McGraw-Hill, 1964, pp. 394–409.

64. Von Dobeln, W., "Anthropometric Determination of Fat-Free Body Weight." *Acta Med. Scand.,* 165:37, 1959.

65. Welham, W. C. and A. R. Behnke, "Specific Gravity of Healthy Men. Body Weight ÷ Volume and Other Physical Characteristics of Exceptional Athletes and of Naval Personnel." *J. Am. Med. Assoc.,* 118:498, 1942.

66. Wilmore, J. H. and A. R. Behnke, "An Anthropometric Estimation of Body Density and Lean Body Weight in Young Men." *J. Appl. Physiol., 27:25, 1969.*

67. Wilmore, J. H., and A. R. Behnke, "Predictability of Lean Body Weight through Anthropometric Assessment in College Men." *J. Appl. Physiol.,* 25:349, 1968.

68. Wilmore, J. H.; R. N. Girandola; and D. L. Moody, "Validity of Skinfold and Girth Assessment for Predicting Alterations in Body Composition." *J. Appl. Physiol.,* 29:313–317, 1970.

69. Young, C. M.; J. Blondin; R. Tensuan; and J. H. Fryer, "Body Composition Studies of 'Older' Women, Thirty to Seventy Years of Age." In *Body Composition. Ann. N.Y. Acad. Sci.,* 110:589, 1963.

70. Zuti, W. B. and L. A. Golding, "Equations for Estimating Percent Fat and Body Density of Active Adult Males." *Med. and Sci. in Sports,* 5:262–266, 1973.

STUDY QUESTIONS • Chapter 8

1. Why is it important for the physical educator to understand the health implications of obesity and why should he or she be familiar with techniques for measuring body fatness?

2. Respond to the statement "a fat baby is a healthy baby."

3. What is the meaning of the terms:

adipose	precursors
edema	hypothalamus
obesity	hydrostatic weighing

4. Explain the difference between the concept of "overweight" and "overfat."

5. According to your text, about what per cent of people past age 30 are sufficiently obese for their health to be impaired?

6. Obesity is associated with what diseases?

7. What possible physiological explanation is there for exercise depressing appetite?

8. A boy's weight in air is 140 lb. His weight in water is 6 lb. What is his specific gravity? Show your work.

9. Describe one of Mayer's experiments on exercise and weight control.

10. What useful functions does subcutaneous fat serve?

11. Among obese children, approximately what percentage will become obese adults?

12. The four major components of the body for the purposes of weight analysis are:

1. _____   3. _____

2. _____   4. _____

13. What is the best practical method of assessing body fatness in schools and recreation programs?

14. Respond to the following statements:
    a. Obese girls tend to underestimate the exercise they get.
    b. Most young children who are obese will outgrow this condition and will not be obese in later life.
    c. Skinfold thickness at different sites on the body are highly correlated with each other.
    d. If animals are kept in restricted living quarters they will not become fat because they will adjust their food intake.
    e. A moderate amount of exercise (for example, one-half hour per day) decreases appetite.
    f. Most of the water in the body is contained outside the cells, i.e., in the tissue spaces.

15. Why is weight control now a more important health problem than it used to be?

16. In what sports and physical education activities are overly fat children particularly handicapped? In which ones are they least handicapped?

17. Is obesity that comes on in the adult years the most serious kind or that which begins during childhood? Why?

18. Does fatness run in families? Why?

19. Respond to the statement: Most cases of excess body fatness are due to a hormone abnormality.

20. If a parent or child says to you, "It doesn't do any good to exercise to lose weight because one has to do so much exercise to burn a pound of fat," what is your response? About how many calories equal a pound of body fat? About how long would the average man (say 160 lb) have to walk at 4 miles per hour to use up this many calories?

21. Respond to the statement: It doesn't do any good to exercise to lose weight because your appetite is increased in proportion to the exercise.

22. Under what circumstances should we be concerned about body hydration as it affects estimates of body fatness?

23. When is a change in body weight not a good estimate of a change in body fatness? Give examples.

24. Can body dimensions decrease without weight decreasing? Explain.

25. Why are most age-height-weight standards not accurate for athletes?

26. What evidence can you cite that skinfold thickness gives a better estimate of body fatness than height-weight ratios (i.e., relative weight)?

27. Why are skinfold calipers designed to give a constant pressure? What is the standard pressure used?

28. Compare the Lange and Harpenden skinfold calipers.

29. How long should skinfold calipers be applied before a reading is taken?

30. List at least four sites where skinfolds are commonly taken.

31. What two methods were used to determine whether or not the skinfold thickness actually measures the fat thickness at that site? Explain.

32. Do you recommend taking skinfolds at ten sites rather than at four sites? Why?

III

Sports

INTRODUCTION TO SPORTS SKILLS TESTING

9

John A. Faulkner
Kathryn Luttgens

Definition of sports

The connotation of "sports" varies greatly. A very limited definition is based essentially on the inclusion of the sport in a highly competitive varsity athletic program. In some schools, this would limit "sports" to football, basketball, and baseball. A much broader concept includes the whole broad spectrum of physical activity organized for competitive purposes, whether in physical education, recreation, or varsity athletics. The broader concept is used throughout the following chapters.

Sports have been classified as individual, dual, and team. Individual sports are defined as those in which participants perform independently of their opponents, as, for example, golf. That close competition in individual sports may motivate the participants to better their performance is accepted. However, the interaction is indirect. Dual sports are defined as those in which the participant responds directly to the performance of the opponent and cannot perform in the sport without an opponent. Tennis is an example. Sports that can be played as both singles and doubles are included in the dual sports.

Sports in which more than two players compete on each team are classified as team sports. In these sports, the teams compete directly against each other and react to the play of the opposing team, as in basketball or football. Participants in individual and dual sports may be identified with a team. In such circumstances, the team score is the sum of the points awarded to the team members. Team championships in gymnastics, track, and wrestling are determined in this manner. This does not affect, however, the basic quality of the competition as being between individuals.

In modern automated society, sports provide an enjoyable way of gaining the benefits of regular, vigorous activity, and as such are important throughout one's life. Varying from the low organization games of childhood through the team games of adolescence, to the individual and dual sports of adulthood, each sport has its contribution to make to the well-being and happiness of the individual. Some will argue that sports do not provide the total body development as quickly or as efficiently as do specific exercises. This has been substantiated by data (6). However very few adults have the desire to maintain a regular program of calisthenics. Divorced from the high motivation of training for athletic competition, for most people, calisthenics are not pleasurable enough to be self-sustaining. The requirement then becomes an activity that is sufficiently enjoyable to ensure regularity of performance, strenuous enough to stress the cardiopulmonary system, and of sufficient duration to control body weight. A variety of sports can satisfy these requirements. The evidence which supports the role of sports and physical activity in modern living has been summarized in the May 1960 Supplement to the *Research Quarterly* under the title "The Contribution of Physical Activity to Human Well-Being" (2).

The development of sports skills testing

Records based on rigid standards of performance are an innovation of the nineteenth century (1). Technically, such athletic records and game statistics were the forerunners of sports skills tests. Whereas athletic records and game statistics are recorded in the actual game situation, the sports skills test isolates the skill under controlled circumstances.

Sports skills tests were developed in response to the need for evaluation of the teaching process, as well as for the measurement of individual ability. A few measurement pioneers began to develop sports skills tests in the thirties during the change in physical education programs from European gymnastics to games and sports. David K. Brace, Thomas K. Cureton, Esther French, and Gladys Scott published early tests and provided continuing leadership (4). Frederick Cozens, Hazel Cubberly, and Neil Neilson developed some of the earliest achievement scales in sports skills (4, 17).

The professional publications of the 1930s and the early 1940s contained a variety of tests and test batteries in a wide range of sports. During the war years, the sports skills tests received less emphasis due to an increased interest in physical fitness tests. Unfortunately, the postwar research workers have not followed up on the leads of the earlier studies with the possible exception of Master Degree candidates whose unpublished theses are unavailable to the profession at large. Consequently, many of the best sports skills tests published are twenty to thirty years old. Improvements in measurement techniques and changes in rules and playing procedures make many of these tests obsolete.

Although the teaching and practice of sports skills comprise the largest percentage of class time in physical education, the gap between measurement theory and practice is greater in sports skills testing than in any other area. There are no national norms available in any sports skills comparable to the AAHPER Youth Fitness Test norms (11) and even regional norms based on adequate populations are scarce.

Unlike most subject areas, physical education is almost completely unstructured. In mathematics, physics, chemistry, English, or French, approximately the same material is being presented in the same grades at the same time. A teacher knows what constitutes a good, bad, or indifferent student at each grade level. In physical education, the teacher frequently does not know when to start and when to stop instruction in a particular sport or when to introduce more advanced skills.

National norms on basic skills tests are vitally needed in each sport. These data would provide criteria for the grade placement of sports. Although sufficient diversity would be required to cover a wide range of sports, a procedure similar to the reading readiness tests appears feasible. The most advantageous time to start teaching a sport and the time when diminishing returns warrant its discontinuance could both be determined. It is ironic that physical education with the most objective test possibilities should be so subjective a field.

Nature of sports skills tests

Sports skills tests are designed to measure the basic skills used in the playing of a specific sport. Because of the wide range of skills in most sports, a selection of the most important skills is invariably necessary. The selection is usually based on jury technique or statistical analysis and the skill items collectively are called a test battery.

Sports skills tests may vary in discriminatory ability. A simple one-item test might suffice for a gross classification into homogeneous teaching groups yet be wholly inadequate for diagnostic, grading, or research purposes. Conversely, a statistically determined, extensive test battery would be most suitable for the grading purposes yet too involved and time consuming for the gross classification.

The emphasis in the skill test is on the ability to perform a fundamental sports skill and does not take into account the many other variables that affect play in a game situation. Therefore, a sports skill test is not necessarily predictive of playing ability except insofar as the ability to perform the specific skill in question affects playing ability. Under game conditions, factors other than the specific skill in question affects playing ability. The factors of motivation, aggressiveness, and cooperation cannot be ignored as determinants of maximum physical performance. The highly trained and highly motivated competitor will tend to reduce the gap between his psychologic and physiologic limit (12). The teacher and test administrator must, therefore, make every effort to motivate the participants.

All sports skills tests require some degree of strength or endurance. Certain tests items have tended to overemphasize these elements. When a sports skills test overemphasizes strength or endurance, it is no longer clear whether the participant attained a specific score because of physical fitness or because of sports skill. A 60-second wall volley test may result in local fatigue of the forearm muscles. In elementary and junior high school, muscle strength rather than sports skill may be the cause of low scores on a basketball shooting test from the foul line or beyond. Cardiopulmonary condition may well be the limiting factor in tests which involve large muscle activity for 30 seconds or more. It is always advisable to obtain as pure a measure as possible and to test for strength and endurance separately. Sports skills tests can thus be differentiated from physical fitness tests.

Since the early motor educability tests, many physical educators have been intrigued with the concept of a general motor capacity test comparable to the psychologist's intelligence quotient (IQ) test (17), but to date, no such entity as general motor ability or innate motor capacity has been isolated. It is apparent that a number of different abilities and capacities are called into play and approximate their potential only under highly specific conditions (18). A skilled gymnast may not be able to shoot baskets, a varsity basketball player may be a nonswimmer, and a world class miler may not be able to punt a football. Such skills are highly specialized and require prior exposure. Skill in one activity does not presuppose skill in the other. This does not preclude, however, the possibility of one's being skilled in a variety of sports, or that the transferrable skills of running, jumping, throwing, catching, dodging, kicking, hitting will also make some contribution in any test.

Certain basic qualities such as speed, balance, and coordination are also common to a variety of sports. In reality, although designated by the same noun, performance dependent on these basic qualities varies greatly from sport to sport. Speed means the ability to move quickly. To demonstrate this quality in one sport does not guarantee that it will be evidenced in another sport. The 100-yard dash champion may be slow in handball. A fullback with outstanding balance in football may not be able to stand up on skates or skis. An athlete may be an agile guard in football yet an extremely awkward basketball player. If there is no general test of speed, balance, agility, or coordination, then each must be measured under the specific conditions required by a particular sport.

Criteria of good sports skills test

The construction of a sports skills test begins with the selection of the most important fundamental skills in the sport. The initial selection may be based on subjective observations of games, objective tabulations of game play, surveys of the literature, or expert opinion. Historically, expert opinion has been the most popular approach.

Following the selection, the skill is placed in a test situation that will result in a reliable, objective, and valid measure. This requires adherence to principles of good test construction as follows:

1. Only one performer should be involved at a time. The addition of a second performer, as in Borleske's Touch Football pass defense and pass catching test, seriously affects the objectivity of a test.

2. The most accurate measurement technique feasible should be used. At shorter distances, timing over a set distance is generally more reliable and administratively easier than distance over a set time. At longer distances where gross differences will occur (5-minute swim for distance) reliability is unaffected and the set time is administratively more economical.

3. Extraneous variables in the test should be kept to a minimum. If running speed is to be measured, the stand-up start reduces the variance due to starting techniques.

4. A skills test should be simple. There has been a tendency to make sports skills tests too complicated. The complexity often results from an attempt to measure several aspects of a skill at the same time. This may take the form of scoring the number of successful trials and the time required to perform a set number of trials. A similar procedure is to award bonus points for performing a skill in a particular manner. Such procedures invariably result in meaningless distributions since one distribution is inevitably superimposed on the other. Tests must measure primarily one aspect of a skill while other aspects are held relatively constant.

5. The skill, form, and technique required of a performer in a test should approximate as nearly as possible that needed in the game situation. For example, the testing of a tennis serve skill should not sacrifice speed for accuracy since both are of consequence under game conditions.

6. The test should provide a suitable degree of differentiation. A simple count of consecutive air juggles will classify students grossly into homogeneous groups for a tennis class. Such a test will not, however, fulfill the other functions of motivation, evaluation, and interpretation previously discussed. To meet these requirements, a more sophisticated instrument is necessary.

7. The test should be suitable for the levels at which it is used. In school systems, it may be advantageous to use the same tests from grade to grade and from school to school to facilitate longitudinal and cross-sectional comparisons. This may aid in the grade placement of sports and in determining

the approximate time to discontinue them. If a test is used in this way throughout a range of grade levels, it is imperative that its validity and reliability be checked at each level. A test may be valid or reliable at one grade level and invalid and/or unreliable at another.

8. The test should have comprehensive and meticulously followed instructions. The most carefully constructed test will lose value if it is not administered as specified. Furthermore, statistics on validity, reliability, objectivity, and achievement scales are then no longer appropriate.

9. Although the test construction may fulfill the foregoing principles, the full value of the test is unknown and its use is limited unless *statistical evidence* of its reliability, objectivity, and validity is reported.

The *reliability* of sports skills tests has been reported routinely, particularly in recent years. Test-retest and split halves methods have been the most widely used procedures.

The *objectivity* of sports skills tests is rarely reported. Apparently it is presumed that a test with high reliability will not suffer loss of objectivity when handled by different administrators. Unpublished studies of the data collected by undergraduate and graduate students and observations of testing in various school systems do not support this assumption.

Test items may be *validated* against such criteria as subjective evaluation of jurors, game statistics, round robin play, other validated tests or a combination of methods. Psychologists have popularized the concept of "face validity," which may also be helpful to physical educators if interpreted correctly. There is no question that the number of lay-up shots made in 30 seconds measures the ability to make a lay-up shot unmolested by an opposing guard and this is a prerequisite to making a lay-up shot under game conditions. It is questionable that this would be a useful measure at high levels of skill and competition where the individual variance in the basic skill approximates zero and intervening variables determine success in the game situation. The solution involves the analysis by partial correlations of all the factors impinging on the performance of the skill under game conditions. More often than not this is the problem of the coach rather than the physical educator.

Although criteria for validating tests have been discussed in a previous chapter, one of the criteria, game statistics, requires further consideration. Two types of descriptive statistics are associated with sports: the scoring statistics that actually determine the outcome of the contest and supplementary game statistics that refer to specific aspects of the play. The scoring statistics are the elapsed time from start to finish in track, the distance in field events, the total points from field goals and foul shots in basketball, the goals in soccer, or the points in tennis. Game statistics are not directly involved in the outcome of the event. They do, however, provide supplementary data for comparisons of individuals or teams on various elements within the context of the overall game. Examples of game statistics are splits or lap times in track or swimming, assists and rebounds in basketball, first downs and yards rushing or passing in football, and errors and double plays in baseball. Game statistics have been carried to questionable lengths on occasion, particularly in the spectator sports of baseball, basketball, and football. National player rankings have been publicized in statistics that are neither comparable nor of any consequence in the play of the team.

The objectivity of scoring and of game statistics varies greatly from sport to sport. Track, field, swimming, and skiing performances are highly objective. These events are timed and other competitors can exert only indirect influence on the score through the intensity of the competition they provide. World class athletes in these sports are able to repeat peak performances again and again. Although other competitors do not influence the performance in gymnastics and diving, the judging in these events is extremely subjective. In the finals of the National Collegiate Athletic Association Gymnastic Championship, negative correlations between judges have been recorded (9). In team sports, objectivity is lost due to the effect of both teammates and opponents on the scoring and game statistics of a player.

Although meaningless for the determination of national rankings, game statistics can be of assistance to the coach who interprets them fully within the context of a particular game or season. Elbel and Allen (8) utilized an extensive range of positive and negative game variables to evaluate team and individual performance in basketball at the University of Kansas. By a similar procedure, Forest Anderson, while head coach at Michigan State University, determined a "Basketball Profile" (3) based on game statistics.

Scoring and game statistics may also be used as evaluative criteria for sports skills tests. Each test item may be correlated to total performance or a specific aspect of performance under game conditions. Data on basketball shooting tests may be correlated with game shooting percentages, and batting skill with batting averages.

Measurement technique

The same sports and sports skills may be performed in the varsity athletic program, intramural program, and general physical education program. Measurement in these sports differ considerably in the three programs due to the variation in the degree of differentiation required.

Good measurement technique for collection of data with a valid test has two equally important aspects. Data must be collected in a reliable and objective manner, yet with administrative economy. Optimal administrative economy changes with the range of ability in the population tested. When variability is minimal, as with varsity athletes, measurement techniques must be more discriminating than when variability is great, as with students in physical education classes. To use the highly discriminatory techniques of varsity athletics in the instructional physical education class would be poor measurement technique. It is not necessary to time a 60-yard dash performed by 6th grade students electronically to obtain satisfactory results. Conversely, the less discriminatory techniques suitable for the heterogeneous class population are inappropriate in the varsity program.

Objective measurements

Number

The number of successful performances made in a set period of time or in a prescribed number of trials is a technique frequently used in objective tests. The Dyer Tennis Test (Chapter 10) is an example. The score is the number of times the ball strikes the wall above the net line during the 30-second test period. Johnson (Chapter 11) used a prescribed number of trials in his test of foul shooting accuracy. One point is scored for each shot made out of ten attempts.

To ensure objectivity, scorers need to be told the criteria for a successful trial and an unsuccessful trial. Tests should be constructed so that the two can be clearly differentiated. The test period or the number of trials must also be adequate to obtain an adequate range of scores.

Accuracy

This technique involves some type of target and points are awarded for successfully striking the target or a particular portion of the target. The Cornish Front-Wall Placement Test in handball uses this technique (Chapter 10). The front wall is divided into areas. Each area is assigned a value. The contestant strokes the ball five times with either hand and his score is the total number of points recorded.

Accuracy tests require more trials to obtain reliability than any other type of test. If target areas are not clearly differentiated and large enough, objectivity may also be lost. Where the test involves a rebound from the target, scorers should stand where they may have an unobstructed view of the missile rebounding from the target area.

Time

Time is used most frequently to measure speed in running, swimming, skating, or skiing. It is the elapsed time between the beginning and successful completion of the particular task. Dribbling in basketball or soccer, stick handling in hockey, and broken field running in football have also been measured in this way.

Instrument and/or human errors may create bias in the timing of speed events. Watches should be synchronized against each other prior to use.

Watches used to time record performances should be returned to the factory annually for calibration.

Human errors in trained timers have been demonstrated experimentally (7). An average bias of 0.3 seconds between watch time and true time was due mainly to a delay in the timer starting his watch. Other contributing factors were anticipating the finish and inaccuracies of the watch itself. The error of 0.3 seconds is equivalent to approximately 9 feet in a sprint event.

A variety of techniques have been subjectively advocated to increase the reliability of stop watch timing. The techniques include (a) taking up of the slack in the stem prior to starting or stopping the watch, (b) depression of the stem with the index finger rather than the thumb, (c) placement of the stem on the knuckle rather than the fleshy part of the finger or thumb, and (d) holding the arm steady rather than moving it down as the stem is depressed. There are limited data which reject the removal of slack in the stem as a means of increasing reliability (15). Support or rejection of the other recommendations is similarly based on limited data (7).

The estimates of true time will be enhanced if (a) watches are checked regularly for instrument errors, (b) timers are trained to react to the visual signals of the gun shot, (c) the mechanics of handling a watch are evaluated objectively and the best mechanics implemented, (d) timers are placed with an unobstructed view of the start and of the finish, (e) each timer reads his own watch without the influence of other officials, competitors, or spectators, and (f) timers are familiar with the calibration of their watches to eliminate read-out errors in reading off the time actually recorded on the watch.

Distance

The distance is the linear range covered by a performance such as a throw, a hit, a jump, or a vault. Speed may also be measured by reversing the usual process and scoring the distance covered in a set time. The 5-minute swim for distance is an example. The more common distance measurements are, however, the shot put, the discus throw, the broad jump, the softball throw, the pole vault, and the high jump.

Linear measurements are used to determine the order of finish in the broad jump, shot put, discus, javelin, high jump, and pole vault. Although records are kept in fractions of inches, the accuracy of the measurement is considerably less than this. Measurement errors may be due to differences in the terrain and the inability of the judges to determine the exact point of impact. Judgments are complicated by variance in the distance of the judge from the point of impact and by the skidding of the projectile on impact.

In 1937, P. H. Kirkpatrick (13) questioned the measurement procedures of distance in field events. He described erroneous measurements due to inaccurate leveling, hardness of ground, variations of the force of gravity, and effect of rotation of the earth. The effect of latitude and altitude alone are such that a 50-foot shot put at sea level in Norway would travel an additional 3 to 4 inches with identical impetus on a mountain at the equator.

Many measurements could be facilitated by improved instrumentation. In the running broad jump, a calibrated metal track fixed in the ground with a hinged movable arm could provide instantaneous measurements. The hinged arm would be moved opposite the break in the ground, swung down, adjusted, and the distance read. Such an instrument has been used intermittently in international contests.

In reality, the high jump and the pole vault are not measurements of the height jumped but the height of the bar over which the competitor jumped. The linear measurement in high jumping is made from the ground surface below the bar vertically to the lowest point of the upper edge of the crossbar. In pole vaulting, the measurement is from the top edge of the box vertically to the lowest point of the upper edge of the crossbar. Variances in terrain and in the sag of the crossbar can result in major differences in the height the jumper must attain to clear the bar without dislodging it. The procedure of determining the order of finish in the event of a tie by the number of misses at the previous height, or if still tied by the number of misses throughout the event, has never been statistically analyzed in the published literature.

Summary

Objective measurements are used extensively in all phases of sports competition and sports skills testing. Few of these measurement procedures have been subjected to statistical analysis or objective study. Timing, judging, and linear measurements are replete with inconsistencies and errors. Further, modern instrumentation has rarely been used to advantage in sports or sports skills testing. Consequently, the area presents a multitude of opportunities for research.

Subjective measurement

Ranking

Subjects are ranked in numerical order from best to worst on the basis of performance. Two types of rankings are widely used in sports. One or more experts may rank players on total playing ability in a particular sport. Tennis rankings, although aided by objective game scores, are determined by this technique. Players in team sports may also be ranked subjectively on the basis of their total game play. The validity of such a procedure is improved if judges use a common set of criteria upon which to base their evaluation.

Finish judges (1) select either the competitor who finished in a specified position (first, second, third, etc.) or, in National Collegiate Athletic Association Swimming events, the judge determines the specific position attained by the swimmer in the judge's lane (16). Each involves a subjective judgment, and objectivity is low when fine discriminations are required. Although the two procedures differ in the technique the judge must use in the determination of his judgment, each is subject to the same problem of the degree of discrimination.

The degree of differentiation varies greatly from race to race. When yards or feet separate the competitors as they finish, accurate judgments are easily made. However, when the distance is reduced to inches, the speeds of the competitors differ, and the body angles vary, valid judgments are sometimes impossible. In swimming, such judgments may be further complicated by the distance between competitors and by under- and above-water touches. Modern electronic and photographic instrumentation appears to be the solution for varsity and international competition.

Pass-fail rating

Sports skills tests in diving and gymnastics (Chapter 10) use progressive lists of skills which are performed by the subject. If the subject performs the skill "successfully" he is passed, otherwise he continues practice on it before trying again. The degree of objectivity of pass-fail ratings depends on the clarity of instructions and agreement beforehand. If clear-cut criteria are established and test administrators are trained to apply them, this technique can have reasonable objectivity. Statistical analysis of pass-fail ratings in diving and fencing (Chapter 10) support the usefulness of this technique.

Rating scales

Rating scales are used in competitive diving, gymnastics, boxing and wrestling, and in such other activities as dance, posture, fencing, and swimming in the instructional program. Judges award points on the basis of observed performance on a variety of different scales. In diving, the judges' scores are multiplied by a subjectively determined weighting factor (16). The poor agreement among judges' ratings in some events in the National Collegiate Association Gymnastic meet has been noted by Hunsicker and Loken (10) and by Faulkner and Loken (9).

Where the pattern is not set by some governing body, as it is in competition, the number of judges and the combination of their scores may vary depending on the use and validity needed. Equally important as the number of judges and the method of combining the scores are the instructions accompanying the rating scale; the more comprehensive and specific, the greater chance for objectivity in its use.

Knowledge testing in sports

Knowledge is a vital factor in the optimum performance of a sports activity. Recognized and often quoted as an important objective of physical education, knowledge acquisition should similarly be evaluated when possible with *objective and validated measuring tools.* More generally used to measure middle or end-of-course achievement, it can also be used for motivation or the determination of knowledge of students at the beginning of a course.

To be worthwhile the knowledge test should be carefully constructed, include supporting statistical evidence of worth, and have the emphasis properly placed on the amount and relative importance of the various phases of knowledge. Even when the first two criteria are satisfied, the last criterion is frequently violated in sports knowledge tests. The relative emphasis placed on rules usually far exceeds that justified in terms of curricular emphasis. This unwarranted emphasis is undoubtedly due to the easier construction of written items related to rules interpretation rather than to those related to analysis of skill, game strategy, or team tactics. This temptation should be avoided and the distribution of content of the test planned according to a carefully identified table of specifications. The table of specifications should list the main topic areas, concepts, or phases of instruction presented in the course and the relative per cent of weighting given each according to its estimated worth in terms of total course content. The proportion of test items related to any one phase of instruction should correspond, then, to the proportion given that phase in the table of specifications.

In selecting any of the standardized knowledge tests available in the literature, teachers should be careful that its content emphasis corresponds to theirs. Otherwise it should not be used, at least not in its entirety. Only those items that are appropriate should be selected. Caution should also be exercised in selecting only those tests that are suitable for the desired sex, age, and skill level.

Research needed

Many of the published tests of sports skills do not meet adequate criteria of reliability, objectivity, and even "face validity" in the sports and for the same sport at different grade levels. Some existing sports skills tests were initially worked out with great care and attention to statistical analysis. Changes in rules, playing skills, and coaching techniques have made some of these obsolete. Such tests merely require modifications to be brought up to date.

In other sports there are no adequate test batteries. New or completely revised test batteries are necessary in these instances. Where objective tests seem inappropriate, validated subjective tools, such as the skills standards approach, are necessary. There is also a great need for well-designed, objective sports knowledge tests which include coverage of history, rules, strategy, and technique.

Subsequent to the development of satisfactory sports skills and knowledge tests, age norms for a large, representative, national sample are urgently required. If stratified on objective measures of program content, these data could provide insight as to what constitutes a physically educated child in specific sports at specific ages. Such information is available in the majority of school subjects.

In summary, the research needs in sports skills tests are for adequate batteries in all sports, age group norms based on a national sample, more objective collection of data in the schools, and evaluation of the students, program, and instruction based on test results.

REFERENCES

1. Amateur Athletic Union, *Official A.A.U. Track and Field Handbook.* New York: The Union, 1962.

2. American Association for Health, Physical Education and Recreation. *Res. Quart.*, Supp., May 1960.

3. Anderson, F. A., *Basketball Profile.* Peoria, Ill.: Statistics Charts Co., 1955.

4. Bookwalter, K. and C. Bookwalter, "Sports Skills." *Measurement and Evaluation Materials in Health, Physical Education and Recreation.* Washington, D.C.: AAHPER, 1950.

5. Campbell, W. R. and R. H. Pohndorf, "Physical Fitness of British and United States Children." In *Health and Fitness in the Modern World.* Chicago: The Athletic Institute, 1961.

6. Cureton, T. K., "How To Get the Physical Fitness Ingredient into Sports Education to Improve in Sports and Fitness." *College Physical Education Proc.*, 60th Annual, pp. 286–297, 1957.

7. Cureton, T. K. and T. E. Doe, "An Analysis of the Errors in Stop Watch Timing." *Res. Quart.*, 4:94–109, 1933.

8. Elbel, E. R. and F. C. Allen, "Evaluating Team and Individual Performance in Basketball. *Res. Quart.*, 12:538–555, 1941.

9. Faulkner, J. A. and N. Loken, "Ob-

jectivity of Judging at the National Collegiate Athletic Association Gymnastic Meet: A Ten-Year Follow-up Study." *Res. Quart.*, 33:435–486, 1962.

10. Hunsicker, P. and N. Loken, "The Objectivity of Judging at the National Collegiate Athletic Association Meet." *Res. Quart.*, 22:423–426, 1951.

11. Hunsicker, P. A. and G. G. Reiff, *A Survey and Comparison of Youth Fitness: 1958–1965.* Ann Arbor: University of Michigan, 1965, p. 174.

12. Ikai, M., and A. H. Steinhaus, "Some Factors Modifying the Expression of Human Strength." *J. Applied Physiol.*, 16:157–163, 1961.

13. Kirkpatrick, P. H., "Erroneous Measurements in Track and Field." *Res. Quart.*, 8:28–31, 1937.

14. Leighton, J. R., "Flexibility Characteristics of Three Specialized Skill Groups of Champion Athletes." *Archives, Phys. Med. and Rehab.*, 38:580–583, 1957.

15. Meyers, C. R., "Comparison of Two Methods of Using a Stop Watch." *Res. Quart.*, 33:491–493, 1962.

16. National Collegiate Athletic Association. *Official Collegiate Scholastic Swimming Guide.* New York: The Association, 1963.

17. Phillips, M. and A. J. Wendler,

"General Motor Skills." In *Measurement and Evaluation Materials in Health, Physical Education and Recreation.* Washington, D.C.: AAHPER, 1950.

18. Seashore, H. G., "Some Relationships of Fine and Gross Motor Coordination." *Res. Quart.,* 13:259–274, 1942.

STUDY QUESTIONS · Chapter 9

1. When measuring speed in running short distances, is it easier to measure distance covered in a fixed time or time to cover a fixed distance?

2. In timing a hundred yard run with a stop watch, is there a tendency for the watch time to be greater (longer) or shorter (less) than true time? If so, in which direction? Why?

3. Why should a backboard volley test last no longer than 30 seconds or a minute?

4. In which sports, if any, do we have national norms?

5. Is strength or endurance involved in performance of sports skill tests? Explain or give examples to support your answers.

6. Are there tests of general motor ability (ability in many sports)? If so, how valid are they?

7. Why should a sports test involve only one performer?

8. Why is a stand-up start recommended in measuring running speed in physical education?

9. Why should sports test items be simple?

10. Describe several examples of game statistics.

11. What is meant by the statement, "When variability is minimal, as with varsity athletes, measurement techniques must be more discriminating."

12. List three ways of improving accuracy in starting and stopping a stop watch.

13. Explain the difference between rating and ranking.

14. For what purposes might you use written tests in sports?

INDIVIDUAL AND DUAL SPORTS SKILLS TESTS

10

John F. McCabe
William D. McArdle

Individual sports are classified as those in which a competitor may participate alone. Examples are gymnastics, skiing, swimming, and track. Dual sports are those in which competition is essentially between two participants. However, most dual sports can also be played as doubles (four persons). Examples are badminton, handball, tennis, and wrestling. These sports require the direct involvement of at least one opponent and cannot be played alone. In this chapter, the individual and dual sports have been listed together in alphabetical order.

Archery

Target archery is an individual sport with a scoring system that makes its own best objective measure of skill. The archery literature lists several types of rounds used in competition which could be used to test objectively subjects of various age groups. Such rounds are the American Round, Junior American Round, Columbia Round, Junior Columbia Round, Scholastic Round, Junior Scholastic Round, Range Round, and Miniature Round. The Columbia Round, probably the most common round, was used by E. Hyde (1, 2) to determine standards of achievement for college women. Although these achievement scales were published in 1937, no comparable study updates them and they still prove to be a useful standard.

Hyde archery standards (1, 2)

Procedures for construction

Data were obtained from 1400 women students from twenty-seven colleges in sixteen states. Standard procedures and equipment were used for shooting an official Columbia Round. Three achievement scales in the form of sigma values with score scales from 0–100 were constructed. The first scale is for the first Columbia Round, which is shot after a minimum practice of 120 arrows at each distance. The second is a scale for a Columbia Round after unlimited practice toward the end of the season. In the third scale, scores are presented for each distance in the Round after unlimited practice. Since the third scale was constructed from the final or highest Columbia Round scores, beginners should be expected to fall relatively low on this scale.

Administration

Equipment. A standard 48-inch target with the center of the gold placed 4 feet from the ground. Matched arrows are used.

Description. A Columbia Round is shot. This consists of four ends of 6 arrows each from 50 yards, 40 yards, and 30 yards for a total of 72 arrows. One practice end is allowed at each distance. The whole round need not be completed on one day, but any one distance should be completed at a session.

Scoring. Standard target archery scoring is used with one exception. An arrow that passes through, or rebounds from the target, scores 5 points instead of 7 points. This deviation from regular target archery scoring is due to a rule change in scoring that occurred after the construction of the standards. Scores for the round, as well as each distance in the round, should be totaled.

Comments

The Achievement Scales, suitable for college women, are listed in reference 2. These scales provide a means for evaluating both beginning and advanced archers. Hyde reports that scores at 40 yards yield the best measure of a beginner's ability, whereas scores at 50 yards are preferred for the advanced archer. Unfortunately, no such scales exist for other than college women and test reliability has not been reported.

AAHPER archery test

The AAHPER Archery Test is part of the battery of AAHPER Sport Skills Tests. It is similar to other archery tests in that the performance of the sport itself provides an objective measure of the skill level. In this test the target used is the standard 48-inch target, 4 feet from the ground. Two ends of 6 arrows each are shot at distances of 10, 20, and 30 yards.

Because of the relatively short distances used in the test, it may perhaps be best utilized as a practice device or as a test for students in beginning archery.

Badminton

A review of the literature reveals that a number of attempts have been made to analyze the skills important for success in badminton, and to provide tests that measure proficiency either in selected skills of the game or in overall performance. Specific tests exist for the short serve, long serve, high, clear, and smash stroke, and footwork. Overall performance has been measured by wall volleys as well as by combining specific skills tests into statistically determined batteries. Each of these tests has been analyzed statistically and figures are reported for reliability and validity.

Of all the badminton tests available, the only tests included in this section are those that do not require an interaction between two performers (i.e., high clear from a serve). In addition, the footwork tests are essentially tests of agility, which is important in badminton but not necessarily specific to the game. For this reason, these tests of agility will not be described here.

Miller wall volley test (5)

Procedures for construction

A careful study was made of the number of times each stroke was used during the matches at the U.S. Amateur Badminton Championships in 1959. It was discovered that the clear was the most important stroke both in singles and doubles play. By use of cinematographical analysis, the author determined the optimum distances for restraining lines for a wall volley test of the clear. These results indicated that the player taking the test must be behind a 10-foot floor restraining line and must clear the shuttlecock above a line on the wall 7 feet 6 inches in height.

Reliability was determined by test-retest within a one-week period of 100 college girls of varying ability ($r = 0.94$). Validity of the clear stroke is established by the fact that the game requires performance of the clear, and test specifications were determined from a cinematographical analysis of the clear during high-level competition. To determine the relationship of the test to total playing ability, 20 players were given the test and then participated in a round-robin tournament consisting of 380 single games ($r = 0.83$).

Administration

Equipment. Badminton racquet in good condition, a new Timpé outdoor shuttlecock (sponge end), a stop watch, and score cards are used. There should be a 1-inch line extending across the wall 7 feet 6 inches above and parallel to the floor. A smooth-surfaced wall space is used which is at least 10 feet wide and a minimum of 15 feet high. There should be a timer who gives starting and stopping signals, a scorer who counts the number of legal hits, and a recorder.

Description. The player is given a chance to practice for one minute before the first trial. A 30-second rest period should be allowed between trials with practice between trials. On the signal "Ready, Go," the player serves the shuttlecock in a legal manner against the wall from behind the restraining line. The player continues to return the rebounds to the wall for 30 seconds. If the serve hits on or above the line, the hit counts as one point, as does each subsequent rebound made on or above the wall line, provided the player is *behind* the 10-foot floor line. The player may step in front of the restraining line to keep the shuttlecock in play, but the hit does not count if any part of the player's foot is on or over the restraining line or if the shuttlecock goes below the wall line. A chalk line 3 inches behind the 10 foot floor line is suggested to help the player stay behind the restraining line. Any stroke may be used to keep the shuttlecock in play. A "carry" or a double hit counts as "good" if the shuttlecock goes above the line.

Scoring. The individual's score is the sum of three 30-second trials.

Comments

If properly executed, wall volleying is excellent practice for wrist action. The test itself can be used as motivation, and for pre- and postseason classification and evaluation.

The data below were obtained by Miller in an administration of the test to college students. Men were tested on a smooth brick wall; women were tested on a smooth cement surface.

115 college men	Range = 20–118, M = 76.33, S.D. = 21.7
100 college women	Range = 9–113, M = 41.69, S.D. = 19.6

The author cautions that wall surfaces and other conditions vary and that different situations may require norms specific to individual conditions. A disadvantage of this test is its use of a special type of sponge-end shuttlecock, necessary for sufficient rebound from the wall. A regulation indoor shuttlecock will not provide sufficient rebound.

French short serve test (6, 4)

Procedures for construction

Originally an unpublished test by Esther French, this test was part of a study of achievement examinations conducted by a research committee of the Central Association of Physical Education for College Women. From the test, administered to 149 beginners, the committee obtained a reliability coefficient of 0.77.

The following additional figures are a summary of results obtained from various administrations of this test over a period of years: test-retest reliability = 0.51 to 0.88, validity (i.e., correlation coefficient) = 0.41 to 0.66 with judges' ratings of playing ability the criterion.

Administration

Equipment. New shuttles and tightly strung racquets are used. A clothesline rope is stretched 20 inches directly above the net and parallel to it. Using the intersection of the short service line and the center line as a midpoint, a series of arcs are described in the right service court at distances of 22, 30, 38, and 46 inches from the midpoint, including the width of the 2-inch line. These lines are extended from the short service line to the center line. (See Figure 10–1).

Description. The player stands diagonally opposite the target in the service court and attempts to serve 20 shuttlecocks between the rope and the net onto the target. The scorer records the value of each service according to the area of the target in which the shuttlecock lands.

Scoring. The player's score is the total number of points for 20 trials. No score is given for any trial which fails to go between the rope and the net, or which fails to land in the service court for the doubles game, or which is served illegally. A shuttle landing on a line dividing two areas receives the value of the higher area.

Comments

This test can be used as a very good practice device for the short serve. If targets are set up in areas off the court, valuable playing space will not be lost for extended periods of time. As a test, it has merit for measuring skill in the low serve, not as a measure of all-round playing ability. As with most skills involving accuracy, reliability increases as the skill of the player increases. Moreover, finesse in the low serve is of more importance to the skilled badminton player than to the beginner. Therefore, it is suggested that the test be used only as a practice device, if at all, with beginners. Norms for college women are available in reference (4).

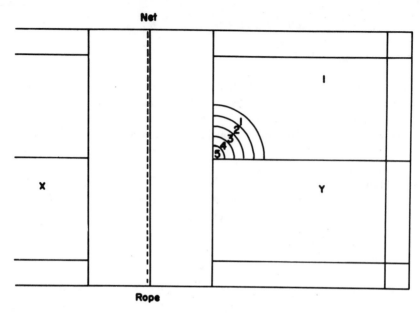

FIGURE 10–1.   Floor markings for badminton serve test.
From Scott (6).

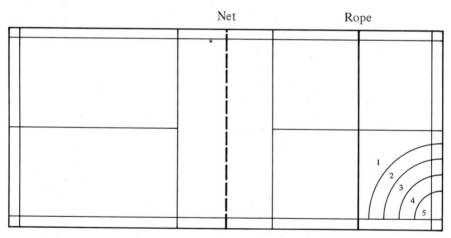

FIGURE 10–2.   Floor markings for badminton long serve
test.   From Scott and French (7).

Scott and French long serve test (7)

Procedures for construction

The test was originally administered to two different groups of freshman and
sophomore women at the University of Iowa.   The subjects were tested on
20 trials.   For the first group of 45 women, the reliability coefficient was

determined to be 0.77 on odd-even trials. On a larger group of 332 players, the coefficient was computed to be 0.68. The validity of the test was determined by correlating subjective ratings of performance by three judges with the test results. The validity coefficient was computed to be 0.54.

Administration

Equipment. A clothesline rope is stretched 8 feet high and 14 feet behind and parallel to the net. New badminton shuttlecocks and tightly strung racquets should be used. Using the intersection of the long service line and the left side boundary line for singles as a midpoint, a series of arcs are described in the left service court at distances of 22, 30, 38 and 46 inches from the midpoint, including the width of the 2-inch line. These lines are extended from the singles long service line to the singles side line. (See Figure 10–2).

Description. The player stands diagonally opposite the target in the service court and attempts to serve 20 shuttlecocks over the rope and onto the target. The scorer records the value of each serve according to the area of the target in which the shuttlecock lands.

Scoring. The player's score is the total number of points for 20 trials. No score is given for any trial which fails to go over the rope, or which fails to land in the singles service court, or which is served illegally. A shuttlecock landing on a line dividing two areas receives the value of the higher area.

Comments

This test can be readily used as practice for the long serve. In addition, volleyball standards can be conveniently used to support the rope at the normal height of 8 feet (men's volleyball). Because of the difficulty of the test, it may not be wise to use it for grading purposes in a beginning badminton class. Originally this test and the short service test (French, 6) allowed illegal serves to be repeated. In this text, it is advised to count illegal serves as 0 points.

Bowling

Bowling is another activity in which the score of the game itself serves as an objective measure of an individual's ability. Consequently, norms based on scores achieved in sequential lines of bowling would have considerable comparative and motivational value in the usual instructional course in bowling. Two such sets of norms exist. M. Phillips and D. Summers (9) developed norms and analyzed learning curves in bowling for college women, and J. D. Martin (8) has established norms useful in classifying college men and women.   Because their data were collected from a much larger and more diverse sample and because they have established norms at more ability levels, including intermediary, the Phillips and Summers norms are recommended for use with college women.

Phillips and Summers bowling norms

With the cooperation of 22 colleges, Phillips and Summers obtained data for construction of norms from scores of 3,634 college women who had each bowled 10–25 lines.   The average of the first 5 lines determined the initial skill level.   Eight ability levels were identified with average initial scores ranging from 50 to 129.9.   Each of the eight classifications was further subdivided into five qualitative ratings of superior, good, average, poor, and inferior, based on the distribution of six standard deviations.   Norms were established at each of the eight ability levels at the end of 10 lines and every 5 lines thereafter up to 25 (four intervals).   Norms for lines 1 to 10 were based on a cumulative average.   In subsequent intervals the average of the 5 lines in the interval was used.

Martin bowling norms

The subjects were 704 freshmen and sophomore male and female students at the University of California, Los Angeles.   Students were classified into three ability groupings after two weeks of instruction according to the average score on the initial 5 lines of bowling.

Ability Grouping	Men	Women
Beginning	120 and under	98 and under
Intermediate	121–145	98–119
Advanced	146 and over	120 and over

If an individual indicated he or she had never bowled before, this person was put in the "beginner" category and was not given the test.

The data were gathered over a three-year period in college service classes. The determined norms were based on the final cumulative averages after 26 lines bowled during a thirteen-week course of instruction.   The cumulative averages were computed by dividing the total number of pins knocked down in each three-game series by the number of lines bowled.   The norms are reproduced in Table 10–1.

Comments

Both of these sets of norms have use for initial and final classification and motivation.   Those constructed by Phillips and Summers allow for more in-

TABLE 10–1
Bowling Norms for College Men and Women

Rating	Scores					
	Beginning		Intermediate		Advanced	
	Men	Women	Men	Women	Men	Women
Superior	127 & above	113 & above	150 & above	125 & above	162 & above	None
Good	116–126	101–112	140–149	120–124	157–161	
Average	107–115	93–100	126–139	115–119	152–156	
Poor	96–106	81–92	115–125	110–114	147–151	
Inferior	95 & below	80 & below	114 & below	109 & below	146 & below	
N	162	292	155	58	37	
Range	86–132	70–123	107–155	101–135	143–174	
M	111.26	97.31	134.42	117.11	154.46	
SD	8.22	8.18	7.33	4.02	4.41	

From Martin (8).

dividual discrimination, but unfortunately are limited to college women. Neither one of these norms nor any norms based on the total game is of much diagnostic value in helping the student determine the specific weaknesses in his or her game. A continuous record of performance on specific setups that occur frequently in a game would provide a worthwhile supplementary evaluative technique.

Diving

Bennett diving test

The official method of scoring dives has little application in a physical education class. Consequently, L. M. Bennett (10), in an attempt to provide an objective method of measuring the achievement of beginning divers, proposed a list of fifty items progressing from simple to complex. The individual's score is the number of items passed.

Procedure for construction

No explanation for the selection or ordering of dives is given. Apparently, the battery was devised empirically. The items are not weighted and the degree of difficulty in progressing to the next dive is assumed to be approximately equal at all levels. The score on each dive is either 0 or 1. The more difficult dives are divided into parts. A subject may progress to the next item without passing the previous one and unlimited attempts may be made at one item.

The sample used to develop the test consisted of 26 college women between 18 and 23 years of age registered in elementary diving classes at the University of California. The validity of the test was determined by correlating the number of items passed during a semester of diving and a rating of expert judges using the official scoring system to judge 8 dives. The correlation coefficient was 0.94. The reliability was determined by the split-halves method. The sum of the scores on the odd items correlated 0.90 with the sum of the even items. Thus, the reliability coefficient is estimated to be 0.95 for the complete test.

Test objectivity was determined by the simultaneous ratings of three judges who rated 4 divers on 42 dives. Of the 168 possible chances for agreement, the three judges agreed on 148 (88.9%), and the two most experienced judges agreed on 156 (92.9%).

Administration

Entrance into the water "head first" means that the hands enter the water first, then the head, then the hips. These must be consecutive, not simultaneous. As long as the hands and head hit the water first this requirement is met even though the dive may be quite flat or the knees bent or the legs apart, etc. In other words, any headfirst entry short of a "belly flop" counts. "Straight head first" implies an excellent entry into the water in this consecutive order: hands, head, hips, knees, feet, with no body bends at waist, hips, or knees. The feet must enter at the same place in the water as the head.

Entrance into the water "feet first" means the feet enter the water first, then the hips, and then the head, in consecutive order, not simultaneously. "Straight feet first" implies an excellent entry into the water in this consecutive order: toes, knees, hips, shoulders, with body straight and no bend at the waist, hips, or knees; and with hands touching the sides of the body. The head must enter at the same place in the water as the feet.

Test items

1. Standing dive from pool edge—enter straight head first.
2. Standing dive from pool edge with return to surface—enter straight head first, keeping hands and arms in same relative position until return to surface.
3. Standing dive from pool edge to bottom of pool—enter straight head first and touch the bottom at an 11-foot depth.
4. Sitting tuck position with fall into the water from the 1-meter board—remain completely tucked (hands grasping shins, and forehead on knees which are drawn up to chest) until under the water. Any starting position.
5. Standing dive from board—enter straight head first.
6. Standing feet-first dive—body must be in the straight feet-first position in air and at entry. Jump from board, do not step.
7. Forward approach—must include at least three steps and a hurdle, landing on both feet. Accompanying arm motion must be smooth —no pauses in entire approach. Toes must be pointed to the board during the hurdle before landing on the end of the board.

8. Running feet-first dive—combine requirements of numbers 7 and 6.

9. Springing the board—rise from the board at least 6 inches with five consecutive jumps, using the arms to help in gaining height.

10. Rocking chair—sit on the end of the board facing the water, and by rocking backward with feet over head, gain enough momentum to rock forward and execute head first dive into the water.

11. Springing the board with a double tuck position—same as number 9 except that a tuck position must be assumed when in the air. Knees must be bent when hands touch shins in tuck position. Do four consecutive tucks.

12. Running front-tuck dive—enter straight head first after assuming a tuck position in the air (knees bent, hands on shins).

13. Forward dive over pole hip high—enter straight head first, clearing the pole.

14. Elementary front jackknife dive (standing)—bent enough at the hips to have the hands below the knees (though not necessarily touching the legs) at the time of the bend. Enter head first.

15. Running jackknife dive—enter straight head first. Keep knees together and straight after leaving the board. Wrists below knees at time of jackknife bend.

16. Advanced jackknife dive—same as number 15 except for these requirements; actually touch ankles, or top of arch, and enter water within 6 feet of the end of the board.

17. Elementary back jackknife dive (taken to the side of the board)— enter head first with the head entering the water behind the starting point. Must have some bend at hips.

18. Back jackknife dive—same as number 17 except that the dive is taken straight back from the end of the board.

19. Advanced backjackknife dive—same as number 18 except that there must be a straight head first entry and knees must be kept together and straight after leaving the board.

20. Back approach—must include at least three steps, correct direction of turn (free leg swings out over the water, not over the board), and no hesitations.

21. Back spring to the water feet first—use arms in the spring-up from the board; jump, do not step, from the board, and enter the water straight feet first.

22. Back spring to the board—from the back stance, spring upward from the board (using arms smoothly to assist) with knees straight and toes pointed to the board. Toes must be at least 6 inches above the board when in the air. Return to the board.

23. Back bend—from the back stance position, bend backward and enter the water head first.

24. Elementary back dive—same as number 23 but hold straight head-first position in air and at entry.

25. Back dive—same as number 24 but use some preparatory spring with smooth use of arms.

26. Advanced back dive—same as number 25 but done in two parts:
    (1) keep the head up, eyes forward, as body is rising from the board, then
    (2) head is thrown back when the crest of the height is reached. Enter straight head first within 6 feet of the board (no twist). Toes pointed throughout the dive.

27. Standing forward dive with an arch—when in the air, look distinctly forward and up. Look down just before entering straight head first. Lead with hands throughout the dive.

28. Butterfly dive—same as number 27, either running or standing, but with hands on hips when in the air. Enter straight head first.

29. Running swan dive—must have the body arched in the air. No body bends, arms above shoulder height and extended to sides, head up. The regular position of the swan dive in the air must be attained even if only for a moment. Enter head first.

30. Advanced running swan dive—same as number 29, entering straight head first.

31. Running forward half twist, feet first—turn at least 180 degrees, and enter straight feet first.

32. Quarter twist—assume a distinct swan position in the air, followed by a turn on the long axis of the body of at least 90 degrees (shoulders determine degree of turn). Enter head first.

33. Half twist—same as number 31, but turn at least 180 degrees.

34. Jackknife with a quarter twist—assume a distinct jackknife position in the air, followed by a turn of at least 90 degrees. Enter head first.

35. Elementary jackknife with a half twist—same as number 34, but turn at least 180 degrees.

36. Neck stand—lie with back to board and head at the "water" end of the board. Bring the feet up over the head, aim them toward the water, and enter the water feet first. Hands must be at sides at time of feet-first entry.

37. Handstand dive—enter straight head first. Entire body must clear the board.

38. Handstand feet-first dive—enter feet first, after assuming the handstand position on board and holding on until feet complete the arc and point toward the water.

39. Rocking chair (see number 10) from 3-meter board—enter head first.

40. Neck stand (see number 36) from 3-meter board—enter feet first.

41. Forward fall dive from 3-meter board—from an erect forward standing position with arms extended over head, fall forward, entering the water head first. Remain perfectly stiff throughout the fall.

42. Backward fall dive from 3-meter board—same as number 41 except that the fall is taken from a backward standing position.

43. Tuck and roll with a spring from edge of pool (a forward somersault in the air from the edge of the pool, turning in the tuck position)—turn at least far enough forward so that the head clears the water and the back strikes the water first.

44. Forward somersault from 1-meter board—turn a forward somersault in the air so that the feet enter the water first.

45. Backward somersault—turn a backward somersault in the air so that the feet enter the water first.

46. Half gainer—only requirement: enter head first.

47. Full gainer—only requirement: enter feet first.

48. Back half twist—from the back stance position, make a half twist, entering the water straight head first. Do not twist until after leaving the board.

49. Forward one-and-one-half somersault—only requirement: enter head first.

50, 51, 52, etc. Perform any of the standard dives (including also the handstand dive and the handstand feet first dive) from the 3-meter board. No requirements as to form except that the dive is recognizable to the judges, and has a head-first or feet-first entry depending on the dive selected. If, for instance, a jackknife dive is done with very little bend at the hips, it would not be evident to the judges whether it was intended to be a jackknife or a plain forward dive.

A question may arise concerning the necessity of a distinction to be drawn between those who pass a test item on the first trial and those who require many trials. The subject who passes on the first trial goes on to the next test item, thus passing more items with an equal number of trials than the poorer diver. The test is unlimited for a beginning class in that all the standard dives may be attempted from the high board. It is to be understood that the subject who fails a test item may go on to the next one without passing the previous item; a person may make one or more attempts at all the tests.

It was not desired to weigh any of these test items, as the progressive steps are approximately equal. The more difficult dives are divided into parts as, for example, the forward jackknife dive in tests 10, 11, and 12. A very elementary performance of this dive is passed under test 10; a better performance under test 11, and an advanced performance under test 12. Perfect performance in the somersaults, gainers, and high board dives is not required. The front somersault dive, for example, requires only that the subject make one turn in the air and enter the water feet first.

Comments

Although statistical evidence will be required to provide the final answer, the 50 dives included in this test battery appear to span an ability range from beginner to advanced in all age groups for both sexes. In a club or a school system, cumulative records could be maintained to enable the instructor to build on the data of the previous year.

The use of cumulative data would facilitate temporary classification of students each year. Some of the items previously passed by a classification grouping could be repeated during the early lessons as a review and to provide opportunities for each diver to work at his own skill level even within a fairly homogeneous squad. Motivation is enhanced through references to age group percentile ranks and through reference to one's own previous score.

There are no norms available.

Fencing

As yet, no completely objective and valid test of fencing skill exists in the literature. The reason for this may be twofold. First, fencing plays a minor role in most physical education programs. Second, it appears difficult to measure objectively the finesse, accuracy, and speed involved in the successful execution of fencing skills. Success in the bout itself could certainly be used as a measure of achievement for the intermediate or advanced player. A performance chart with provision for recording the number of times specified attack or defense skills were used during a bout would have considerable diagnostic value as well as give evidence of skill achievement. A rating scale can also be of use in assessing individual fencing skills. L. Emery (11) has developed such a scale for beginning foil fencing skills.

Emery performance chart (11)

Procedures for construction

The basic techniques and a description of each were selected and submitted to the 1956–1958 DGWS Fencing Committee. The skills and their analyses included in the rating scale were selected by the majority of committee members. A jury of experts rated each subject on each skill. The sum of the judges' scores when correlated with scores received on the rating scale resulted in a 0.80 coefficient. This validity coefficient refers to the individual items on the scale and does not express a correlation of the rating scale with success in fencing competition. No reliability or objectivity figures are reported.

Administration of rating scale

One student at a time is tested except when attacks and parries are evaluated. A check is placed by the skill analysis if a specific part is present. Each of the seven skills is assigned a number value: 3 = good, 2 = fair, 1 = poor. To receive a "good" rating no more than one part of each skill should be lacking. A perfect score is 21. Letter grades and T-scores are presented in Table 10–2.

TABLE 10–2
Standards for Emery Fencing Performance Test

Raw Score	21	20	19	18	17	16	15	14	13
Letter Grade	A	B	B	C	C	C	D	D	F
T-score	74	68	62	56	48	44	38	32	26

RATING SCALE FOR EMERY BEGINNING FENCING SKILLS

Directions:

A. Check in the space provided each skill with a subjective rating of good, fair, or poor.

B. Use a check to indicate correct performance and a minus for incorrect performance on the breakdown of each skill (use space provided).

C. Additional comments may be written in the space on the extreme right.

Items:

   I. On Guard   Good——; Fair——; Poor——.   Comments on form performance:

      A. Foil arm
      —— 1. Elbow, comfortable distance from waist
      —— 2. Pommel, flat on wrist
      —— 3. Hand, supinated
      —— 4. Point, in line with opponent's eyes

      B. Non-foil arm
      —— 5. Upper arm parallel with floor
      —— 6. Forearm at right angles
      —— 7. Hand relaxed toward head

      C. Upper body
      —— 8. Hand, supinated
      —— 9. Trunk erect, head toward opponent
      ——10. Hips tucked under

      D. Lower extremities
      ——11. Feet at right angles
      ——12. Distance two foot lengths
      ——13. Right foot toward opponent
      ——14. Knees over insteps
      ——15. Right knee toward opponent

  II. Advance: Good——; Fair——; Poor——.

      A. Lower extremities
      —— 1. Right foot lift first, heel touches first
      —— 2. Left foot one movement
      —— 3. Both feet move close to floor, no sliding

 III. Lunge: Good——; Fair——; Poor——.

      A. Foil arm
      —— 1. Extended shoulder high
      —— 2. Hand supinated

B. Non-foil arm

_____ 3. Arm straightened

_____ 4. Palm turned up

C. Lower extremities

_____ 5. Right foot forward, straight line toward opponent

_____ 6. Right knee over instep, toward opponent

_____ 7. Left foot flat on floor

_____ 8. Left knee and leg straight

IV. Disengage: Good_____; Fair_____; Poor_____.

_____ 1. On-guard position

_____ 2. Foil arm extended

_____ 3. Drop foil arm around opponent's bell guard in same movement as arm extension

_____ 4. Lunge

_____ 5. Movement continuous and done with fingers

V. Parry–lateral: Good_____; Fair_____; Poor_____.

_____ 1. On-guard position

_____ 2. Hand half-supination throughout

_____ 3. Middle of blade against middle of opponent's blade

_____ 4. Blade moved enough to cover line being attacked

_____ 5. Hand level no change

VI. Parry–counter: Good_____; Fair_____; Poor_____.

_____ 1. On-guard position

_____ 2. Circle made by finger action

_____ 3. Small circle

_____ 4. Last three fingers

_____ 5. Counter parry quarte counter-clockwise

_____ 6. Counter parry sixte clockwise

_____ 7. Hand level no change

VII. Riposte–simple: Good_____; Fair_____; Poor_____.

_____ 1. On-guard position

_____ 2. Follows successful parry, no delay

_____ 3. Arm extended if needed

_____ 4. Lunge if needed

Field events

Some field events have been included in motor ability and physical fitness test batteries (12). The tests that are appropriate for the development of achievement scales are the standing broad jump, the running broad jump, the running high jump, the pole vault, the shot put, and the discus throw. Additional information on equipment is available in the men's and women's track and field guides (13, 14). Due to its inclusion in the AAHPER Youth Fitness Test, achievement scales are available for the standing broad jump.

Six field events have been selected for inclusion here on the basis of expert judgment and trial and error experience in school programs. No reliability, objectivity, or validity coefficients or percentiles have been reported for any of the events with the exception of the standing broad jump (12).

Pole vault (boys only)

Equipment. A vaulting pole, pole vault uprights, a cross-bar, a pole vault takeoff box, and a vaulting pit.

Description. The subject performs the event as specified in the rules of the Official NCAA Track and Field Guide.

Three trials are allowed at each height and the bar may be raised 3, 4, or 6 inches at a time depending on the degree of skill discrimination required.

Scoring. The greatest height successfully vaulted constitutes the score.

Discus throw

Equipment. Discus, tape measure, and an 8 foot 2½ inch diameter circle which serves as the throwing area.

Description. The subject performs the event as specified in the rules of the Official NCAA or DGWS Track and Field Guide.

Three trials are allowed and the distance of the throw is measured from the inside of the discus ring to the nearest break in the turf.

Scoring. The score is the best of three throws in feet and inches measured to the nearest inch.

Running long jump

Equipment. The jumping pit is 6 feet wide and 15 feet long, filled level with sand. A take-off board is placed approximately 4 to 12 feet from the pit. The board is preceded by a smooth runway approximately 100 feet in length.

Description. NCAA or DGWS track and field rules govern throughout. One practice jump and three trial jumps are allowed. Measurement is taken as described in the rules for this event.

Scoring. The best of three trials in feet and inches (to the nearest inch) is recorded as the contestant's performance.

Shot put

Equipment.   One or several regulation shots is used (8-pound shot for elementary and junior high boys and girls and high school girls, 8 pound 13 ounce for high school boys and college women, 12-pound shot for college men). The shot is put from within a circle 7 feet in diameter.

Description.   Track and field rules must be observed in putting and in determining fouls.   Three warm-up puts are permitted followed by three trial puts.

Scoring.   The contestant's score is the best of the three puts recorded in feet and inches.

Standing broad jump

Equipment.   Mat, floor or outdoor jumping pit, and tape measure are required.

Description.   Subject stands with feet several inches apart and toes just behind the take-off line.   Preparatory to jumping, the subject swings the arms backward and bends the knees.   The jump is accomplished by simultaneously extending the knees and swinging the arms forward.

Three trials are used and the distance is measured from the take-off line to the heel or other part of the body that touches the floor nearest the take-off line.   When the test is given indoors, it is convenient to attach the tape measure to the floor at right angles to the take-off line and have subjects jump along the tape.   The scorer stands to the side and observes the mark to the nearest inch.

Scoring.   Record the best of three trials in feet and inches to the nearest inch.

Running high jump

Equipment.   Test equipment consists of a set of high jump standards, a crossbar, and a jumping pit.

Description.   This event is conducted as it would be in a track and field meet. The bar is started at a height that all contestants can successfully jump and is then raised an inch at a time.   To save time, the bar may be raised 2 or 3 inches at a time.   NCAA or DGWS track and field rules shall govern.

Scoring.   The highest jump recorded in feet and inches is the contestant's score.

Comments

Achievement scales in the field events can be used as a self-testing device when supervised by squad leaders in a track and field teaching unit. Considerable interest is generated through students constantly attempting to better their previous best score.

Test stations administered by trained testers may be set up during the final few periods to obtain data for grading purposes.

Golf

Golf skill tests based on research findings deal primarily with measuring the skill of beginning golfers. The golf score itself is considered a valid measure of ability of the more advanced player. The literature available on golf skill tests may be divided into two categories: outdoor tests calling for standard golf equipment and game-like situations; and indoor tests which require some modifications in equipment and the utilization of situations unlike the actual game. Where equipment and facilities permit, outdoor tests are preferred. However, indoor tests require less space and time for administration and therefore should not be entirely discounted.

Outdoor golf tests for woods and long irons tend to use targets with parallel lines to indicate scoring areas, thus placing primary emphasis on hitting for distance. The lateral deviations of a hook or a slice penalize the performer by reducing distance achieved. Approach shot tests, designed to measure accuracy, usually have targets of concentric circles. Outdoor golf testing unfortunately requires large areas, a great number of trials for reliable results, and considerable time for administration and scoring. Nevertheless, it is desirable to include one such test in the beginning and intermediate golf unit if there is no opportunity to play several holes on a regulation course. The indoor tests (16) are relatively easy to administer and score, but low reliabilities and validities indicate that their use would be limited to practice or motivation and not for individual evaluation.

Vanderhoof indoor golf test (16)

Procedures for construction

An indoor target area suitable for testing ability to loft a plastic golf ball with a two wood, a five iron, or a seven iron was developed. Since the area specifications for all three clubs are the same, the test for the five iron will be described here. Administered to 110 women at the University of Iowa, the reliability coefficient on the five iron test was 0.84 and the validity coefficient was 0.66 when the criterion was a rating of form by three judges.

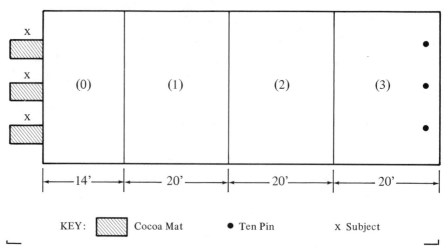

FIGURE 10–3.   Indoor test for five iron shot.
From Vanderhoof (16).

Administration

Equipment.   Test equipment includes plastic pee-gee practice golf balls, number five iron golf clubs, cocoa mats, ten pins or indian clubs placed as targets at the far end of the gymnasium, and high jump standards placed 14 feet from a line at which the balls are hit.   Between the standards, a rope is stretched 8 feet above the floor.

Description.   The subject may take as many practice swings as he wishes and hit 2 or 3 practice balls to warm up.   When ready, he hits 15 full-swing trials toward the target.

Scoring.   Each trial is scored according to the point value of the area in which the ball lands (Figure 10–3).   Two successive topped balls (balls not going over the 8-foot-high rope) are recorded as one trial with a zero score. The total score for the test is the sum of scores for 15 trials.

Comments

Although the original test calls for a rope 14 feet from the subject and 8 feet above the ground, it was found impossible to loft the plastic balls over this height from the specified distance with the specified clubs.   Experimentation by Davis (15) without the rope yielded similar results in reliability and scoring to that reported by Vanderhoof.   Davis therefore concluded that the rope should not be used.   The test administrator is also cautioned that a different type of practice ball may produce entirely different results.

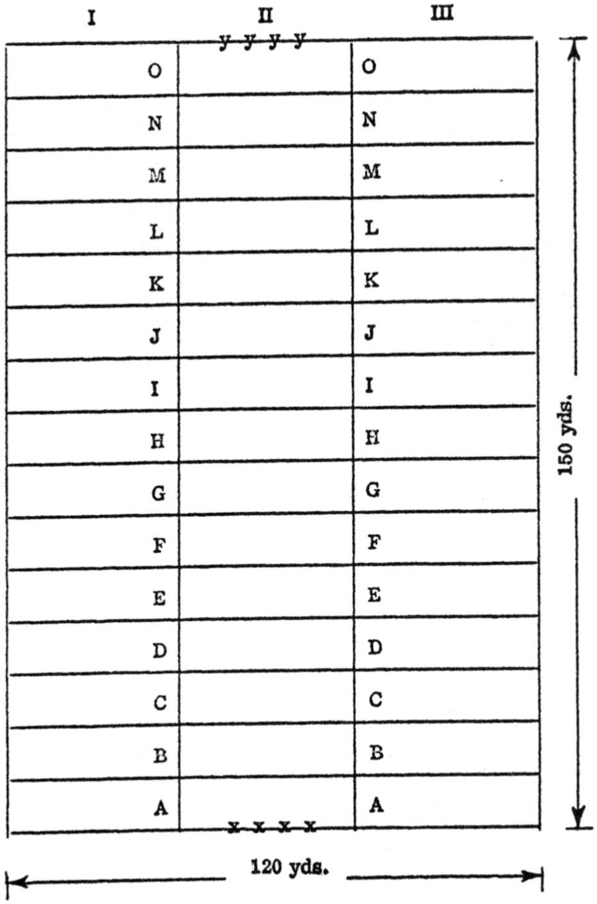

I	II	III
O		O
N		N
M		M
L		L
K		K
J		J
I		I
H		H
G		G
F		F
E		E
D		D
C		C
B		B
A		A

y y y y

x x x x

150 yds.

120 yds.

FIGURE 10–4. Field diagram of outdoor golf test. From Davis (15).

Davis outdoor golf test (15)

Procedures for construction

The test was developed to test the ability of the subject to hit a full swinging five iron shot for distance and accuracy. It was administered to 67 women at the University of Michigan. The test had an estimated reliability of 0.80 for the full length of the test. The design and scoring procedure used gave the test face validity as a measure of distance and accuracy with a five iron.

Carol Davis experimented with two methods of scoring. Method A penalized shots to the right and left of the center 40-yard area of the field, whereas Method B did not. Both methods of scoring yielded the same reliability figures. Correlation of scores computed by Method A with those computed by Method B yielded a correlation coefficient of 0.87. This relationship is high enough to indicate that in testing beginning golfers, penalties in scoring errors to the right and left beyond that imposed by the parallel lines are not necessary.

Administration

Equipment. A level field is used with parallel lines marked at 10-yard intervals across the field (Figure 10–4). It is desirable for the field to be at least 150 yards long. Equipment consists of eight number five iron clubs, eight sets of test balls with each set marked with a different colored pattern, sixteen unmarked balls, two sets of signs on 4-by-8-inch cards staked out along each side of the field to indicate the scoring area, and score cards.

Description. A testing station is set up at each end of the lined field. Four subjects are tested simultaneously at a station. Each subject is allowed an unlimited number of practice swings and 2 practice hits with unmarked balls before hitting the test balls. Two 10-ball trials are taken by each subject, with a period of rest intervening. In order to equalize the effects of hitting from any one of the hitting stations, each subject should hit 5 balls from each of the four hitting stations at his end of the field. At no time should subjects hit toward each other! Following the completion of each 10-ball trial, the balls in each are gathered to the center of that area. On individual score cards, each subject records the area in which her balls are found.

Scoring. The score for the test is the sum of the number of balls in each area multiplied by the score for that area (Figure 10–5). No norms are available for this test.

Gymnastics

In terms of student interest and progress, teacher time and energy, and class time and equipment, the gymnastic standards or achievement progression method of teaching and testing is among the best. In gymnastic standards, movements are selected from the great variety that are possible on each piece of apparatus and arranged in order of simple to complex. Each skill on each apparatus is judged on a pass-fail basis, and cumulative records can be kept from year to year. Although objectivity coefficients have not been determined, it appears that trained squad leaders in junior or senior high school can make successful judgments under careful supervision.

The standards included were initially developed at Glebe Collegiate, Ottawa, Ontario (17). The skills were initially selected and arranged in order of difficulty on the basis of expert judgment. Since that time, they have been modified and rearranged through trial and error. However, the standards have not been validated using official judges' ratings as a criterion, nor has

12	14	12
11	13	11
10	12	10
9	11	9
8	10	8
7	9	7
6	8	6
5	7	5
4	6	4
3	5	3
2	4	2
1	3	1
1	2	1
	x	

FIGURE 10–5. Scoring chart for outdoor golf test. From Davis (15).

any statistical data been presented as to the reliability or the objectivity of the standards approach to gymnastics testing.

Horizontal bar

1. Back circle to front support
2. One half-circle forward, skin the cat
3. Single knee hang, swing head above bar 3 times
4. Assisted swing dismount—3 swings
5. Two chin-ups—each grip
6. Single knee hang, 2 swings, single knee mount
7. Single knee circle forward (reverse grip)
8. Left half of right half left, double knee circle backward
9. Double knee swing dismount

10. Short underswing dismount 5 feet (1-foot take-off)
11. Jump to single knee uprise (mixed grip)
12. Forward knee circle (reverse grip)
13. Left half right or right half left, double knee circle backward, double knee swing dismount
14. Four chin-ups each grip
15. Back circle to front support, hip circle, underswing dismount
16. Hook heels on bar between hands, forward circle mount
17. Short underswing, left half right, angle swing, unhook and underswing dismount
18. Five chin-ups—each grip

Side (pommel) horse

1. Flank vaults, right and left
2. Right leg half circles forward and back, left leg half circles forward and back
3. Squat to back rest, right half right, left half left, right half left, left half right
4. Pivot to front rest on neck, left half left
5. Pivot to front rest, kneel on, jump off
6. Straddle vault running
7. Hitch-kick mount to front riding seat
8. Right half right, left half right, right half left, left half left, right half right
9. Right full right to a feint left and flank vault
10. Thief vault
11. Flank vault to back support, pivot to neck of horse
12. Left half left, to zig-zag travel, pivot to front support-center
13. Left half right, right half left, left half left, right half right
14. Left full right to a rear support
15. Feint left and rear vault
16. Front rest right half left, left half right, right half right, left half left
17. Left full left to a rear support
18. Right full left to a half double left; push-off
19. Hitch kick mount at croup, horizontal travel
20. Left half left turn to straddle seat; swing and scissors to straddle seat, facing out, scissors, dismount

Tumbling

1. Standing front roll
2. Standing back roll

3. Frog balance to frog headstand
4. Front roll to headstand
5. Drop back to feet and side roll
6. Neck spring off cushion
7. Front roll to long sitting position, roll back on shoulders, neck spring to feet
8. Attention fall, shoot, back roll
9. Front roll to headstand, roll out
10. Jump-turn, head spring off cushion
11. Neckspring
12. Attention fall, straight leg drop up to headstand
13. Chest roll, shoot
14. Handspring from cushion
15. Neckspring
16. Handspring
17. Headspring
18. Pike, back roll without up shoot
19. Front roll to headstand, chest roll, shoot, nip-up, front roll out

Parallel bars

1. Hand walk 3 turns (front rest to cross rest to front rest to cross rest)
2. Inside cross seat travel ¾ length
3. Swing to outside cross seat turn straddle seat
4. Straddle travel length front dismount
5. Two shoulder dips
6. Lazy man kip
7. Outside cross seat travel to straddle seat. Repeat three times
8. Straddle travel backwards
9. Two-hand jumps to center, swing outside cross seat
10. Rear vault over both bars
11. Three shoulder dips
12. Back circle to front thigh rest
13. Single leg front jump to straddle seat
14. Shoulder stand pike
15. Front roll to straddle seat, straddle dismount
16. Five shoulder dips
17. Front vault at center to straddle seat
18. Front support swing to a shoulder stand
19. Shoulder hang, swing to pike and kip to front support
20. Long underswing, kip to front support
21. High front dismount
22. Seven shoulder dips

Comments

The gymnastics standards approach enables each student to progress at his own ability level and at his own learning rate on each piece of apparatus. Achievement scales on each piece of apparatus should provide for a wide range of age groups. Student leaders can keep records of the skills passed on each piece of apparatus throughout the teaching block. To perform this function effectively the leaders must be trained to recognize the criteria of successful performance in each skill. This procedure for marking motivates the student to improve his own status. It also eliminates the time-consuming procedures usually associated with testing in gymnastics. To avoid long lines of students waiting to be tested, squads should not be larger than 6 to 8 students per leader. The instructor can then circulate and give assistance where needed in either skill learning or testing. When higher skill levels are attained, it is advisable to have the instructor supervise the testing.

Handball

Several handball test batteries were developed during the thirties. The items were selected on the basis of empirical judgment and the data were not statistically analyzed. Since it is the only test available with established validity, the Cornish Test of Handball Ability has been the most widely used.

Cornish handball test (19)

Procedures of construction

Five tests were selected by the author and administered to 134 students who were enrolled in handball classes at Louisiana State University. The tests were administered after one week of instruction. Three class periods were required to administer the battery. The tests were readministered after ten weeks of practice and play.

Validity, determined by the multiple correlations of the five tests with the total number of "plus points" (points scored in 23 games minus points scored by opponents), was found to be 0.69. The highest individual correlation with the criterion was the Power Test, 0.58. The lowest correlation with the criterion was the Back-Wall Placement, 0.38. A combination of the Thirty-Second Volley and the Service Placement Test correlated 0.67 with the criterion. The lowest test item intercorrelations were Service Placement Test with Front-Wall Placement Test and the Service Placement Test with Back-Wall Placement Test. No reliability or objectivity has been reported and data on college men include only means and standard deviations.

Administration

Thirty-second volley. The contestant, standing behind the service line, bounces the ball and then strikes it continuously against the front wall for 30 seconds. The ball must rebound far enough from the wall for the contestant to remain behind the service line. If the ball fails to return, he may step into the front court to strike the ball, but must return to the service line for the succeeding stroke. If the ball is missed, another is handed to him by the judge and play continues. A point is recorded each time the ball strikes the front wall, and the total points are recorded at the end of 30 seconds.

Front wall placement test. The front wall is divided into scoring areas. After much experimentation, the scoring areas selected were found to range from very easy to very difficult. The smaller and more difficult areas are of greater scoring value than the larger ones.

Starting from the service line, the subject tosses the ball to the front wall below a line drawn 6 feet above and parallel to the floor. On the rebound, he strikes the ball, striving to place it in the area with the largest scoring value. The contestant follows this procedure five times with the right hand and five times with the left hand. The total number of points is recorded. After striking the ball on the rebound, the ball is tossed to the front wall on each succeeding try.

Back wall placement test. The judge tosses the ball so that it strikes the back wall approximately 3 feet above the floor on each try. The ball is then stroked by the contestant who attempts to place the ball in the higher scoring areas on the front wall. The same number of trials is used as in the front wall placement test and scoring is identical.

Power Test. The floor of the court is divided into five areas. Standing in the service zone, the subject tosses the ball to the front wall, allowing it to bounce before striking it. The ball has to strike the front wall below a line 6 feet above the floor. In the event that it strikes the wall above the line or the subject steps into the front court, another trial is allowed. Five strokes are made with the right hand and five with the left hand. Each stroke is given the point value of the area in which it lands. The total number of points are recorded.

Placement-service test. The back court floor is divided into areas as shown in Figure 10–6. The contestant is allowed ten legal services. Five must be cross-court services and all are executed with the hand normally used in serving. The total score is recorded.

Comments

The five-item battery can be used as a self-testing device to measure skill improvement or to motivate students. It is too time consuming to use with test

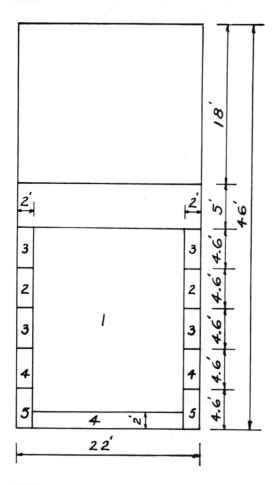

FIGURE 10–6.   The value placed on various positions of the
back court relative to service placement in handball.   From
Cornish (19).

administrators.   A two-item battery composed of the 30-Second Volley and
Service Placement tests correlated 0.67 with the total number of "plus points,"
and is recommended.   The addition of the other three items adds very little
to the validity.

In an effort to develop a measure of handball ability, Pennington and
colleagues (20) have recently studied the relationship of strength, motor
ability, and handball skills in 37 male undergraduate students.   A multiple
correlation of 0.80 was obtained between the criterion (average score per
game in a partial round robin tournament) and slightly modified versions of
the service accuracy, wall volley and back wall placement tests by Cornish.
The highest correlation coefficient for any single item was 0.71 between the
service placement test and the criterion.

Ice skating

At the present time, there are no published tests with appropriate validity and reliability scores available in ice skating. However, the Ice Skating Institute of America (ISIA) has developed a series of skill tests for its award program (21). This skill test series is included here.

Assuming that the required skills are in a progression of increasing difficulty, the highest skill performed, or the total number of skills performed, should be indicative of ice skating skill proficiency.

The progression of skills is:

1. Forward stroking
2. Forward crossover (right foot over left)
3. Forward crossover (left foot over right)
4. One foot snowplow stop
5. Backward stroking
6. Backward crossover (right foot over left)
7. Backward crossover (left foot over right)
8. T-stop (right foot outside edge)
9. T-stop (left foot outside edge)
10. Right forward outside three turn (one foot turn)
11. Left forward outside three turn
12. Right forward inside open Mohawk turn followed by backward outside Mohawk turn (change foot turn)
13. Left forward inside open Mohawk turn followed by backward outside Mohawk turn
14. Hockey stop

Comments

One of the difficulties in making use of skill performance as a test is that the tester must make a subjective determination of whether the skill has been adequately performed. To help alleviate this problem it is suggested that a checklist of the components of each skill be used during the test.

Paddleball and racquetball

A validated test for paddleball and racquetball is yet to be developed. However, A. J. Kozar (22) at the University of Tennessee has had some success using a "Continuous Around the Wall" test to evaluate playing performance. This test requires the subject to continuously pass the ball with a forehand stroke so that the ball when hit in front of the service line goes to the left side wall, front wall, right side wall and back to the player. The score is the number of times the subject can continuously hit the ball without its stopping. Kozar, Grambeau, and Riskey (22) also suggest specific areas in which to serve, as well as a continuous volley test off the front wall.

Swimming

The assessment of achievement in swimming presents diverse measurement problems. If either the time to swim a set distance or the distance swum in a specified time is used, regardless of the age group, a certain portion of the distribution will not be able to obtain a score. In spite of their inability to appear in a time or distance distribution, the nonswimmers will present a skill distribution within their own ranks. This kind of distribution is extremely difficult to handle by traditional achievement scales. Raw scores of different swimming abilities also tend to be negatively skewed with the curve trailing off toward the lower end.

A wide variety of tests have been devised by such organizations as the Red Cross, Camp Fire Girls, Girl Scouts, American Playground and Recreation Association, and the Young Men's and Women's Christian Associations. The majority of these tests have not been scientifically formulated or analyzed.

The most useful swimming achievement scales are those developed for wartime swimming, for college men, and for high school swimming by Jack E. Hewitt at the University of California, Berkeley. The scales provide an effective means of classifying students into capability groups, of motivating learners, and of grading.

Hewitt achievement scales (23–25)

Procedures of construction

Instructors from six high schools in the San Francisco Bay area participated in setting up and administering this test. The crawl, the flutter kick, the elementary back stroke, the side stroke, the breast stroke, and an endurance swim were selected as the fundamental strokes in a high school swimming program. The sample used to construct the scales consisted of 1,093 high school students of whom 647 were girls. The college sample consisted of 4,000 men at the University of California.

Since no external criterion of swimming ability was available, the total test battery score was used as a criterion and correlations were obtained between each test item and the total score. A random sample of 124 boys were retested in the five items a week after the first test without an intervening instruction. Correlation coefficients were determined (Table 10–3).

Objectivity has not been reported. Data are available on high school boys and girls with no stratification on age. In the college achievement scales,

TABLE 10–3

Item	Validity Coefficient	Reliability Coefficient
50-yard crawl	0.65	0.92
25-yard flutter kick	0.60	0.89
10-minute endurance swim	0.59	0.89
25-yard elem. back*	0.88	0.96
25-yard side stroke*	0.94	0.90
25-yard breast stroke*	0.77	0.93

From Hewitt (23)
*Number of strokes required to complete a 25-yard distance.

a 50-yard distance is used in place of 25 yards and the endurance swim was increased to 15 minutes. Norms for college men are reported in T-scores.

Administration

The following test should be given to all students who can swim:

1. Fifty-yard Crawl for time. Use a racing dive. Swim the crawl stroke for 50 yards. Scoring: Record to closest tenth of a second.

2. Twenty-five-yard Flutter Kick for time with water polo ball. Start in the pool holding onto the gutter with one hand and with the other hand to ball. Start at the word "Go." Use a regulation push off. Stop when ball touches end. Scoring: Record time to closest tenth of a second.

3. Glide and Relaxation Ability for 25 yards for the Elementary Back Stroke, Side Stroke, and Breast Stroke. Only one leg action and one arm action are allowed per stroke. Scoring: Count push-off plus strokes used for total distance.

   a. Elementary Back Stroke: Start in the water using a regulation push-off at the start with arms at sides of body and legs together. Use inverted breast stroke kick. Arms must remain in the water at all times, but they may be raised above the shoulders on the recovery. Maximum glide is recommended. No arm or leg action is allowed on the push-off.

   b. Side Stroke: Push-off into gliding position with lower arm extended over the head and upper arm along side of the hip. No arm or leg action is allowed on the push-off. Only one leg action is allowed per arm action while stroking. Use single under-arm or underwater side stroke and not the over-arm side stroke.

   c. Breast Stroke: Start in water using regulation above-water push-off for start and for turn. Push-off into gliding position with arms extended over head and legs together. No arm pull or leg kick allowed on push-offs. Use regulation breast stroke. The butterfly kick is not permitted. Only one arm and leg action is allowed per stroke.

After the test has been explained, students can count their own strokes. If the pool is not large enough for the entire class, divide into two sections and have the students on the bank count the strokes. It saves time to record results of the whole class.

Comments

The achievement scales in swimming may be used to classify students into homogeneous groups at the beginning of a teaching block in aquatics. They are also useful as self-testing devices throughout the teaching block. Administered at the end of a block of swimming classes, the achievement scales may be used to measure improvement or to determine a grade.

Tennis

The backboard test of tennis ability was developed by J. Dyer at Teachers College, Columbia University, in 1932. Extensive data were collected during the next three years and published in the *Studies in Physical Education* sponsored by the School of Education of Boston University, Supplement to the *Research Quarterly,* March 1935.

Due to ease of administration, similarity to game skills, and practice possibilities, the test has been widely adopted. Dyer revised the test in 1938 (27) by instituting a restraining line 5 feet from the wall and simplifying the scoring. A 27.5-foot restraining line has been proposed by Scott and French (31), whereas Hewitt (29) recommends the use of a 20-foot line. A 20-foot restraining line has been in use for the past decade at the University of Michigan. It appears that a restraining line 20 to 30 feet from the wall provides a better test of stroking ability.

Recently, a rally test of tennis skill has been proposed by J. Kemp and M. Vincent (30). In this test, the students rally as in a game situation. A relatively short time period is involved, and no special equipment or court markings are needed. Due to the game-like quality, ease of administration and relatively high validity and reliability of this test, the author will consider it below.

In addition, J. DiGennaro (26) constructed a battery of tennis tests (Tennis Tests of Achievement) to measure skill in the forehand drive, backhand drive, and service. Because specific tennis skills are evaluated, these tests are included here.

Dyer backboard test (27)

Procedures for construction

The test was initially designed for classification of students. For the first publication, 736 women at nineteen colleges were tested. Data on men were obtained prior to the second publication in 1938.

The sum of three trials was correlated with ranking by three experts and with a round robin tournament of 20-point games. Correlations ranged from 0.86 to 0.92 in samples of from 13 to 37 women.

A variety of test-retest reliabilities were determined in different populations. The coefficients range from 0.84 to 0.90. Since opinions and subjective judgments are not involved and testing media are kept constant, the author assumes high objectivity. Means, standard deviation, ranges, and T-scores for college women are presented. Limited data on a small sample of college men are also available.

Administration

Equipment. Tennis racquet, dozen tennis balls, a wire basket or cardboard box, and a stop watch are required.

Description. Use a flat wall (at least 10 feet high and 15 feet wide) with a line 3 feet high at the front wall and a restraining line 20–30 feet from the wall and parallel to it.*

Place the cardboard box or wire basket containing the balls on the floor at the left of the playing area for right-handed players (opposite side for left-handed players).

Divide the class into groups of three with one person in each group designated as the timer, one as scorer and one as subject. These assignments are to be alternated until all three have been tested.

The subject takes a position behind the restraining line and approximately midway between the side lines. He should hold two tennis balls in one hand and the racquet in the other hand.

On the signal "Go," the subject drops one tennis ball and hits it on the first bounce so that it strikes the front wall above net height. He then attempts to keep this ball in play by hitting it against the front wall above net height and from behind the restraining line. A subject scores one point for each shot that is hit in this manner. If the subject loses control of the ball, he is free to put another ball in play. When a ball is first put in play, it is dropped and then hit on the bounce. After this, it may be hit on a volley or on any bounce as long as the subject is standing behind the restraining line. A testee may use any number of balls during the test period. The object of the test is to make as many good returns as possible in the 1-minute time period.

Scoring. The scorer gives the subject 1 point for each good shot. The timer gives the signal "Go" at the outset and shouts "Stop" at the end of 1 minute.

*Note: A 5-foot restraining line was used in the original study (26).

Comments

It should be noted that in other studies using the Dyer test the validity and reliability have not been as high as originally reported by Dyer. Fox (28) obtained a validity coefficient of 0.53 between the Dyer test and the subjective ratings of skill of beginning players. Thorpe (32) reported test-retest reliabilities of from 0.49 to 0.82, and Hewitt (29) found validity coefficients for the Dyer test that ranged from 0.12 to 0.34 for beginning players and 0.68 to 0.78 for advanced players when compared to rankings in a round robin tournament. With the use of a 20-foot restraining line, reliability increased to 0.82 for beginners and 0.93 for advanced players in Hewitt's study. Validity coefficients for the Hewitt revision were 0.71 to 0.73 for beginners and 0.84 to 0.89 for advanced players.

Although the optimal distance for the restraining line in the backboard test needs to be determined, a distance of 20 feet probably would be more suitable for beginners and novices, whereas distances closer to 30 feet would better serve the skill level of intermediate and advanced players. We have found that the 5-foot restraining line as recommended in the original study encourages poor stroking technique in that most subjects tend to use a "wristy" or badminton-type stroke at this distance.

The test is useful as a practice drill. Although no statistical evidence has been advanced, the test also provides possibilities of evaluating consecutive forehand and backhand volleys and alternating forehand and backhand volleys.

Kemp-Vincent rally test (30)

Procedures for construction

The test was constructed to overcome the criticisms of tennis skills tests: namely, that current tests do not measure skills under game conditions, they require the use of special equipment or line markings, and they demand considerable time for administration.

The purpose of this test is to classify students and rate achievement in playing skill as measured by rally ability in a simulated tennis game. In evaluating the test, the authors employed two forms of validation. In the first, 54 men and women (30 intermediate and 24 beginners) were ranked according to round robin tournament play. Comparing tournament and skills test rankings yielded a correlation coefficient* of 0.84 and 0.93 for beginners and intermediate players, respectively. In the second validation, the skills test scores of 362 male and female players of varied ability levels were compared to scores on the Iowa modification of the Dyer test. The validity (correlation) coefficients were 0.86 for beginners and 0.90 for intermediate players.

*Spearman Rho formula for ranks. This coefficient is interpreted like the usual correlation coefficient.

Administration

Equipment. A stop watch, regulation tennis singles court, four good tennis balls per court, and a tennis racquet for each student are the only equipment necessary for this test.

Description. Two players of similar ability take position on opposite sides of the net. Each player has two tennis balls. On the signal "Go," one player bounces the ball from behind the baseline and puts the ball in play with a courtesy stroke. The players keep the ball in play for as long as possible within the 3-minute test period. If a ball is hit into the net or out of bounds so that it is not playable, another ball is put in play by a courtesy stroke from behind the baseline. Any stroke may be used and players are responsible for retrieving the balls after the original four have been used.

The following are considered errors and affect the score:

1. Failure to get ball over net on courtesy stroke.
2. Failure to get ball over net on rally.
3. Failure to start a new ball from behind the baseline.
4. Failure to keep ball within singles area.
5. Failure to hit ball before second bounce.

Balls landing on a boundary line are in play. Balls hitting the top of the net and landing over the net and in bounds are good and in play. A player may play a ball on which his partner had made an error if it is believed advantageous to keep the ball in play. This would include an out-of-bounds ball if it could be played faster than putting a new ball in play.

Scoring. A trial test is administered prior to the actual testing. For a 3-minute rally period the total number of hits for the two players are counted regardless of whether an error is made on a hit. Each courtesy stroke counts as a hit. From the combined total number of hits for both players, each player subtracts the number of his errors to arrive at a final rally score.

Three scorers are recommended: one scorer to count the total number of hits by both players, and one scorer for each of the participants to score the individual errors.

Comments

The main difficulty with this test is the adequate pairing of participants on playing ability. A participant capable of consistently placing a rally so that it might easily be returned would tend to have the effect of spuriously over-rating his partner's ability score, and the opposite would be true if the participant was of poor caliber. This is the main problem in skills tests which involve more than one participant. However, in view of the reported figures for the reliability and validity of this test, plus its ease of administration and game-like characteristics, the authors feel this test warrants consideration as a measure of tennis ability.

Tennis tests of achievement (26)

Procedures for construction

The Tennis Tests of Achievement (TTA) were constructed to provide an evaluation of three specific skills in tennis, rather than some overall measure of tennis-playing performance.

Basically, the TTA requires the student to hit the tennis ball into targets of concentric circles using forehand drive, backhand drive, and service.

The subjects for evaluating the TTA were 64 male college students enrolled in three beginning tennis classes. Test-retest reliability coefficients were 0.67 for the forehand drive test, 0.66 for the backhand drive test, and 0.80 for the service test. Validity of the TTA was determined by judge's ratings of performance on the specific skills during a round-robin tennis tournament (N = 15). The validity coefficients attained were 0.40 for the forehand drive, 0.78 for the backhand drive and 0.66 for the service.

Administration

Equipment. A tightly strung tennis racquet and tennis balls, and a rope stretched 3 feet directly above the top of the net and parallel to it are needed. The drive target should be marked on a regulation tennis court 6 feet from the baseline at the center of the court with concentric circles of 5, 10, and 15 feet in diameter. The center of the service target is at a point 4 feet from the service end line and the service side line. Service target circles are 4, 8, and 12 feet in diameter. (See Figure 10–7.)

Description. For the drive tests (forehand and backhand) the subject should stand 2 feet in front of the baseline at the center of the court facing the net. The tester drops a tennis ball from about 6 feet above the court and in front of the subject. The subject, after allowing the ball to bounce, attempts to drive it over the net and under the rope so that it lands as close to the center of the target as possible.

In performing the service test the subject attempts a legal overhand serve at the baseline and 4 feet to the right of the center court. For the drive tests and the service test the score is determined by the area of the respective targets in which the ball lands.

Scoring. The player's score is the total number of points for 20 trials. Each player is given 5 practice trials. If the ball goes over the restraining rope, the subject is given half value for that trial. Point scoring for the drive test is 10 for the bulls-eye, 8 for the next circle, 6 for the outside circle, 4 for a hit outside the target circles but landing in the backcourt, and 2 for the forecourt. For the serve, point scoring is 10 for the bulls-eye, 8 for the next circle, 6 for the outside circle, and 4 for a hit outside the target circles but landing in the right service box.

Service Target   Drive Target

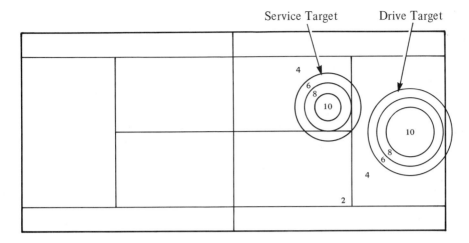

FIGURE 10–7. TTA testing station. From DiGennaro
(26).

Comments

As for most sport skills tests, these tests can be used as practice sessions during
the instructional part of the course. If the targets are drawn on sheets of
canvas, setting up the testing area is considerably easier. A possible change
in the administration of the drive tests would be to have the player drop the
ball himself before hitting it.

Track events

Track events have traditionally been included in physical fitness test batteries
as speed or endurance measures (33). The lack of achievement scales with
the exception of physical fitness items is indicative of how seldom boys and
girls are instructed and trained in the skills of sprinting and pacing. Each
of these skills is a prerequisite of a physically educated child. Since the optimal distance for evaluation of sprint and distance running has not been
determined, selections had to be made on empirical grounds.

The 50-yard dash has been selected by the authors as the sprint item
rather than the traditional track distance of 100 yards. The 100-yard distance
provides a closer tie with track meets and interscholastic athletics; however,
it has limitations when advocated as a test for all ages in all schools. Decisive
factors in the selection of the 50-yard distance were (33) the extensive data
available in the AAHPER Youth Fitness Test Manual for this distance, (2)
the availability of a 50-yard straightaway over reasonably smooth terrain in
most school facilities, (3) the suitability of 50 yards as a sprint distance for

all age groups, and (4) that this is a distance long enough not to be seriously affected by reaction time in starting.

The 880-yard run has been selected as the distance over which to train individuals in pacing. This distance is long enough to require pacing. The 880-yard run was also selected as one item in the physical fitness test for high school and college men developed under the sponsorship of the U.S. Office of Education in 1943 (36). The distance has been used extensively with boys of widely varying age and is equally appropriate for girls.

50-yard dash

Administration

Equipment. Two stopwatches or one with a split-second timer.

Description. It is preferable to administer this test to two pupils at a time. Have both take positions behind the starting line. The starter will use the commands "Are you ready?" and "Go!" The latter will be accompanied by a downward sweep of the starter's arm to give the timer a visual signal.

Scoring. The score is the time between the starter's signal and the instant the pupil crosses the finish line. Record to the tenth of a second.

Half-mile run

Administration

Equipment. A quarter-mile running track or suitable area where a distance of a half-mile can readily be measured.

Description. To save time, subjects run in groups of 15 to 20 or less.

Scoring. Time is taken from the word "Go" until the runner crosses the finish line when the time is called out in minutes and seconds thus, "Two-thirty-seven," "Two-thirty-eight," etc. Runners shall not cut in until they are two full running strides ahead of their nearest competitor. Time is recorded to the nearest second.

Comments

The administration of a sprint and a distance running test within the framework of a track and field teaching unit has a different emphasis and a different purpose than that associated with their presence in a physical fitness test battery. In the track teaching unit, the emphasis is on the present status and subsequent improvement in the skill measured, not on extrapolating from this measure to some underlying variable. Consequently, the testing and the guidance based on the test results is directed towards improvement in running style, in sprinting ability, and in pacing. Very few youngsters are trained to run, in spite of the national interest in endurance. The problem is that attention has been directed toward the test and test data rather than toward development of the skills of running and pacing.

Wrestling

A statistically validated test of the sports skills of wrestling has yet to be published. The only wrestling test that has appeared is an unpublished master's thesis on potential wrestling ability. The two-item test battery consists of a stunt-type test and a sustained grip strength test. No tests of sports skill are included.

Wrestling appears to lend itself to the same type of achievement scale approach as diving and gymnastics. The skills could be arranged from simple to complex and then be scored on a pass-fail basis. Such a test could be validated against actual wrestling performance within different weight classifications. Considering the growing popularity of wrestling in physical education programs, it is unfortunate that subjective evaluative criteria are not available.

REFERENCES

ARCHERY

1. Hyde, E. I., "National Research Study in Archery." *Res. Quart.*, 7:64–71, 1936.

2. ———, "An Achievement Scale in Archery." *Res. Quart.*, 8:109–116, 1937.

3. American Association for Health, Physical Education and Recreation, *Skills Test Manual: Archery for Boys and Girls.* Washington, D.C.: The Association, 1967.

BADMINTON

4. French, E., and E. Stalter, "Study of Skills Tests in Badminton for College Women." *Res. Quart.*, 20:257–272, 1949.

5. Miller, F. A., "A Badminton Wall Volley Test." *Res. Quart.*, 22:208–213, 1951.

6. Scott, M. G., "Achievement Examinations in Badminton." *Res. Quart.*, 12:242–253, 1941.

7. Scott, M.G., and E. French, *Measurement and Evaluation in Physical Education.* Dubuque, Iowa: Brown, 1959, pp. 145 and 147.

BOWLING

8.   Martin, J. L. S., "Bowling Norms for College Men and Women." *Res. Quart.,* 31:113–116, 1960.

9.   Phillips, M. and D. Summers, "Bowl-ing Norms and Learning Curves for College Women." *Res. Quart.,* 21:382–384, 1950.

DIVING

10.   Bennett, L. M., "A Test of Diving for Use in Beginning Classes." *Res. Quart.,* 13:109–115, 1942.

FENCING

11.   Emery, L., "Criteria for Rating Selected Skills of Foil Fencing." *Bowling/Fencing/Golf Guide, 1960–62.* Washington, D.C.: The Division for Girls' and Women's Sports, American Association for Health, Physical Education and Recreation, p. 74.

FIELD EVENTS

12.   American Association for Health, Physical Education and Recreation, *Youth Fitness Test Manual.* Washington, D.C.: The Association, 1965.

13.   Division for Girls and Women's Sports, *Track and Field Guide.* Washington, D.C.: American Association for Health, Physical Education and Recreation, 1972–1974 (or most recent revision).

14.   National Collegiate Athletic Association, *Official NCAA Track and Field Guide.* New York: National Collegiate Athletic Bureau, 1973 (or most recent revision).

GOLF

15.   Davis, C. M., "The Use of the Golf Tee in Teaching Beginning Golf." Unpublished Master's thesis, University of Michigan, 1960.

16.   Vanderhoof, E. R., "Beginning Golf Achievement Test." Master's thesis, University of Iowa, 1956. Eugene, Ore.: Microcard Publications, University of Oregon, 1956.

GYMNASTICS

17.   Faulkner, J. A., and R. E. Thornton, "Methods in Gymnastics." Mimeographed material, University of Western Ontario, London, 1957.

18.   Hall, R. M., "Gymnastic Standards at Pickering High." *J. Canad. Assoc. for Health, Physical Education and Recreation,* 25:27–29, 1958.

HANDBALL

19.   Cornish, C., "A Study of Ability in Handball." *Res. Quart.,* 20:213–222, 1949.

20.   Pennington, G. G.; J. A. P. Day; J. Drowatzky; and J. F. Hansen, "A Measure of Handball Ability." *Res. Quart.,* 38:247–253, 1967.

ICE SKATING

21. Jomland, E.; R. Priestley; J. Waldo; and M. Kirby, *How To Improve Your* *Ice Skating.* Chicago: Athletic Institute, 1963.

PADDLEBALL and RACQUETBALL

22. Kozar, A. J.; J. B. Rodney; and E. N. Riskey, *Beginning Paddleball.* Bel-mont, Calif.: Wadsworth, 1967, p. 53.

SWIMMING

23. Hewitt, J. E., "Achievement Scales for Wartime Swimming." *Res. Quart.,* 14:391–396, 1943.

24. _____, "Swimming Achievement Scale Scores for College Men." *Res.* *Quart.,* 19:282–294, 1948.

25. _____, "Achievement Scale Scores for High School Swimming." *Res. Quart.,* 20:170–179, 1949.

TENNIS

26. DiGennaro, J., "Construction of Forehand Drive, Backhand Drive and Service Tennis Courts." *Res. Quart.,* 40: 496–501, 1969.

27. Dyer, J. T., "Revision of the Backboard Test of Tennis Ability." *Res. Quart.,* 9:25–31, 1938.

28. Fox, K., "A Study of the Validity of the Dyer Backboard Test and the Miller Forehand-Backhand Test for Beginning Tennis Players." *Res. Quart.,* 24:1–7, 1953.

29. Hewitt, J., "Revision of the Dyer Backboard Tennis Test." *Res. Quart.,* 36:153–157, 1965.

30. Kemp, J. and M. Vincent, "Kemp-Vincent Rally Test of Tennis Skill." *Res. Quart.,* 39:1000–1004, 1969.

31. Scott, M. G. and E. French, *Evaluation in Physical Education.* St. Louis: Mosby, 1959.

32. Thorpe, J., "Intelligence and Skill in Relation to Success in Singles Competition in Badminton and Tennis." *Res. Quart.,* 38:119–125, 1967.

TRACK EVENTS

33. American Association for Health, Physical Education and Recreation, *Youth Fitness Test Manual.* Washington, D.C.: The Association, 1965.

34. Division for Girls and Women's Sports, *Track and Field Guide.* Washington, D.C.: American Association for Health, Physical Education and Recreation, 1972–1974.

35. National Collegiate Athletic Asso-ciation, *Official NCAA Track and Field Guide.* New York: National College Athletic Bureau, 1973 (or most recent revision).

36. U.S. Office of Education, Federal Security Agency, *Handbook on Physical Fitness for Colleges and Universities.* Washington, D.C.: U.S. Government Printing Office, 1943.

WRESTLING

37. Sievers, H. L., "The Measurement of Potential Wrestling Ability." Unpublished Master's thesis, State University of Iowa, 1934. (Cited in C. H. McCloy, and N. D. Young, *Tests and Measurements in Health and Physical Education.* New York: Appleton-Century-Crofts, 1954.

STUDY QUESTIONS · *Chapter 10*

1. In what sports are pass-fail skill tests frequently used?

2. What is the best criterion for validating:
   a. a table tennis test
   b. a golf ability test
   c. a gymnastics test

3. How can you improve the reliability of accuracy (i.e., target-type) tests?

4. What is meant by a "dual" sport?

5. What is a test battery?

6. If you think a badminton test measures badminton ability, how would you determine its validity? What criterion would you use?.

7. Describe a published test of ability in the following sports:
   a. badminton   e. bowling
   b. diving   f. fencing
   c. golf   g. gymnastics
   d. tennis

8. A Columbia Round is used in what sport?

TEAM SPORTS SKILLS TESTS

11

John F. McCabe
William D. McArdle

Most team sports provide no built-in objective method to evaluate the individual's efforts. Skills tests are particularly helpful in the class situation where the skill level is low or intermediate, the number of pupils large, and instructional units short. However, at the present time, of all the available tests or combinations of tests designed to measure some aspect of skill in a team sport, none should be used as the sole device. Along with skill tests, subjective ratings of game performance, performance or incidence charts, and achievement progressions should be used for the most complete profile of the individual's skill. At the varsity level, some of the best evaluation can be accomplished subjectively by skilled coaches who have the opportunity of constant observation of small numbers, of supplementary aid by numerous assistants, and of analysis of game movies.

Basketball tests for boys and men

Test batteries for basketball are among the most numerous of all the sports skills tests. L. W. Johnson's three-item test battery (2), developed in 1934, has been widely accepted and used. The advantages of Johnson's battery are that it is short and simple. The simplicity is apparent in both the construction and administration of the items. Each item objectively measures predominantly one aspect of the game. Many tests of more recent vintage are too complex. The result is that several variables contribute to the eventual score and the teacher is at a loss as to which requires more instruction and practice. An example is a dribble-and-shoot test in which a poor score may be due to poor dribbling ability, poor shooting ability, or both.

Johnson basketball battery

Procedures for construction

Johnson's total test battery includes the three-item test of basic skill and four items of potential ability. The Iowa-Brace, footwork, jump and reach, and dodging run tests which purport to measure potential ability are not included here since the validity of these test items has not been established.

The validity and reliability coefficients cited in the following sections are based on data obtained from 180 high school boys. The boys were divided into a "good" group who made the basketball squad and a "poor" group who did not. There were 50 boys in the "good" group and 130 boys in the "poor" group. Johnson used a biserial correlation coefficient* to report the validity coefficients between each test item and the total battery and the criterion of the boy's ability to make the squad.

Test	Validity	Reliability
Basket shooting	0.73	0.73
Throw for Accuracy	0.78	0.80
Dribble	0.65	0.78
Three-Item Battery	0.88	0.89

The objectivity has not been reported.

Administration

Field-goal speed test. The subject may assume any position he desires under the basket. On the signal "Go," he starts making "layup" shots as fast as he can. At the end of 30 seconds, the signal "Stop" is given. One point is scored for each basket made.

Dribble. Place the chairs as shown in Figure 11–1. On the signal "Go," the subject starts dribbling from the starting line and continues in the prescribed route for 30 seconds. The number of chairs passed in the time allotted comprises the score.† Two trials should be given.

*Interpreted like the usual correlation coefficient.
†It is preferable to measure the elapsed time between the start and finish of the course.

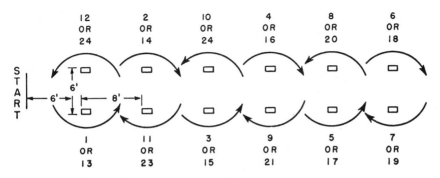

FIGURE 11–1. Diagram for basketball dribble test. From Hunsicker and Montoye (1).

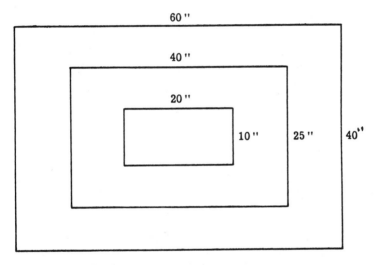

FIGURE 11–2. Wall marking for target in basketball passing test. From Hunsicker and Montoye (1).

Passing test. Hang the target (Figure 11–2) so that the 60-inch length of the outer rectangle is parallel to the floor and the bottom border of this rectangle is 14 inches above the floor. Draw a restraining line 40 feet from the target. The subject is given ten trials with either an overhand or hook pass at the target from behind the restraining line. Three points are granted for hitting the inner rectangle and line, two for the middle one and line, and one for the outer rectangle and line.

Comments

The three-item basketball test battery is short enough to administer to the whole class before and after (or at least after) a block of teaching in basketball. The test results can be used for diagnosis and guidance of individual strengths and weaknesses. The validity and reliability of the whole battery are adequate for classification and grading. The effectiveness of teaching may also be assessed through reference to the average improvement of a class during the teaching block. However, there appears to be some question as to the face validity of the passing test, since a 40-foot pass test may not be indicative of passing ability in a game situation. A 30-foot pass is preferable. Very few norms are available in percentile ranks. Johnson's data on high school boys were originally reported in a form somewhat similar to T-scores. Hunsicker and Montoye (1) provided percentile ranks for college men in their now out-of-print laboratory manual.

AAHPER basketball test

A nine-item basketball skills test for boys (3) has been presented as part of the battery of AAHPER Sport Skills Tests. The test consists of items to measure shooting, passing, jumping, and dribbling. Several items are quite similar to those which appear in previously validated tests of basketball skill. Separate manuals are available for use with boys and girls. The test items are the same for both groups with the exception that the restraining lines are moved closer to the target for girls in the side shot and overarm and push-pass for accuracy tests.

The main limitation of this test lies in the fact that no data on reliability and validity are presented for either the individual test items or the entire test. Therefore, it is difficult to evaluate the relative merit of each item to assess basketball performance, and administration of the entire nine-item test requires considerably more time than previously validated basketball tests. It would be impractical to test an entire class with the nine-item test. However, these test items appear to meet the criteria of face validity in that shooting, dribbling, jumping, and passing are important basketball skills.

The main value of this test battery is that it provides the student with the opportunity to practice, in a test situation, important basketball skills and compare his or her results to norms. This test is not recommended for grading purposes.

Basketball tests for girls and women

The game of basketball for girls has changed considerably in the last thirty years. The change from the three-court game of the 1930s to the full court game of the 1970s has resulted in a much faster-moving, faster-passing game.

One attempt to update skill testing in women's basketball was made by Lambert (6), who altered the bounce and shoot test of Glassow et al. (5). This revised test is included with two other skills tests thought to have merit in evaluating the performance of female basketball players.

The professional studies and Research Committee of the Midwest Association of College Teachers of Physical Education for Women, in 1954, reported achievement levels in basketball skills for women physical education majors (7). To obtain data for these skill norms they selected three tests chosen on the basis of a study by Leilich of all basketball tests appearing in the literature. Leilich found four factors to be basic to all these tests: basketball motor ability, speed, ball handling involving speed and accuracy, and ball handling involving goal shooting. The three tests selected to measure these factors were the Johnson Half-Minute Shooting Test (8), the Push-Pass (4), and the Bounce and Shoot (5) with revisions (6).

Girls' basketball battery

Administration

Half-minute shooting test. The subject may assume any position she desires under the basket. On the signal "Go," she starts shooting baskets as fast as she can for 30 seconds. If the ball has left her hands before the signal to stop, the basket, if made, counts. Two trials are given and the test score is that of the better trial. This is the same as the boys' test except that two 30-second trials are given. Norms for high school girls and college women may be found in Scott and French (8).

Bounce and shoot test. The equipment includes two chairs, two basketballs, a stop watch, and regulation backboard and basket arranged as indicated in Figure 11–3.

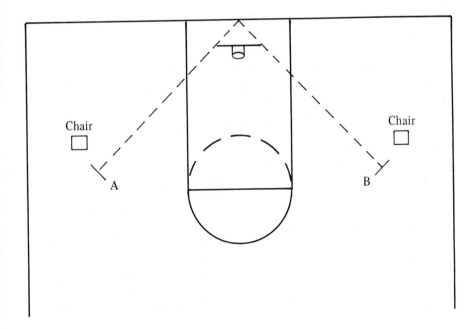

FIGURE 11–3. Floor diagram for the bounce and shoot test. From Glassow et al. (5).

On either side of the basket at an angle of 45 degrees, an 18-foot dashed line is drawn from the center of the end line. Perpendicular to the 18-foot lines, 24-inch lines are added. Starting from a point 1 foot behind and 30 inches to the outside of the 18-foot lines, additional lines 18 inches are drawn. On each of the 18-inch lines, a chair with a ball is placed.

The subject starts on line B. On the signal "Go," she picks up the ball from the chair, bounces, shoots, recovers the rebound and passes it back to a person standing behind chair B. She then runs to chair A, picks up the ball, and repeats the sequence for a total of ten shots (five on each side). The timer is responsible for recording the total time (nearest 0.1 second) until the ball is caught after the tenth trial. The scorer records the points made on the shooting and notifies the timer on the ninth shot. The test score consists of a score for accuracy and a score for time. The accuracy score is as follows: 2 points for each basket and 1 point for hitting the rim but missing the basket. The time score is the total time to the nearest tenth of a second. Lambert (6) suggests that scoring be either the total time or twice the time plus the accuracy score.

The original source for this test (5) indicates a reliability coefficient of 0.82 for 51 college women. The Lambert revision of the test has a reliability coefficient of 0.92 based on 25 subjects and a validity coefficient with game performance of 0.65 (time score only) and 0.60 (twice time plus accuracy score). The Lambert revision eliminates from the score subjectively imposed penalties for number of bounces and the initiation point of the dribble, which were contained in the original version of the test.

Push-pass. The subject stands behind a restraining line 10 feet from the wall and parallel to it. On the signal "Go," she makes a push-pass (two-hand chest pass) to a target on the wall (Figure 11–4). She recovers the ball and continues to pass to the target from behind the restraining line for 30 seconds. Her score is the total number of target "points" obtained before the "Stop" signal is called. Points are given according to the area of the target in which the ball lands as indicated on the diagram. Line hits are awarded the value of the inner circle. No points are recorded for a pass in which the feet are on or over the restraining line. The test score is the best score of two trials. No figures for reliability, validity, or objectivity are given.

Comments

Fifty-nine schools in the United States contributed scores toward the calculation of the T-score and percentile norms for female physical education majors. The norms of the Half-Minute Shoot represent 1,812 subjects, the Bounce and Shoot, 1,645, and the Push-Pass, 1,646.

A nine-item skills test of basketball for girls was developed as part of the Sports Skills Test project of AAHPER. Test manuals with norms in percentiles are available. See details under Basketball, Men.

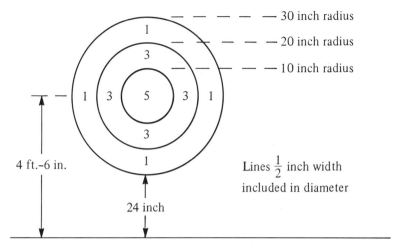

FIGURE 11–4. Target for the basketball push-pass test.
From Glassow et al. (5).

Football (touch)

A touch football test battery is included since the skills taught and practiced in physical education relate to this game rather than to tackle football.

In an unpublished master's thesis at the University of California in 1936, Stanley E. Borleske developed and analyzed a touch football test that was subsequently published by Cozens in the *Research Quarterly* as part of the Ninth Annual Report of the Committee on Curriculum Research (9). It has been widely referred to in textbooks as the Borleske Touch-Football Test.

Borleske touch-football test

Procedures of construction

Forty-six physical education instructors in the San Joaquin Valley provided judgments as to the elements comprising touch football. Based on these judgments, eighteen tests were identified and classified under five elements. The five elements were passing, catching, kicking, running, and pass defense. The eighteen-item test battery was administered to eighty-seven men in the required program of Fresno State College.

A three-item battery (forward pass for distance, punt for distance, and running 50 yards carrying the ball) correlated 0.88 with the sum of the scores of the eighteen-item battery. The original eighteen-item test correlated 0.85 with the opinion of experts subjectively rating performance.

Reliability and objectivity have not been reported. Data are presented on college men only.

Administration

Forward pass for distance.   A football field or playground is needed, with lines marked every 5 yards, and with markers every 10 yards, so that subjects may throw from both ends of the field.   One to six pairs of passers (depending on width of field) may throw at the same time.   A new regulation football is used.

Subjects throw in pairs.   After a 1-minute warm-up, each contestant is allowed three throws from behind the endline.   The best throw is counted. Each throw must be preceded by the catch of a pass from the center.* Partners of subjects who have just thrown should immediately spot the point where the ball hits without attempting to retrieve the ball until the distance has been estimated to the nearest yard.   The best of three throws is the score.

Punt for distance.   A football field or playground is marked as for "Forward Pass for Distance."   A new regulation football is used.   One-minute warm-up is permitted.   Kickers work in pairs, each man standing behind a line at least 7 yards behind center when he kicks.   The ball must be kicked within two seconds after the snap from center.   Each subject is allowed three punts for distance, and distance is measured to the nearest yard.   The best of three punts is the score.

Running: straight-away, speed, or sprint.   The football field or playground is marked as for "Forward Pass for Distance."   New regulation football is used.   The contestant catches the ball from center from a point 5 yards back of the center and from a backfield stance (i.e., three-point stance) and carries it a total distance of 50 yards, running as fast as possible.†   Any form of carrying the ball used in football is permissible.   One minute is allowed for warm-up.   One trial is allowed and the time in seconds is the score.

Comments

The three-item battery, composed of forward pass for distance, punt for distance, and running 50 yards carrying the ball, has adequate validity to be used for classification and grading.

AAHPER football test

Test items designed to measure passing, catching, running, dodging, kicking, blocking, charging, and ball handling are part of the ten-item AAHPER Foot-

---

*A more objective test procedure is to eliminate the center and simply have the subject throw or punt for distance.

†A more objective test procedure is to eliminate the center and simply have the subject run.   Cozen's article does not clarify the timing procedure.   It appears that the watch is started with the snap of the ball and ends as the runner crosses the 50-yard mark.

ball Skills Test (10). The test items are designed to cover the fundamental skills of football and could be used as "practice tests" for skill improvement. To this end their use would appear justified, since a variety of football skills would be covered and norms are available for both motivation and individual comparison. However, since no statistical data on reliability and validity are presented, it is impossible to evaluate the degree to which scores on these tests actually relate to performance of football skills in the game situation. In addition, the administration of the entire ten-item test would require considerable time and would not appear justified in terms of the length of time usually devoted to a particular skill unit.

Field hockey (11)

Several tests exist for the measurement of field hockey skills. Unlike most tests thus far presented, the one selected includes several skills and is an example of a single test designed to predict game-playing ability.

Strait field hockey test

Procedures for construction

Data were obtained from 56 Smith College freshmen and sophomores, 19 members of the Hampshire Field Hockey Association and 30 members of the 1951 USFHA Northeast Section first, second and third teams. The test was designed to incorporate the essential skills of the drive, the dribble, fielding, turning to the right, and dodging, and to take advantage of the use of a backboard. Originally, the combination of techniques and their selection was determined empirically but after preliminary testing the items were modified. Test scores when correlated with the judges' ratings resulted in the following validity coefficients:

56 Smith College students	validity = 0.61
30 Sectional players	validity = 0.60
86 combined group	validity = 0.76

The greater the range in playing ability, the higher the validity coefficient. The author also noted that the test afforded a significant discrimination when teams of varying ability were compared. The reliability coefficient obtained on test-retest data for 62 subjects was 0.86.

Administration

The equipment needed includes a hockey stick for each participant, hockey ball, stop watch, a backboard 12 feet by 18 inches, and a closely cut grass

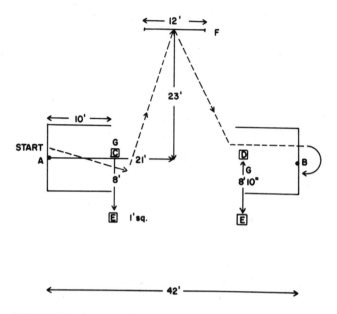

FIGURE 11–5. Diagram of equipment and procedure for
the field hockey dribble and pass test. From Strait (11).
C, D, and E are 1-foot squares. Lines at A and B are 3 feet
9 inches in length.

field, marked according to Figure 11–5. The minimum amount of space
needed is an area 32 by 62 feet.

On the signal "Go," the subject at stake A stays in the alley and dribbles
the ball toward (C), where a motionless assistant stands holding a hockey
stick (G). Any legal dodge may be executed around the assistant. The ball
is then driven to the backboard (F) and the rebounding ball fielded. The
ball is dribbled to stake (B) and a turn made around the stake (circular
tackle). The player is now in the alley and repeats the same order of events
as she returns toward stake (A), i.e., dribble, dodge, drive, field, and turn
around stake (A). A trial consists of two continuous circuits ending when
the player dribbles the ball past stake (A) for the second time. The assistant
to be dodged stands on the square (C) nearest (A) as the test is begun and
then moves to the square (D) nearest (B) in time for the player's return trip.
The shifting from end to end continues for the second half of the trial.

If a driven ball misses the backboard and travels behind it, the performer
goes to the nearest ball enclosure (E) for another ball, drives the ball to the
backboard and continues from there. If the ball fails to reach the backboard
on the drive, the performer must run forward and drive the ball again. Failure
to keep feet within the lane during the dribble prior to the dodge means the
trial must be repeated. One practice trial should be given. The time for
the best of three trials, excluding the practice trial, constitutes the final score.

Comments

This test does require that special equipment be set up and maneuvers are relatively complicated. However, the test measures dribbling, dodging, driving, receiving, and a circular tackle, the most used skills in the game. Unfortunately, the test does not provide individual scores for each of the skills it measures. Once the test is set up, it is not time consuming and scoring is relatively easy. It can serve as an excellent practice as well as testing device, for it provides a game-like situation that involves important skills, change of direction, footwork, and speed. The author notes that there was no significant difference between the scores of defense and attack players.

Ice hockey

Recently, the first statistically validated test of the sports skills of ice hockey has appeared in the literature (13). Prior to this, a test of ice hockey skills for women was proposed by H. Brown (12). The three-item battery included puck handling, goal shooting, and speed skating with the puck. The test, which was published in 1935, did not include any norms, nor was the validity or reliability reported. The test did, however, provide some direction and it is unfortunate that few have followed up on this early lead.

. Several pertinent factors probably explain the dearth of test data on ice hockey. Ice hockey is rarely taught in the physical education program in the United States. Skills are developed in after-school programs or community leagues. Consequently, physical educators have not felt the need to evaluate the skills of the sport. Also of consequence is the fact that Canadian schools of physical education, which should be the most interested in evaluating the skill levels in their national winter sport, have only recently instituted graduate programs. It is hoped that future research will provide achievement scales for valid and reliable tests of the skills of this exciting winter sport.

Merrifield-Walford ice hockey test

Procedures for construction

Six skill test items were developed to measure the basic skills of ice hockey. The selection of the items was based on the subjective judgment of the two investigators. The tests involved forward skating speed, backward skating speed, skating agility, puck carry, shooting, and passing. Fifteen male college students who were members of the Ithaca College Hockey Club served as subjects. They represented various levels of hockey ability. The battery of tests was administered after one week of practice and was repeated one week later. Reliability as determined by the Spearman rho* formula ranged from 0.37–0.94 with reliability lowest in the shooting and passing test; 0.62 and 0.37 respectively. These two items were not considered further. When the four skills test items with high reliability were correlated with subjective ratings by the hockey coach the validity coefficients ranged from 0.75 to 0.96. Inter-correlations among the test items indicated that the skating agility and backward skating speed tests were measuring similar aspects of hockey ability. The puck carry test was found to have a significant relationship to each of the other three tests and was most highly correlated with skill ratings by the hockey coach ($r = 0.96$). The authors concluded that although the forward skating speed test, the puck carry test and either the backward skating speed test or skating agility test may be used as measures of ice hockey skills, the puck carry test would be the best single-item test for determining overall ability.

Administration

Puck Carry. Regulation ice hockey stick and puck, stopwatch and seven wooden obstacles placed on the ice in a straight line 30 feet apart are needed. The first obstacle is at the 4-foot start-finish line (Figure 11–6).

The skater stands behind the start-finish line with the puck resting on the line to the left of the obstacle. On the signal "Go," the skater zig-zags through the course passing to the left of the first obstacle. If two or more obstacles are knocked down the skater must repeat the test. Control of the puck must be maintained throughout the test. The subject is allowed to go through the test half-speed for practice. The score is the time to the nearest 0.1 second from the command "Go" to the skater's first skate touching the finish line.

Forward skating speed. Two parallel lines 120 feet apart are painted on new-surfaced ice (Figure 11–6). The line nearer the end of the skating rink is the starting line. The subject starts facing the finish line with both feet behind the starting line. On the signal "Go," the subject skates for the finish line. Scoring is the same as in Puck Carry.

Backward skating speed. This test is exactly as the Forward Skating Speed Test except that the subject starts with his back to the finish line. Scoring is also the same.

Skating agility. A 2-foot starting line is marked on the ice 14 feet from the goal cage and perpendicular to the goal crease. A 4-foot finish line is marked perpendicular to the starting line and extended to 23 feet away from the goal cage. Three wooden obstacles 30 inches in height with a 2-by-4-inch base are used. One obstacle is placed 4 feet in front of the starting line, one 10

---

*Interpreted like the usual correlation coefficient.

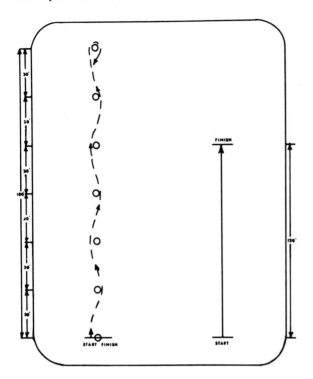

FIGURE 11–6.   Ice markings for puck carry and speed
skating tests.   From Merrifield and Walford (13).

feet to the right of the first obstacle, and the other 10 feet closer to the goal
cage.   Two lines each 4 feet in length are placed 8 feet apart and centered in
front of the goal cage (Figure 11–7).

On the signal "Go," the subject skates by the first obstacle, passing it on his
right, loops the second obstacle by passing just to the left, and returns to loop
the first obstacle and continues to the 4-foot line in front of the goal cage.
He stops at this line and then starts to the next 4-foot line located 8 feet away.
He repeats the stop-start.   He then passes behind the goal cage and skates
around the far obstacle (to the finish), performing a turn to skate backwards,
backward skating, and a turn to skate forward.   The subject is allowed to
go through the course at half-speed to assure familiarity with the test procedure.
Scoring is the same as in Puck Carry.

Comments

If a subject falls during a test he repeats the trial.   The subject must carry the
hockey stick with both hands below shoulder level.   In addition to the fact
that each test item is a good measure of ice-hockey ability, each is also an
excellent self-testing and motivational activity in which actual game skills are
utilized.

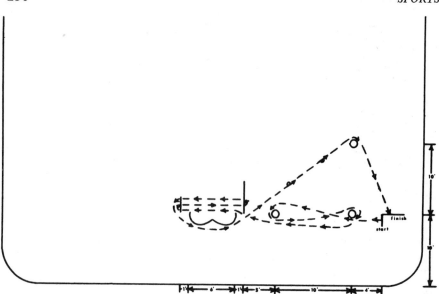

FIGURE 11–7.   Ice markings for skating agility test.   From
Merrifield and Walford (13).

Lacrosse

To date there are no published tests for lacrosse.   This probably can be
attributed to the fact that interest in lacrosse in the United States has been
limited almost exclusively to a small section of the country.   However, dis-
ciples of the sport are increasing in number and a geographic appeal is notice-
able at this time.   This, then, is an area in which the development of sound
skills would be most welcome.

Kate Barrett (14) has experimented with a wall volley test as a measure
of general lacrosse ability.   The test was administered at the Bouvé-Boston
School to 55 female physical education and physical therapy students who had
learned to throw, catch, and cradle.   The reliability coefficient on repeated
trials was found to be 0.86.   The validity with a criterion of judges' ratings
was 0.71.

Barrett lacrosse test

Administration

Equipment.   The equipment needed includes one crosse of the subject's own
choosing, a box of five balls, stop watch, individual score cards, a clear wall
area at least 15 feet high and 24 feet wide with a floor space in front of 36
inches or more.   A restraining line is drawn 26 feet and 10 inches from the

wall and to the right or left of the 24 foot fall area depending upon the handed-
ness of the player.

Description. The subjects are given a thirty-second practice trial prior to
the test. The subject stands behind the restraining line with a ball in her
crosse. On the signal "Go," she throws the ball to the wall and catches it on
the rebound as many times as she can within a thirty-second period. There
is no limit to the number of times the ball may bounce *after* it has hit the wall,
but it must first hit the wall on the fly. The subject may cross the restraining
line to retrieve her ball, but no hit will count unless thrown from behind the
line. If the subject looses control of the ball she may retrieve it or get another
one from the box. Any number of balls may be used. The ball must be
caught by the crosse, not the hands.

There should be a timer, a scorer, a ball retriever, and a recorder. The
scorer should warn the subject if she crosses the restraining line.

Scoring. The score is the sum of the number of hits for 3 thirty-second trials.
Subjects should alternate so that there is a rest between each trial. There are
no norms available.

Soccer

McDonald wall volley

Procedures for construction

The wall volley frequently appears as the best single skill test of general ability
for many sports. L. G. McDonald (18) studied such a test as a measure of
general soccer ability, using 18 freshmen, 18 junior varsity, and 17 varsity
players as his 53 subjects. The subjective ratings of three coaches were correlated with test scores to obtain the following validity coefficients: Varsity
players, 0.94; junior varsity players, 0.63; freshmen varsity players, 0.76; and
combined groups, 0.85. No reliability is reported, nor are any norms given.

Administration

Equipment. A restraining line is drawn on the floor, 9 feet from and parallel
to a kickboard or wall 30 feet long and 11½ feet high. Three balls inflated
to 13 pounds are used. One ball is placed on the restraining line and two 9
feet behind it in the center of the testing area.

Description. At the command "Go," the subject kicks the ball at the kickboard from behind the restraining line for thirty seconds, rebounding it as
quickly as possible, using any type of kick and control method. To be scored,
the kick must be performed with the supporting leg behind the restraining line.

A lost ball must be retrieved with either hands or feet but must be placed behind the restraining line to continue the test. If control of the original ball is lost, reserve balls may be used by moving them, using hands or feet, into kicking position behind the restraining line.

Scoring. Four trials are administered and the final score is the sum of the fair "kicks" of the *three* best trials.

Comments

Although this test has been designed for and developed using men, it seems equally appropriate for women. A similar wall volley with dimensions suitable for 4th, 5th and 6th grade children is also available (17), as is one for high school and college girls (19). This last one has a different type of floor boundary. Norms, in the form of T-scores and percentiles, are listed for the elementary school children and T-scores for the high school and college girls.

Bontz soccer test

Procedures for construction

A soccer test developed by Jean Bontz (15) measures the important skills of dribbling, passing, and trapping. If one has the time and space, this would make an excellent second test. The test was administered to 124 5th and 6th grade children from two school systems, yielding a reliability coefficient of 0.93 by the odd-even method. The validity coefficients were 0.92 for one group of 92 subjects and 0.53 for the remaining 32 subjects with a criterion of subjective rating.

Administration

Equipment. Needed equipment includes fully inflated soccer balls, two goal posts or standards, playing surface 55 yards long, a rebounding surface 12 feet by 30 feet, and a field marked according to the accompanying diagram (Figure 11–8).

Description. The ball is placed on the starting line (B). On the signal "Go," it is dribbled toward the goal, being kept to the right of the restraining line. When nearing the target the ball is passed diagonally toward it with the right foot. The rebound is recovered and the player dribbles toward the goal until close enough to kick for a goal. The kick must be performed before crossing the line in front of the goal. The trial is completed when the ball passes through the goal. Four trials are given with the wall on the left for right-footed passes and four more with the wall on the right for left-footed passes. Two practice trials are allowed for each side.

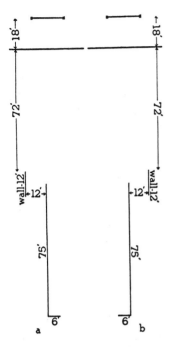

FIGURE 11–8. Field markings for soccer combination of skills test. From Bontz (15).

Scoring. The test score is the total time required for eight trials. Time should be recorded to the nearest half-second.

Comments

This test has the advantage of being game-like in nature and challenging to the subject. It measures several skills important to the game and provides a good device for practicing them. Although developed and tested with elementary school children, it is also useful for high school and college-age groups and would be equally appropriate for men and women.

If one is interested in measuring separate skills, the Heath and Rodgers test (16), one of the earliest skill tests reported, consists of tests for dribbling, place kick for goal, a throw-in, and kicking a rolling ball. It was designed for upper elementary school boys.

Softball

Subjective and objective measures complement one another in obtaining the best indications of an individual's ability to perform softball skills. Responses to the special responsibilities of diverse positions and on-the-spot judgments called for in the game can be judged best subjectively. Objective measurements provide a good evaluation of the skills that can be performed where the situation is similar for everyone. Even though not all positions in softball require the same skills, a variety of skills are required by all. The problem becomes one of choosing those skills most representative of general softball playing ability. They are batting, catching and fielding, throwing, and running. Although the softball throw for distance or repeated throws tests are cited most frequently as the most useful and valid single measures of softball playing ability, a battery of tests has some advantages compared to a single test. The use of several tests enables evaluation of the many skills involved and makes clearer to the student and teacher the specific area in which additional work and practice is needed.

Softball test batteries for high school girls have been developed by M. N. Fringer (22) and by D. O'Donnell (25). The Fringer battery consists of a throw for distance, fielding grounders, flyball catching, and batting tee and base-running tests. The O'Donnell battery includes fungo batting, overhand accuracy throw, fielding fly balls, repeated throws, and throw-and-catch tests. No softball tests for men or boys are reported in the literature. However, a battery of baseball skill tests for Little League classification by Kelson (23), a baseball battery for 5th and 6th grade boys by Rodgers and Heath (26), and a battery of baseball tests to classify boys between the ages of 7 and 15 are available.

The tests listed below are suggested for use individually or in combination depending on whether a rough screening or detailed evaluation is desired.

Repeated throws test

Procedures for construction

Set up by the Research Committee of the Central Association for Physical Education for College Women, this test is reported by Scott and French (28).

A reliability coefficient of 0.89 was obtained by the odd-even method when the test was administered to 210 college women. The validity coefficient for this test, when a subjective rating of softball ability was used as the criterion, was 0.51 for 173 college women. Fringer obtained a reliability coefficient of 0.87 in a test-retest of 147 high school girls.

Administration

The subject stands behind a restraining line parallel to and 15 feet from the wall. On the signal "Go," a new 12-inch softball is thrown overhand against the wall so that it hits on or above a line 7½ feet from the floor. The player catches the rebound and repeats the process as many times as possible in 30 seconds. One ball is used throughout the test. Throws made while making a foot fault (stepping on or over the restraining line) do not count. The test score is the total number of hits for six 30-second trials. There should be a 2-minute rest between trials.

Comments

This test is objective, reliable, easily administered, and purported to be a valid single measure of softball playing ability. Since it does not require as much space as some of the other softball tests, it may be administered indoors providing the necessary wall space is available.

Throw for distance test

Procedure for construction

When administered to 136 high school girls, Fringer obtained a reliability coefficient of 0.90 using the test-retest method. This test is similar to one reported by Scott and French (28). However, the best of three throws is used as the player's score rather than the best of nine throws obtained from three trials of three throws each. A correlation coefficient of 0.72 was obtained when this test was correlated with the Repeated Throws Test.

Administration

In three successive trials, the player throws a softball as far as she can. The player is limited to *one* step before throwing and this must be taken behind a restraining line. Any type of throw is allowed and the score (to the nearest foot) of the best trial is recorded. The field should be marked with parallel lines at 5-yard intervals and intermediate markings at 5-foot intervals. Each line is marked with a flag indicating the footage. A 5-foot Bamboo pole with distances marked off to the nearest foot helps to record the distance that the ball is thrown. Small pegs should be used to mark where the farthest ball lands until all three trials have been performed. This test is believed by many to be the best single measure of softball playing ability.

Fielding grounders test

Procedures for construction

This is one of the tests included in the Fringer softball battery. The test was administered to 151 girls in grades 10–12. The test-retest reliability coefficient was 0.72. Correlation with the Throw for Distance Test and Repeated Throws Test yielded coefficients of 0.62 and 0.70 respectively.

Administration

For the wall and floor markings consult the diagram in Figure 11–9. On the signal "Go," the player quickly moves to either of the two bases from which she throws a softball at the 5-foot circular wall target. She then re-

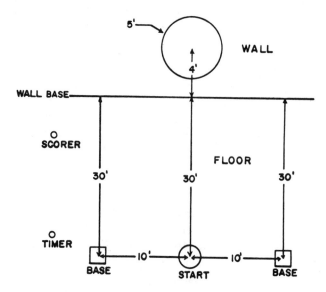

FIGURE 11–9.   Field markings for softball test for fielding grounders.   From Fringer (22).

trieves the ball, goes to the other base and again throws at the target.   This procedure continues for 45 seconds.

The player's foot must be on the base while the ball is thrown and she must alternate bases after each throw.   The number of balls hitting in the target or on the target circle are recorded.   The test score is the total hits for two trials.   A rest period should be allowed between trials.   It is possible to administer this test indoors or outdoors if the necessary wall space is available.   One advantage of this test over the type of repeated throw target tests where the player is stationary is that it requires the player to move to retrieve the ball and to move to tag the base as is often required in the game.

Batting tee test (22)

Procedure for construction

This test uses homemade adjustable batting tees made from 1½-inch radiator hose, 1-inch iron piping and a circular metal stand.   When administered to 137 high school girls as part of the Fringer Battery, a test-retest reliability coefficient of 0.74 was obtained.

Administration

The same field markings used for the softball throw for distance are used for this test.   An adjustable batting tee is placed on the restraining line.   The player is allowed five practice hits and ten test hits.   Each hit is recorded to the nearest foot where the ball first lands. Complete misses are counted as a trial and recorded as zero. The test score is the sum of the distances of ten consecutive trials. Disadvantages of this test are that it is time consuming, and that batting from a tee is quite different from batting a pitched ball. How closely these two skills are related is not known.

It would be interesting to have a comparison of scores from fungo hitting, batting-tee hitting, hitting from a pitching machine and hitting averages. Such a study has not yet been undertaken. The need for a valid, reliable, and efficient batting test still exists.

Comments

Tests similar to those presented have been studied for their appropriateness with elementary and junior high school students. Latchaw (24) reports an adaptation of the Repeated Throws Test for 4th, 5th and 6th grades. Reliability coefficients varied from 0.77 to 0.85 depending on sex and grade. Norms are listed in T-scores and percentiles. Broer (21) determined that for junior high school girls an adequate reliability can be obtained on the Batting Tee Test with just five trials. Similarly, the Throw for Distance required only one trial. Achievement scales for the Softball Throw for Distance for ages 10–18 years are published in the AAHPER Youth Fitness Test Manual (20).

AAHPER softball test

An eight-item test of softball skill for boys and girls is part of the battery of sports skills developed by AAHPER. The specific test items include measures of throwing, pitching, running, batting, and fielding. Items are the same for both boys and girls although distances have been shortened for the girls in the accuracy tests and a different test is used to measure the ability to catch a fly ball.

On the basis of face validity, the majority of test items appear to measure important softball skills. However, no data are reported on validity and reliability and it is therefore difficult to evaluate the relative merit of each item as an indicator of a particular softball skill or of softball ability in general.

The throwing tests for distance and accuracy are similar to items used in other skills tests. Considerable variability may exist in performance in the tests of batting, fielding, and catching fly balls that would not be reflected in the test score. The degree to which fungo hitting is related to the ability to hit a pitched ball or catching balls thrown from a second-story window reflects the ability to catch a batted ball remains to be demonstrated. This lack of established validity makes it difficult to justify the use of these items for grading purposes. The test items do provide for a means for students to practice important skills in a competitive atmosphere and evaluate their performance in relation to others of the same age.

Speedball

Speedball is a combination of soccer and basketball as well as some kicking elements of football. All soccer skills and all ball-handling skills of basketball except the bounce-to-self and the dribble are used in speedball. The only skills peculiar to speedball are those of converting a ground ball to an aerial ball, i.e., the kick-up or lift to self or teammates. Probably the most important skills in the game are dribbling and passing the ball with the foot, throwing and catching, and the kick-up-to-self. Tests to measure these skills were constructed by Miller (31).

Miller speedball test

Skills important to the game of speedball were selected and tests to measure these skills were either adapted from existing tests or newly devised tests. Six tests are presented: Dribble and Pass, Speed Toss, Kick-up-to-Self, Foot Pass to Wall, Wall Zone Pass, and Zone Toss. Of these, the Kick-up-to-Self and the Speed Toss are selected here as measuring those skills most appropriate to Speedball, within the framework of administrative feasibility. Previously described soccer tests may substitute for the other soccer-type tests in the Miller battery.

The tests were administered to 64 college women. The criterion for validity was the sum of subjective ratings of four judges. Using a nine-point scale, the judges rated the subjects on nine separate items and on over-all general playing ability. Validity coefficients are given for various combinations of the six items in the whole series and range from 0.70 to 0.56. The reliability coefficient for the Kick-up-to-Self was 0.92 and for the Speed Toss was 0.82. The multiple correlation for the two items described here is 0.56. No norms are listed. These tests are designed for use with high school and college girls.

Administration

Speed Toss Test. A soccer ball, two 7½-foot standards, a 20-foot rope, and a stop watch are needed. The standards are placed 18 feet apart with the rope, 7½ feet above the ground, stretched taut between them. A 3-inch-wide line is marked on the ground between the two standards. Speedball or soccer goal posts may be substituted for standards, and the cross bar for the rope. The subject stands on one side of the line. On the signal "Go," she tosses the ball over the rope, steps across to the other side of the line, and catches the ball. The procedure is repeated for thirty seconds. If control of the ball is lost, it is recovered by a legal kick-up. The kick-up counts as a caught ball. The catch does not count if the ball passes under the rope or if the subject's feet are not on the same side of the line as the ball when the catch is made. The test score is the total number of catches for three trials. A practice trial of four tosses should precede the test.

Kick-up-to-self test. Soccer balls, a stopwatch, and an unobstructed wall space approximately 6 feet wide are needed for each test station. A restraining line is drawn on the floor, 5 feet 7 inches from the wall. A ball is placed on the restraining line. On the signal "Go," the subject passes the ball to the wall with her feet and controls it on the rebound by executing a one- or two-foot kick-up. The ball is quickly replaced on the restraining line and the test continued for thirty seconds. If the ball does not rebound beyond the restraining line, it may be retrieved by hand and returned to the restraining line for the next pass. The test score is the total number of successful legal kick-ups for the best two out of three trials. A practice trial of two passes to the wall and two kick-ups should precede the test.

Comments

These tests are easy to set up and administer and can be used for diagnosis of student difficulties, motivation, classification, practice, and grading. If only one test is to be used, the kick-up-to-self is recommended. It should be remembered that in a total evaluation of speedball skills, soccer-type tests should also be included. There are no norms available.

Volleyball

The most useful and valid test for volleyball appears to be that which employs the wall volley. The Brady test (32) is the only test for men reported in the literature. Recently, this test has been revised for use with high school boys (35). In addition, two wall volley tests for women have been reported (33, 34). Also included in this section is a test for the chest pass which appears to warrant consideration (37).

Brady volleyball test (32)

Procedure for construction

After experimenting with several volleyball test items, Brady selected the wall volley as the most valid measure of volleyball skill. Reliability by the test-retest method for 522 men college students and 15 members of a championship team was 0.92. The validity coefficient, obtained by correlating the test scores with ratings of playing ability by four judges, was 0.86. No norms are published.

Administration

A regulation volleyball is used. A horizontal line 5 feet long and 11½ feet above the floor is marked on a smooth wall. Vertical lines extend upward toward the ceiling from the ends of the 5-foot horizontal line. The subject stands anywhere in front of the target and on the signal "Go" throws the ball against the wall. When the ball returns, the player volleys it against the wall within the boundaries of the target. If the ball is caught or goes out of control, it is started with a throw as at the beginning of the test. The player is timed for 1 minute, and the score is the number of legal volleys that hit within the target.

Comments

We believe that this test is most reliable when used with college men and reliability decreases with younger subjects or those with very poor skill. If the test is used as a method of grading, improvement must be considered. To this end, Brady suggests that scores made on the first test be subtracted from scores made on the last test and this value be added to scores on the last test. The author also indicates that this test is of value as a drill practice device. One of the difficulties with a volleyball wall volley test is that an evaluation of the legality of the passes is necessary during the test administration.

A slight modification of the Brady test for use with high school boys was employed by Kronqvist and Brumbach (35). The test consists of three 20-second trials. The horizontal wall line is 5 feet wide and 11 feet above the ground. No restraining line is used and the score is the best two out of three trials. Validity was determined by comparing test scores of 71 subjects from grades ten and eleven with ratings of three experienced volleyball teachers. The correlation coefficient was 0.77. Test-retest reliability was 0.82.

Clifton volleyball test (33)

Procedure for construction

Forty-five freshman and sophomore women students enrolled in general college volleyball classes at UCLA were tested in the middle of a fourteen-week volleyball class and again one week later. Although the author experimented with three trials and restraining lines of 5 feet and 7 feet, it was determined that the combination producing the highest coefficients of reliability (0.83) and validity (0.70) occurred when the test score was the sum of two trials with the restraining line at 7 feet.

Administration

A regulation volleyball is used. A one-inch horizontal line, 7½ feet above the floor is marked the length of a smooth wall. A corresponding line 7 feet from the wall and parallel to it is marked on the floor. The wall space for each subject should be 10 feet wide and a minimum of 15 feet high. On the signal "Go," the ball is thrown underhand against the wall from behind the 7 foot restraining line. Using the single volley, the ball is volleyed to the wall above the 7½-foot line. If the ball is caught or drops, it may be restarted with an underhand throw from behind the 7-foot line. If the ball is put in play or volleyed below the 7½-foot line or one, or both feet step on or over the restraining line, or the ball is considered "held" prior to a volley, the ball may be kept in play but the hit is not included in the score. The final score is the total number of *legal* volleys made on or above the 7½-foot line from behind the 7-foot restraining line within two thirty-second trials.

Comments

This test is similar to and incorporates elements of previous tests. However, since it takes into consideration the change in women's volleyball rules, it is currently the preferred test for women.

Recently, Cunningham and Garrison (34) utilized a high wall volley test to measure volleyball playing ability in 111 college women. The target area was formed by three lines consisting of a horizontal line 3 feet long and 10 feet above the floor with 3-foot vertical lines at each end. No restraining line was used. When the better of two 30-second trials was compared to judges ratings of playing ability the validity coefficient was 0.72. Test-retest reliability was 0.87.

Liba and Stauff volleyball test (36)

Procedure for construction

By use of cinematographical analysis, the desired vertical height and linear distance of a well-executed chest pass were determined. Optimum distances were determined for college women and junior high school girls. The test utilizes ropes to measure the height of ball clearance, and a ground target to measure horizontal distance.

Reliability coefficients obtained by testing seventh grade girls and college women on separate days was 0.90 and 0.85 respectively. Validity is accepted as face validity, since ability in the chest pass is being measured and this is an important volleyball skill. There are no norms currently available for the test.

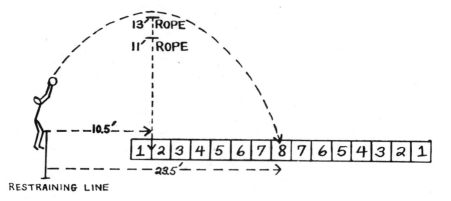

FIGURE 11–10.   Floor markings and procedure for the
volleyball pass test.   From Liba and Stauff (36).

Administration

Ropes are placed at heights of 13 feet and 11 feet and are located 10.5 feet
away from a floor restraining line.   A canvas strip target, 2 feet* by 30 feet,
is placed on the floor so that the center of the target (area "8") is 23.5 feet
away from the passer (Figure 11–10).   Properly inflated volleyballs are
placed behind the restraining line.   (For junior high school girls, the ropes
are placed at heights of 12 and 10 feet and are placed 6.5 feet away from the
restraining line.   The target is 28 feet long and has a maximum score of 7
instead of 8).

The subject standing behind the restraining line sets up the ball to herself,
and performs a chest pass attempting to pass the ball over the 13-foot line and
into the target area marked "8."   A pass hitting a rope is taken over.   The
subject is given two practice trials followed by ten test trials.   Scoring is as
follows:

a. Height: 3 points if ball goes over 13-foot rope
             2 points if ball goes over 11-foot rope
             1 point if ball goes under 11-foot rope
             0 points if ball fails to reach rope
b. Distance: The distance score is the number of the area in which
    the ball lands.   A ball landing on a line is given the higher score.
c. The total trial score is the height score times the distance score.   The
    total test score is the sum of the scores of the ten trials.

Comments

The purpose of this test is to assess ability in the performance of the volleyball "chest" pass.   The authors of the test consider this pass to be the fundamental skill in volleyball and the basis for good team play.   The test is

*Correspondence with the senior author indicates that the balls that land within a dis-
tance of 2 feet either side of the 2-foot strip are counted as falling within the target.
Therefore a 6-foot target area is recommended.

scientifically developed and sound, and has use as an evaluative tool as well as an excellent practice device. Cunningham and Garrison (34) obtained a validity coefficient of 0.60 when this test was compared to judge ratings of physical ability. It would be interesting to see how scores on this test would correlate with scores on the wall volley test, since they seem to measure the same ability. Still lacking in the literature are objective and valid tests for measuring ability in attack play.

AAHPER volleyball test

A test battery of volleyball skills for use with boys and girls has been presented by AAHPER (37) as part of their Sports Skills Test Project. The test battery consists of four items which purport to measure ability in passing, volleying, serving, and performing the set-up. Many of the test items are similar to the progressions used in teaching the fundamental skills of volleyball. As with most of the AAHPER skills tests, a strong enticement for their use is that norms in percentiles have been established for each test item. However, since estimates for reliability and validity have not been reported, it is difficult to evaluate the degree to which each item measures a specific volleyball skill as it is related to game performance.

The wall volley test and serving test are slight modifications of existing tests with established validity. The tests designed to measure passing and set-up ability are complicated by the fact that more than one individual is involved in the test (a thrower and passer or set-up man). This would introduce extraneous factors which would not be reflected in terms of the test score. If the items are regarded as "practice tests" intended as a means of improving abilities in the fundamental skills of volleyball, their use is justified.

REFERENCES

BOYS' BASKETBALL

1. Hunsicker, P. A. and H. J. Montoye, *Applied Tests and Measurements in Physical Education.* New York: Prentice-Hall, 1953.

2. Johnson, L. W., *Objective Tests in Basketball for High School Boys.* Un-published Master's thesis, State University of Iowa, 1934.

3. American Association for Health, Physical Education and Recreation, *Skills Test Manual: Basketball for Boys.* Washington, D.C.: The Association, 1966, p. 47.

GIRLS' BASKETBALL

4. Cozens, F. W.; H. Cubberly; and N. P. Neilson, *Achievement Scales in Physical Education Activities for Secondary School Girls and College Women.* New York: Barnes, 1937, p. 23.

5. Glassow, R.; V. Colvin; and M. Schwarz, "Studies in Measuring Basketball Playing Ability of College Women." *Res. Quart.*, 9:60–68, 1938.

6. Lambert, A. T., *A Basketball Skill Test for College Women.* Unpublished Master's thesis, University of North Carolina, 1969.

7. Miller, W. K., et al. "Achievement Levels in Basketball Skills for Women Physical Education Majors." *Res. Quart.,* 25:450–455, 1954.

8. Scott, M. G. and E. French. *Measurement and Evaluation in Physical Education.* Dubuque, Iowa: Brown, 1959, pp. 158–159.

FOOTBALL

9. Cozens, F. W., "Ninth Annual Report of the Committee on Curriculum Research of the College Physical Education Association." *Res. Quart.,* 8:73–78, 1937.

10. American Association for Health, Physical Education and Recreation, *Skills Test Manual: Football.* Washington, D.C.: The Association, 1966, Pp. 48.

FIELD HOCKEY

11. Strait, C. J., *The Construction and Evaluation of a Field Hockey Skills Test.* Unpublished Master's thesis, Smith College, 1960.

ICE HOCKEY

12. Brown H. M., "The Game of Ice Hockey." *J. Health & Physical Education,* 6:28–30, 1935.

13. Merrifield, H. H. and G. A. Walford, "Battery of Ice Hockey Skill Tests." *Res. Quart.,* 40:146–152, 1969.

LACROSSE

14. Barrett, K., "A Lacrosse Test for General Ability." Unpublished study, Bouve-Boston School, 1956.

SOCCER

15. Bontz, J., "An Experiment in the Construction of a Test for Measuring Ability in Some of the Fundamental Skills Used by Fifth and Sixth Grade Children in Soccer." Unpublished Master's thesis, State University of Iowa, 1942. (Cited in M. G. Scott, and E. F. French, *Measurement and Evaluation in Physical Education.* Dubuque, Iowa: Brown, 1959, pp. 195–198.

16. Heath, M. L. and E. A. Rodgers, "A Study in the Use of Knowledge and Skill Tests in Soccer." *Res. Quart.,* 3:33–53, 1932.

17. Latchaw, M., "Measuring Selected Motor Skills in Fourth, Fifth, and Sixth Grades." *Res. Quart.,* 25:439–449, 1954.

18. McDonald, L. G., "The Construction of a Kicking Skill Test as an Index of General Soccer Ability." Unpublished Master's thesis, Springfield College, 1951. (Cited in D. Mathews, *Measurement in Physical Education.* 2d ed., Philadelphia: Saunders,, 1963, p. 177).

19. Scott, M. G. and E. French, *Measurement and Evaluation in Physical Education.* Dubuque, Iowa: Crown, 1959, pp. 187–190.

SOFTBALL

20. American Association for Health, Physical Education and Recreation, *Youth Fitness Test Manual.* Washington, D.C.: The Association, 1965.

21. Broer, M., "Skill Test for Junior High School Girls." *Res. Quart.*, 29:139–145, 1958.

22. Fringer, M. N., "A Battery of Softball Skill Tests for Senior High School Girls." Unpublished Master's thesis, The University of Michigan, 1961.

23. Kelson, R. E., "Baseball Classification Plan for Boys." *Res. Quart.*, 24:304–307, 1953.

24. Latchaw, M., "Measuring Selected Motor Skills in Fourth, Fifth and Sixth Grades." *Res. Quart.*, 25:439–449, 1954.

25. O'Donnell, D., "Validation of Softball Skill Tests for High School Girls." Unpublished Master's thesis, Indiana University, 1950. (Cited in R. Weiss, and M. Phillips, *Administration of Tests in Physical Education*. St. Louis: Mosby, 1954, pp. 247–253.

26. Rodgers, E., and M. Heath, "An Experiment in the Use of Knowledge and Skill Tests in Playground Baseball." *Res. Quart.*, 11:113–31, 1931.

27. Sheehan, F. E., "Baseball Achievement Scales for Elementary and Junior High School Boys." Master's thesis, The University of Wisconsin, 1954. (Eugene: Microcard Publication, University of Oregon, 1954).

28. Scott, M. G. and E. French, *Measurement in Physical Education*. Dubuque, Iowa: Brown, 1959, pp. 199–202.

29. American Association for Health, Physical Education and Recreation, *Skills Test Manual: Softball for Boys*. Washington, D.C.: The Association, 1966, p. 44.

30. Waglow, F. and F. Stephens, "A Softball Knowledge Test." *Res. Quart.*, 26:234–243, 1955.

SPEEDBALL

31. Miller, S. B., "A Battery of Speedball Skill Tests for College Women." Unpublished Master's thesis, University of Nebraska, 1959.

VOLLEYBALL

32. Brady, G. F., "Preliminary Investigations of Volleyball Playing Ability." *Res. Quart.*, 16:14–17, 1945.

33. Clifton M. A., "Single Hit Volley Test." *Res. Quart.*, 33:208–211, 1962.

34. Cunningham, P. and J. Garrison, "High Wall Volley Test for Women's Volleyball." *Res. Quart.*, 39:486–490, 1968.

35. Kronqvist, R. A. and W. Brumbach, "A Modification of the Brady Volleyball Skill Test for High School Boys." *Res. Quart.*, 39:116–120, 1968.

36. Liba, M. and M. Stauff, "Test for the Volleyball Chest Pass." *Res. Quart.*, 34:56–63, 1963.

37. American Association for Health, Physical Education and Recreation, *Skills Test Manual: Volleyball for Boys and Girls*. Washington, D.C.: The Association, 1969, p. 36.

STUDY QUESTIONS

1. Respond to the statement: A touch football skills test that is valid for college males can be accepted as valid for junior high school boys.

2. List two other factors which enter into basketball ability besides specific skills in the game.

3. Describe two soccer tests discussed in your text.

4. Describe the AAHPER skills project. What has this produced? What are some of the limitations of this project?

5. Describe a published test of ability in the following sports:
    a. basketball   f. softball
    b. touch football   g. volleyball
    c. lacrosse   h. speedball
    d. field hockey   i. ice hockey
    e. soccer

6. Give three ways of improving the reliability of a test score such as the score in the dribbling test in basketball or the field hockey test.

IV

Paper and Pencil Tests

MEASUREMENT OF KNOWLEDGE AND UNDERSTANDING

12

M. Gladys Scott

Introduction

W ritten and verbal tests are not a new procedure in physical education. However, two or three decades ago such testing was characteristic of much of the testing in education in general. It measured the student's ability to parrot back information given by the instructor, the exchange of teacher and pupil "on the two ends of the learning log." Further evidence of lack of a clear purpose in this type of measurement is revealed in the terminology used. The earliest term in vogue was "pencil-and-paper" test which later evolved into one with little more meaning, "written test."

If such testing was in connection with learning a sport, the questions most likely covered rules, probably phrased in the words of the rule book. Behavioral learning of that day was largely rote memory.

Educational goals have changed. Probably the best overall expression of goals is given in the publication edited by Bloom (3), which deals with processes of the cognitive domain. The six types of learning set forth in that volume are knowledge, comprehension, application, analysis, synthesis, and evaluation.

Even though newer texts on test construction such as Ebel (5) or Bloom,

Hastings, and Madaus (4) may approach the problem a little differently, the terminology of taxonomy is still a worthwhile guide.

Let us look at the areas of instruction in Physical Education and behavioral objectives as they relate to this terminology. First consideration will be for students learning a sport.

TAXONOMY	EXAMPLES OF OBJECTIVES
A. Knowledge (*recall* of specifics)	To be able to express terms To understand terminology in class or in reading To be able to use and respond to terms used for equipment and game situations
B. Comprehension (*understanding* of what is presented)	To be able to describe game situations as legal or illegal in terms of rules To describe a skill as it should be performed To translate a rule into a game situation To interpret a game situation in a diagram To translate a game score into a game situation
C. Application (*use* of ideas, generalized rules, or procedures)	To relate principles to action or new situations To judge applicability of generalization to a situation To solve problems on the basis of theory and principles
D. Analysis (*breakdown* of elements, relationships, or principles)	To infer from materials to assumptions or conditions that exist To relate an entire situation to some component part(s)
E. Synthesis (*constructing* a plan of action from parts or ideas)	To put parts or action together to create a new pattern or sequence To organize known facts or ideas To solve a problem or task at hand To develop explanations to account for a given situation
F. Evaluation (*judgments* about value)	To recognize completeness or accuracy of a proposition To judge conclusions To distinguish between valid and nonvalid generalizations To apply criteria to the assessment of a situation

EXAMPLES OF QUESTIONS IN EACH CATEGORY.

A. Knowledge

   1. Which is a foul in volleyball?

      a. Hitting the ball with the fist
    *b. Hitting the ball with the head
      c. Hitting the ball with the wrist
      d. Backing away to avoid the ball

   2. From which line is the tennis serve made?

      a. Service line
      b. Center line
      c. Side line
    *d. Base line

B. Comprehension

   1. Which of the following statements about a forehand tennis drive is *not* true?

      a. A good reach contributes to the speed of the ball.
    *b. The easiest position from which to make a return is close to the bounce.
      c. A firm wrist aids in accuracy.
      d. Follow-through should be toward the top of the net.
      e. Over-reaching on the back swing is apt to result in the ball going to the right out of bounds.

   2. What does a score of 6–4, 4–2 mean in tennis?

      a. A has won 10 points to B's 6.
      b. A won 6 points in the first game and 4 in the second.
      c. A has the advantage score in set.
    *d. A won first set and is ahead in second.
      e. First set was deuce, second probably won't be.

C. Application

   1. When should the drives be used in tennis?

    *a. When playing behind the base line
      b. When playing just in front of the service line
      c. When playing net position
      d. When playing midcourt, with ball coming directly toward one's feet

   2. Receiver has difficulty with returns because the ball always seems to bounce at her feet. What is the most probable cause of difficulty?

      a. Player is not watching the ball.
      b. Player is too slow to change stance.

    c.   Player swings to avoid it.
    d.   Ball does not bounce straight.
*e.   Player is playing too far in court.

D. Analysis

1. Which parts of the stroke add most to the accuracy of the placement of a forehand drive when carefully controlled?

   *a.   Transfer of weight, angle of racquet face
   d.   Waiting position, playing ball immediately off the bounce
   c.   Firmness of grip, position on court
   d.   Speed of the ball, facing opposite player while stroking

2. When would the ball *not* rebound upward from the tennis racket?

   *a.   Played at top of bounce, racket face closed
   b.   Played at knee level, swing is under ball
   c.   Played at waist height, racket face open
   d.   Played over head, wrist relaxed

E. Synthesis

1. Your canoe is crushed while you are on a remote lake. It seems necessary to build a raft to get across the lake. With your knowledge of canoe safety, which would be *least* desirable?

   a.   Select smooth, dry logs.
   b.   Lash logs together closely.
   c.   Make the raft broad.
   d.   Taper the front end of each log.
  *e.   Mount a seat on top of the raft.

2. Your opponent has a good forehand, poor backhand, and is moderately good in footwork. Which would be best strategy?

   *a.   Serve to the right-hand court, make next return to deep backhand service court.
   b.   Serve from right to right of center line.
   c.   Serve from left to just left of center line.
   d.   Serve just beyond short-service line and make next return to same point.

F. Evaluation

1. Which is the most appropriate statement concerning the contribution of tennis at the beginners' level to the general fitness of the individual player?

   a.   Has no contribution
   b.   Builds arm strength
   c.   Is excellent for conditioning feet
   d.   Reduces the waist line
  *e.   Value depends on frequency and duration of playing sessions

2. You are becoming fatigued. Which procedure would give you the best opportunity to reduce the tempo of the tennis game and gain a chance to recover?

    a. Stall as long as possible between serves.
    b. Reduce speed on your drives.
    c. Play further forward on the court.
    d. Play mid-court only.
  *e. Play only back court, with slow, well-placed returns.

Constructing the examination

The above discussion deals with the mental organization and procedures for dealing with content and concepts. There are certain other decisions that must be made in constructing the classroom test. These are presented briefly.

1. What type of questions or tasks may be used to measure student knowledge?

There are several choices: essay, multiple choice, alternate response, recall.

2. Isn't essay the most economical and effective way to let the student demonstrate knowledge and understanding?

3. What type of test item should be used? The multiple choice question is best suited to provide items dealing with the last four categories in Bloom's taxonomy. The process of dealing with alternatives is a real life experience, for which each item serves as a model. It also offers many forms.

The alternate response encourages guessing and taking chances rather than thinking because blind guessing can yield approximately 50% right answers.

The recall encourages the "cut-and-paste" procedure in construction, and blind memorization on the part of the student. It is most appropriately used if the course objective is memorization of terms, facts, and names.

Essay is economical only if one considers the time involved before the examination is given. But good essay questions require time to prepare too. When the examination has been given the time investment begins. The time required for grading is a minimum of ten to fifteen minutes per paper. Total time is the number of minutes times number of papers. Later discussion will outline ways of producing a partially objective evaluation.

4. What type of question is most economical?

The multiple-choice and alternate response are both faster to score than recall. However, they are usually a little more time consuming to construct.

The multiple-choice requires a little more time for the student to read, but more alternate response items are needed to make the scores reliable.

5. What type is best to use?

There is no one answer that can be made for all classes, all ages, and all situations.

Consistent use of multiple choice discourages the student from trying to memorize "just enough to get by."

Hopefully, education encourages the student to think, solve problems, weigh values and consequences. The examination should reflect this purpose and multiple choice is the most preferable form.

Multiple choice requires more paper and stencils but this should never be a criterion in decision making.

6.   What content is to be covered in the exam?

The achievement examination is usually planned around the course and the concepts with which the students have been working. The diagnostic examination is designed to determine the relative strengths and weaknesses of each student on some array of concepts. The placement test is closely related to the diagnostic but is usually confined to the concepts incorporated in each successive level of a curriculum.

Each of these three exams has one thing in common, known concepts that can be stated and items that can be written which require the respondent to use these concepts and which can discriminate between those who use the concept well and those who have not acquired it or can not use it.

Thus a blueprint for the exam must be written before starting to construct items for the examination. This blueprint is usually called a *table of specifications*.

Constructing the table of specifications

The following material is essential for this table.

1.   Concepts to be covered
2.   Objectives of the course or learning experience
3.   Objectives in terms of taxonomy
4.   The relative emphasis or fraction of the total exam to be used for the various concepts and use of the concepts
5.   Proportion of the exam to be devoted to each concept and goal
6.   The purpose of the examination
7.   The length of the examination

The table of specifications for a beginners' tennis examination for measuring achievement might read as follows:

	%	TAXONOMY AIM
Technique of performing strokes:	45	
forehand—backhand drives		D, E
serve		D, E
volley		D, E
footwork		D, E

Game play and strategy	30	
singles—doubles		B, C
covering court		C, D
assessing opponent's ability and style		F
Terminology of the game	15	
with respect to racket		A, B
with respect to court		B, C
with respect to game and competition		B, C
Rules	10	
scoring		A, B, C
serving		A, B, C
returns (singles and doubles)		A, B, C

Construction of items

Content and student behavioral goals should be studied to determine the kind of item to use in the examination. Most situations in physical education, safety in relation to sports, and health practices fit well into the multiple-choice format.

Multiple choice

In a multiple-choice question, the student must choose between several alternatives, or foils, offered as an answer to the question asked. Each foil should have some plausibility and must appeal to a few students as an optimum answer. Both the question (stem) and the foils must be carefully written.

Guidelines for construction

1. The stem should be a short direct question.
2. Avoid textbook or rule book wording throughout the item.
3. Foils should be of similar length.
4. Foils should be of same grammatical form.
5. Foils should each be clear in meaning.
6. There should be a basis, in terms of the question asked, on which one alternative constitutes a better answer than any of the others.
7. The instructions should point out to the student that the *best* answer for the question should be sought in each item.
8. The correct foil should be randomly placed in the sequence of items in the examination.
9. The process the student is expected to use in answering determines the form of the question more than the content with which it deals.
10. If a negative question is asked, underline the negative word.
    For example,
    Which player does <u>not</u> guard an opponent in the scoring area?

Which is <u>least</u> apt to occur as a result of raising the head while doing a back float?

11. Each and every foil must be plausible to several members of the group being tested.

12. Each item must have at least three foils. Use more unless you are sure each will function in the item. Five is usually the maximum; do not exceed that number if an answer sheet planned for five foils is used. You may use a variable number of foils for different items.

13. Avoid giving grammatical clues to the correct answer. Incomplete statements serving as the stem often provide a clue to the answer.

There are several variations of multiple-choice questions. The reasoning required for successfully dealing with the question is essentially the same. The mechanics of arranging the material and of answering are the characteristic differences.

ALTERNATE FORMS OF MULTIPLE CHOICE

A. Unit item

In which of the following leaves must there be pin deflection to pick up a spare?

a. 2–8
*b. 5–10
c. 3–10
d. 4–5

Which of the following strokes most nearly resemble each other?

a. Volley–drive
*b. Smash–serve
c. Lob–volley
d. Smash–drive

B. Single array of foils

(a) Foul (on player)
(b) Foul (on team)
(c) Violation
(d) Legal play

1. Player places both hands on the ball simultaneously during a dribble across the floor.

2. Player involved in a jump ball catches the ball before it is tapped.

3. Two players on one team have the near spots on each side of the basket during a free throw.

C. Cluster questions

Several questions may be based on a single situation depicted in a drawing or a verbal statement. For example, an accident involving several persons is described. There follow three or four questions based on the accident. Each question must be independent of the others.

Alternatively, a diagram of a game situation may be drawn. Several questions on strategy may follow covering offense and defense of both teams.

D. Matching

Select the item from column A to answer each question in column B and place the letter of the answer on the line to the left of the item in A.

A		B	
——— 1.	Spare	a.	Term for knocking down all the pins with first ball
——— 2.	Frame	b.	Term for rolling two balls at the 10 pin set-up
——— 3.	Leave	c.	Term for ball which goes in gutter
——— 4.	Split	d.	Term for a 1–2 leave
——— 5.	Sleeper	e.	Term for knocking down all the pins on second ball
		f.	Term for any pin left after first ball
		g.	Term for a 7–10 leave
		h.	Term for a 3–9 leave

A		B	
——— 1.	Keel	a.	Structure to hold the canoe in shape
——— 2.	Bang plate	b.	Part which helps to prevent canoe from capsizing
——— 3.	Thwart	c.	Structure to strengthen canoe
——— 4.	Ribs	d.	Structure to prevent leaking
		e.	Structure to minimize damage when coming into docking area
		f.	Structure to provide a seat
		g.	Device for making canoe more buoyant

Alternate response

These items provide for an "either-or" answer, i.e., true-false or yes-no to an interrogation or statement.

Guidelines for construction:

1. Make each item brief and as direct as possible.
2. Avoid qualifying words such as *usually* or *always*.
3. Avoid double phrases or double meanings.
4. Avoid answering one question by the wording of another one.
5. Have an approximately equal number in the exam of each alternate, and in a random sequence.
6. Avoid items obvious to all.

ALTERNATE FORMS OF ALTERNATE RESPONSE

A. True-False

1. Letting the toe cross the line dividing the lane and the approach does <u>not</u> affect the count for that frame.
2. The height of the backswing has <u>no</u> effect on the speed of the ball delivered.
3. The center arrow on the lane should be used as the point of aim for the first ball.

B. Yes-No

1. Should a novice bowler attempt to roll the ball as fast as possible?
2. Do right- and left-handed bowlers use the same foot for the initial step in approach?

C. Multiple response (check all foils which apply)

There are runners on first and second. The batter hits a ball into the outfield a little left of the right fielder. What can be expected to happen?

    a) Runner to first is out.
    b) Runner to home is out.
    c) Runner to second is out.
    d) Batter has a ball called.
    e) Batter is credited with a two-base hit.

Recall

There is a danger in this type of question that it covers the trivial and depends on rote learning. The sentence completion form should be avoided for this reason.

If the purpose of the test is to elicit specific recall, then a direct question, asking for a direct brief answer, is appropriate.

Avoid asking the student to draw diagrams. They are frequently poorly drawn and poorly proportioned. Seldom can they be judged objectively. There is justification for this form *only* when used as a self-study aid, particularly if working on correction of spatial concepts.

Guidelines for construction:

1. Be sure there is only one answer.
2. Ask questions that call for answers of only one or two words.
3. Provide a short space for the answer to discourage the student from "talking around" the question.

ALTERNATE FORMS OF RECALL QUESTIONS

A. Word or phrase

What is the term for a golf stroke that sends the ball in an abrupt curve to the right?

B. Sentence answers or enumerations

What are the factors on which par for a hole is set?

1.
2.
3.

C. Diagram answers

On the following outline of a singles tennis court, draw in the optimum area for placement of the serve for the left-hand service area with a right-handed opponent.

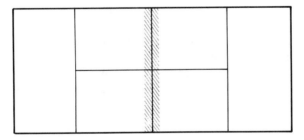

These three examples illustrate a progression toward nonobjectivity and should be couched in some other form. These forms do have value in the self-study evaluation process where the student can check the answer. For example, the task requested may lead to a modification of his concept of placement of a serve.

Putting the examination together

1. Check items against the table of specifications to determine the appropriateness of the spread of content.
2. Check the process of answering the items against the categories in taxonomy to determine the spread of mental involvement in answering.

3.   Make sure the time necessary for reading and answering is consistent with the time available in the writing period.   At times, the examination may be planned so that the less knowledgeable students will not finish.   In that case, care must be taken to have the most difficult questions in the last 10–20% of the examination.   This procedure avoids having student scores massed at the top because the exam is too easy and too short.

4.   Try to put the entire examination into not more than two forms.

5.   Write instructions for the examination, or for parts if they differ. If there is doubt about the students' acquaintance with the form and process, provide an example.

6.   Consider the advisability of using an answer sheet.   Answer sheets save time for the scorer but are sometimes inconvenient for the student.

7.   If answers are to be placed on the examination copy, be sure all answers are in a column along the margin.

8.   Match the difficulty of the examination questions with the group for which it is written.

9.   Avoid making the examination too difficult, as it will yield a cluster of scores near the bottom of the range of scores.

10.   Include some difficult questions or the examination will yield a cluster of scores near the top of the range.

11.   If used for contractual learning, include difficult questions as motivation.   Also, pay particular attention to the category of taxonomy to which the process of correct solution should be assigned.   These categories should be consistent with objectives of the learning unit.

12.   Plan the page format of the answer sheet.   Usually two parallel columns to a page save space and are easier to read unless the responses are to be written on the examination copy.

13.   Use of diagrams is helpful.   They save reading time by saving long descriptions of a situation, or long foils.   Keep them simple so each will be understood.

Essay examinations

An essay examination may be used if one is interested in the students' ability to express themselves as well as solve the problems presented.   Be prepared as a scorer for long hours of careful reading to ensure fair interpretation of each paper.

Essay questions also require careful construction to elicit the type of response for which they are designed.

Scoring can be done subjectively only.   Prior to reading the papers, the types of acceptable answers should be outlined, expectation for content coverage noted, and the number of points should be set for optimum presentation. In grading, each question is evaluated on that predetermined plan, with the question given optimum credit or some fraction thereof.   The examination score is then the sum of points assigned each question and a distribution of sums can be made for grades.

Scoring the examination

Most questions are scored simply as right or wrong and the total number of correct answers is the score for the exam. Recall questions may be scored as half-points or as 2 points if two answers are expected. This avoids the use of the half-score.

The final grade for the paper may be assigned on the basis of predetermined scores for pass-fail or for satisfying a contract for learning, or on the basis of a frequency distribution of scores and a percentage allotment to each grade.

After the papers are scored, a prompt report of scores to students should be effective motivation for most. The report can also be used for class discussion and to encourage further learning.

Evaluating the quality of the examination

Two functions of an examination are 1) to determine each student's level of understanding, and 2) to aid in the learning process. These purposes can not be achieved unless the items in the examination are properly constructed. The effectiveness of the examination is judged by the following criteria applied to each item:

a) difficulty
b) index of discrimination
c) functional foils

Difficulty refers to the percentage of the total group writing the examination who answered the item correctly. Index of discrimination is a validity estimate. Since the purpose of a test is to differentiate between those who know and those who do not, it leads to two types of computation.

The score on the total examination is considered an adequate estimate of knowledge, or criterion, for this computation. If the index is calculated by computer, the index used is usually a correlation, probably a point biserial, between response on the item and the total score. Schmeiser, Stewart, and Whitney discuss use of the item analysis (10).

An alternative method for determining this index involves tallying the responses. The writers of papers at the upper end of the total score distribution are assumed to be most knowledgeable, and those at the lower end of the total score range are least knowledgeable. Therefore, the upper and lower quartiles or the upper-lower 27% of the papers are used. However, an observational analysis of the tally sheet may be quite adequate for many examinations.

The sample below indicates several points about the worksheet.

	a	b	c	d	e	Omit
1	卌 ǀ 卌 卌	卌 卌 ǀǀǀǀ ǀǀ	卌 卌 ǀ	ǀǀ ǀǀǀ	ǀǀǀ ǀǀǀǀ	
2		卌 ǀǀ ǀǀǀǀ	卌 ǀ ǀǀǀ	卌 ǀǀ 卌 卌 卌	卌 ǀǀǀ	

1. Each question has one line across for the record of responses on that question.
2. Each question has the upper 27% tallied in the top of each cell; the lower 27% in the lower part of each cell. (An additional aid is to use different colored pencils on each group.)
3. The correct answer is indicated by a heavy box around the cell. That cell is used to determine the difficulty rating and the index of discrimination.
4. A nonfunctioning foil is indicated in 2a.

The difficulty rating is the percentage of papers in the two groups with correct answers. This total is a known constant. In the example above, the total $N = 50$. Therefore, each tally yields 2%. If the total N were 100, each tally would be 1%. The difficulty rating can be interpreted immediately, knowing the percentage value of each tally.

The index of discrimination does not need to be computed exactly. The discriminating item is one in which a significantly larger number of correct responses is given by the upper group than by the lower group. A rough guide is a difference of at least two, preferably three or more. The greater the difference, the more discriminating the item.

In the illustration given above, question 1 has a difference of 12, and therefore differentiates clearly between those who know and those who do not. On the other hand, question 2 has 8 more in the lower group answering correctly than in the upper group. This means the item is producing a reverse differentiation. The index is labelled negative. Such negative and near zero items are detrimental for separation of those knowing and not knowing as much. Such items should be discarded or revised. Experience in writing items, followed by study of the item analysis, should help one develop the ability to produce functional items.

Standardized tests

Standardized knowledge examinations in physical education are very few. Standardization requires large numbers for purposes of item analysis and norms. Very few attempts of this sort have been made. From time to time tests have been published, many without an item analysis. Most of these examinations have been designed for college students.

The scarcity of examination of this refinement reflects the lack of commitment to test usage, lack of understanding of test construction, and lack of underwriting to finance such developments and marketing. Two early attempts were designed for college women in professional preparation, and another for use with common activities in college women's programs. All would need revision before use today. The study by Ley (7) was an attempt to demonstrate that items could be written in the upper categories of taxonomy in the period before Bloom's work had made much of an impact on physical education testing.

One example of leadership in this respect was a project carried out by a committee of the American Association for Health, Physical Education, and Recreation, and sponsored by that Association. The result of committee effort was of two types: 1) a manual on content for physical education at elementary and secondary levels (1), 2) collaboration with Educational Testing Service of Princeton, New Jersey on preparation, norming, and distribution of tests in physical education, based on content outlined in the manual. The tests are included in the STEP tests, marketed by ETS, designed for use primarily at 6th, 9th, and 12th grades as a diagnostic analysis of educational progress in the schools. For a time, ETS marketed an advanced physical education test for graduate students. It was discontinued at the time their advanced tests in all disciplines were discontinued.

Summary

In this period of emphasis on individualization of learning, acceleration of individual learning rates, granting of advanced standing, and accountability of education, knowledge tests of good quality can be a meaningful tool. There is an indication that the professional attitude is improving in this respect and that young teachers will be better prepared in constructing tests and using them, and that in-service training programs will reach the experienced teacher who may need help. Improvements of testing procedures could build better rapport with students, parents, colleagues in education, and social administrators.

REFERENCES

1. American Association for Health, Physical Education and Recreation, *Knowledges and Understandings in Physical Education.* Washington, D.C.: The Association, 1970.

2. Barrow, Harold M. and Rosemary McGee, *A Practical Approach to Measurement in Physical Education.* Philadelphia: Lea & Febiger, 1971.

3. Bloom, Benjamin S., ed., *Taxonomy of Educational Goals: Cognitive Domain.* New York: McKay, 1956.

4. ———, J. Thomas Hastings, and George F. Madaus, *Handbook on Formative and Summative Evaluation of Student Learning.* New York: McGraw-Hill, 1971.

5. Ebel, Robert L., *Essentials of Educational Measurement.* Englewood Cliffs, N.J.: Prentice-Hall, 1972.

6. ———, *How to Judge the Quality of An Objective Classroom Test.* Technical Bulletin no. 6. Iowa City: The University of Iowa, 1970.

7. Ley, Katherine L., *Constructing Objective Test Items to Measure High Levels of Achievement in Selected Physical Education Activities.* Ph.D. dissertation, The University of Iowa, 1960.

8. Neilson, N. P. and Clayne R. Jensen, *Measurement and Statistics in Physical Education.* Belmont, Calif.: Wadsworth, 1972.

9. Safrit, Margaret J., *Evaluation in Physical Education.* Englewood Cliffs, N.J.: Prentice-Hall, 1973.

10. Schmeiser, Cynthia B.; James T. Stewart; and Douglas R. Whitney, *Understanding and Using Item Analysis, Technical Bulletin* #17. Iowa City: The University of Iowa, 1974.

STUDY QUESTIONS · Chapter 12

1. Give two examples of "knowledge" questions in:
   a. basketball
   b. gymnastics
   c. field hockey
   d. physical fitness

2. Give two examples of questions in the area of "comprehension" for:
   a. touch football
   b. golf
   c. swimming
   d. dance

3. Give two examples of questions concerning "application" in:
   a. weight control as related to exercise
   b. endurance
   c. track and field
   d. bowling

4. Give two examples of questions in the category of "analyses" in:
   a. softball throw
   b. dance
   c. archery
   d. muscular strength

5. Give two examples of questions concerning "synthesis" in:
   a. soccer
   b. circulatory-respiratory fitness
   c. wrestling
   d. volleyball

6. Give two examples of questions on "evaluation" in:
   a. endurance
   b. dance
   c. flexibility
   d. softball

7. Describe some of the advantages and disadvantages of the following kinds of questions:
   a. essay
   b. multiple choice
   c. alternate response
   d. recall

8. What is a "foil" as used in multiple-choice questions?

9. Describe the several alternate forms of multiple-choice questions.

10. Give three examples of different kinds of an "alternate response" question.

11. Define (a) difficulty, (b) index of discrimination, and (c) functional foils, as these terms relate to evaluating an examination.

12. Describe the advantages and disadvantages of standardized written tests in physical education.

V

Operational
Practices

STATISTICAL CALCULATIONS

13

Henry J. Montoye

Introduction

In a previous chapter, the product moment coefficient of correlation (or simply, the correlation coefficient) was discussed as one way of expressing quantitatively the validity, reliability, or objectivity of a test. There are, of course, many other statistical techniques for measuring these three characteristics of a test, but the correlation coefficient has been used much more frequently in physical education than any of the others. So, at the least, a teacher should understand this method. The discussion in Chapter 3 provided some theoretical and geometric insight into the correlation coefficient (abbreviated *r*). However the formula given in that chapter for r, although technically correct, does not lend itself well to the actual calculation. Yet, it is felt that the student will develop a better understanding of this statistical technique if he or she calculates the correlation coefficient from data.

It will be noted from Chapter 3 that the mean and standard deviation are intimately related to the correlation coefficient. Therefore, procedures for calculating these will be presented first. Excellent electronic desk calculators have become readily available in recent years and they are relatively inexpensive. Therefore, methods of calculating the mean, standard deviation, or correlation coefficient from grouped data are not as important now as they were a few years ago. Nevertheless, some instructors believe the student develops better insight if he or she goes through this process. Hence, examples using ungrouped data (so-called long method) and grouped data (short method) are given. Data are provided at the end of the chapter as exercises for the student.

Mean: grouped and ungrouped data

The mean, or, more precisely, the arithmetic mean, is the most widely employed measure of central tendency. In nonstatistical discourse or writing, it is commonly called the "average." Geometrically, the mean represents the point on the x-axis where a distribution would balance on a knife edge.

Examples

The mean may be calculated in two ways. If the data are not grouped, the mean may be calculated by dividing the sum of all the scores by the number of scores. For example $3 + 8 + 6 + 9 + 10 + 4 + 2 = 42$. $42/7 = 6$. The formula for this operation is

$$M_x \text{ or } \overline{X} = \frac{\Sigma X}{N} = \frac{42}{7} = 6$$

Where M_x or $\overline{X}$ = the mean
X = any score
ΣX = sum of the scores*
N = number of scores.

While the ungrouped method is the most precise method of obtaining the mean, it becomes unwieldy when a large number of cases are involved. This is especially true if there are no electrical or mechanical calculators available. To facilitate the calculation of the mean for a large number of scores, the grouped method has been devised.

The first step in the calculation of the mean by this method is to group the data into class intervals. While there is no universally accepted practice for developing class intervals, neither accuracy nor simplicity are severely compromised if the scores are divided into ten to twenty class intervals. The approximate size of the class interval may be determined by dividing the range by the desired number of class intervals. For example, the grip strength scores of a group of boys varied from 37 to 134 pounds. The range of scores was 97 pounds. Suppose the approximate number of intervals desired is 15. Then the size of the class intervals will be: $97/15 = 6.5$ pounds. To simplify tabulation the interval size could be rounded to 5 pounds.

*Σ, or sigma, means "the sum of," or the command, "add up."

TABLE 13–1
Standing Long Jump Scores in Inches
4th Grade Boys
(Unpublished Data)

65	58	50	56	56	62
59	47	52	63	65	59
60	57	55	67	69	65
60	72	58	55	67	67
66	65	65	68	58	67
66	54	60	65	60	49
61	58	53	61	64	69
63	67	41	53	68	62
62	62	58	52	56	56
67	60	57	68	58	60
63	59	72			

High Score = 72   Low Score = 41   Range = 31

Conversely, if a class interval of a specific size is easier to work with, or better expresses the data, the range may be divided by the desired class interval size to determine the approximate number of intervals. For example, using the grip strength data given above, with a desired interval size of 5 pounds, the approximate number of intervals that will be formed is: $97/5 = 19.4$.* Since there cannot be a fraction of an interval, the number of intervals would be twenty.

In the following example, the standing long jump scores of Table 13–1 are arranged in a frequency distribution. The first column of the frequency table (Table 13–2) contains the class interval limits arranged so the best scores will be tabulated at the top of the column. The second column contains the tabulation marks, one for each score that falls within the interval. The third column contains the sum of the tabulations in the second column.

The next step in determining the mean is the selection of a class interval in which the mean might be expected to fall. This generally is the class with the greatest frequency and/or the class which is near the center of the distribution. The boundaries of this class (58–60) have been overscored to identify this assumed mean interval. The "d" stands for the deviations of other class intervals from the assumed mean interval. The row containing the assumed mean is given the value of zero in the "d" column and the class deviations then increase positively by 1 in the direction of the higher scores and negatively by 1 in the direction of the lower scores. For example, the class interval 70–72 is 4 deviations from the assumed mean, i.e., interval 58–60 (see Table 13–2). The "fd" values in the last column are calculated by multiplying the figures

*The true limits of class intervals should be clearly understood. For example, an interval of 85 to 89 pounds used in grouping grip strength scores includes all scores from 84.50 to 89.499+. If, on the other hand, pull-up scores are being tabulated, an interval of 3.0–5.0 includes all scores from 3.0 to 5.99+, since partial attempts are not recorded as complete pull-ups.

TABLE 13-2
Frequency Table for Calculating the Mean
Standing Broad Jump

Inches	Tabulation			f	d	fd
70-72	11			2	4	8
67-69	HTI HTI	1		11	3	33
64-66	HTI 1111			9	2	18
61-63	HTI 1111			9	1	9
58-60	1111 1111	1111		15	0	68/−34
55-57	HTI 111			8	−1	−8
52-54	HTI			5	−2	−10
49-51	11			2	−3	−6
46-48	1			1	−4	−4
43-45				0	−5	0
40-42	1			1	−6	−6
				63		34

in the f-column by the corresponding figures in the d-column, e.g., for class interval 70–82, f = 2, d = 4, fd = 8.

Next, the sum of the fd-column (Σ fd) is obtained. The plus fd-values above the assumed mean and the minus fd-values below the assumed mean are added separately. The algebraic difference between these two sums is Σ fd.

The mean (X) is calculated by substituting the above values in the following formula:

$$M_x \text{ or } \overline{X} = M' + \left(\frac{\Sigma \text{ fd}}{N} \cdot i \right)$$

Where M_x or $\overline{X}$ = the mean

M' = the assumed mean (i.e., the center of the class of the assumed mean)

Σ fd = algebraic sum of column fd

i = size of class intervals

N = total number of scores

Thus in the example:

$$\overline{X} = 59 + \left(\frac{34}{63} \right) \cdot 3 = 59 + (.54 \cdot 3)$$

$$\overline{X} = 59 + 1.62$$

$$\overline{X} = 60.62 \text{ inches}$$

Since the scores lose their exact identity in grouping, there is a small error in calculating the mean in this way. For example, compare the mean above,

60.62, with the arithmetic mean calculated by the "long" method, namely 60.59.

The mean generally defines the concentration of data (i.e., central tendency). It has the disadvantage of being influenced by extreme scores, a disadvantage not shared by certain other measures of central tendency. When a distribution is markedly skewed (i.e., more scores near one of the extremes), the mean, interpreted as a measure of central tendency, is apt to be misleading. In physical education, however, these instances are rare and the mean generally is a good measure of central tendency.

Standard deviation: ungrouped data

Whereas the mean is the most important measure of concentration of the data, the standard deviation is the most important measure of variation. The symbol for the standard deviation of a total population is σ while the symbol generally used to represent the standard deviation of a sample of a population is written s or *S.D.* The standard deviation may be computed for distributions of any shape. However, when it is to be used in the construction of standards and interpreted in terms of percentiles, the shape of the distribution must be known.

The standard deviation may be computed using the following formula:

$$ s = \sqrt{\frac{\Sigma X^2}{N} - \left(\frac{\Sigma X}{N}\right)^2} $$

Where
$\Sigma X =$ the sum of the raw scores
$\Sigma X^2 =$ the sum of the squares of the raw scores
$N =$ the total number of raw scores

Table 13–3 contains data taken from a report on the relationship of post-exercise breath-holding ability to the duration of exercise. Each raw score in the X-column is the mean of three trials. The squares of the raw scores are in the X^2-column and the calculations are in the third column.

The standard deviation is an important measure of variability since it gives some indication of the distribution of the scores around the mean. It also has the advantage of being relatively stable from sample to sample.

Frequently the standard deviation of a sample is used as an estimate of the standard deviation of the total population. A more accurate estimate may be had if the sum of squares is divided by $N - 1$ instead of N.

Standard deviation: grouped data

Frequently the teacher or researcher must calculate the mean and standard deviation of a large number of scores. Unless he has a computer at his disposal, or at least a rapid electric calculator, he will have a long and tedious task

TABLE 13–3
Mean Breath-Holding Time After Exercise (in Seconds)
*College Men**
(N = 33)

X	X²	Computations
12	144	
26	676	
21	441	
12	144	
8	64	
19	361	
17	289	
21	441	
29	841	$s = \sqrt{\dfrac{\Sigma X^2}{N} - \left(\dfrac{\Sigma X}{N}\right)^2}$
38	1,444	
17	289	
27	729	
25	625	$s = \sqrt{\dfrac{14614}{33} - \left(\dfrac{656}{33}\right)^2}$
30	900	
12	144	
16	256	
14	196	$s = \sqrt{\dfrac{14614}{33} - (19.7585)^2}$
12	144	
20	400	
20	400	$s = \sqrt{442.85 - 395.17}$
21	441	
22	484	
17	289	$s = \sqrt{47.68}$
28	784	
12	144	$s = 6.9$ seconds
15	225	
18	324	
15	225	$X = \dfrac{656}{33} = 19.9$ seconds
14	196	
22	484	
15	225	
29	841	
32	1,024	
ΣX = 656	ΣX² = 14,614	

*From Montoye, H. J. "Analysis of Breath-Holding Tests." *Res. Quart.* 21:322–330, 1950.

calculating the mean and standard deviation using the ungrouped data technique. Earlier in this chapter, a method of calculating the mean by grouping data is explained. The standard deviation may also be calculated from grouped data.

Table 13–4 contains the same tabulations as Table 13–2 plus one additional column, fd². This column, fd², is obtained by multiplying f by the square of d. The sum of the fd²'s is obtained by adding the values in this column.

The standard deviation is then calculated by substituting the appropriate values from Table 13–4 in the following formula:

TABLE 13–4
Frequency Table for Calculating the Standard Deviation
Standing Long Jump Scores

Class Interval (Inches)	Tabulation	f	d	fd	fd²
70-72	11	2	4	8	32
67-69	⊔⊔⊤ ⊔⊔⊤ 1	11	3	33	99
64-66	⊔⊔⊤ 1111	9	2	18	36
61-63	⊔⊔⊤ 1111	9	1	9	9
58-60	⊔⊔⊤ ⊔⊔⊤ ⊔⊔⊤	15	0	68/−34	0
55-57	⊔⊔⊤ 111	8	−1	−8	8
52-54	⊔⊔⊤	5	−2	−10	20
49-51	11	2	−3	−6	18
46-48	1	1	−4	−4	16
43-45		0	−5	0	0
40-42	1	1	−6	−6	36
Σ		63		34	274

$$s = i \sqrt{\frac{\Sigma fd^2}{N} - \left(\frac{\Sigma fd}{N}\right)^2}$$

Where
s = the standard deviation
i = size of class interval
Σfd = sum of fd-column
Σfd^2 = sum of fd²-column
N = total number of scores

In this example:

$$s = 3 \sqrt{\frac{274}{63} - \left(\frac{34}{63}\right)^2}$$
$$= 3 \sqrt{4.35 - (.54)^2}$$
$$= 3 \sqrt{4.35 - .2916}$$
$$= 3 \sqrt{4.0584}$$
$$= (3)\ (2.014)$$
$$= 6.042 \text{ inches}$$

The standard deviation, when computed from grouped data by the short method, is subject to several errors. These are so small as to be of minor significance. Sheppard's correction may be used to compensate for the most important of these, the error introduced when all scores within a class are assumed to be at the mid-point of that class. When the number of classes is small, less than ten or twelve, the correction is of some consequence, but becomes less important as the number of classes is increased. In terms of intervals, the corrected standard deviation is as follows:

$$s \text{ corrected} = \sqrt{s^2 - \frac{1}{12}}$$

and in terms of units:

$$s \text{ corrected} = \sqrt{s^2 - \frac{i^2}{12}}$$

In the example given (Table 13–4), the corrected s would be

$$s = \sqrt{s^2 - \frac{1}{12}} = \sqrt{4.0584 - \frac{1}{12}} = 1.99 \text{ (intervals)}$$

$$s = \sqrt{s^2 - \frac{i^2}{12}} = \sqrt{36.5058 - \frac{9}{12}} = 5.96 \text{ inches (units)}$$

Product-moment coefficient of correlation: ungrouped data

No statistical procedure has been utilized more frequently than the coefficient of correlation for determining the validity, reliability, and objectivity of tests. Consequently, a clear understanding of this term is essential for evaluating most existing tests in health, physical education, and recreation. Correlation generally involves scores on two tests for each of the subjects. The tests may be the same, as is the case when the reliability coefficient of a test is desired, or the tests may be totally different. In any event, the scores on each test represent separate groups of data with separate distributions, means, and standard deviations. Generally the two sets of scores are for a single group of subjects. In only rare instances does one correlate data from one group of subjects with data obtained from a second group of subjects. The problem of correlation is essentially one of determining the relationship between two variables. Frequently, this may be stated in the form of a question: Do boys who score high on one test consistently tend to also score high (or low) on a second test? The coefficient is a quantitative measure of this tendency. Its numerical value may range from minus one (perfect negative correlation) through zero (no correlation) to a plus one (perfect positive correlation). Any fractional value between these points is possible.

When only a small number of cases is involved, the correlation coefficient may readily be calculated by the ungrouped method. Table 13–5 shows how the data should be arranged to facilitate calculations.

In Table 13–5, the times have been converted from minutes and seconds to minutes and fractions of minutes, i.e., 20 minutes, 30 seconds becomes 20.50 minutes, 21:40 = 21.67 minutes.

TABLE 13–5

*Pulse Rates and Performance Times
for Cross Country Runners*

Sub-ject	Pulse Rate	Perfor-mance*	Sub-ject	Pulse Rate	Perfor-mance	Sub-ject	Pulse Rate	Perfor-mance
1	45	20.58	17	68	21.75	33	72	22.75
2	54	20.67	18	52	21.77	34	56	22.78
3	52	20.98	19	56	21.80	35	65	22.92
4	72	20.88	20	52	21.83	36	56	23.20
5	54	21.17	21	52	21.90	37	52	23.32
6	60	21.25	22	56	21.92	38	60	23.40
7	52	21.27	23	58	21.95	39	64	23.48
8	68	21.32	24	60	21.97	40	62	23.75
9	64	21.35	25	60	22.12	41	58	24.37
10	56	21.40	26	60	22.17	42	76	24.50
11	62	21.42	27	52	22.18	43	64	24.53
12	50	21.58	28	57	22.42	44	72	24.98
13	58	21.60	29	64	22.45	45	73	24.98
14	60	21.62	30	67	22.57	46	77	25.48
15	51	21.63	31	64	22.60			
16	66	21.67	32	64	22.65			

*Times in minutes

The formula used to calculate the correlation coefficient for ungrouped data is:

$$r_{xy} = \frac{\Sigma XY - \dfrac{(\Sigma X)}{N}\dfrac{(\Sigma Y)}{N}}{\sqrt{\left[\Sigma X^2 - \dfrac{(\Sigma X)^2}{N}\right]\left[\Sigma Y^2 - \dfrac{(\Sigma Y)^2}{N}\right]}}$$

Where: r_{xy} = coefficient of correlation

ΣX = sum of first group of scores (x-variable)

ΣY = sum of second group of scores (y-variable)

ΣX^2 = sum of squared scores in first group (x-variable)

ΣY^2 = sum of squared scores in second group (y-variable)

ΣXY = sum of the products of the two scores for each subject

N = total number of subjects

The initial calculations appear in Table 13–6. The sums at the bottom of this table are substituted in the formula above. Thus,

$$r_{xy} = \frac{62{,}248.06 - \dfrac{(2773)}{46}\dfrac{(1028.88)}{46}}{\sqrt{\left[169{,}675 - \dfrac{(2773)^2}{46}\right]\left[23{,}079.19 - \dfrac{(1028.88)^2}{46}\right]}}$$

TABLE 13–6
Initial Calculations for Raw Data Presented in Table 13–5

Subject Number	Pulse Rate (X)	Performance (Y)	X^2	Y^2	XY
1	45	20.58	2025	423.54	926.10
2	54	20.67	2916	427.25	1116.18
3	52	20.98	2704	440.16	1090.96
4	72	20.88	5184	435.97	1503.36
5	54	21.17	2916	448.17	1143.18
6	60	21.25	3600	451.56	1275.00
7	52	21.27	2704	452.41	1106.04
8	68	21.32	4624	454.54	1449.76
9	64	21.35	4096	455.82	1366.40
10	56	21.40	3136	457.96	1198.40
11	62	21.42	3844	458.82	1328.04
12	50	21.58	2500	465.70	1079.00
13	58	21.60	3364	466.36	1252.80
14	60	21.62	3600	467.42	1297.20
15	51	21.63	2601	467.86	1103.13
16	66	21.67	4356	469.59	1430.22
17	68	21.75	4624	473.06	1479.00
18	52	21.77	2704	473.93	1132.04
19	56	21.80	3136	475.24	1220.80
20	52	21.83	2704	476.55	1135.16
21	52	21.90	2704	479.61	1138.80
22	56	21.92	3136	480.49	1227.52
23	58	21.95	3364	481.80	1273.10
24	60	21.97	3600	482.68	1318.20
25	60	22.12	3600	489.29	1327.20
26	60	22.17	3600	491.51	1330.20
27	52	22.18	2704	491.95	1153.36
28	57	22.42	3249	502.66	1277.94
29	64	22.45	4096	504.00	1436.80
30	67	22.57	4489	509.40	1512.19
31	64	22.60	4096	510.76	1446.40
32	64	22.65	4096	513.02	1449.60
33	72	22.75	5184	517.56	1638.00
34	56	22.78	3136	518.93	1275.68
35	65	22.92	4225	525.33	1489.80
36	56	23.20	3136	538.24	1299.20
37	52	23.32	2704	543.82	1212.64
38	60	23.40	3600	547.56	1404.00
39	64	23.48	4096	551.31	1502.72
40	62	23.75	3844	564.06	1472.50
41	58	24.37	3364	593.90	1413.46
42	76	24.50	5776	600.25	1862.00
43	64	24.53	4096	601.72	1569.92
44	72	24.98	5184	624.00	1798.56
45	73	24.98	5329	624.00	1823.54
46	77	25.48	5929	649.23	1961.96
Σ	2773	1028.88	169,675	23,079.19	62,248.06

$$r_{xy} = \cfrac{62{,}248.06 - \cfrac{2{,}853{,}084.24}{46}}{\sqrt{\left[169{,}675 - \cfrac{(7{,}689{,}529)}{46}\right]\left[23{,}079.19 - \cfrac{1{,}058{,}594.05}{46}\right]}}$$

$$r_{xy} = \frac{62{,}248.06 - 62{,}023.57}{\sqrt{[169{,}675 - 167{,}163.67] \quad [23{,}079.19 - 23{,}012.90]}}$$

$$r_{xy} = \frac{224.49}{\sqrt{[2511.33] \quad [66.28]}}$$

$$r_{xy} = \frac{224.49}{\sqrt{166{,}450.9524}}$$

$$r_{xy} = \frac{224.49}{407.98}$$

$$r_{xy} = 0.55$$

It should be carefully noted that ΣX^2 is not the same as $(\Sigma X)^2$. In the first case, ΣX^2, each score, X, is squared and the resulting squares are summed. With $(\Sigma X)^2$, on the other hand, the raw scores, X, are summed and the total thus obtained is squared. A similar distinction should be made between ΣY^2 and $(\Sigma Y)^2$. Also, ΣXY is not the equivalent of $(\Sigma X)(\Sigma Y)$. The first sum, ΣXY, is obtained by multiplying each subject's X-score by his corresponding Y-score and summing the products thus obtained. However, $(\Sigma X)(\Sigma Y)$ is the result of summing all the X-scores and then separately summing all the Y-scores and multiplying these two sums together.

Often the coding of data can reduce the size of the numbers to shorten the time spent in calculating correlation coefficients and other statistics. One method of coding is accomplished by subtracting a constant from all of the scores for one variable. This reduces the mean by the size of the constant, but it does not change the standard deviation or the correlation coefficient.

In Table 13–7, the performance times (column 3) of Table 13–6 have been coded by subtracting 20 minutes from each score. In addition, these values were rounded off from two decimal places to one. It can be seen that these procedures did not alter the final value of r, at least to the second decimal place. Coding does not introduce any error but rounding off occasionally does. The savings in time and labor justify the small error resulting from rounding off.

One last point should be mentioned. The values in the last three columns of Tables 13–6 and 13–7 are not needed, except to obtain the sums of these columns shown at the bottom of the tables. With most calculators, these sums can be obtained without recording the individual values in the last three columns. In fact, with many calculators the five sums appearing at the bottom of Tables 13–6 and 13–7 may be obtained simultaneously.

Calculations using the coded scores in Table 13–7 follow.

$$r_{xy} = \frac{6827.0 - \dfrac{(2773)}{46} \dfrac{(109.5)}{}}{\sqrt{\left[169,675 - \left(\dfrac{2773}{46}\right)^2\right]\left[327.2 - \left(\dfrac{109.5}{46}\right)^2\right]}}$$

$$r_{xy} = \frac{6827.0 - 6600.9}{\sqrt{167,001.45}}$$

$$r_{xy} = \frac{226.1}{408.7}$$

$$r_{xy} = 0.55$$

In the example given above, a correlation coefficient of 0.55 was obtained. This coefficient indicates that there is a trend for the better runners to have lower heart rates. However, it would be impossible to predict with a great deal of accuracy a runner's time from his resting heart rate. This is true because one way of interpreting the correlation coefficient is to square it and multiply the result by 100. This figure, under several reasonable assumptions, represents the percent of the variance of one group of scores that is explained by its association with another group of scores. For example, the coefficient 0.55 explains only 30% of the variance (s^2). That is $(0.55)^2 = 30.25$, or 30% of the variance in running times is accounted for by their relationship with heart rate.

Had the correlation been negative (i.e., −0.55) it would have indicated that the runners who had the best performance times also had highest resting heart rates, or that the poorest runners had the lowest resting heart rates.

Product-moment coefficient of correlation: grouped data

When the correlation coefficient is to be calculated for scores on a large number of subjects (for example, 100 or more), and particularly when a calculator is not available, it is expedient to group the scores as outlined in this exercise. If done correctly, the slight error introduced by grouping does not affect the final value of the correlation coefficient significantly. There is another advantage to this method, namely, a scatter-diagram is one of the results. (Why is this important?)

Table 13–8 contains body weight (lb) and grip strength scores (lb) on 135 college men. These data are from a study by Tinkle and Montoye (1). Using a work sheet the various steps outlined below were followed to calculate the correlation coefficient for the data of Table 13–8. The tabulations and

TABLE 13–7
Initial Calculations for Coded Raw Data

Subject Number	Pulse Rate (X)	Performance (Y)	X²	Y²	XY
1	45	0.6	2025	.36	27.0
2	54	0.7	2916	.49	37.8
3	52	1.0	2704	1.00	52.0
4	72	0.9	5184	.81	64.8
5	54	1.2	2916	1.44	64.8
6	60	1.3	3600	1.69	78.0
7	52	1.3	2704	1.69	67.6
8	68	1.3	4624	1.69	88.4
9	64	1.4	4096	1.96	89.6
10	56	1.4	3136	1.96	78.4
11	62	1.4	3844	1.96	86.8
12	50	1.6	2500	2.56	80.0
13	58	1.6	3364	2.56	92.8
14	60	1.6	3600	2.56	96.0
15	51	1.6	2601	2.56	81.6
16	66	1.7	4356	2.89	112.2
17	68	1.8	4624	3.24	122.4
18	52	1.8	2704	3.24	93.6
19	56	1.8	3136	3.24	100.8
20	52	1.8	2704	3.24	93.6
21	52	1.9	2704	3.61	98.8
22	56	1.9	3136	3.61	106.4
23	58	2.0	3364	4.00	116.0
24	60	2.0	3600	4.00	120.0
25	60	2.1	3600	4.41	126.0
26	60	2.2	3600	4.84	132.0
27	52	2.2	2704	4.84	114.4
28	57	2.4	3249	5.76	136.8
29	64	2.5	4096	6.25	160.0
30	67	2.6	4489	6.76	174.2
31	64	2.6	4096	6.76	166.4
32	64	2.7	4096	7.29	172.8
33	72	2.8	5184	7.84	201.6
34	56	2.8	3136	7.84	156.8
35	65	2.9	4225	8.41	188.5
36	56	3.2	3136	10.24	179.2
37	52	3.3	2704	10.89	171.6
38	60	3.4	3600	11.56	204.0
39	64	3.5	4096	12.55	224.0
40	62	3.8	3844	14.44	235.6
41	58	4.4	3364	19.36	255.2
42	76	4.5	5776	20.25	342.0
43	64	4.5	4096	20.25	288.0
44	72	5.0	5184	25.00	360.0
45	73	5.0	5329	25.00	365.0
46	77	5.5	5929	30.25	423.5
Σ	2773	109.5	169,675	327.15	6827.0

TABLE 13-8
Weight and Grip Strength Measurements
College Men
(N = 135)

Subject Number	Weight (lb)	Grip Strength (lb)	Subject Number	Weight (lb)	Grip Strength (lb)	Subject Number	Weight (lb)	Grip Strength (lb)
1	162	145	46	154	152	91	174	132
2	157	162	47	154	132	92	180	119
3	171	150	48	164	130	93	165	140
4	159	137	49	162	142	94	140	109
5	192	130	50	143	122	95	170	155
6	133	113	51	181	120	96	137	130
7	163	120	52	130	119	97	136	140
8	179	150	53	139	115	98	155	111
9	171	121	54	149	122	99	150	116
10	118	110	55	147	148	100	166	148
11	160	171	56	159	154	101	145	110
12	183	129	57	146	140	102	160	150
13	158	132	58	163	136	103	150	145
14	166	112	59	175	128	104	170	124
15	111	118	60	160	141	105	162	119
16	142	150	61	180	145	106	158	119
17	140	150	62	145	100	107	160	119
18	165	160	63	175	154	108	162	139
19	187	160	64	142	115	109	161	141
20	176	130	65	146	137	110	175	145
21	141	123	66	165	146	111	140	128
22	129	120	67	170	126	112	165	135
23	138	116	68	180	150	113	160	131
24	134	120	69	170	148	114	185	150
25	134	110	70	135	116	115	229	162
26	133	132	71	175	151	116	135	119
27	162	132	72	172	122	117	138	140
28	158	113	73	152	121	118	162	158
29	152	119	74	150	122	119	205	160
30	188	152	75	160	152	120	170	142
31	159	117	76	210	158	121	150	106
32	154	121	77	160	148	122	155	117
33	135	112	78	128	110	123	140	132
34	140	100	79	118	144	124	140	142
35	150	109	80	145	126	125	155	150
36	145	121	81	150	140	126	165	122
37	150	139	82	160	120	127	195	162
38	142	112	83	150	132	128	145	122
39	175	145	84	160	129	129	170	140
40	127	101	85	130	128	130	170	160
41	178	140	86	190	139	131	175	158
42	136	115	87	185	116	132	180	124
43	167	138	88	180	142	133	148	103
44	155	150	89	155	142	134	170	139
45	167	128	90	150	120	135	120	115

calculations are shown in Figure 13–1. In following the example below, refer to Figure 13–1 at each step.

Step 1. One of the series of scores (grip strength) was designated as the X-axis variable and the other (body weight) as the Y-axis variable. The names of these variables are written in the spaces provided at the top and left sides of the work sheet.

Step 2. The size of the step interval for each variable is determined in the same manner as before. The limits of the step intervals are shown in the first row of squares at the top and along the left side of the work sheet. The scores were arranged so that the larger ones are at the right side of the X-variable and at the top for the Y-variable.

Step 3. The paired scores for each subject were next tabulated by placing a small tally in the square forming the intersection of the row and column corresponding to these scores. The correct square was found by locating the subject's Y-score (weight) in the appropriate class in the left-hand column and following horizontally across the chart until the column corresponding to the subject's X-score (grip strength) was located. The tally was then placed in the intersecting square.

Step 4. The number of tallies in each *row* was counted and the totals written in the column marked fy.

Step 5. The number of tallies in each *column* was counted and the totals written in the row marked fx.

Step 6. A class (column) in which the mean of the X-variable (grip strength) might be expected to fall was selected (135–139). This is called the "assumed mean." Similarly, a class (row) in which the mean of the Y-variable (weight) might be expected to fall was selected (160–169). The boundaries of these classes were then overscored with a colored pencil.

Step 7. The deviations of columns and rows from the assumed means were recorded in row dx and column dy, respectively. This was done as follows. The row and column containing the assumed means were marked 0. The class deviations then increase by 1 positively in the direction of the higher scores and negatively in the direction of the lower scores.

Step 8. The fydy values were determined by multiplying the values in the fy column by the corresponding values in the dy column. Similarly, the fx-values were multiplied by dx values to secure the products in the fxdx row.

Step 9. The values in the $fydy^2$ column were determined by multiplying the figures in the dy column by corresponding figures in the fydy column. The same procedure is followed for computing the products in the fxdx² row.

Step 10. Next, the cross-products were obtained. This was done for every square (junction of row and column) that contains one or more tallies and does not fall in the column or row of the assumed mean. The algebraic product of the class deviations (dx and dy) of a given square is computed and this value is then multiplied by the number of tallies in the square. The final product is written in the square and circled. The sign (+ or −) for this value is easily assigned since all figures in the first quadrant (to the right and above the assumed means) and in the third quadrant (to the left and below the assumed means) are positive. The values in the other two quadrants are negative. An example follows. There were 2 scores in which the subject's weight was 180–189 (dy value of +2) and whose grip strength was 120–124 (dx value of −3). The encircled cross product (−12) was obtained by multiplying the dy value (+2) by the dx value (−3) and this product (−6) by the number of scores in that cell (2).

Step 11. The encircled positive products were then summed by rows and these totals are placed in the right-hand column marked "+" under X'Y'. The sum of this column is 590. The encircled negative values were also summed by rows and the totals placed in the column marked "−" under X'Y'. The sum of this column is −102. The difference between these two sums, with sign retained, is the value X'Y' or 488.

Step 12. The following column and row totals were then computed: Σfy (135), Σfydy (−77), Σfydy² (553), Σfxdx (−115), Σfxdx² (1535).

Step 13. Finally these sums were substituted in the formulae below. "C" stands for corrected or adjusted, "ç" means the same for interval units.

$$\varsigma x = \frac{\Sigma fxdx}{N} = \frac{-115}{135} = -.852$$

$$\varsigma y = \frac{\Sigma fydy}{N} = \frac{-77}{135} = -.570$$

These are correction terms to be added or subtracted (as in this case) to the assumed mean. The means are not needed for the calculation of the correlation coefficient but they may be calculated as follows:
For grip strength:

$$C_x \text{ (the correction term in score units)} = \varsigma_x i_x = (-.852) \ (5)$$

$$= -4.25$$

$$M_x = AM_x \text{ (assumed mean)} + C_x = 137.0 - 4.25 = 132.75 \text{ lb}$$

For body weight:

$$C_y = ç_y i_y = (-.570)\ (10) = -5.70$$
$$M_y = AM_y + C_y = 164.5 - 5.70 = 158.8 \text{ lb}$$

The standard deviation in intervals (s′) is needed in the formula for the correlation coefficient. For grip strength this is:

$$s'_x = \sqrt{\frac{\Sigma f_x d_x^2}{N} - ç_x^2} = \sqrt{\frac{1535}{135} - .7259} = \sqrt{10.6445} = 3.26$$

You will note that

$$\sqrt{\frac{\Sigma f_x d_x^2}{N} - ç_x^2} \text{ is equivalent to}$$

$$\sqrt{\frac{\Sigma fd^2}{N} - \left(\frac{\Sigma fd}{N}\right)^2}$$

Similarly for body weight

$$s'_y = \sqrt{\frac{\Sigma f_y d^2_y}{N} - ç_y^2} = \sqrt{\frac{553}{135} - .3249} = \sqrt{3.7714} = 1.67$$

Correlation tabulation chart — X AXIS VARIABLE: GRIP STRENGTH; Y AXIS VARIABLE: WEIGHT

Right-hand summary columns (by weight interval): f_y, d_y, $f_y d_y$, $f_y d^2_y$, $\Sigma x'y'$ (+ −)

Weight	f_y	d_y	$f_y d_y$	$f_y d^2_y$	$\Sigma x'y'$ +	−
220-9	1	6	6	36	30	
210-9	1	5	5	25	20	
200-9	1	4	4	16	20	
190-9	3	3	9	27	15	3
180-9	11	2	22	44	34	32
170-9	21	1	21	21	33	15
160-9	28	0				
150-9	26	-1	-26	26	57	21
140-9	21	-2	-42	84	122	20
130-9	15	-3	-45	135	138	6
120-9	4	-4	-16	64	76	
110-9	3	-5	-15	75	45	5
Totals	135	$\Sigma f_y d_y =$	$\Sigma f_y d^2_y$	590	-102	
		$\overset{..}{z}$ -77	553	$\Sigma x'y' = 488$		

Bottom summary rows (by grip strength interval):

	100-9	105-9	110-4	115-9	120-4	125-9	130-9	135-9	140-9	145-9	150-9	155-9	160-4	165-9	170-9	Totals
f_x	4	3	10	18	19	8	12	9	15	10	15	4	7	0	1	135
d_x	-7	-6	-5	-4	-3	-2	-1	0	1	2	3	4	5	6	7	$\overset{..}{z}$ -77 553 $\Sigma x'y' = 488$
$f_x d_x$	-28	-18	-50	-72	-57	-16	-12		15	20	45	16	35		7	$\Sigma f_x d_x$ -115
$f_x d^2_x$	196	108	250	288	171	32	12		15	40	135	64	175		49	$\Sigma f_x d^2_x$ 1535

FIGURE 13-1. Example of tabulations and initial calculations to be followed in computing a correlation coefficient.

The correlation coefficient (r) is then calculated thus:

$$r_{xy} = \frac{\dfrac{\Sigma X'Y'}{N} - \varsigma_x \; \varsigma_y}{s'_x s'_y} = \frac{\dfrac{488}{135} - (-.852) \; (-.570)}{(3.26) \; (1.67)}$$

$$= \frac{3.615 - .486}{5.444} = .57$$

Errors commonly occur in Step 10 when the encircled cell products are calculated. One should also be very careful that the correct sign is attached at each step of the calculations. Frequently C_x or ς_x^2 is used instead of ς_x; or C_y or ς_y^2 is erroneously used in the formula for r instead of ς_y.

The correlation coefficient is not *necessarily* an expression of causal relationship, simply one of concomitant variation. The correlation in evidence *may* be due to the effect of one factor on the other, but it may also be accounted for by the effect of a third influence on both the factors in question.

REFERENCE

1. Tinkle, W. and H. J. Montoye, "Relationship between Grip Strength and Achievement in Physical Education among College Men," *Res. Quart.*, 32:238–243, 1961.

STUDY QUESTIONS

1. Why is it suggested, when dealing with grouped scores, that the assumed mean be in a class near the center of the distribution? Will the computed mean be less accurate if the assumed mean is taken at one of the classes farthest from the center of the distribution?

2. What effect will increasing the number of classes beyond twenty have in the computation of the mean? Of decreasing the number below ten?

3. What distinction is made in statistics between an "average" and the arithmetic mean? What other "averages" are there? What other means are sometimes employed?

4. What other measures of central tendency are sometimes used in physical education? When are they more appropriate than the arithmetic means?

5. What measures of variation or variability, other than the standard deviation, are frequently employed?

6. Write another formula for the standard deviation using ungrouped data.

7. How would a constant error affect the standard deviation (e.g., a certain scale always reads one pound less than the individual's true weight). How would these errors affect the mean?

8. How would variable (chance) errors introduced into the data affect the size of the standard deviation? How would these errors affect the mean?

9. What effect would multiplying each score by a constant have on the mean and standard deviation of the distribution?

10. Explain the significance of a negative correlation coefficient.

11. Assuming all the X-scores to be negative and the Y-scores to be positive, what would be the sign of each of the following?
    a. ΣX
    b. ΣX^2
    c. $(\Sigma X)^2$
    d. $(\Sigma XY)^2$
    e. $(\Sigma X)(\Sigma Y)$

12. What assumption or assumptions are necessary in order to compute a coefficient of correlation and feel certain that it represents the best measure of the relationship between the two variables?

13. When the tallies occur predominantly in the second and fourth quadrants, what is the sign of the correlation coefficient? When the tallies are approximately equally distributed among the four quadrants, the coefficient approaches what value? (Grouped Data.) See Figure 13–1.

14. Which have more influence on the sum of the cross products $(\Sigma x'y')$, the average or extreme values? (Figure 13–1.)

15. Why is Sheppard's correction not important in the calculation of the coefficient of correlation even though the data are grouped?

TEST SCORES AND PERFORMANCE STANDARDS

14

Henry J. Montoye

Tests and measurements in physical education are continually undergoing change. As new knowledge is acquired it is, or should be, assimilated into our programs. However, there are many unanswered questions and there are controversial solutions to some of our problems. The development of achievement standards and the form in which scores should be reported are topics in which there is no unanimity of opinion. These are the topics to be discussed in this chapter.

The teacher's role

The beginning teacher, and, for that matter, even the experienced teacher is rarely directly involved in research as a part of his or her duties. For what purposes then will the teacher need to deal with scores? Usually it will be for one or two reasons. There will be occasions when, in the interest of public relations, it will be necessary to summarize or interpret performance or other data for the school board, for the parent-teacher organization, or for some other group. An elementary knowledge of the methods of descriptive statistics is essential for this task. The teacher should understand how to calculate the arithmetic mean, the range, the median, and perhaps other points in a distribution. High on the list of essential skills is the ability to construct clear and effective graphs of various kinds.

The second important reason for the teacher to be familiar with performance scores is for developing achievement scales. Using such scales, the individual scores may then be interpreted and explained to the students and their parents. Of course, a raw score (for example, a softball throw of 47 feet) can be reported. But there is no indication in this score whether the score is average, above average, or below average.

Achievement scales

In medicine, nutrition, and in certain other fields, there is often a normal range that is desirable. For example, the glucose concentration in the blood should not exceed a certain level, nor should it fall below a certain level. A minimum intake of certain vitamins is essential, but too much, in some instances, can be harmful. In other words, "if some is good, more is not necessarily better." In physical education activities, however, particularly with healthy children, if some is good, more generally *is* better. It is usually desirable to throw a ball farther or more accurately, to run faster, to be stronger, to jump higher, etc. Hence, it is not sufficient to set some minimum or to have a normal range. Instead, it is desirable to develop achievement scales so that individual performances may be accurately compared. One might argue, of course, that, for a middle-aged man, some physical activity is desirable, but more could be harmful. This is a special case, but even in this age group a higher level of skill in sports or dancing, even in work capacity is often desirable.

There are many forms of achievement scales. In other words, raw scores may be converted to other kinds of scores by various mathematical manipulations. Other tests and measurement texts often contain achievement scales in the form of standard scores (i.e., converted into standard deviation scores). At other times, T-scores, which are also derived from the standard deviation, are employed. In advanced statistical techniques (generally used for research), there are some mathematical advantages to such transformations. Although others may not agree (6, 7), there appears to be no practical use for such scores in the everyday duties of a teacher. Percentiles are, by far, the most useful form of achievement scales (8).

The use of the standard score in physical education presents several difficulties. Of most importance is the fact that the standard score lacks a common, readily understandable interpretation. Have you ever attempted to explain a σ-score to a ninth-grade boy or girl, or to their parents? The computation of the standard deviation, and hence, scores based on the standard deviation, requires no assumptions as to the shape of the distribution. However, if the mathematical equation for the distribution is not known, scores having the standard deviation as a basis lack meaning. A boy receives a

σ-score of, say 2.9, in "sit-ups." You can probably explain to him that his score is above the mean since it is positive but he does not know how many of his peers may be expected to have a higher score or how many a lower score. Yet, this is precisely what the boy wants to know.

Would it not be more valuable to the teacher and pupil alike to convert raw scores into percentile ranks? Little difficulty is encountered in explaining percentile ranks to children or adults providing they understand simple percentage. If a boy performs 63 "sit-ups" and is given a percentile rank of 85, he knows immediately that approximately 15% of his peers excel him in this event and approximately 85% have done poorer than he.

The computation of percentile ranks is simple and expedient and involves no assumptions as to the distribution of scores. A percentile rank may be computed individually for each raw score, or percentile standards may be constructed from a smooth ogive curve that has been fitted to grouped or ungrouped data. The next section will outline the procedures for calculating percentile scores.

When scores on several tests are available, their corresponding percentile ranks can be averaged. The interpretation of the mean of several percentile ranks probably comes closer to the common connotation of the term "average" than does the mean of standard scores. A case in point: A boy received raw scores of 164 pounds and 4 pull-ups in two tests with corresponding σ-scores of $+7.6$ and -1.2 and percentile ranks of 100 and 30. His mean σ-score of $+3.2$ placed him near the top in "average ability," yet one of his two scores was distinctly below average. The mean percentile rank of 65 in this case is a more logical expression of his average ability. The situation is comparable to the use of the median in preference to the mean when a distribution is skewed as, for example, in reporting average financial incomes.

Percentile scales may be constructed manually, i.e., with a desk calculator, or by means of a high speed computer. The undergraduate student in tests and measurements should learn how to construct percentile scales manually unless he or she is already familiar with the technique. The use of an electronic computer in the calculation of percentile scales is discussed in a later chapter.

Construction of percentile achievement standards

Percentile scores for large groups of subjects may be computed by the graphic method. The first step in constructing percentile scores is to group the data (raw scores) into intervals which will facilitate computations. This process was described in Chapter 13.

Table 14–1 contains data on college males for the triple jump (formerly called the hop, step, and jump). These data will be used to illustrate how

TABLE 14–1
Triple Jump Scores*
College Men N=150

28-0	33-7	35-1	32-3	30-6	33-2
30-6	34-11	34-5	34-0	32-4	31-8
31-0	33-7	29-7	31-6	30-3	36-1
30-6	32-11	34-0	29-6	27-1	30-0
29-7	33-10	25-0	32-0	30-9	33-3
28-8	32-6	30-0	30-1	36-10	34-10
31-8	31-8	26-9	30-10	29-3	30-5
32-6	32-3	30-3	28-3	31-9	35-3
37-3	34-7	31-2	30-0	31-10	35-4
32-3	29-0	26-7	37-6	29-11	38-8
31-8	33-0	33-7	27-5	35-2	29-10
30-9	31-0	32-7	27-10	35-0	31-6
30-11	32-7	31-6	32-3	37-11	25-5
33-4	34-11	32-6	31-8	35-3	31-4
30-6	29-8	36-3	33-9	31-2	30-3
30-9	36-7	28-11	35-8	30-6	29-9
34-9	39-1	31-7	34-4	36-3	28-11
36-1	34-7	31-5	23-7	29-6	34-10
29-8	30-8	34-8	30-6	29-1	32-6
32-0	29-10	31-6	32-3	28-10	32-2
33-6	28-10	32-10	30-5	34-11	26-2
31-10	32-1	28-8	31-5	24-6	33-2
30-10	29-9	25-10	33-9	26-8	31-1
32-5	30-4	29-7	30-10	30-11	38-3
28-3	34-9	31-2	27-11	36-6	33-9

*Scores are given in feet and inches. Unpublished data.

percentile scores are calculated. First, class intervals are established as follows:

$$\text{Range} = 39'1'' - 23'7'' = 15'6''$$

$$\text{Estimated size of class interval} = 15'6'' \div 15 = 1.03$$

Class interval size rounded to 1 foot for convenience.

Next, the triple jump scores of Table 14–1 are arranged in a frequency distribution. The first column of the frequency table (Table 14–2) contains the class interval limits arranged so the best scores will be tabulated at the top of the column. The second column contains the tabulation marks, one for each score that falls within the interval. The third column contains the sum of the tabulations in the second column. The fourth column is labeled "Cumulative Frequency": The cumulative frequency distribution is formed by starting from the bottom and adding each frequency to the next above and recording these sums in Column 4 of Table 14–2. The cumulative frequency of any class interval is equal to the sum of the frequencies in that interval plus the sum of the frequencies in all the intervals below it. The percentile ranks

TABLE 14–2

Cumulative Frequency Tabulation for Triple Jump Data

Class Boundaries Feet & Inches	Tabulation					Frequency	Cumulative Frequency	Percentile Ranks (Upper Limits)
39'0" — 39'11"	1					1	150	100.0
38'0" — 38'11"	11					2	149	99.3
37'0" — 37'11"	111					3	147	98.0
36'0" — 36'11"	1111	11				7	144	96.0
35'0" — 35'11"	1111	11				7	137	91.3
34'0" — 34'11"	1111	1111	1111			14	130	86.7
33'0" — 33'11"	1111	1111	111			13	116	77.3
32'0" — 32'11"	1111	1111	1111	1111		19	103	68.7
31'0" — 31'11"	1111	1111	1111	1111	11	22	84	56.0
30'0" — 30'11"	1111	1111	1111	1111	1111	25	62	41.3
29'0" — 29'11"	1111	1111	1111			14	37	24.7
28'0" — 28'11"	1111	1111				9	23	15.3
27'0" — 27'11"	1111					4	14	9.3
26'0" — 26'11"	1111					5	10	6.7
25'0" — 25'11"	111					3	5	3.3
24'0" — 24'11"	1					1	2	1.3
23'0" — 23'11"	1					1	1	0.7

which appear in the last column of Table 14–2 correspond to the upper limits of each class. By upper limit is meant the limiting value of the class in the direction of the best score numerically, whether it be the highest or lowest. The percentile points are computed by the following formula:

$$\text{Percentile rank} = \frac{S}{N} \cdot 100$$

Where S = the cumulative frequency up to and including the particular class interval

N = total number of scores

For example, the percentile rank corresponding to the upper limit of the interval 32'0" — 32'11" is

$$\frac{103}{150} \cdot 100 = 68.7\%.$$

After the percentile points for each upper limit have been computed and recorded in column 5, Table 14–2, these same percentile points are plotted on a graph. The percentile points are plotted along the ordinate and the raw scores (i.e., upper limits of each class interval) are plotted along the abscissa. (See Figure 14–1 for a graph based on the triple jump data given in Tables 14–1 and 14–2.) A smooth curve is then fitted to the plotted points with the aid of a French curve. It is not necessary for the fitted line to pass through each point.

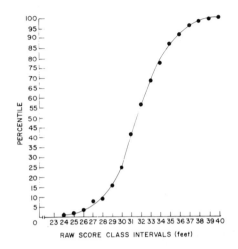

FIGURE 14–1. Graph of Tables 14–1 and 14–2.

The final step is to construct a table, such as Table 14–3, with percentile ranks appearing in the first column and the corresponding raw scores in the second column. This is done by finding the raw score equivalent on the curve which corresponds to each of the percentile ranks listed in Table 14–3.

TABLE 14–3
Achievement Standards for Triple Jump Data

Percentile Rank	Raw Scores (Feet – Inches)
95	36-6
90	35-5
85	34-9
80	34-2
75	33-8
70	33-2
65	32-9
60	32-4
55	31-11
50	31-7
45	31-3
40	30-10
35	30-6
30	30-3
25	29-11
20	29-6
15	29-0
10	28-3
5	26-9

Caution should be exercised with swimming or track times or any data in which smaller scores indicate better performances. The data are handled in much the same way except that the upper limit of a class is the smallest possible value rather than the largest possible value in the class.

Effects of age, height, and weight

As children become older they also become heavier, taller, and more skilled in physical education activities. It is also well known that bigger children and adults tend to be stronger when strength is measured in absolute terms, as, for example, in the maximum weight lifted or force exerted on a dynamometer. This is why weight classes exist in competitive wrestling and weight-lifting and why champion shot-putters tend to be big. However, in most physical education activities, a performer must move his own body weight. Also, skill is often more important than size. For these reasons, one might question the necessity of correcting for height or weight. Nevertheless, it is sometimes the practice in schools to use combinations of age, height, and weight to establish standards of performance for physical education activities. In both national surveys of youth fitness in the United States, percentile standards were reported by age and by a classification system based on age, height, and weight (2, 5).

Since chronological age is related to maturity, which is in turn related to performance in children, most people will agree that children of various ages should not be compared. If there were simple, practical, and accurate measurements of maturation, perhaps this would be a better way of comparing children.

The Tecumseh Community Health Study (9) provided an opportunity to study the advisability of including age, height, and weight in establishing performance scales. In Tecumseh, Michigan, 99% of the children in grades 4 through 12 were given the AAHPER fitness tests and a trunk flexion and trunk extension test. Their ages, heights and weights were also recorded. In all, 1224 boys and 1061 girls were tested. Correlation coefficients between age, height, and weight and the various test scores were calculated. These are shown in Table 14–4. From Table 14–4 it appears that age is at least as clearly related to the fitness measurements as either height or weight. Furthermore, a boy or girl cannot alter his or her age or height, so if there is an appreciable correlation of either or both of these with the fitness scores, it seems logical to consider age and/or height in establishing standards. Therefore, the next step is to determine how much better the correlation would be if height is also considered with age rather than age alone. The statistical method by which this was done need not trouble the student. The results are shown in Table 14–5. The figures in this table can be interpreted as percentages and are derived from the correlation coefficients as explained in Chapter 3. Thus, the correlation of age and pull-ups for boys is 0.49 (Table 14–4). When this coefficient is squared and multiplied by 100 we get the first figure

TABLE 14–4
Correlation Coefficients between Age, Height, and Weight
and the Fitness Tests

Measurement	Ht	Wt	Pull-up arm hang	Tr. flex	Tr. exten.	Long jump	Shut. run	Sit-ups	50-yd run	Soft. throw	600-yd run
Boys											
Age	.85	.76	.49	.21	.38	.72	−.63	.25	−.73	.74	−.66
Height	—	.86	.34	.16	.41	.70	−.59	.25	−.69	.75	−.62
Weight	—	—	.18	.18	.32	.52	−.42	.13	−.50	.67	−.40
Girls											
Age	.74	.66	.02	.25	.36	.38	−.36	−.15	−.47	.51	−.25
Height	—	.77	−.04	.20	.38	.41	−.40	−.13	−.48	.49	−.24
Weight	—	—	−.28	.14	.23	.15	−.16	−.24	−.19	.41	.07

in Table 14–5, namely 24. This means that 24% of the variance in pull-ups is associated with age. The next column shows the percentage of the variance in pull-ups that is associated with age and height, namely 26%. The third column indicates how much of the pull-up score is associated with age, height, and weight.

The inclusion of weight in a classification index could be questioned regardless of its correlation with the fitness test scores because part of one's weight is constituted by bone and muscle, but part is attributed to fat. By considering body weight in the classification index, one is then, to some extent, giving the advantage to fat children, that is, raising the percentile rather than allowing the excess fat to lower the relative performance or score.

A study of Table 14–5 will indicate that in the case of boys, age and height or a combination of age, height, and weight accounts for very little more of the variance than simply age alone. In the case of girls, this is also true for most of the tests with regard to the addition of height. The addition of weight, however, accounts for considerably more of the variance in the flexed arm hang, the 600-yard run, the standing long jump and the 50-yard run, than does age and height alone. In almost every case, weight is negatively related to performance when the effects of age and height are taken out. Arm strength and speed over the ground as measured in these tests is thought of in terms of one's ability to move his own body weight. Correcting for body weight (i.e., including weight in a classification index) is therefore a questionable procedure.

In the case of boys, it is quite clear that if achievement standards are developed for each age, it is not necessary to be concerned about differences in height or weight among the children. Even with girls, age accounts for almost as much of the variance in fitness scores as does age and height. In the standing long jump, the shuttle run and the 50-yard run, height makes its greatest contribution, but even in these instances the increase in the amount of variance accounted for by the addition of height is only 4%. To demonstrate this in a very practical way, age-specific percentile ranks were developed

TABLE 14–5
Percent of the Variance in Fitness Test Score That Is
Associated with Child's Age, Age and Height, or Age,
Height, and Weight.

	Age	Age and height	Age, height, and weight
Boys:			
Pull-ups	24	26	33
Tr. flexion	5	5	5
Tr. extension	14	17	18
Stand. long jump	52	55	58
Shut. run	40	41	45
Sit-ups	6	7	10
50-yard run	53	55	59
Soft. throw	55	61	61
600-yard run	43	45	53
Girls:			
Arm hang	0	1	18
Tr. flexion	6	6	7
Tr. extension	13	16	17
Stand. long jump	14	18	26
Shut. run	13	17	24
Sit-ups	2	2	7
50-yard run	22	26	36
Soft. throw	26	29	29
600-yard run	6	7	25

for girls in these events. Next, the girls within each age group were subdivided into two groups using the median height as the dividing point. Percentile ranks were then developed for the lower half of the height distribution and also for the upper half, for each age group. Results of several representative ages for two of the events are shown in Tables 14–6 and 14–7. If we disregard height, we would use the middle column marked "all subjects" for age 11 in Table 14–6. A girl whose standing long jump score is 52 inches would be at the 50th percentile. If, on the other hand, she were in the lower half of the class in stature, we would use the left-hand column in age group 11. In this instance, 52 inches in the long jump would still place her at the 50th percentile. If she were among the taller girls in the class, a score of 52 inches would place her in the 45th percentile when compared to other girls in this half of the height distribution. Thus, if we were to develop two percentile achievement standards, one for the taller and one for the shorter girls, it would make a difference of about 5 percentile points. This is also true of the other two events and various age groups.

TABLE 14–6
Percentile Ranks for the Standing Long Jump
(in Inches). Girls: Age 11 and 15.

Percentile	Age 11			Age 15		
	Lower half of height distribution	All subjects	Upper half of height distribution	Lower half of height distribution	All subjects	Upper half of height distribution
95	66	67	68	77	78	79
90	64	64	65	73	74	75
85	60	61	63	71	70	69
80	60	60	61	68	68	68
75	59	59	60	65	64	64
70	59	59	59	64	64	63
65	56	58	58	64	63	61
60	54	56	56	63	61	60
55	53	54	55	61	60	60
50	52	52	54	59	59	58
45	50	51	52	58	57	57
40	48	49	50	55	55	55
35	48	48	49	55	55	55
30	45	47	48	53	54	54
25	45	45	46	51	52	53
20	44	44	44	50	51	51
15	43	43	43	49	49	49
10	40	41	41	46	46	43
5	38	38	37	44	41	37
N =	67	132	65	55	107	52

From the results presented, it appears clear that one can disregard height and weight, if achievement standards in these fitness tests are established for specific ages and for boys and girls separately.

This is essentially the conclusion of Gross and Casciani (4) and Espenschade (3). In the published national percentile tables for Canada using almost the same battery of tests (1), height and weight were disregarded and the tables appear only for sex- and age-specific groups.

A Word of Caution Many performance tests in physical education are not well standardized. If the gym floor is slippery, scores are poorer in such tests as the shuttle run or basketball dribble. Similarly, the ground surface out of doors affects running events significantly. The subjective grading of gymnastic skills—even some fitness tests—varies depending on the instructor. Hence, published standards in many tests should be accepted with caution or not at all. Furthermore, the methods of sampling on which published standards are based frequently leave something to be desired. Therefore, for many purposes it would behoove conscientious teachers to calculate performance standards using data from their own classes.

TABLE 14-7
Percentile Ranks for the Shuttle Run (in Seconds).
Girls: Age 12 and 16.

Percentile	Age 12				Age 16		
	Lower half of height distribution	All subjects	Upper half of height distribution	Lower half of height distribution	All subjects	Upper half of height distribution	
95	10.0	10.1	10.2	10.2	10.0	9.9
90	10.4	10.3	10.3	10.5	10.3	10.2
85	10.6	10.5	10.4	10.7	10.6	10.4
80	10.7	10.6	10.5	10.9	10.8	10.6
75	10.8	10.7	10.6	11.0	10.9	10.8
70	10.9	10.9	10.8	11.1	11.0	10.9
65	11.0	11.0	10.9	11.2	11.1	11.0
60	11.1	11.1	11.1	11.2	11.2	11.1
55	11.2	11.2	11.2	11.4	11.2	11.2
50	11.4	11.3	11.3	11.5	11.2	11.2
45	11.5	11.4	11.4	11.6	11.4	11.2
40	11.6	11.5	11.5	11.6	11.6	11.3
35	11.8	11.6	11.5	11.7	11.6	11.5
30	11.9	11.8	11.6	11.9	11.8	11.7
25	12.1	11.9	11.8	12.0	11.9	11.8
20	12.2	12.1	12.0	12.1	12.0	12.0
15	12.4	12.3	12.1	12.5	12.3	12.2
10	12.8	12.8	12.8	12.9	12.8	12.7
5	13.2	13.1	13.1	13.4	13.1	13.2
N =	66	136	70	47	97	50

REFERENCES

1. The Canadian Association for Health, Physical Education and Recreation, "The CAHPER fitness-performance test manual." Toronto: The Association, 1966.

2. American Association for Health, Physical Education and Recreation, *AAHPER Youth Fitness Test Manual.* Washington, D.C.: The Association, 1958.

3. Espenschade, A. S., "Restudy of Relationships between Physical Performance of School Children and Age, Height, and Weight." *Res. Quart.,* 34:144–153, 1965.

4. Gross, E. A. and J. A. Casciani, "The Value of Age, Height and Weight as a Classification Device for Secondary School Students in the Seven AAHPER

Youth Fitness Tests." *Res. Quart.,* 33: 51–58, 1962.

5. Hunsicker, P.A. and G. G. Reiff, "A Survey and Comparison of Youth Fitness, 1938–1965." U.S. Office of Education, Report of Cooperative Research Project No. 2418. Ann Arbor: University of Michigan, 1965.

6. Massey, B. W., "The Use of T-Scores in Physical Education." *Physical Educator,* 10:20–21, 1953.

7. Miller, K. D., "A Plea for the Standard Score in Physical Education." *Physical Educator,* 8:49–50, 1951.

8. Montoye, H. J., "A Plea for the Percentile Rank in Physical Education." *Physical Educator,* 8:112–113, 1951.

9. Montoye, H. J.; M. E. Frantz; and   Fitness for Children." *J. Sports Medicine*
A. J. Kozar, "The Value of Age, Height   *and Physical Fitness,* 12:174–179, 1972.
and Weight in Establishing Standards of

PROBLEMS · Chapter 14

1. Using the following 440-yard run times of 120 17-year-old boys, construct percentile achievement standards (i.e., a table similar to Table 14–3) giving the corresponding raw scores for each percentile listed. The times are given in seconds.

77	79	67	68	80	73	58	59	82	69
62	65	67	51	68	57	59	58	72	74
58	64	73	74	66	62	60	73	74	70
64	73	71	62	68	66	75	57	67	68
70	58	68	64	62	62	72	58	77	72
66	68	65	76	67	66	63	64	61	60
66	77	77	75	63	72	67	71	61	71
74	61	53	83	66	62	74	64	67	75
72	66	66	73	80	62	66	68	72	76
73	66	68	85	74	66	73	65	65	74
64	67	67	66	80	70	67	69	75	79
75	61	67	63	68	52	64	58	65	72

2. Construct percentile ranks similar to Table 14–3 for the following grip strength measures giving the corresponding raw scores for each percentile as was done in Table 14–3. These data are from a study of the effects of varying the setting of an adjustable grip dynamometer on the grip strength scores of men and women. The scores below are those scores made by 135 males tested in the study ranging in age from 5 to 52 years. The scores are for the dominant hand and are measured to the nearest one-half kilogram.

45.0	11.0	12.0	25.0	43.0	51.5	46.0	63.5	74.5
57.0	07.0	18.5	16.5	49.0	50.0	44.0	63.5	15.0
58.0	06.5	22.0	20.0	39.0	34.5	46.0	36.5	18.0
60.5	21.0	13.0	22.0	51.5	37.0	54.0	73.0	14.0
58.0	18.0	18.5	24.0	44.0	50.0	55.0	40.0	61.0
51.0	21.0	12.0	24.5	30.0	44.5	54.5	61.0	56.0
56.5	16.0	17.0	19.0	45.0	60.5	31.0	53.5	49.0
71.0	15.5	13.0	24.5	45.0	46.5	48.5	43.0	60.5
68.0	21.5	25.0	20.5	29.5	34.5	61.0	42.0	13.0
78.0	20.0	26.5	18.0	43.5	39.0	53.0	38.0	19.0
32.5	16.5	22.5	20.0	46.0	28.5	43.0	35.0	45.0
48.0	18.0	25.0	25.0	55.0	40.5	51.5	32.5	46.0
44.5	15.0	14.0	27.0	46.0	51.0	48.0	34.5	34.0
65.5	15.5	14.5	28.0	63.0	68.5	53.5	69.5	36.0
62.5	22.0	14.5	35.0	35.0	49.0	45.0	70.5	54.0

(From: Montoye, Henry J. and John A. Faulkner, "Determination of the Optimum Setting of an Adjustable Grip Dynamometer." *Res. Quart.,* 31:1:29–36, March 1964.)

3. The data presented below are from the Tecumseh study (unpublished data). They are trunk flexion measures on 107 eighth-grade girls. Construct percentile ranks for these data, giving the corresponding raw scores for each percentile listed as in Table 14–3. The scores are given to the nearest one-half inch.

12.0	13.0	12.0	8.0	16.0	16.5	13.0	10.5
13.5	12.5	12.5	13.0	8.0	16.5	11.0	9.5
17.0	11.0	10.5	14.0	13.0	13.5	13.0	12.5
15.0	12.0	13.0	9.5	13.0	13.5	12.0	13.5
14.5	10.5	14.0	13.5	11.0	10.5	13.0	12.0
14.5	11.0	14.5	14.0	14.5	10.5	10.5	16.0
13.5	11.5	11.5	13.0	16.0	11.0	14.0	12.5
13.0	12.0	15.0	9.0	13.5	14.0	14.5	10.0
13.0	13.5	13.0	12.0	16.0	12.5	13.0	14.5
12.5	15.0	16.5	10.0	9.0	12.0	15.0	
12.0	8.0	11.0	11.0	13.0	14.0	12.0	
13.5	9.0	16.0	13.5	9.0	11.5	13.0	
13.0	14.5	14.0	11.0	11.0	14.5	15.0	
11.0	16.0	12.0	12.5	14.5	14.5	10.5	

STUDY QUESTIONS • Chapter 14

1. Why is it necessary to be able to calculate percentile scores?

2. In dealing with scores on various tests, as, for example, broad jump, mile run, and push-ups, why should the raw scores not be averaged to determine an average score?

3. What are the advantages of percentile standards for use in school programs as compared to other types of scores?

4. If you desired grades on the Triple Jump to be distributed as follows:

   15% A (Excellent)   20% D (Inferior)
   20% B (Good)   15% E (Failure)
   30% C (Fair)

   what would be the raw score limits for each of these grade categories? Use the data presented in Table 14–3 and Figure 14–1.

5. How would you use mimeographed or printed achievement standards as a permanent profile record of each child?

6. For what purpose may percentile ranks be used other than grading?

7. Do you plan to group children on the basis of height or weight to develop percentile standards? Why?

8. In boys grades 4 through 12, which is more closely related to the AAHPER fitness tests, age, height, or weight? How do these relationships compare in girls in these grades?

9. Why is it unwise to raise the score on a fitness test because a boy or girl weighs more than the average?

TEST INTERPRETATION AND GRADING

15

Paul Hunsicker

Test interpretation

During the past decade, there has been a tremendous increase in the use of tests in physical education. The work of the American Alliance for Health, Physical Education and Recreation, and the President's Council on Physical Fitness have both contributed to the promotion of the Youth Fitness Test and in general have stimulated a nationwide interest in testing. While no precise figure is possible, it has been conservatively estimated that upward of 25 million boys and girls have been tested in physical fitness over the past ten years. While the discussion in this chapter will not be restricted to the interpretation of the Youth Fitness Test, the author has had an excellent opportunity to discuss problems of testing while directing the two national surveys of 1958 and 1965. Many of the comments offered represent a distillation of these discussions. The second part of the chapter will be concerned with problems of grading. A final section will touch on some recent developments in measurement and evaluation.

Traditionally, tests are given for any one or more of the following reasons:

1. To diagnose pupil's knowledge and performance abilities.
2. To improve instructional technique.

3. To serve as a basis for counseling and guidance.
4. To serve as a basis for grades.
5. To classify and group pupils.
6. To motivate pupils.
7. To provide data for reports of program progress.
8. To provide information for improving public relations.
9. To provide data for research.

The list is not in a priority order and may not be definitive, but in general covers most of the reasons for conducting testing programs. At this juncture, the reader should be reminded that no teacher should launch a testing program without some rather clearly defined objectives for so doing. Testing just for the sake of having a testing program is a waste of time for both pupil and teacher. The useless collection of data has not aided the utilization of tests in school programs.

To make tests truly functional, the results should be helpful in attaining the objectives of the program. The pupils should be told the results of the test and what relevance it has to their progress. Several basic principles should be mentioned at this point.

Know what the test measures

The teacher or consumer should certainly be aware of what is being measured by the test. This ties in with the basic concept of validity. While there is general agreement that validity refers to a test measuring what it purports to measure, there are inherent limitations in this definition. In the first place, a test may be valid at a particular maturation or skill level and invalid at a different one. Think of a scale used to weigh a baby which has a weight range of perhaps 25 or 30 pounds. Regardless of the precision instrumentation and the ounce gradation between pounds, the instrument is useless for a first-grader. The same criticism could be made of a sports skill test that has been developed for classroom use and then is applied to varsity players. In essence, the test is too simple and everyone makes a perfect score. To be useful, tests must discriminate ability levels!

Knowing the validity is extremely important in interpreting the results of a test. One can be considerably more secure in interpreting height, weight, and other objective measures than one can in interpreting subjective data. This is not to imply that you should avoid subjective test data, but remember to temper your interpretations accordingly. After all, when you, as a teacher, are asked to write a letter of recommendation for a student, many of the important attributes—loyalty, honesty, dedication—are evaluated subjectively. Can you imagine a prospective employer not being interested in these traits?

Know the reliability of the test

Test reliability refers to consistency on repeated trials. Obviously, any instrument used for quantitative measurement must have this characteristic. When dealing with human traits and abilities, it must be recognized that some are inherently more stable than others and consequently yield higher reliability coefficients. For instance, a person's body weight fluctuates considerably less during the course of the day than his pulse, blood pressure, or ability to throw a baseball. Consequently, any test-retest measure of weight should be more reliable than a similar comparison of pulse rate, blood pressure, or baseball throwing abilities. This is not to imply that because performance measures vary, they are necessarily unreliable. Basically, a good performer is a good performer on repeated trials although his scores may not be identical. After all, if people could perform athletic feats with precisely the same result on repeated trials there would be no need for a track meet. The coaches could get together and compare scores for the various events and points could be awarded accordingly. The fact that individual variance may be as great as it is makes a track meet or a horse race possible. In these instances, the variance is inherent in the performer and not due to the measurement device. Obviously, a tape measure or stop watch is a fairly reliable instrument.

Tests are fairly specific

Teachers and administrators all too frequently look for a three-item or four-item test battery that will meet all their test needs. This is impossible when viewed against the broad panorama of activities taught in physical education classes. When one thinks of a single objective like physical fitness it soon becomes apparent that any three-item or four-item test battery has limitations. Even single traits such as reaction time or flexibility are highly specific and the thought of using a single test as an indicator of all types of reaction time or flexibility is at best precarious.

Trying to measure something as complex as general motor ability and using the results in any meaningful specific sports instruction is time wasted in this writer's opinion. Sports skills are fairly specific and if you want to know how well pupils are able to perform in baseball you should measure them with a baseball skill test, not a general motor ability test. The same holds for swimming, basketball, football, or any other sports skill.

Tests are indicators

A physician taking a patient's temperature is not interested in temperature *per se*. But if the reading is above "normal" he recognizes the possibility of an infection being present. This is frequently the case in interpreting physical fitness test scores.   The number of pull-ups a pupil might be able to do is important as an indicator of arm and shoulder girdle strength.   If the pupil's score is low, a teacher does not recommend merely practicing pull-ups, but outlines a program that involves rope climbing, work on the side horse, rings, or parallel bars, or some weight training activities.   The same logic should be applied to other test data.

Test scores are samples

Because of time and staff limitations, it is virtually impossible to test every aspect of a field of interest.   People developing tests know this and the technique of weighing components statistically is one method of coping with the problem. The very selection of a test item for inclusion in a test battery attaches a priority and importance to this particular item.   The test battery that includes the most important aspects of the trait tested does the best job of measuring that ability.

Another facet of testing is the number of times the pupil is tested.   A single exposure, or "one-shot," testing program has serious limitations and any interpretation based on a test of this sort should certainly be guarded.   This leads to the next topic, namely, serial testing.

Serial testing

This refers to the administration of tests on a regular basis, even if only annually.   If one is interested in assessing a pupil's ability in baseball batting, he does not arrive at an answer by giving the pupil merely one time at bat.   The same holds true for interpreting any test.   One obvious advantage of serial testing is the possibility of establishing a baseline for the individual pupil.   This is better than comparing the pupil's score with a group norm.   Serial testing can have life-long implications and can sensitize the pupil to the desirability of retaining certain baseline figures.   A good example of this is weight control, where it would be possible to establish a desirable weight for a college senior that he could keep in mind through life.   Once this is fixed it is a relatively simple matter to check weekly or monthly and take whatever steps are necessary to keep weight within a few pounds of the desired limit.

The single index score

All too often teachers or administrators want to combine test scores into a single index.   For example, they will average the seven test scores in the AAHPER Youth Fitness Test to obtain a single index of fitness.   This is a precarious procedure and should not be encouraged for several reasons.

First, the interrelationships among the seven tests are not high. If they were, there would be no point in administering seven tests—one or two would suffice! Each test is an indicator of a different component of fitness and by using a composite, such as the average, one loses the diagnostic possibilities of the individual test item. Retaining the separate scores permits the teacher to spot specific components of fitness that are low and with this information make suggestions for improvement.

Second, the tests are not statistically weighted as to their contribution to fitness. By averaging the test scores, one assumes that each test contributes equally to the measure of physical fitness. This is highly unlikely.

While the thought of having a single index score to represent a wide variety of traits has appeal, at least from an administrative viewpoint, the practice should be discouraged because it is usually unsound.

Grading

Grading is probably the phase of teaching that has been slighted the most in physical education. This represents a grave professional error. Here is one way of communicating with the parents that in all too many instances has been either ignored or done poorly. This section will examine some facets of the grading process and explore possibilities for improving current practices.

As a point of departure, ask a college admissions officer to look at a high school student's transcript and give you an interpretation of what the grades in physical education represent. The possibilities defy the imagination! In the first place, he would have no idea what the content of the course was unless he happened to be personally familiar with the particular whims of the teacher in question. Secondly, he would have no idea what the teacher included in his grading plan.

Grades have been awarded for such diverse attributes as attendance, dress, taking a shower, physical fitness, rules interpretation, posture, good citizenship, effort, improvement, and performance. In a few instances, teachers almost apologize for the last item. When one recognizes that in the majority of school systems a single letter or numerical grade is awarded, one can appreciate the hopelessness of trying to derive anything meaningful from what appears on the transcript. To add to the chaos, teachers seldom agree on the weighting they place on the factors that go into a grade. Actually, the situation need not be so grim when one reviews some of the following points.

Many of the activities we teach can be measured with a tape, a stop watch, or other objective measuring technique. For instance, a score in bowling, golf, or archery, to name a few, should be the same regardless of who did the scoring. Certainly the task is simpler than that which confronts the teacher of English, history, or any of the other social studies where testing is apt to be more subjective. The problem of establishing any anchoring reference point in these disciplines is certainly more difficult than in physical education. In sports performance, for example, the field is full of meaningful reference points; the .300 hitter or 20-game winner in baseball, the par golfer, or the 4-minute miler are suggestive of the possibilities. Obviously these represent top-flight levels of performance that are appreciated by any sports enthusiast but equally objective performances could be established for the less talented. Certainly obtaining objective performance data in our field should not be a problem.

As a general principle, it is probably wise to have the grading plan in physical education conform to that of other courses in the school. That is, if a letter system is used in other courses, this should be the pattern for physical education. Don't settle for a plan that sets your field off as an outcast!

A pupil should not be penalized because teachers differ. This can happen in large systems where multiple sections are taught and where the teachers have not reached some consensus on the method of awarding grades. While human differences in personality are always present in any faculty, every effort should be exerted to minimize their effects on the pupil's grade.

Another point that is frequently overlooked in grading is the failure to inform pupils of the bases for their grades. Not only should they be apprised of the factors that will be considered in arriving at a grade but they should also be aware of how much each contributes to the final outcome. This information should be made available at the start of the semester at which time it would be appropriate to invite student input into the grading system. Now it might be appropriate to discuss pertinent factors related to the procedure of arriving at a grade and some of the reasons for awarding one.

Few teachers view grading as an easy assignment but rather look on the process as a "thorny chestnut" that has to be dealt with. While many educators have vented their views on the shortcomings of grades, the possibility of eliminating them before anyone suggests a better method is remote. Basically, the grade symbolizes the teacher's judgment of how well the pupil has performed in mastering what the teacher believes important. It sounds simple enough, but here are some of the complications. Does one use an absolute standard or a relative one? The former presupposes that the objectives have been clearly delineated and the possibility of every pupil earning the top grade does exist. The other alternative, a relative standard, places the pupils in competition with one another with the thought that the variance in performance will result in some type of "curve" suitable for grading. This method usually meant that the bulk of the grades would be C's with some D's and B's and a few A's and perhaps E's. The performance of the group is actually the anchoring reference for the system and each pupil is in competition with his fellow-pupils. Strict adherence to this procedure has been criticized and it has been suggested that the pupil be in competition with standards of excellence rather than with his classmates. The climate for learning under those conditions lends itself more readily to having pupils assist one another. This procedure for grading enjoys its greatest popularity in lower-level college courses in large universities where course enrollments may run over a thousand students. While "curve grading" may still exist at these institutions in advanced courses, the "curve" is tempered by reducing the number of Ds and Es.

Another possibility, and one that is practiced by many teachers, is a combination of absolute and relative standards. In fact, it is extremely difficult to envision a purely absolute standard. It could be absolute for a particular class or group but is undoubtedly relative to some human performance of the past. In the case of relative standards, adjustments are frequently made to conform with the teacher's concept of goals and course objectives. Every experienced teacher realizes that there will be some year-to-year differences in performance and that one class will not be as capable as another. This is usually reflected by the grading system—the overall average is not identical nor is the variance. It is apparent that all grading systems have some pitfalls and the reader may well pose the question, "What would you suggest?"

A number of years ago the author had the opportunity of devising a Performance Record for the Summer Youth Fitness Program at The University of Michigan. This was to be mailed to the parents at the conclusion of the six-week session. The task was accepted as a genuine challenge to develop something out of the ordinary. In reflecting on the problem, the following thoughts seemed to be germane to the topic: In any worthwhile educational experience, some change is going to take place. The nature of the change may be obvious, such as a pupil becoming stronger or more highly skilled. On the other hand, it could be equally meaningful, but quite subtle, such as a change in a person's philosophy or value system. In any event, a Report Form should reflect the change whenever possible. Along with this, some evidence as to where a pupil's performance is in relation to a peer group should be shown. Parents and pupils are also interested in the amount of improvement that has taken place (this goes back to reflecting the change). A copy of the end-result appears as Figure 15–1. Colored paste-on dots can be used in place of the symbols making the chart more attractive.

At the outset of the program, the boys and girls are given the performance tests indicated on the Record. These are graded Superior, Above Average, Average, Below Average, and Poor and the indicated color assigned to the performance. This is posted by means of a colored gummed dot in the cell marked "0–0" and outlined by the heavy black lines. During the last week of the program, the boys and girls are retested and a percentage change from the initial test is calculated. These performances are also classified Superior, Above Average, etc., and the appropriate color selected to indicate the level of performance. The location of this colored gummed dot (lower border) indicates the percent change according to the scale at the left of the chart. When the Performance Record is completed, it is possible to tell at a glance the changes that have occurred, the level of performance in comparison with a peer group, and the individual strengths and weaknesses.

The procedure described has been in operation for a number of years and has been well received by parents. Some teachers have questioned the feasibility of the process because of the seemingly large amount of clerical work needed. In actual practice, you could have the pupils assume a good share of this and keep the record as a personal performance record. The items tested would have to be adapted to the program, but the thought of hav-

THE UNIVERSITY OF MICHIGAN
DEPARTMENT OF PHYSICAL EDUCATION FOR MEN
YOUTH FITNESS PROGRAM

Performance Record of ______________________________

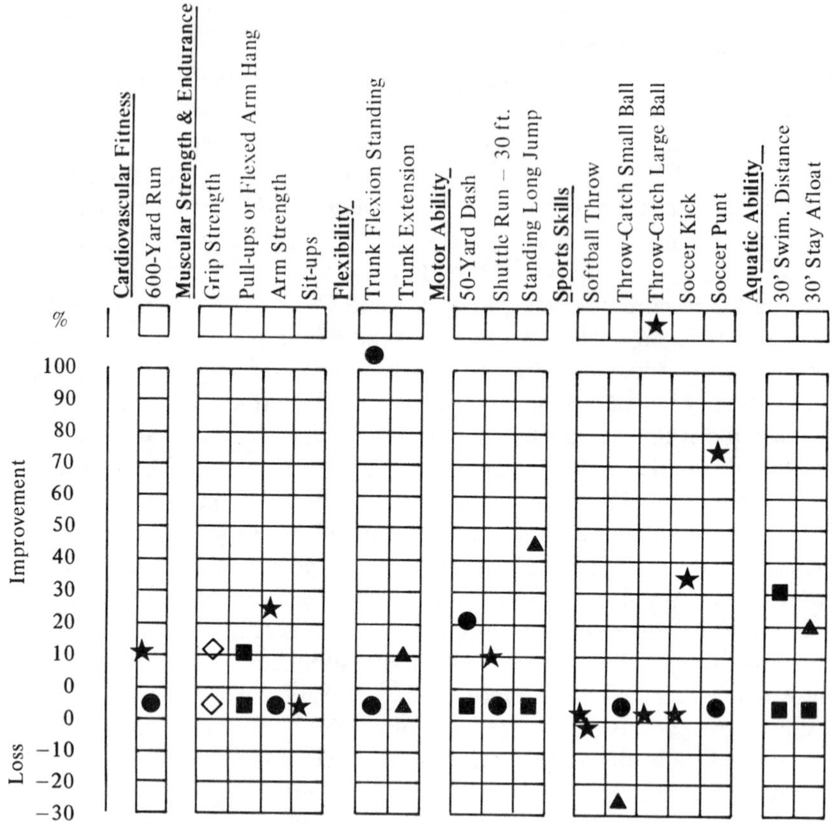

GYMNASTIC SKILLS: Successfully performed 14 stunts for a rating of ▲
AQUATIC SKILLS: Successfully performed 8 skills for a rating of ■

Explanation of Grading:

1. The cell marked "0–0" and outlined by the heavy black lines indicates the child's score at the beginning of the program. This is coded in the following manner:

Superior	★
Above average	●
Average	▲
Below average	■
Poor	◇

2. The child's improvement or loss is calculated in terms of percentage with his initial score as a base

$$\% \text{ change} = \frac{FS - IS}{IS} \times 100$$

FS = Final Score IS = Initial Score

The location of the colored dot (lower border) indicate the percent change according to the scale at the left of the chart. The color of the dot indicates your child's classification on the final test according to the above categories.

FIGURE 15–1. Performance record. Youth Fitness Program, Department of Physical Education, University of Michigan.

ing a reporting form which tells the parents where the pupil stands in relation to a peer group and the change that has occurred during the time period does have appeal.

As a final plea, please recognize the value of a meaningful grading system as a means of communication to pupils, parents, and school administrators. Remember whatever you single out as the bases for grading should be the factors you consider important.

Recent challenges in tests and measurements

During the last decade, a variety of new developments in education have posed additional challenges for educational measurement specialists. One concept, performance contracting, had a brief appeal to school boards several years ago but has lost some of its glitter as the result of several trial programs. Other ventures might prove more lasting.

The general demand by the public for greater educational accountability and the attendant innovations in budget procedures should stimulate greater interest in testing and evaluating programs. Some systems are using Planning, Programming and Budgeting Systems (PPBS) as a means of identifying the cost of the outputs of a program. The need for better tests that will quantify outputs should be obvious.

A brief look at the problem should convince the reader of the magnitude of the challenge. While it is relatively simple to quantify performance that can be measured with a stop-watch, a tape-measure, or a numerical count, the task of measuring sportsmanship, as one example, is considerably more complex. Other traits, equally as important, compound the challenge.

Several other recent developments add to the future demands for better tests and evaluative criteria. It is not the purpose of this chapter to give any in-depth treatment of these topics but they should be mentioned.

A number of schools and state departments of public instruction are developing Performance Based Teacher Education programs for the universities and Performance Objectives for the elementary and secondary schools. If this trend continues, the demand for functional testing programs will be staggering. If the need is met with high quality tests, these programs should have a salutary effect on the field.

REFERENCES

1. Avedisian, C., "PPBS—Its Implications for Physical Education." *Administrative Theory and Practice in Athletics and Physical Education.* Chicago: Athletic Institute, 1973, pp. 111–118.

2. Chauncey, H. and J. E. Dobbin, *Testing: It's Place in Education Today.* New York: Harper and Row, 1963, p. 224.

3. Cureton, L. W., "The History of Grading Practices." *NCME,* Vol. 2, No. 4, May 1971.

4. David, F. B., *Educational Measurements and Their Interpretation.* Belmont, Calif.: Wadsworth, 1964.

5. Doherty, V. and W. Hathaway, "Goals and Objectives in Planning and Evaluation: A Second Generation." *NCME,* Vol. 4, No. 1, Fall 1972.

6. Doppelt, J. E. and H. G. Seashore, "How Effective Are Your Tests?" *Test Service Bulletin,* No. 37, New York: Psychological Corp., June 1949, pp. 4–10.

7. Educational Testing Service, *New Approaches to Individualizing Instruction.* Princeton, N.J.: ETS, p. 142.

8. Jansen, U. H., "Marking and Reporting Procedures in the Secondary Schools of Texas." Texas Study of Secondary Education, *Research Bulletin,* No. 32, December 1960.

9. Jarrett, C. D., "Marking and Reporting Practices in the American Secondary School." *Peabody J. of Education,* 41: 36–48, July 1963.

10. Lessinger, L., *Every Kid a Winner: Accountability in Education.* New York: Simon and Schuster, 1970, p. 239.

11. Lindquist, E. F. (ed.), *Educational Measurement.* Washington, D.C.: American Council on Education, 1963, p. 819.

12. Lyman, H. B., *Test Scores and What They Mean.* Englewood Cliffs, N.J.: Prentice-Hall, 1963, p. 223.

13. McGraw, L., "Principles and Practices for Assigning Grades in Physical Education." *JOHPER,* 35:24–25, February 1964.

14. McLaughlin, K. F., *Interpretation of Test Results.* Washington, D.C.: Office of Education, *Bulletin* No. 7, p. 63, 1964.

15. May, Robert E., "A Dean of Education Speaks," *JOHPER,* 36:49+, September 1965.

16. Michigan Department of Education, *Minimal Performance Objectives for Physical Education in Michigan.* Lansing, Mich.: The Department, 1974, p. 116.

17. Moughamian, H., "General Overview of Trends in Testing: Interpretation of Scores." *Rev. of Ed. Res.,* 35:10, February 1965.

18. Needham, John, et al., "Improving Test Interpretation Through Films." *Voc. Guid. Quart.,* 12:141–44, Winter 1963–1964.

19. Rothney, John W. M., "Evaluating and Reporting Pupil Progress." American Educational Research Association Series, "What Research Says." No. 7, March 1955.

20. Schutz, Richard E., "Measurement Aspects of Performance Contracting." *NCME,* Vol. 2, No. 3, March 1971.

21. The University of Michigan, The Center for Research on Learning and Teaching. Memo No. 4, "The Assignment of Grades" (John Milholland). January 1964.

22. The University of Michigan, The Center for Research on Learning and Teaching. Memo No. 18, "Grades." June 1966.

23. The University of Michigan, The Center for Research on Learning and Teaching. Memo No. 46, "Grading and Evaluation." October 1971.

STUDY QUESTIONS • Chapter 15

1. Give an example of how one might use tests to accomplish each of the nine purposes of testing listed in the second paragraph of this chapter.

2. What is meant by serial testing?

3. Why does the author discourage the concept of a "single index score"?

4. In light of current practices in grading in physical education, what might a grade of "B" in a high school physical education course mean? What might enter into the determination of the grade? Is grading uniform in different schools?

5. What is meant by absolute and relative standards? What are the advantages and disadvantages of each?

6. What are the main features of the Performance Record for the University of Michigan Summer Youth Fitness Program?

7. Discuss the advisability of including each of the following in a grading plan in physical education at the Junior High School level.

   a. attendance
   b. taking a shower
   c. physical fitness
   d. rules of sports
   e. sportsmanship
   f. posture
   g. attitude
   h. good citizenship
   i. effort
   j. improvement
   k. performance

8. You are teaching six classes of physical education three times per week, 30 children per class (two 4th grade, two 5th grade, and two 6th grade classes). You have complete freedom in reporting the performance (or grade) to the parents. What factors would you include in the grade? Why? What form would the report to the parents take? Why?

ORGANIZATION AND ADMINISTRATION OF TESTS AND MEASUREMENTS IN A SCHOOL PROGRAM

16

James Oestriech

The primary purpose of a school testing program is to provide opportunities for learning. The most important attitude to develop is that each student apply himself to the best of his abilities, learn more about himself and the skills being taught, and realistically appraise his own progress in skill development. His final score, his performance in relation to other students, or his position in comparison to standardized scores are of secondary importance. This is true for the simple self-testing stunts at the lower elementary level as well as for the highly competitive fitness tests in high school.

Before a testing program can be initiated, two important questions must be answered. *Why* are measurements desired? For grouping pupils for instruction, grading, or determining pupil status and progress? Many testing programs have failed because the teacher did not give proper consideration to the *why* of tests and measurements. The second question is: *What* should be measured? Skill level, fitness, growth, or knowledge? The success of any testing program depends on the clarity and preciseness with which these two questions are answered.

An effective tests and measurements program frequently may: (1) improve student knowledge, (2) evaluate student progress, (3) evaluate the

Appreciation is expressed to Elizabeth Flinchbaugh for her contribution to the chapter as it appeared in the first edition and to Greg Kingdon for his help in preparing the revision.

physical education and health program in the school, (4) provide for integration with other areas of the school curriculum, and (5) involve and inform the parents and community. All of these goals can be reached through proper planning.

Guides for administering a testing program

Orientation

Before an intelligent approach can be made to any problem, one must familiarize oneself with the situation. No one set of rules can be established that will cover all situations, but once the purpose for testing has been determined, some general suggestions are in order. Keep in mind at all times the relative importance of accuracy and economy of time. The orientation process can be divided into two categories; orientation for the teachers, and orientation of the students.

Orientation for the teacher

1. Selection of tests. The initial consideration is what is to be measured and for what purpose. Is it to measure pupil progress for diagnostic or grading purposes? Is it to measure the effectiveness of the class activity for the purpose of evaluating the educational program? Next, one must consider the factors of reliability and validity and time required. These factors should be weighed carefully in terms of the objectives for testing. For more details concerning the selection of tests, refer to Chapter 3.

2. Know the tests. Complete understanding is necessary to administer the tests properly. Before a person administers any test, he or she should be aware of the limitations of that test, taking into consideration the age group for which the test is best suited, the equipment and facilities necessary, and the best method for administering the tests. Also, it is a good idea to find out if norms are available. If not, it is possible to construct norms. Norms are valuable in interpreting results but the value of national norms for particular school systems should not be overemphasized.

3. Arranging equipment and facilities. Attention should be given to course layout and necessary markings. (See Figures 16–1 and 16–2.) These should be reasonably accurate within the level desired. Any modification of course may affect the interpretation of scores. In setting up equipment, there are a number of things that should be taken into consideration. The equipment required and the way in which it is set up will vary depending on the conditions under which the tests are going to be administered. Careful placement of equipment is important to allow for ease of scoring and smooth flow during the testing. Also, factors of safety should be carefully considered. At the elementary level, test markings should be painted on the outdoor hard-surface

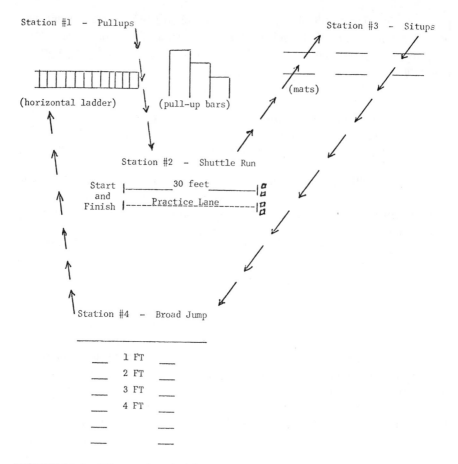

FIGURE 16–1.   Diagram for administering the Youth Fitness
Test: Indoor stations.   (Example of test battery layout.)

play area so the children can make use of them at recess and after school for
self-testing.

Failure to recognize the importance of the steps outlined here may result
in too much time being spent for a particular test.   The natural tendency is to
blame the design of the test whereas, in truth, the fault frequently lies with the
teacher and his or her failure to realize the necessity for orientation.

Orientation of students

Good student orientation will make conduct of the testing smooth and elicit
maximum effort.   The students should be informed of the purpose of the test
and how the test results will be used.   Explain what is being measured and
why it is important.   Familiarize students with equipment required and correct
procedure for performing the tests.   Advance demonstration and practice
should be used whenever possible.

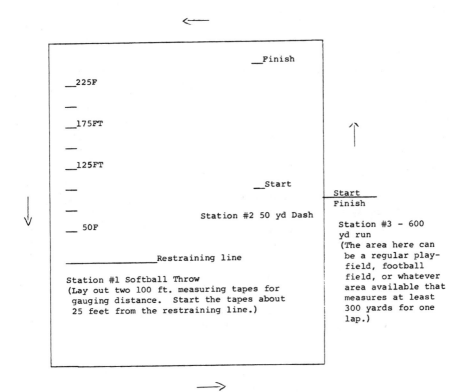

The students should rotate to the next station as they complete the
testing at the previous station. For the 600 yd. run test 4-6 students
at a time. Under ideal conditions, half the class may take the test
at one time while partners in the other half of the class note the
running times.

FIGURE 16–2. Diagram for administering the Youth Fitness
Test: Outdoor stations.

Students should be motivated to put forth maximum effort. At some
age levels it is necessary to encourage the students to greater effort. Older
girls, particularly, tend not to care about excelling. A pupil will do better
when told the general purpose of the test and method of scoring. If assistants
are to be used, they should be given definite suggestions on how to motivate
the students to maximum effort. Some suggestions are: (1) showing an
interest in the pupil's performance; (2) using words of encouragement; (3)
praising good performance; (4) repeating certain key words to remind the
pupil of the correct technique; and (5) recognizing increased proficiency. The
poorly skilled should not be embarrassed.

Many times, it will be necessary to use students to administer tests and
record results. The amount of training necessary depends to a great extent on
the type of tests to be given. The importance of accuracy should be impressed
on the students at all times.

If student assistants are used, they should be trained in: (1) procedures
for properly administering the tests; (2) techniques of each individual item;

and (3) the method of scoring. Detailed instruction on the use of special equipment, such as stop watches or dynamometers, is very important.

Standardized directions should be developed and they should be simple and concise. If possible, the directions should be written out. The student assistants should go through the entire test as subjects. This will help them become familiar with the correct techniques and also help them feel that they are a part of the testing program.

Mechanics

Once the why and what of testing have been answered, thought must be given to how the tests will be conducted. All procedures concerning the mechanics of administering the tests should be carefully planned in advance. Nothing should be left to chance. All ways and means for economical administration of tests should be studied. Many teachers cringe at the thought of all the mechanics involved in testing. Actually it is only after these factors have been considered that tests can be conducted in an effective and economical way. The major areas requiring detailed planning are class organization, the order for giving the tests, demonstration of techniques and procedures, the recording of scores, and provisions for safety.

Class organization. The basic organization for testing would depend primarily on two factors—the type of test, and the characteristics of the group being tested. The most commonly used systems will be discussed.

Mass testing. In this method one examiner can explain and demonstrate all test items and administer them to all students. The students are paired and while one-half of the group takes the test, the partners score. This method saves time and should be used whenever the items and purpose of the test are appropriate.

Squad method. If squads are already set up in class, it is simple to have each squad tested on a particular item by the squad leader or a trained assistant. After all squad members have been tested, the squad can rotate to another test station. If permanent class squads are not already designated, temporary groups may be established.

Station-to-station method. Frequently with large groups, this is the best method of organization. Here students rotate from one station to another as they complete the tests. It may be that one or more items are slower to administer than others. In this case, two stations may be organized for the slower items.

Task orientation. When administering self-testing items, especially at the elementary level, it may be appropriate to give directions for a task-orientated approach, for example, "You must do three testings today. After you do these, you may retest on them if you wish."

Combination.   Occasionally it is best to combine two of the above methods. For instance, in many cases it is expedient to have the squads rotate from one test to another on a station-to-station basis.   Often, the mass technique may be used for one or two items and then a shift made to the squad for a station-to-station method for the others.   No one plan or organization will suit all situations.   In any event, all test items should be explained and demonstrated to all members of the class before the testing is started.

Order of tests.   When the order of test items has not been suggested by the author of the test battery, an order must be established.   Make sure the test items that are close together in order do not require using the same set of muscles in the same way.   Adjacent test items should complement each other. For example, don't give pull-ups, then push-ups, then sit-ups.   A better order would be pull-ups, sit-ups, and then push-ups.   At the elementary level, motivation may be so high that there may be a need, to avoid fatigue, to limit the number of tests administered on a given day.   If an endurance test is given as part of the battery (the 600-yard run-walk, for example) that should be the only test for the day.   Under these circumstances, it would be advisable to have a low organized activity that children can join into as they finish the testing, such as kickball.

Recording scores.   One of the most important considerations in testing is the recording of scores.   This must be done quickly and accurately.   All scoring forms should be designed and prepared in advance.   Some suggested methods are:

Class roll sheet.   The class sheet may have the names of all class members and spaces for the scores and other necessary data.   This method can be used when there is one examiner who administers and scores all tests.   Sometimes such cards are used as cumulative records when scores from individual cards are transferred to them.

Squad cards.   The squad card is used when the squads rotate from station-to-station.   The squad card goes with the squad.   It is a smaller version of the class roll sheet.

Individual score card.   In many instances the best method is the individual score card which each pupil carries from station to station.   It is designed for the specific test battery and might have spaces for the pupil's name, class, age, weight, height, and scores.   This card is used when the students score each other or when they rotate from station to station and are scored by a trained tester.

NAME			TEACHER		CLASS
1	2	3	4	5	6
PT ____	PT ____	PT ____	PT ____	PT ____	PT ____
FT ____	FT ____	FT ____	FT ____	FT ____	FT ____
KT ____	KT ____	KT ____	KT ____	KT ____	KT ____
____	____	____	____	____	____
____	____	____	____	____	____
____	____	6 WK Gr. ☐	____	____	6 WK Gr. ☐
____	____	SEM.	____	____	SEM.
GRADE ☐	GRADE ☐	GRADE ☐	GRADE ☐	GRADE ☐	GRADE ☐
CODE:	PT – Performance Test	FT – Fitness Test	KT – Knowledge Test		

FIGURE 16–3a. Health and physical education grade card.

Student help can be effectively utilized for recording scores. Three main methods of scoring are:

By partners. This method is generally used when the tests are administered on a mass basis. One administrator administers the tests but they are scored by the partner who is not taking the test at that time. It is possible to have partners scoring within the squad.

By squad leaders. When tests are administered on a squad basis, generally they are administered and scored by a squad leader. The training of the squad leader should be done before the day of testing.

Trained testers. When tests are administered on a station-to-station basis, scoring is generally done by trained testers who have been instructed in the method of scoring at a training session before the day of testing. The outstanding advantage of this method is the greater uniformity in scoring that is generally achieved. Parent volunteers can be used as testers/recorders. This is an excellent means of promoting community involvement and understanding.

Self-recording. This method can be used when the instructor is confident that the students completely understand the test and can show their level of proficiency when called on.

Previous years' scores should be made available so that students can see their progress.

Demonstration. A demonstration of each test item is usually desirable. Demonstration techniques should be planned and learned in advance. The

HEALTH FITNESS RECORD

NAME							CLASS	
	1		2		3		4	
	Raw Score	%ile	Raw Score	%ile	Raw Score	%ile	Raw Score	%ile
Age								
Height								
Weight								
Pull-ups								
Sit-ups								
50 Yd. Dash								
600 Yd. Run								
Shuttle Run								
Broad Jump								
Vertical Jump								
Softball Throw								

RATING _____

FIGURE 16–3b. Health fitness card.

demonstration may accompany the explanation or follow it. The person demonstrating should have the attention of all the subjects. He should present the test first as a whole and then stress the important details. The class members should be placed so they can easily hear the explanation and see the demonstration. It is usually a good idea to demonstrate all the items before any testing is done. An opportunity should be given the students to ask questions during or shortly after each demonstration.

Safety. Testing is usually greeted by pupils with excitement and enthusiasm. They like self-testing activities and the challenge of most tests. Safeguards must be observed to prevent accidents. A warm-up period is desirable to prevent pulled muscles as well as to insure maximum performance. Leaders should be warned to look for certain hazards, and the class should be instructed in special precautionary procedures. Make sure that the whole testing area is under direct eye observation and that students watch each other. If necessary, medical examinations should precede the administration of all strenuous physical tests. When exercise is contraindicated or where there is doubt, a student should be excused. It is advisable to check in advance with other school professional staff members—teachers, counselors, nurses, and administrators—to identify health problems that should limit student participation or performance.

How much time does it take?

Certainly the amount of time necessary to administer a test is one of the factors that should be taken into consideration. However, when one considers that taking many tests in physical education is a learning experience, the amount of time spent is of secondary importance.

Most established tests, along with indicating the equipment and facilities necessary and the proper technique and procedures for administering the tests, also will give the average amount of time necessary to administer the tests properly. This time is based on a properly organized and effective approach to the testing. This means that the amount of time spent on organization before the tests are actually administered will determine how effectively time will be used during the testing. Here is a check list of ten items that help in the effective administration of tests.

Ten checks for the effective administration of tests

1. The basic purpose of the test is to measure _____
    _____

2. The test results are to be used for _____

3. Equipment and facilities needed

    Stop watches _____   Others

    Tape measure _____

    Chalk   _____   _____

    Pencils   _____   _____

    Score cards   _____   _____

4. Time required to administer the complete test   _____

5. Basic organizational details

    a. Class organization   b. Order of test time

        _____ Mass testing   1.   5.

        _____ Squads   2.   6.

        _____ Station-to-station   3.   7.

        _____ Combination   4.   8.

A diagram showing the location of each station might be very helpful. (Figures 16–1 and 16–2)

6. Student motivation (a strong statement giving a meaningful explanation of the reason for the testing)
7. Explanation and demonstration of:
    a. Proper technique for performing each test item
    b. Method of scoring
    c. Standardized directions for order of tests, rotation, etc.
8. Training student assistants on
    a. Procedure for administering the tests
    b. Techniques of individual items
    c. Method of scoring
9. Method of handling scoring

Recorded on	Recorded by
_____ Class roll	_____ Partner
_____ Squad card	_____ Squad leader
_____ Individual score card	_____ Trained tester
_____ Other	_____ Other

10. Safety factors (list general and special precautionary procedures)

After the tests have been administered, time should be spent, using this check sheet as a guide, evaluating the effectiveness of the test. Some questions that should be asked are: If I were to give this test again, what changes would I make? Was this the best test to use? Were the test items arranged in the best possible order? Was it necessary to include all the items? Was this the best method of class organization in scoring? Was the amount of time spent proportionate to the amount of learning that took place? This check sheet and your evaluation should then be filed away for future reference.

Practical application

Some common pitfalls

A formal treatise on tests and measurements in a school program can be very misleading. The inexperienced person often becomes frustrated by the time and energy required to prepare for and administer Test Battery "X" as outlined in the college text. Teachers can negatively influence students by creating a do-or-die atmosphere in their presentations. The testing program should be approached and presented as an integrated, on-going part of the total program. Taking tests should be a learning experience in itself.

With due consideration to the underlying scientific principles of the tests, there is no harm in the teacher modifying tests to better fit the particular situation. The researcher, in administering the 600-yard run as a test of endurance, may time each participant separately to obtain the most accurate measurement. What does the physical education teacher do when he or she has 40 students in a class? Run one student at a time? If the teacher runs them in groups of 10 or 20 and calls off the times as they cross the finish line, this will cause hardly a sufficient amount of error to render the test invalid.

Using tests in a meaningful way

Tests need not always be given at the beginning or end of a unit of instruction. Tests can also be used throughout the unit as a learning experience. This can be done in a number of ways:

Let students take skill or performance tests as they feel ready.

Allow for retesting as much as possible.

Analyze students' performance as they are tested to help them better understand the fundamentals necessary for improving performance.

Tests should indicate to the teacher what progress is being made by the students and when reteaching is necessary.

Integrating fitness tests into the teaching unit

There is much to be said for administering a battery of tests at one time. One might, for example, want to survey the fitness level of a group of students at a particular time. The beginning or end of a school year might be such a time. There can also be value in testing specific fitness items at the time the class is involved in a discussion of the relationship between the activity and its contribution to fitness. Whenever feasible, testing should be administered in such a way as to reveal a meaningful relationship to the over-all curriculum. The average basketball enthusiast would be quick to rate this sport high in terms of its contribution to strength of the arms and shoulders. The administration of the pull-up test at the beginning and end of a basketball unit should furnish some interesting data. Does basketball, as an activity, help to develop strength of the arms and shoulders? How about soccer for endurance? Wrestling for agility? Swimming for leg power? Field hockey for strength of the abdominals? Stunts and tumbling for flexibility?

Interpreting physical education through testing

Students are curious about how they rank when compared to others. Tests are available that can readily measure level of skill, fitness, or knowledge of a particular sport or activity. These tests give convincing results to indicate strengths and weaknesses of the individual or a class as a whole. The results can serve as an argument for having calisthenics, for a program which includes a variety of activities, for discussion and explanation concerning rules, strategy, etc.

Evaluating the total program through
tests and measurements

One of the major purposes of tests and measurements should be to evaluate the effectiveness of the physical education program. This is effectiveness in terms of meeting the goals of the program. A good program will have clearly defined goals of both an immediate and long range nature. Tests can measure:

The present level of performance of a student.

The amount of learning (change) that a student has experienced over a specified period of time. This also reflects the effectiveness of the teaching.

Tests show:

The strengths of a program.

The need to expand or reduce a program.

The worth of a particular method of teaching.

The need for more emphasis on a particular phase of a program.

Relation to the total school curriculum

Tests and measurements in the area of physical education should serve to shed light on other subject areas in the curriculum. A strong total school curriculum can only result when there is a constant interplay between all the individual subject areas. In some situations, the information obtained in one area of instruction might provide facts that give meaning to a topic when discussed under the jurisdiction of another subject area. Some specific examples are:

Use of age, height and weight measurements by the classroom teacher when discussing growth and development or the guidance counselor when analyzing student progress.

Use of knowledge of bones, muscles, joints, etc., as discussed in the science class and by the physical education teacher in explaining basic principles of movement, use of bones for support, and use of levers in throwing.

Use of basic mathematical principles as explained in the mathematics class and by the physical education teacher when interpreting the results of tests, the meaning of standardized scores, and percentile ranking.

Reporting to parents

The job is not done when the program is organized and administered in such a way that the students and teachers in the school have a complete understanding. The parents should, and in most cases do, want to know what's happening and why. This can be accomplished in a number of ways:

Give a demonstration at a PTA meeting. If you want to go a step further, have the parents participate by taking some of the tests.

Periodically make a complete report to the parents as to what's happening in your program. This can be done through the PTA Newsletter. If your PTA does not have one, make a newsletter of your own. The local newspaper can also be used.

Supplement the standard reporting of "A," "B," "C," "Satisfactory," or "Unsatisfactory," or whatever system you use, with a personal summary of the tests given, the students' scores, and what they mean. (See Figures 16–3a, 16–3b, 16–4, and 16–5 for some examples of forms that have been found to be successful.)

FIGURE 16–4 ELEMENTARY PHYSICAL EDUCATION PROGRESS CHECK LIST (For use with the Fall Parent-Teacher Conference for students in the primary grades)

STUDENT_____ LEVEL_____ TEACHER_____

In our physical education program we have selected activities which we hope will help develop specific skills. The results recorded here are not taken from a formal testing situation. They have resulted from observation by the classroom and special teacher of the student during the regular physical education activity program. The check marks indicate a satisfactory performance has been demonstrated by the student. Ability to:

_____ Run to a given mark and back without stopping (approximately 15 feet)

_____ Skip to a given mark and back without stopping (approximately 15 feet)

_____ Hop to a given mark and back without stopping (approximately 15 feet)

_____ Catch a large ball with the hands

_____ Throw a large ball 15 feet

_____ Perform simple stunts on playground apparatus

_____ Kick a stationary and rolling ball

_____ Take turns

_____ Accept decisions of leaders

_____ Follow directions for games and drills

_____ Perform basic exercises involving use of arms and shoulders

_____ Perform basic exercises involving flexibility

_____ Perform basic exercises involving agility and cooordination

_____ Perform basic exercises involving trunk and abdominals

_____ Understand game concepts and move with purpose

FIGURE 16–5   ELEMENTARY PHYSICAL EDUCATION
PROGRESS CHECK LIST (For use with the Fall Parent-
Teacher Conference for students in grades 5–6)

STUDENT_____ GRADE_____ TEACHER_____

 In our physical education program, we have selected activities which we hope will develop specific skills.   The ratings are based on the observation of the classroom and special teacher of the student during the regular physical education activity program.   The check marks indicate a satisfactory performance has been demonstrated by the student.

_____ Ability to perform basic soccer skills (dribble, pass, kick, trap).

_____ Understanding of the rules and team play concepts of soccer.

_____ Ability to perform basic speedball skills (drop kick, punt conversion skills).

_____ Understanding of the rules and team play concepts of speedball.

_____ Accepts decisions of leaders (teacher or student).

_____ Ability to achieve a satisfactory rating (50th percentile) on each item of the physical fitness tests.   (See the Individual Physical Fitness Test Record for the breakdown of scores and ratings).

Other Comments:

When the parents have a knowledge and understanding of a program, they will generally support it.   If this understanding is lacking, usually one is treading on thin ice.   Sometimes the results of this lack of understanding are tragic. In a community where the money available to schools is limited and a school millage issue fails, sometimes the tendency is to cut back the physical education program.   If the citizens in the community have a high regard for the physical education program, they will generally not allow any curtailment to take place.   The teacher's responsibility to cultivate a positive attitude on the part of the parent toward his program becomes obvious.

What are you doing right now?

When was the last time you were in a school to observe a physical education program?   As a college student, one can easily become so engrossed in course work that all the learning experiences are confined to the immediate "campus." Vast reading and discussion pertaining to the organization and administration of tests and measurements in a school program certainly has great value, but often it takes on no practical significance unless we can observe these concepts as they are functioning in a real situation. Students often point the finger of blame at college instructors for emphasizing "theory with no practical implications." What initiative have you shown to get some practical experience? Have you contacted your tests and measurements instructor to make arrangements to visit a local school system? If the time is right, you may find a school would welcome a group of college students to take an active part in administering a battery of tests. If you are going to visit a school, prepare yourself to take advantage of this experience.

STUDY QUESTIONS · Chapter 16

1. What two fundamental questions should a teacher answer before initiating a testing program in physical education?

2. What should you do in advance when students are to be used in administering the testing program?

3. In the organization of a tests and measurements program, distinguish between (a) mass testing, (b) squad method, (c) station-to-station method, (d) task orientation, (e) combination. What are the advantages and disadvantages of each?

4. What should be considered in deciding the order to give tests on a particular day?

5. Describe the various methods of recording scores:
    a. Class roll sheet
    b. Squad cards
    c. Individual score card
    d. Self-scoring

6. What safety precautions should one take in connection with a testing program?

7. You have a six-lane track and one stop watch. How might you time 6 7th-grade children in the 50-yard dash simultaneously?

8. How can you use test results in physical education to interpret the program for parents and PTA groups?

COMPUTERS AT THE SERVICE OF THE PHYSICAL EDUCATION TEACHER

17

Ray T. Hermiston

Automation in industry and computerization in business have been instrumental in forcing a movement toward computer usage in the educational domain. Both the rapid influx of computer hardware (machines) and software (computer programs) have caused considerable anxiety about the computer age in education. Some of the anxiety is certainly justified, but anxiety about computer errors indicates naiveté on the part of the user.

In the past few years, most educational institutions have acquired computer keypunches, eliminating a major problem, the entry of masses of data. In fact, computer technology has advanced the data entry spectrum to include mark-sense cards, optical scan data sheets, and, most recently, a machine that actually reads typewritten pages. With the data entry barrier alleviated, it is time to consider what you, as a physical educator, can do to improve your physical education program through computer-assisted teaching, marking, and program development.

Digital computers are used to analyze great volumes of data. You can utilize these amazing devices to eliminate the boredom of producing profile report cards, scoring multiple-choice questions, calculating the finances of your

Revision of article by R. T. Hermiston, A. J. Kozar, and H. J. Montoye, "Computers at the Service of the Physical Education Teacher," *J. of Health, Physical Education and Recreation,* September 1968. Reproduced with permission of the publisher.

program, taking stock and controlling stock inventory, classifying students, computing complex statistics, and calculating particular algorithms that may interest you, such as percent body fat, skeletal age, IQ, etc.

Until very recently, few teachers or school administrators had ever used the computer, yet our recent graduates have grown up in the computer age. In fact, in most universities these students now fill in computer cards to register for their courses. In community colleges and universities, computer courses are being offered as workshops during the summer months. Hopefully, this approach will acquaint more physical education teachers with computers and their operation. A tests and measurements course is often required in most physical education curricula. Yet very few public or parochial schools are involved in extensive testing and evaluating of either their students or their programs. There are many conscientious teachers and area supervisors who believe that their instructional program could be improved. Yet, they are reluctant to expand their testing program for a variety of reasons. One of the reasons frequently mentioned is the time required for data analysis. Even the relatively straightforward task of developing percentile ranks requires considerable time—time the busy teacher does not have. Second, the teacher may not have the training or inclination to work with numbers. Many teachers are dedicated and capable, but many also have little ability to analyze numeric data. Third, the courses in tests and measurements and/or statistics that these teachers may have had were probably concerned with statistics as a research technique. Perhaps much of the time was spent on complicated analytical procedures far beyond the immediate needs of teachers in physical education. Furthermore, the teacher may have been trained before the advent of modern computers capable of dealing with thousands of scores as easily as they can perform operations on a few scores.

The teacher may wish to increase his effectiveness but may not be sophisticated in mathematical analysis or have little time or energy left at the end of the day for routine arithmetical tasks. Computers, however, are capable of not only performing arithmetical calculations; they can, for instance, identify individuals with certain characteristics (for example, high or low scores). The computer also checks the data it processes and, if errors are detected in the calculations that the computer has made, these calculations are redone, and checked again until correct.

The ways in which computers may be of service to the physical educator are really only limited by the imagination of the user. Certainly, only the surface has been scratched. One day, data on school children stored on magnetic tape may be rapidly recalled for counseling the child or to study the effectiveness of teaching or administrative procedures. With the aid of the computer, tests will be subjected to item analysis as a routine procedure. Administrators may use the computer for scheduling or improving efficiency in using facilities. However, such applications will require study and a great many man-hours will be needed for writing and testing programs. The simpler and more urgent needs of the classroom physical education teacher, however, are already within the scope of developed programming.

Teachers who administer skills tests or physical fitness tests generally consider the calculations of percentile scores desirable. This percentile ranking may properly interpret each child's raw scores. Computer programs are available for calculating percentile scores. Since many physical skills and abilities are correlated with maturation and chronological age, such percentile scores should be age specific. At most ages, the performance of boys and girls is quite different, requiring sex-specific percentile norms. After further study, it may be found necessary to correct for body size as well.

At a minimum, teachers need a tabulation of raw scores and corresponding percentile scores for their classes. A computer can do this very easily; it will provide alphabetical or other listing of the boys and girls of a particular age, giving percentile scores for each child. In addition, these percentile scores are well typed as the secretary (computer) makes very few errors and can type approximately 1500 lines a minute.

The Tecumseh, Michigan, experiment

Tecumseh, Michigan, is the focus of a large scientific research effort—an ecologic investigation of an entire American community. The main research objectives are to appraise the health status of residents and discover the earliest signs of impaired health. Tecumseh is a community of about 7,000 inhabitants. These people, together with approximately 3,000 additional participants who live in the rural area immediately outside the town, comprise the study population. The school system includes almost the same geographical area. Over 80 per cent of the residents of the study area have been participating in the health investigation, which includes periodic medical examinations. This provides a unique opportunity to study physical performance, physical fitness, school achievement, athletics, and physical exercise as they relate to health.

Between February and June, 1966, a team of investigators administered fitness tests to almost all the children in the school system, most of whom also are participants along with their parents in the Tecumseh Community Health Study. The testing program also provided the opportunity to develop computer programs to analyze and feed back useful information to the school system. These programs were written with sufficient flexibility to be applicable to any size school or school system. Although a research team in this instance did the testing, local school personnel or even student leaders could be used.

In the experiment, the AAHPER Youth Fitness Test battery was administered in grades 4 through 12. Test items were administered exactly as described and the proper number of repetitions of a particular test was included. In addition, a trunk flexion and truck extension test were given. Age (as of last birthday), height, weight, and grade were recorded. There were eight elementary schools (including one parochial school), one junior high school, and one senior high school in the study population. For various reasons some students did not take particular tests. However, the percentage of participation was very high.

TABLE 17–1
Tecumseh School System. Testing Done January
Through June, 1966.
Tecumseh School Girls 10 Years of Age.

	Flexed Arm Hang (Sec)	Trunk Flex- ion (Inches)	Trunk Exten- sion (Inches)	Shut- tle Run (Sec)	Sit- Ups (Max. 50)	Soft Ball Throw (Ft)	
95	29	14.0	19.0	10.8	50	81	95
P 90	23	13.0	17.0	11.1	50	70	90 P
E 85	17	12.5	16.5	11.5	50	64	85 E
R 80	13	11.5	16.0	11.7	45	60	80 R
C 75	13	11.5	15.5	11.8 ****	40	60	75 C
E 70	10	11.0	15.0	11.9 ****	38	54	70 E
N 65	9	11.0	15.0	12.0	35 ****	54 ****	65 N
T 60	8 ****	11.0	14.5	12.1	30 ****	48 ****	60 T
I 55	7 ****	10.5	14.5	12.2	30	48	55 I
L 50	6	10.5	14.0	12.4	28	45	50 L
E 45	5	10.0	13.5	12.5	26	45	45 E
40	4	10.0	13.5	12.5	25	45	40
35	3	9.5	12.8	12.7	22	42	35
R 30	3	9.0	12.5	12.9	20	39	30 R
A 25	1	9.0	12.0	13.1	19	36	25 A
N 20	1	8.5	11.4	13.3	18	33	20 N
K 15	0	8.0	10.5	13.5	16	32	15 K
S 10	0	7.0	9.4	13.9	13	30	10 S
5	0	5.5	8.5	14.5	8	27	5
Mean	8.8	10.0	13.7	12.5	29.9	48.5	
Std Dev	9.6	2.5	3.5	1.1	14.2	15.6	
Number	130	130	130	130	127	130	

****indicates the median scores.

After these data were tabulated on mimeographed forms, the scores, together with the school identification, grade, and student's last name and first
initial, were punched on the IBM cards. The data were then processed by
the programs described above which are now contained in the Physical Education Computer Program Library at the University of Windsor, Windsor,
Ontario.

Examples of the results of these programs are shown in Tables 17–1 to
17–4. Table 17–1 is an example of percentile norms for six of the nine tests
used. These norms are for 10-year-old girls only. In addition to percentile
scores, the means, standard deviations, and numbers of girls in Tecumseh
from which these percentile scores were calculated are given at the bottom
of the sheet. There are asterisks above and below a particular value in all

TABLE 17–2
Tecumseh School System.
Testing Done January Through June, 1966.
Tecumseh School Girls 10 Years of Age.

Name: Student 1		Height (Ins): 58.0		Weight (lb): 85	Age: 10	Grade: 4	
	Flexed Arm Hang (Sec)	Trunk Flexion (Inches)	Trunk Extension (Inches)	Shuttle Run (Sec)	Sit-Ups (Max. 50)	Soft Ball Throw (Ft)	
	****		****				
95	29	14.0	19.0	10.8	50	81	95
	****		****				
P 90	23	13.0	17.0	11.1	50	70	90 P
E 85	17	12.5	16.5	11.5	50	64	85 E
				****		****	
R 80	13	11.5	16.0	11.7	45	60	80 R
				****		****	
C 75	13	11.5	15.5	11.8	40	60	75 C
E 70	10	11.0	15.0	11.9	38	54	70 E
N 65	9	11.0	15.0	12.0	35	54	65 N
T 60	8	11.0	14.5	12.1	30	48	60 T
I 55	7	10.5	14.5	12.2	30	48	55 I
L 50	6	10.5	14.0	12.4	28	45	50 L
		****					
E 45	5	10.0	13.5	12.5	26	45	45 E
		****		****			
40	4	10.0	13.5	12.5	25	45	40
				****			
35	3	9.5	12.8	12.7	22	42	35
R 30	3	9.0	12.5	12.9	20	39	30 R
A 25	1	9.0	12.0	13.1	19	36	25 A
N 20	1	8.5	11.4	13.3	18	33	20 N
K 15	0	8.0	10.5	13.5	16	32	15 K
S 10	0	7.0	9.4	13.9	13	30	10 S
5	0	5.0	8.5	14.5	8	27	5

Data Processed by Research Dept. School of P. and H. Educ. Univ. of Windsor

but two of the test items. The values bracketed in this way are median scores (50th percentile) for the United States nationwide sample. These values are interpreted as follows: the median value for the total United States sample of 10-year-old girls on flexed arm hang is 7 seconds (asterisks above and below), whereas the median (50th percentile) for the Tecumseh group is 6 seconds. Similarly, in the softball throw the median for the United States sample is 48 feet whereas the Tecumseh median is 45 feet. The other test items are interpreted in a similar manner.

Table 17–2 is an individual report card in the form of a profile record for Student Number 1, a 10-year-old girl. Her height, weight, age, and grade are shown on the top of the sheet. From Table 17–2, her raw score of 29 seconds on the arm hang is equivalent to the 95th percentile, making her per-

FIGURE 17–3
Tecumseh School System. Testing Done January
Through June, 1966.
Tecumseh School Girls 10 Years of Age.

Flexed Arm Hang (Sec)	Trunk Flex-ion (Inches)	Trunk Exten-sion (Inches)	Shut-tle Run (Sec)	Sit-Ups (Max. 50)	Soft Ball Throw (Ft)	
34	10.0	21.0	11.7	25	60	Student 1
0	11.0	12.5	13.0	26	24	Student 2
4	6.5	16.0	10.8	50	48	Student 3
4	14.0	13.5	14.8	18	33	Student 4
9	6.5	14.5	14.2	27	33	Student 5

TABLE 17–4
Tecumseh School Girls 10 Years of Age.

Flexed Arm Hang (Sec)	Trunk Flex-ion (Inches)	Trunk Exten-sion (Inches)	Shut-tle Run (Sec)	Sit-Ups (Max. 50)	Soft Ball Throw (Ft)	
95	45	95	80	40	80	Student 1
15	70	30	25	45	5	Student 2
40	5	80	30	95	60	Student 3
40	90	45	95	20	60	Student 4
65	5	30	5	45	20	Student 5

formance superior to 95% of the 10-year-old girls on this test. Similarly, her sit-ups score was 25, which placed her at the 40th percentile for ten-year-old girls. The program available provides a record of this kind for each child in Tecumseh.

One of the computer print-outs also provides the teacher with reports similar to that shown in Table 17–3. In this example of girls age 10, the list contains each girl's identification number and name, together with her raw scores. The pupils can be listed alphabetically instead of by identification number. This print-out provides the teacher with a tabulation of all children and their raw scores with the children grouped by age, by sex and age, by age and grade, or by age, sex, and grade. The mean, standard deviation, and number of participants for each test item is given at the bottom of the list for each grouping. As an illustration, the first child, identified as Student 1, scored 34 seconds on the arm hang, 10.0 inches on the trunk flexion, 21 inches on trunk extension, etc.

Table 17–4 is another list for the teacher similar to the one in Table 17–3 which was just described. However, in Table 17–4 the scores for each child are in the form of percentile scores. Student Number 1, the first 10-year-old girl on the list, had a percentile rank of 95 for arm hang, 45 for trunk flexion, 95 for trunk extension, etc.

Finally in the Tecumseh experiment, it was of interest to know which children scored at or above the 85th percentile on all seven items of the youth fitness test. The percentile ranks in this case were the age and sex-specific 1964–1965 norms produced by the second United States survey. Scoring on or above the 85th percentile on all tests qualified the child for the Presidential Fitness Award. A feature was built into the program to ferret out the names of these children and to print their names and identification numbers on a separate sheet.

Physical education class assignment experiment

Enrollment in most required physical education programs is based on a combination of student selection and course availability. Some schools use test data to aid in the counselling assignment of students for required physical education classes. However, many administrators have not used test results because of the considerable administrative effort involved in processing the data.

Since physical education potentially deals with highly objective data, physical educators could make extensive use of computers for the accurate and efficient processing of test data. Such processing does not preclude the development of tests or the determination of criteria for assignment to required programs in terms of either the needs of different students or the philosophies of different individuals or groups.

Nine tests were selected for this experiment and these were divided into five program categories: 1) Cardiovascular Condition—heart rate during the last 10 seconds of an 8-minute submaximum step test performed at 24 steps per minute on a 14–inch bench; 2) Weight Control—fatfold measures at the subscapular, triceps, suprailiac, and umbilical sites, 3) Strength—bent arm pull (3); 4) Sports Skills—a) tennis wall rally (2), b) badminton wall volley (5), c) volleyball wall volley (1), d) basketball layups (4), and e) basketball throw for distance (3); and 5) Swimming Ability—5-minute swim for distance (3). The raw data were recorded on precoded data sheets and punched on IBM cards. Computer analysis of the data in these five sections was set up to produce four types of charts:

1. **Percentile table.** The raw score equivalents for each decile were calculated for the nine variables and printed in the form of a percentile table (Table 17–5). The computer program accumulated and ordered the scores and at each decile printed out the value of the score immediately above and below each decile. In large samples these scores are invariably the same. If the scores were different, the two scores were averaged to obtain the raw score value for the decile.

2. **Administrative records.** The raw score values for each student were compared to the nine percentile tables and appropriate decile rankings were

TABLE 17–5
Percentile Ranks for 340 University Freshmen
Age 17 Years

Percen-tile Rank	Ex. Hr. (beats/ min)	Fat-folds (mm)	Arm Str. (kg/kg)	Tennis (No)	Bad-minton (No)	Volley-ball (No)	Lay-ups (No)	Sitting Throw (ft)	5-min Swim (yd)
90	128	24	1.547	32	52	36	30	46	285
80	136	28	1.460	29	47	33	27	43	250
70	142	31	1.405	28	43	30	26	41	235
60	146	36	1.340	26	39	27	23	40	225
50	150	40	1.301	24	36	24	22	39	200
40	152	45	1.248	22	33	22	20	37	190
30	158	51	1.207	20	30	19	17	34	175
20	162	59	1.165	19	26	16	14	32	150
10	169	71	1.110	15	21	12	10	29	100

TABLE 17–6
Individual Percentile Rating from Comparison with
Percentile Norm

Ex. HR	Fat-folds	Arm str.	Tennis	Bad-minton	Volley-ball	Lay-ups	Throw	Swim	I.D. number
0	20	20	0	0	0	0	0	0	208,974
80	50	50	0	10	10	30	50	10	296,729
60	30	40	80	60	80	80	40	90	403,829
70	70	0	20	30	0	0	10	20	533,557
10	10	80	50	40	40	60	60	60	675,050

printed out as shown in Table 17–6. This type of print out provides a cumulative record file for the administrator.

3. Counselling records. With the exception of subcutaneous fat thickness and swimming distance, the distribution for each of the nine variables was divided into three groups of equal size. Each group was numbered 1, 2, or 3—1 indicative of a poor score, 2 a fair score, and 3 a good score. An absolute rather than a relative criterion of poor and good was made in the weight control section. A student was classified as "poor" if his total fatfold measure was greater than 55 millimeters. Fifty-five millimeters was arbitrarily set as a reasonable thickness of subcutaneous fatness on the basis of Sloan's data (7). Sloan recommended 14% of body weight composed of fat. On the basis of a previously developed regression equation (% fat = 5.783 + .153 × sum of 4 fatfolds), 55 millimeters of subcutaneous fat is equivalent to 14% of body weight being composed of fat. Swimming was kept separate from the other sports skills. If a student was unable to swim more than 100 yards in 5 minutes, he was classified as a nonswimmer.

A rating of "good," "fair," or "poor" was then assigned to each student in each of the five program categories. The ratings were simply based on the numerical divisions in a single variable in the cardiovascular, weight control,

TABLE 17–7

Individual Ratings in Each of the Five Program Categories

Cardiovascular		Weight control		Arm str.	Sports skills								Swim		Overall assessment		
Exercise heart rate	Rating	Fatfolds	Rating	Rating	Rating	Tennis	Badminton	Volleyball	Lay ups	Sit throw	Sum	Rating	5-Minute Swim	Rating	Total	General rating	Identification number
1	poor	3	good	poor	1	1	1	1	1	5	poor	1	NS	12	poor	208,974
3	good	3	good	fair	1	1	1	2	2	7	poor	1	OK	17	poor	296,729
3	good	3	good	fair	3	2	3	3	2	13	good	3	OK	23	good	403,829
3	good	3	good	poor	2	2	1	1	1	7	poor	1	OK	18	good	533,557
1	poor	1	poor	good	2	2	2	2	2	10	fair	2	OK	16	poor	675,050

strength and swimming categories (Table 17–7). In the sports skill category, the sum of the five sports skills tests provided a composite score out of a possible 15 points. The ratings assigned were 13–15 points—"good"; 10–12 points—"fair"; less than 10 points—"poor."

4. Classification by instructional needs. On the basis of a set of arbitrary criteria, the subjects were arranged into six homogeneous groups.

Group I. Nonswimmers—Students unable to swim more than 100 yards in 5 minutes.

Group II. Overweight—Students with more than 55 millimeters of fat over the four sites.

Group III. Poor cardiovascular condition—Students with an exercise heart rate below the 30th percentile.

Group IV. Low sports skill—Students who scored less than 10 out of a possible 15 on the sports skills test battery.

Group V. Low muscular strength—Students whose arm strength was below the 30 percentile.

Group VI. Physically educated and physically fit—Students whose ratings were above the criteria of the deficiency groups.

Each of the six groups was mutually exclusive. If a student was assigned to Group I, he would not be assigned to any of the subsequent groups. Assignment was therefore on a priority basis.

For each of the six groups, a table was printed out with the identification number and the 18-digit profile of each subject. Each student's 18-digit profile indicated the decile ranking on each of the nine tests (Table 17–6). The classifications are summarized in Table 17–7. These tables provide the administrator with an overview of the status of each student.

In a small experimental group, the students in Group I were assigned to a swimming class, Group II to a weight control class, and Group III to a cardiovascular conditioning class. Students in Groups IV and V were counselled as to their weaknesses and possible methods for improvement. They then personally chose from appropriate courses offered in the required program. Students in Group VI met the program criteria of physically educated and physically fit young men. These students voluntarily selected courses in the required program to learn a new sports skill, improve present competency, or maintain or improve their fitness. If they so desired, they were given credit for the required physical education program with the understanding that they would meet their daily physical activity needs in intramural or personal recreational programs.

The computer program is adaptable to any eleven test items (although only nine were used here) and all eleven tests may be weighted as desired. The tests may also be grouped to conform with the philosophy and curriculum of a specific institution. The procedure is simple, economical, and applicable to programs for all ages and both sexes. It is particularly useful in the division of large numbers of children into homogeneous teaching groups in public schools.

Computer programming of an individual's test data does not necessarily depersonalize the physical education program. The computer print-outs may be modified at any time to conform with changing philosophies and new curricula. The print-outs are best used as a counselling aid to acquaint the instructor and the student with the student's specific strengths and weaknesses. The most appropriate physical education experience for a given student develops when objective test data, the interests of the student, and the experience of the instructor are all involved in the decision. It would appear that computer programming can make a significant contribution to the economy and precision with which a proper assignment is accomplished.

REFERENCES

1. Brady, G. F., "Preliminary Investigation of Volleyball Playing Ability." *Res. Quart.,* 16:14–17, 1945.

2. Dyer, J., "Revision of the Backboard Test of Tennis Ability." *Res. Quart.,* 9:25–31, 1938.

3. Faulkner, J. A.; G. W. Greey; and P. A. Hunsicker, "Evaluation of Health and Physical Education Program in Grand Rapids." Ann Arbor: University of Michigan, Bureau of School Services, 1962.

4. Mathews, D. K., *Measurements in Physical Education.* Philadelphia: Saunders, 1963.

5. Miller, F. A., "A Badminton Volley Test." *Res. Quart.,* 22:208–13, 1951.

6. Phillips, B. M., "Evaluation of Minimum Service Programs." *Res. Quart.,* 26:185–96, 1955.

7. Sloan, A. W., "Estimation of Body Fat in Young Men." *J. Appl. Physiol.,* 23:311–15, 1967.

STUDY QUESTIONS • Chapter 17

1. What is meant by "software and hardware" in computer use?

2. Define *algorithm*.

3. Describe six ways a physical education teacher might use a computer in his or her work.

4. List four reasons more testing in physical education is not done in the schools.

5. Describe how you might use the computer output illustrated in figures 17–1 through 17–4.

6. Can you describe any other ways computers may be used to improve your teaching and coaching?

Percentiles			Age		
	6	9	12	15	18
Neck Flexion-Extension: Females					
95	153	145	167	153	145
90	140	143	160	145	134
80	133	140	150	140	128
70	130	135	145	135	125
60	126	131	140	130	122
50	123	128	134	123	120
40	121	126	130	120	117
30	118	124	126	116	114
20	115	118	120	111	108
10	111	112	112	103	102
5	103	107	107	100	97
N=	50	50	50	50	100
Neck Rotation: Females					
95	184	191	190	184	181
90	181	189	186	180	178
80	178	186	179	173	175
70	175	183	177	170	173
60	173	178	174	166	170
50	170	175	172	163	167
40	167	172	170	161	162
30	164	168	168	158	155
20	160	163	163	155	151
10	156	156	158	137	145
5	151	152	152	131	135
N=	50	50	50	45	100
Left Arm Flexion-Extension: Females					
95	248	242	241	230	232
90	244	238	235	228	230
80	242	233	231	223	223
70	240	227	227	221	221
60	235	224	223	217	218
50	231	223	219	213	214
40	227	221	214	211	209
30	223	220	211	208	206
20	216	216	207	206	203
10	211	213	205	201	201
5	206	210	192	196	195
N=	50	50	50	50	100
Right Arm Flexion-Extension: Females					
95	244	239	236	237	232
90	243	237	233	228	230
80	240	232	228	223	224

Percentiles	Age				
	6	9	12	15	18
70	236	224	224	218	221
60	233	222	218	214	217
50	231	220	214	212	214
40	229	217	211	210	211
30	225	214	208	206	207
20	220	211	205	201	203
10	207	207	201	200	199
5	202	203	197	195	192
N=	50	50	50	50	100

Left Forearm Flexion-Extension: Females

Percentiles	6	9	12	15	18
95	172	171	174	169	165
90	168	169	170	168	163
80	165	167	165	165	159
70	162	165	163	162	157
60	160	163	162	160	155
50	157	162	160	157	153
40	155	160	157	154	152
30	151	158	155	152	150
20	151	156	150	150	147
10	149	152	147	143	145
5	146	148	142	140	140
N=	50	50	50	50	100

Right Forearm Flexion-Extension: Females

Percentiles	6	9	12	15	18
95	168	168	173	167	164
90	166	167	168	163	161
80	163	164	164	161	158
70	160	161	162	158	156
60	158	159	160	156	154
50	156	158	158	155	152
40	155	156	156	153	150
30	152	155	154	152	148
20	150	152	151	150	145
10	147	150	148	145	141
5	146	143	143	138	138
N=	50	50	50	50	100

Left Hand Flexion-Extension: Females

Percentiles	6	9	12	15	18
95	168	176	181	177	175
90	160	170	175	172	169
80	156	166	167	166	164
70	153	162	163	161	159
60	150	159	160	158	157
50	147	156	157	155	154
40	145	153	154	153	152
30	142	150	151	151	148
20	140	145	148	146	143
10	133	141	143	138	136
5	130	135	141	133	131
N=	50	50	50	50	100

Percentiles			Age		
	6	9	12	15	18

Right Hand Flexion-Extension: Females

95	167	175	180	177	170
90	162	168	175	172	167
80	157	163	168	165	163
70	154	158	163	160	159
60	151	155	158	156	156
50	148	152	155	152	151
40	145	149	151	149	150
30	141	146	147	145	147
20	137	142	143	140	143
10	132	136	138	132	138
5	127	128	133	126	132
N=	50	50	50	50	100

Left Thigh Abduction-Adduction: Females

95	64	67	66	66	63
90	61	64	63	62	62
80	56	60	61	58	58
70	53	59	58	57	56
60	51	57	55	55	54
50	50	56	53	53	52
40	48	55	52	51	51
30	45	53	50	50	49
20	43	52	48	48	46
10	40	50	45	45	40
5	38	47	42	41	36
N=	50	50	50	50	100

Right Thigh Abduction-Adduction: Females

95	64	67	68	69	66
90	61	64	67	65	64
80	55	61	63	60	61
70	51	59	59	56	58
60	48	56	57	53	56
50	45	53	54	51	54
40	43	50	50	49	51
30	42	44	47	46	48
20	41	42	45	44	45
10	39	40	42	41	42
5	37	37	40	40	40
N=	50	50	50	50	100

Left Leg Flexion-Extension: Females

95	151	143	139	135	128
90	142	139	137	132	126
80	138	136	134	129	123
70	135	134	131	127	121
60	132	131	129	125	119
50	130	128	126	123	117
40	128	126	124	121	115
30	125	123	122	117	113
20	122	121	119	114	110

Percentiles	Age				
	6	9	12	15	18
10	118	120	115	111	106
5	113	113	110	110	101
N=	50	50	50	50	100

Right Leg Flexion-Extension: Females

	6	9	12	15	18
95	145	143	140	134	132
90	143	141	134	132	129
80	141	137	131	129	124
70	138	135	128	126	121
60	135	131	126	124	119
50	132	128	124	122	116
40	129	125	123	120	114
30	125	122	122	117	112
20	122	119	121	116	109
10	120	115	120	115	106
5	116	111	117	111	103
N=	50	50	50	50	100

Left Foot Flexion-Extension: Females

	6	9	12	15	18
95	90	91	89	87	84
90	88	89	88	83	83
80	84	84	85	79	79
70	82	80	81	77	76
60	79	77	79	74	74
50	77	74	76	72	72
40	74	72	74	70	71
30	71	70	72	67	69
20	68	65	70	65	65
10	65	63	66	60	61
5	61	59	59	56	60
N=	50	50	50	50	100

Right Foot Flexion-Extension: Females

	6	9	12	15	18
95	89	95	93	93	91
90	87	90	88	88	87
80	83	85	84	83	82
70	81	81	82	80	78
60	80	78	80	77	76
50	75	76	78	73	74
40	73	75	75	71	72
30	71	72	73	68	70
20	68	70	70	65	67
10	63	65	66	62	63
5	61	61	64	60	61
N=	50	50	50	50	100

Neck Flexion-Extension: Males

	6	9	12	15	18
95	150	153	150	150	148	177
90	145	151	148	141	145	173
80	140	148	145	133	141	162
70	134	145	143	128	138	157
60	131	143	140	125	135	154

Percentiles	Age					
	10	12	14	16	18	College
50	126	141	136	123	129	151
40	122	138	131	121	126	148
30	119	135	127	118	123	144
20	111	126	124	116	118	140
10	100	122	121	111	111	130
5	90	111	119	108	101	117
N=	100	90	140	90	100	50

Neck Lateral Flexion: Males

95	117	116	109	104	127	155
90	112	109	103	101	120	147
80	106	104	99	96	113	133
70	103	101	96	93	110	125
60	101	98	93	90	101	119
50	98	97	91	89	94	116
40	95	95	89	86	90	114
30	91	93	86	84	86	111
20	85	90	82	79	81	107
10	80	83	70	75	75	100
5	73	80	66	71	72	85
N=	100	90	140	90	100	50

Neck Rotation: Males

95	209	182	179	176	188	208
90	205	178	173	173	183	204
80	197	175	168	168	177	201
70	191	172	165	164	172	194
60	187	168	163	160	168	191
50	183	163	160	158	163	188
40	179	159	157	155	157	184
30	173	154	154	153	151	182
20	166	148	151	150	142	180
10	152	137	145	144	132	167
5	135	127	140	138	110	166
N=	100	90	140	90	100	50

Left Arm Flexion-Extension: Males

95	268	270	274	275	266	245
90	263	264	268	269	262	241
80	256	257	261	267	255	234
70	250	252	256	264	248	230
60	244	248	251	262	242	225
50	239	244	247	260	236	224
40	235	239	244	256	230	220
30	231	236	240	253	225	215
20	226	233	234	250	220	212
10	221	230	227	243	211	207
5	216	225	222	239	203	201
N=	100	82	140	90	100	50

Right Arm Flexion-Extension: Males

95	269	269	275	275	266	243
90	264	263	269	269	269	238

Percentiles	Age					
	10	12	14	16	18	College
80	256	256	259	266	256	232
70	250	251	255	264	252	226
60	244	248	252	261	245	223
50	239	245	249	258	236	220
40	235	242	246	254	229	217
30	230	238	243	251	224	214
20	225	234	240	246	218	211
10	218	230	231	241	208	205
5	213	225	223	236	203	201
N=	100	90	140	90	100	50

Left Arm Adduction-Abduction: Males

	10	12	14	16	18	College
95	199	196	201	195	212	209
90	197	193	197	190	205	206
80	195	189	192	178	197	196
70	192	186	188	177	193	191
60	189	184	186	175	189	187
50	187	182	183	173	186	183
40	184	180	181	171	183	177
30	182	177	177	168	180	173
20	180	174	172	165	176	171
10	172	171	164	161	171	164
5	165	167	154	156	166	161
N=	100	90	140	90	100	50

Right Arm Adduction-Abduction: Males

	10	12	14	16	18	College
95	200	196	198	187	205	199
90	198	192	196	184	195	192
80	194	188	192	179	187	188
70	190	186	188	177	182	183
60	187	184	185	175	178	178
50	185	181	183	173	175	175
40	182	179	182	171	172	170
30	180	176	176	170	170	166
20	175	173	172	165	165	163
10	171	170	166	161	160	162
5	166	166	160	156	153	158
N=	100	90	140	90	100	50

Left Arm Rotation: Males

	10	12	14	16	18	College
95	205	208	189	212	198	238
90	197	198	187	192	192	230
80	190	189	182	182	185	216
70	187	184	179	177	180	209
60	184	180	176	174	174	206
50	181	177	173	170	169	203
40	178	174	170	165	165	200
30	174	171	167	161	160	195
20	171	168	163	156	154	191
10	166	162	160	151	147	185
5	163	160	155	147	142	180
N=	100	90	140	90	100	50

Percentiles	Age					
	10	12	14	16	18	College

Right Arm Rotation: Males

Percentiles	10	12	14	16	18	College
95	205	212	195	212	197	229
90	199	194	190	188	192	225
80	191	185	185	182	185	218
70	187	180	181	177	180	211
60	183	178	178	172	175	205
50	180	175	176	168	171	199
40	176	173	173	165	166	194
30	173	171	171	161	161	188
20	170	170	165	157	155	183
10	164	163	158	151	150	176
5	161	161	153	146	141	172
N=	100	90	130	90	100	50

Left Forearm Flexion-Extension: Males

Percentiles	10	12	14	16	18	College
95	164	162	170	153	167	177
90	161	158	166	150	162	174
80	157	153	160	147	157	168
70	154	150	156	145	154	163
60	152	146	151	144	152	160
50	150	144	147	143	150	158
40	147	142	144	142	147	155
30	145	140	142	141	144	153
20	142	137	139	140	141	151
10	138	135	135	135	137	147
5	136	130	128	131	133	146
N=	100	90	140	90	100	50

Right Forearm Flexion-Extension: Males

Percentiles	10	12	14	16	18	College
95	164	159	169	152	167	177
90	160	156	165	149	162	174
80	157	152	160	146	157	168
70	155	149	155	144	153	163
60	152	147	152	143	151	160
50	150	144	149	142	148	158
40	148	142	146	141	146	155
30	145	140	143	140	143	153
20	141	138	140	138	141	151
10	135	135	136	133	133	147
5	130	132	128	122	125	146
N=	100	90	140	90	100	50

Left Hand Supination-Pronation: Males

Percentiles	10	12	14	16	18	College
95	216	209	203	179	200	217
90	212	204	198	175	193	213
80	208	198	194	170	186	206
70	205	194	187	166	179	200
60	202	190	181	164	172	192
50	198	187	177	161	167	185
40	193	184	172	159	165	178
30	187	181	167	154	161	175
20	180	177	162	151	155	171

Percentiles	Age					
	10	**12**	**14**	**16**	**18**	**College**
10	171	170	158	146	146	162
5	163	168	153	142	138	148
N=	100	90	140	90	100	50

Right Hand Supination-Pronation: Males

95	213	207	201	179	202	225
90	211	203	197	178	193	216
80	208	195	191	175	184	205
70	204	193	186	168	179	197
60	202	190	180	165	172	191
50	199	186	175	162	166	184
40	193	183	170	156	162	178
30	185	180	166	153	158	174
20	179	177	163	151	152	165
10	173	173	158	147	140	162
5	165	168	153	143	136	157
N=	100	90	140	90	100	50

Left Hand Flexion-Extension: Males

95	186	175	167	157	151	188
90	183	168	164	154	146	180
80	178	157	158	146	138	176
70	175	149	149	140	134	173
60	172	146	140	131	130	170
50	169	143	132	127	126	165
40	166	140	126	125	122	160
30	163	135	121	123	118	156
20	161	130	115	120	114	153
10	152	120	110	115	110	150
5	135	111	105	111	98	146
N=	100	90	140	90	100	50

Right Hand Flexion-Extension: Males

95	184	176	167	159	153	181
90	179	170	164	154	144	178
80	177	158	158	145	137	175
70	175	148	149	136	133	172
60	173	145	139	130	129	168
50	171	142	131	126	125	166
40	169	139	125	123	122	163
30	165	135	120	120˙	119	160
20	160	131	115	115	115	156
10	153	121	111	111	111	151
5	140	92	107	106	110	145
N=	100	90	140	90	100	50

Left Hand Abduction-Adduction: Males

95	112	104	97	92	106	107
90	109	100	88	85	101	98
80	105	95	84	83	93	92
70	98	93	81	80	90	87
60	93	90	79	79	86	83
50	89	86	78	77	83	80

Percentiles	Age					
	10	12	14	16	18	College
40	86	84	76	75	80	76
30	83	81	74	73	77	72
20	80	78	72	70	71	67
10	76	74	70	57	66	62
5	73	70	69	53	63	58
N=	100	90	140	90	100	50

Right Hand Abduction-Adduction: Males

	10	12	14	16	18	College
95	116	104	97	90	103	103
90	111	99	90	84	98	95
80	102	93	83	82	95	91
70	97	91	81	80	92	83
60	93	89	79	78	89	81
50	89	87	77	76	85	74
40	86	85	75	75	82	73
30	82	83	73	72	77	71
20	78	80	71	70	70	70
10	76	73	69	60	65	62
5	75	69	67	56	62	60
N=	100	90	140	90	100	50

Thigh Adduction-Abduction: Males

	10	12	14	16	18	College
95	70	76	76	76	72	64
90	65	73	73	68	69	62
80	59	67	71	67	64	58
70	56	63	68	65	61	55
60	54	60	64	64	58	53
50	51	58	60	·61	55	51
40	48	56	53	57	52	49
30	46	53	50	49	50	47
20	43	49	46	47	47	45
10	39	44	43	43	45	40
5	36	42	41	39	40	36
N=	100	90	140	90	100	50

Left Thigh Rotation: Males

	10	12	14	16	18	College
95	135	111	84	99	135	132
90	128	100	81	92	128	127
80	121	91	77	78	110	121
70	117	84	74	74	100	113
60	113	82	73	72	95	107
50	108	80	72	69	87	102
40	104	77	70	66	83	97
30	101	74	67	64	78	92
20	91	70	63	60	73	85
10	84	62	51	56	68	77
5	79	57	42	46	60	73
N=	100	89	140	90	100	50

Right Thigh Rotation: Males

	10	12	14	16	18	College
95	140	108	86	92	135	124
90	127	98	80	90	130	115

Percentiles	Age					
	10	12	14	16	18	College
80	121	89	75	77	110	111
70	117	86	74	73	101	103
60	113	83	73	72	94	101
50	108	79	72	70	87	94
40	104	77	70	68	80	92
30	99	75	69	65	75	91
20	93	70	63	61	72	84
10	85	63	53	54	65	81
5	80	60	42	43	53	80
N=	100	90	140	89	100	50

Left Leg Flexion-Extension: Males

	10	12	14	16	18	College
95	165	158	152	154	148	165
90	160	156	149	152	146	163
80	157	153	145	145	141	161
70	153	151	143	143	137	155
60	150	149	141	141	134	152
50	146	147	139	138	131	150
40	143	146	137	134	128	148
30	138	144	135	129	124	145
20	127	141	130	126	121	140
10	125	138	125	121	118	136
5	118	135	119	118	115	135
N=	100	90	140	90	100	50

Right Leg Flexion-Extension: Males

	10	12	14	16	18	College
95	166	158	158	157	153	165
90	162	157	156	154	149	162
80	156	154	152	150	144	158
70	152	151	148	145	142	155
60	149	149	146	142	140	153
50	145	147	143	140	137	151
40	142	146	141	131	135	150
30	138	144	138	128	132	145
20	134	141	135	125	129	142
10	125	138	127	118	126	140
5	120	136	121	116	122	136
N=	100	90	140	90	100	50

Left Foot Flexion-Extension: Males

	10	12	14	16	18	College
95	100	75	77	82	80	77
90	95	70	75	80	75	74
80	90	64	68	75	72	71
70	87	62	64	64	70	67
60	84	60	62	62	66	64
50	80	58	60	60	64	62
40	77	56	57	59	62	60
30	74	55	55	58	60	54
20	70	52	53	56	55	52
10	64	48	51	55	50	50
5	61	47	50	51	46	46
N=	100	90	140	90	100	50

Percentiles			Age			
	10	12	14	16	18	College

Right Foot Flexion-Extension: Males

Percentiles	10	12	14	16	18	College
95	99	77	80	85	81	79
90	95	74	69	82	76	75
80	91	68	64	71	73	68
70	88	64	60	65	70	66
60	84	62	58	63	67	64
50	80	59	56	60	64	62
40	77	57	54	59	61	60
30	73	54	52	57	59	56
20	69	51	50	56	56	52
10	60	46	45	51	50	47
5	60	46	45	51	50	47
N=	100	89	140	90	100	50

Left Foot Inversion-Eversion: Males

Percentiles	10	12	14	16	18	College
95	64	63	63	59	70	73
90	61	60	60	57	62	68
80	57	55	55	53	56	65
70	55	51	51	48	53	63
60	51	48	49	46	49	61
50	48	46	46	44	45	58
40	46	44	43	42	41	55
30	44	41	40	41	37	52
20	41	38	36	38	30	48
10	40	34	32	35	28	41
5	36	30	23	32	23	37
N=	100	90	140	90	100	50

Right Foot Inversion-Eversion: Males

Percentiles	10	12	14	16	18	College
95	64	63	64	59	72	70
90	60	60	61	54	63	68
80	57	54	57	51	57	65
70	54	49	53	48	52	61
60	50	47	50	46	44	58
50	48	45	43	44	42	55
40	46	42	40	41	40	52
30	44	40	38	39	37	48
20	41	37	36	37	32	43
10	37	35	33	35	26	40
5	35	30	30	32	23	34
N=	100	90	140	90	100	50

Trunk Lateral Flexion: Males

Percentiles	10	12	14	16	18	College
95	121	103	105	123	129	133
90	117	101	100	119	125	123
80	111	97	94	115	112	119
70	108	90	91	105	107	116
60	105	87	89	96	103	114
50	102	84	87	92	99	110
40	99	82	84	90	96	104
30	96	80	82	87	91	100
20	92	77	78	80	82	93

Percentiles			Age			
	6	9	12		15	18
10	87	73	70	77	73	91
5	83	70	61	76	68	83
N=	100	90	140	90	100	49

Trunk Rotation: Males

	6	9	12		15	18
95	158	163	170	154	170	153
90	155	161	168	151	162	145
80	152	157	164	146	150	136
70	149	154	158	143	144	131
60	147	151	153	140	136	125
50	145	148	148	137	134	117
40	143	145	143	135	131	107
30	141	143	140	132	127	102
20	138	140	135	128	124	90
10	134	136	127	124	119	80
5	130	135	97	121	115	71
N=	100	90	131	90	100	50

Index